D1519328

Cold War and Black Liberation

COLD WAR and

BLACK LIBERATION
The United States and White Rule in Africa, 1948–1968

Thomas J. Noer

University of Missouri Press
Columbia, 1985

Library of Congress Cataloging in Publication Data

Noer, Thomas J.
   Cold War and Black liberation.

    Bibliography: p.
    Includes index.
    1. Africa—Foreign relations—United States.   2. United States—Foreign
relations—Africa.   3. Africa—Foreign relations—1945–1960.   4. Africa—Foreign
relations—1960–   .   5. United States—Foreign relations—1945–   .
6. Decolonization—Africa.   7. National liberation movements—Africa.   I. Title.
DT38.5.A35N64   1985   327.7306   84–19665
ISBN 0–8262–0458–9

To Linda

CONTENTS

PREFACE

History is what we select from the past to help us understand the present. As a result, history often follows the headlines. While in theory historians are committed to dispassionate reconstruction of the past, in fact they often pick their subjects with an eye on current issues. From Herodotus's account of the Peloponnesian War to the most recent book on the changing status of gays, historians have always reflected the times in their choice of topics as well as in their interpretations.

This search for relevance is readily apparent in the changing emphasis in studies of American foreign relations. In the past two decades, authors have concentrated on periods and geographic areas that seemed most significant for an understanding of contemporary international issues. In the early 1960s, historians reacted to the triumph of Fidel Castro by directing their attention to U.S. relations with Latin America. They churned out dissertations, articles, and books on past American policies, and grants funded a bevy of institutes, workshops, and programs. With the gradual emergence of Vietnam as the dominant U.S. concern in the middle of the decade, diplomatic historians shifted their focus from the South to the East. Publishers sought material on American involvement in Asia rather than Latin America, and graduate students learned Chinese instead of Spanish.

If this periodic realignment of historical interest continues, Africa should be the next area of attention. While it lacks the proximity of Cuba and the direct military involvement of Vietnam, black Africa now occupies a position nearly analogous to theirs in terms of public interest and international attention. The victory of black nationalists in Angola and Mozambique in the mid-1970s, the continuing problems of the transition to majority rule in Zimbabwe-Rhodesia, and the sustained international pressure on South Africa for an end to its racist policies have stimulated a growing interest in Africa, particularly the southern half.

Recent debate over the importance of human rights and the role of private investments in the making of U.S. foreign policy has also helped focus attention on the region. Although the dispute over human rights and foreign policy is not new, the controversy generated by the Carter administration's commitment to personal freedom centered heavily on southern Africa. The conflict between students and university administrators over the removal of college investments in corporations active in South Africa, the dispute within the corporations themselves over alleged cooperation with apartheid, and the recent revelation of covert U.S. activities in Angola and Mozambique have all contributed to a new awareness of the continent. Politicians, the press, and even the general public now appear conscious of the symbolic significance of and tangible interests involved in U.S. relations with southern Africa.

Despite the contemporary interest in and controversy over current policies, there is no reliable account of past American involvement in the area. Historians have avoided writing about U.S. relations with black Africa for a variety of reasons. Preoccupied with military conflict and great power confrontations, most have dismissed Africa as unimportant to America and concentrated on areas that they assumed had greater strategic, economic, or cultural significance. This has usually meant Europe. The historiography of the Cold War, for example, has centered on its European origins and development. Historians seldom examine American policy in countries outside Europe except at times of intense crisis such as the Cuban revolution, or the wars in Korea, Vietnam, and the Middle East.

To most historians, the only period of African history of any importance to the United States began when Ghana gained independence in 1957. To many professional historians, this is "current events." It may be fit material for journalists, but not for scholars dedicated to research in all relevant sources and detached objectivity that comes from studying events long past. Such prejudice against "instant" history has not prevented the examination of America's role in Asia, Latin America, or Europe, but it has successfully limited efforts on Africa.

Historians have also avoided dealing with Africa out of sheer ignorance. Only recently have undergraduate and graduate curriculums included courses on African history, languages, politics, and economics. While most historians specializing in international relations have had a thorough background in Europe, Asia, or Latin America, they generally have little knowledge of Africa.

As a result of the historians' lack of interest, journalists, political scientists, and former government officials have done most of the work on U.S.–African relations. While they have produced some excellent studies, their efforts suffer from two serious limitations: lack of evidence and a strident, partisan tone. With a few, rare exceptions, these studies have been based exclusively on newspapers, magazines, memoirs, and other published sources. While this may not detract from the accuracy of an author's conclusions, it offers little documentation to support them. Without primary sources, findings are largely assumptions resting on rhetoric rather than evidence. The flaws in existing books on American policy in southern Africa have further alienated professional historians. Despite their failure to explore the topic themselves, historians have been appalled by the unobjective and undocumented results of those who did and have left the subject to the polemicists.

Given their intent and limited research, both critics and supporters have produced simplistic analyses of U.S. actions in Africa. Neither group sees much complexity or any contradictions in American diplomacy. Critics denounce the United States as "racist," "counterrevolutionary," or "imperialistic." Their objective is not the careful analysis of previous policies but their reversal. The past is used only to advance contemporary alternatives. Those supportive of American efforts have been equally partisan. They are similarly didactical, and their works are largely self-serving defenses of diplomatic decisions. They are designed to present critics of U.S. policy as "idealistic utopians" or "dangerous radicals" unaware of the realities of global politics.

In this book, I attempt to use available archival material to describe and analyze U.S. policy toward the white governments of South Africa, Rhodesia, and the Portuguese colonies. The study begins in 1948. In that year the Nationalist party and its policy of apartheid triumphed in South Africa. At the same time, civil rights emerged as a national issue within the United States. While the role of blacks in American society has been debated since the adoption of slavery, the Truman administration's decision to endorse at least limited civil rights for blacks, and the resulting fight over the 1948 Democratic party platform and walkout of southern Democrats, attest to the new importance of domestic race relations. Finally, by 1948 America had achieved near consensus on its Cold War strategy. The acceptance of the global containment of communism was nearly complete with the defeat of Henry Wallace and the Progressive party.

The book concludes in 1968 largely because of an absence of sources. The study is based heavily on material in the Truman, Eisenhower, Kennedy, and Johnson presidential libraries. Although there is as yet no archival material available on the period after 1968, the epilogue sketches shifts in policy in the period 1969–1984. Historians must wait for the documents of the Nixon, Ford, Carter, and Reagan administrations before they can offer a complete account of the recent era.

The major sources for the book include materials in the four presidential libraries, State Department records in the National Archives, and the private papers of former governmental officials. Some documents remain classified by government agencies and others have been "sanitized" (censored). Nevertheless, detailed and candid documents, particularly in the National Security Files and in the personal records of key individuals, provide abundant evidence for an accurate account of policy decisions and their impact. Material now open to scholars reveals the wide range of officials, agencies, and nongovernmental groups concerned about southern Africa.

I have generally used *Rhodesia* rather than *Zimbabwe* or *Southern Rhodesia* as this was the accepted term within the American government in the period of this study. For the same reason, I have used *South West Africa* rather than *Namibia*, and *Capetown* instead of *Cape Town*. I have used *South Africa* throughout, even though the nation was officially the Union of South Africa prior to 1961 and the

Republic of South Africa afterward. The term *African* indicates black African. Although whites in southern Africa consider themselves as "African" as blacks, I have used the term only in reference to the black majorities.

While it is tempting to draw "lessons" from past American actions in southern Africa to guide current policies, I have tried to restrain the impulse to write a "primer" on contemporary diplomacy. Still certain assumptions and tactics developed in the period of this study endure, and, although altered dramatically in the past sixteen years, white Africa remains an issue for America. Although the book does not attempt to predict future African developments or U.S. policy, it does try to show how past actions led to the frustrations and vacillations of recent American diplomacy. It assumes that we can learn from history—if not direct axioms at least the origins of current problems and dilemmas. While history follows the headlines, it is also true that the headlines are the harvest of history.

ACKNOWLEDGMENTS

This project began in a National Endowment for the Humanities Summer Seminar for College Teachers on the Cold War at the University of Texas. Robert Divine, the director of the seminar, helped me define the topic and the other participants, particularly Jerry Simmons, offered critical and useful suggestions at the early stage. Kinley Brauer of the University of Minnesota and Edward Bennett of Washington State University were unflagging in their encouragement. My colleagues in the history department at Carthage College, John Bailey, Robert Frost, Dennis Romano, John Neuenschwander, and Jon Zophy, prodded me to completion. The Carthage College Research Fund, the American Philosophical Society, and the Harry S. Truman Institute all helped fund early research. The Charles Warren Center for American History at Harvard University graciously granted me a resident fellowship that allowed me to complete research. I am greatly indebted to Donald Fleming, then director of the Warren Center, and to the other Warren Fellows. The librarians and research staffs at the Truman, Eisenhower, Kennedy, and Johnson presidential libraries, the National Archives, the Sterling Library at Yale University, and the Widener Library at Harvard eagerly shared their expertise. My greatest debt is to my wife, Linda, who not only endured long stretches in Abilene, Kansas, Independence, Missouri, Austin, Texas, Boston, and Washington, D.C., but also tolerated all the absences and eased all the frustrations.

T. J. N.
December 1984

1. WHITE RULE ON A BLACK CONTINENT | Background of a Diplomatic Dilemma

The American response to white rule in black Africa after World War II reveals a great deal about the objectives and tactics of Cold War diplomacy as well as the changing nature of international relations in the past three decades. The decolonization of Asia and Africa not only increased the number of participants in world politics but also introduced new issues. The bipolar, East-West perspective so dominant in American diplomacy increasingly confronted a world committed to nonalignment, economic development, and racial equality. The product of an eighteenth-century anticolonial struggle came face-to-face with modern liberation movements. While the United States could call for the "liberation" of Eastern Europe from Soviet domination, it faced a dilemma in the "liberation" of southern Africa. Sincere but abstract commitments to "freedom" clashed with immediate and concrete economic, strategic, and political interests. The conflict between such "hard" interests as trade and defense and "soft" issues such as human rights created a tension in America's Cold War diplomacy that was most obvious in its dealings with white Africa. The situation in South Africa, Rhodesia, and the Portuguese colonies of Angola and Mozambique forced America to transform its ideology of self-determination, majority rule, and individual freedom into policies toward governments that deny all three.

American diplomacy in southern Africa also illustrates the complex relationship between domestic considerations and pressure groups and foreign policy. The civil rights and black-power movements, the emergence of liberal, religious, and labor critics of U.S. actions, and well-financed lobbying efforts by agents of the white regimes "internalized" American foreign policy. Diplomats made policies designed simultaneously to silence domestic critics, to retain traditional European allies, to avoid a conservative revolt in Congress, and to gain third-world support. As a result, much of U.S. policy was "posturing" for domestic consumption. Packaging policy for various audiences often resulted in wide discrepancies between statements and action.

The response to black liberation also helps clarify the decisionmaking process within the U.S. government. The foreign policy bureaucracy was deeply split throughout the years between 1948 and 1968 over American efforts in southern Africa. The State Department, executive branch, and military were divided between "Europeanists" who argued for the primacy of the North Atlantic Treaty

Organization and the relative insignificance of Africa for America, and "Africanists" who pushed for a strong stance against white control and for an "Africa first" policy to gain the favor of the emerging nations. The bureaucratic battle intensified as African issues became more crucial and choices more difficult. The inter- and intradepartmental infighting over U.S. priorities is an important aspect of diplomatic history most evident in American relations with white Africa and black opponents of white rule.

The most important influence on American policy in southern Africa, as in all other areas, was anticommunism. Neither governmental officials nor interested citizens debated the objective of U.S. diplomacy: the prevention of communist gains in Africa. They disagreed about the tactics to achieve this goal. Europeanists and Africanists, liberals and conservatives, "realists" and "idealists" argued about the best strategy to insure a peaceful and anticommunist southern Africa. All assumed America had a right to shape African development to insure non-Marxist regimes. The conflict was over the means.

Proponents of a "European" policy contended that the rapid end of white rule would lead to weak, unstable, black governments easily controlled by Moscow or Peking. While the white regimes were repugnant to American ideals, they supported U.S. interests. America must separate ideological yearnings from the realities of the Cold War and either maintain the whites in power as bastions of anticommunism, or at least assure a slow and peaceful transition to majority rule that would protect the rights of the white minority and perpetuate pro-Western governments.

Advocates of an "Africa first" policy also argued from the anticommunist position. They claimed that continued white supremacy would drive Africans to communism as the only means of their liberation. Therefore, Washington must support a rapid shift to black rule not merely for ideological reasons but also to protect its own long-range interests. White control was doomed, and America must assist in its downfall or face the prospect of racial war and a continent totally alienated from the West.

Southern Africa became a laboratory for America's Cold War experiment in containment of communism and the spread of liberty. It tested America's ability to modify white intransigence and to control black nationalism. U.S. involvement stemmed from both an idealistic commitment to majority rule and a coldly realistic recognition of its Cold War interests.

Bringing African issues to the attention of American citizens as well as their policy makers in Washington, however, was hampered by vague impressions of the dark continent. With Tarzan movies, Hemingway short stories, and missionary slides in church basements as the principal sources of information about Africa, most Americans have a minimal knowledge of Africa and Africans. The stereotype of Africa as a land of jungles, cannibals, white hunters, and wild animals is not only wrong but also ignores the diversity of the continent.

Even interested and knowledgeable Americans tend to speak of the area and its peoples with little regard for the vast differences in ethnicity, language, culture, and history. The single image of the black African has been accompanied by a homogenized impression of whites on the continent. To speak of a monolithic "white" Africa is as erroneous as to assume the commonality of blacks. The three intractable white regimes in southern Africa differed markedly in their historical development, governments, and perception of their role in Africa. While they were often conveniently grouped in both the public and official mind, their uniqueness often outweighed their similarities.

A popular joke in the State Department in the early 1960s told of Antonio Salazar, dictator of Portugal, sending three Africans to college. According to the story, he was so pleased with his success that he began planning Portugal's second five-hundred-year plan. Though perhaps a fair critique of the dictator's anachronistic leadership, the State Department's humor reveals American appreciation of Portugal's long history of conquest and colonization. It also recognizes the "civilizing mission" implicit in Portugal's imperial heritage. Salazar followed a long line of Portuguese leaders determined to conquer new lands, to subjugate the native people, and to uplift them with a superior Portuguese culture. Portugal was not alone. Dutch and British explorers set sail for Africa in search of resources and in hopes of shining civilized light on a dark and savage continent. By the time the United States emerged as a world power in the twentieth century, Portugal, the Netherlands, and Great Britain had controlled colonies in Africa for centuries. The descendants of the first explorers and colonists considered the African lands their home and continued white control a necessity. America's diplomatic dilemma becomes clearer when viewed in light of centuries-long development of white rule in Africa.

Portuguese Africa

Portugal's involvement in Africa spanned more than five hundred years. In 1441 Portuguese adventurers explored the African coast in search of gold and the mythical Christian king, Prester John. Later Prince Henry the Navigator sent expeditions to find a route from Europe to India. Portuguese sailors explored the Congo River estuary in 1483 and made contact with the Kongo kingdom of King Nzina. Within a decade King John II had sent traders, priests, and soldiers to establish small settlements along the Congo. The king also sent Bartholomeu Dias on a voyage to India. He sailed around the Cape of Good Hope and brought the Portuguese into contact with East Africa in 1487. Later voyages to the East resulted in the development of trading posts and way stations in Mozambique that served as stepping stones to Portugal's vast mercantile empire in India and the Indies until the beginning of the "Spanish Captivity" in 1580. Under Spain's rule, Portugal lost its Asian empire, and whites in Mozambique were cut off from contact with the mother country. Their communities degenerated into isolated, decadent fiefdoms.

Portuguese involvement in Angola in the sixteenth century soon eclipsed interest in the Congo or Mozambique. Portugal's control of Brazil and the demand for slave labor prompted Angola's development. Under pressure from slave traders and missionaries, King Sebastian ordered Paulo Dias de Novais to lead an expedition inland from the port of Luanda in 1576. Dias met fierce resistance from Africans in the interior, but Portugal managed to establish a foothold in the region for the slave trade. When the Portuguese regained their throne from the Spanish in 1640, they immediately fought off a Dutch challenge for Angola. By 1647, Portugal held firm control of the slave trade and rushed to meet the seemingly insatiable demands of the new world. Over the next two centuries, Portuguese slavers shipped more than three million Africans from Angola until Portugal abolished slave trade in 1836. In 1858, responding to pressure from Great Britain, Portugal ended slavery in its African possessions as well.

With the legal end of the slave trade and slavery, Portugal gradually pushed from the coast toward the interior of Africa in preparation for formal annexation of colonies. The motives for direct colonization were as much nationalistic as economic. The Portuguese wanted to recapture the power and prestige of the fifteenth century through a new colonial empire in Africa. Their goal was an enormous empire uniting Angola on the west with Mozambique on the east through control of central Africa. This grandiose scheme, however, conflicted with the colonial aims of Portugal's more powerful European rivals. As a result, Portugal gained international recognition of its control of Angola and Mozambique but had to abandon its claims in central Africa.

Even with this loss, Portugal emerged from the European scramble for Africa with the third largest empire. When Europeans had finished drawing the map of Africa, Portuguese Angola was over 481,000 square miles and Mozambique nearly 300,000. This empire, however, existed largely on paper, as it remained nearly unexplored and unoccupied. Whites ruled less than 10 percent of the territory and were outnumbered by Africans more than one hundred to one. Throughout the early twentieth century, Lisbon attempted to expand its area of occupation, to increase the white population, and to cultivate cash crops. It generally failed in each goal. Efforts to attract whites were disastrous. Portuguese chose to emigrate to America rather than Africa. By 1920 over one million Portuguese had left for the United States, while only thirty-five thousand had gone to the African colonies. Because the white population was so tiny, most of Angola and Mozambique remained nearly unaffected by European control.

Lisbon was also unable to solve the problem of fixed agriculture. With the abolition of slavery, whites turned to forced labor for their cotton, cocoa, and coffee plantations. By the early twentieth century, exposés of Portuguese impressment, whippings, and mutilations rivaled accounts of Belgian exploitation of the Congo.

By the early 1930s, Portugal's African empire seemed such a burden for the small nation that some European diplomats argued that a more powerful state should seize it. The empire not only remained in Portuguese hands but also became a crucial part of the nation's identity. The triumph of Dr. Antonio de Oliveira Salazar and his quasi-fascist "New State" in 1932 totally altered the importance of the African possessions for Portugal. Salazar saw the colonies not as a burden but as a symbol of the glory of Portugal's past and its vehicle for remaining a world power. While Mussolini could only dream of reviving the Roman empire, Salazar could point to the "overseas possessions" as the heritage of Portugal's greatness. They were tangible proof of the nation's importance in the world and of the mystical "civilizing mission" ordained for the Portuguese people. To Salazar, the importance of the empire was not as much economic as nationalistic and even spiritual. Continued control was necessary for the morale of the people, the international status of the state, and the legitimacy of the government. Until his retirement in 1968, Salazar never abandoned his conviction that the end of the empire would lead directly to the collapse of the Portuguese nation.

Salazar developed elaborate justifications for continued control of the African territories. He argued that the possessions were not colonies but integral parts of Portugal. Angola and Mozambique were "overseas possessions," not colonies. They were as much a part of the nation as Lisbon. The mother country and the empire were a single "pan-Lusitanian" community bound by Portuguese language, culture, and law. There were no colonies but "one state, one race, one faith, and one civilization."

Just as there were no colonies there were also no "Africans." All in the empire were "Portuguese." The theory of "lusotropicalism" put forth by Salazar claimed that all individuals in the possessions were Portuguese citizens. There were no distinctions based on color but only on "merit." All who were "civilized" deserved legal rights. Thus, Lisbon could and did argue that there was no racial prejudice in their possessions. They only distinguished between "civilized" and "uncivilized."

Lusotropicalism was somewhat similar to the early French colonial policy of "assimilation"—the idealistic attempt to unite the French empire in a common language and culture regardless of regional differences. The Portuguese, however, absolutely refused to adjust their ideas to the growth of nationalism after World War II. Salazar's belief in the crucial importance of the empire and his mystical defense of his policies locked Portugal into a view of the colonies that was unfathomable to other European nations and repugnant to black Africans.

Those outside Portugal were perplexed by Salazar's ideas of empire and pointed to the results of Lisbon's rule. Despite the rhetoric about racial equality and the "civilizing mission," the Portuguese had done little to improve the plight of the African. Angola and Mozambique remained impoverished, ignorant, and exploited by white masters. In 1950, only thirty thousand of the four million Angolans were considered "civilized," while the remaining "uncivilized" *idigenas* had no political or civil rights. Less than 1 percent of the Africans in the Portuguese colonies had ever attended a school. Salazar's grand theories of Portugal's mission did little to alter the squalor in Africa.

Portugal's continued presence in Africa posed a series of problems for America in the Cold War period. As Great Britain, France, and Belgium made plans to part with their African colonies, Portugal steadfastly refused even to consider any program for independence. Lisbon argued that there was no need to prepare for independence as Angola and Mozambique were already a part of Portugal. The decolonization of black Africa left Portugal as the lone European nation on the continent. U.S. support of continued Portuguese rule would alienate independent Africa and the rest of the third world, while pressures for decolonization would strain relations with Lisbon.

Salazar's personality compounded Portugal's rigidity and sensitivity. He was convinced of the cultural superiority of Portugal and the growing decadence of the rest of the West. He viewed twentieth-century Westerners as hopelessly materialistic and uncultured. Salazar spent his happiest moments cultivating his garden in the country or reading theology in his candle-lit study. He despised the dehumanizing tendencies of technology, refused to have a telephone in his office, and banned the use of typewriters by his secretaries. A self-proclaimed "nineteenth-century man" (critics argued sixteenth-century), Salazar puzzled Americans. U.S. officials considered him an anachronism and ridiculed his defense of Portugal's "civilizing mission." Salazar, in turn, saw America as the prime example of the debasement of modern times. Its materialism, aggressiveness, and arrogance appalled him. To alter Portugal's African policy, America would have to change Salazar's ideas about the empire, pressure him into abandoning the colonies, or remove him. Eventually, Washington tried all three.

Strategic and military considerations also influenced U.S. actions. Militantly anticommunist and a member of the North Atlantic Treaty Organization, Portugal controlled a key military base in the Azores islands. Demands for African independence had to be weighed against the possible loss of a faithful Cold War ally, a weakening of the European defense pact, and possible eviction of U.S. forces from the Azores base.

Ironically, Portugal's own failure to educate the African or create a stable economy in its colonies restrained American demands for decolonization. U.S. diplomats were dismayed by the lack of preparation for self-rule in the Portuguese territories and feared that if independece were obtained too rapidly it would lead to chaos and weak nations that would invite communist inroads. There was even concern in Washington that the sudden loss of its colonies might so shake Portugal that it, too, would fall under communist influence.

American policymakers thus adopted a middle road between support of Portugal and active assistance to independence movements. Defense of continued rule by Lisbon would alienate black Africa (and black America) and violate U.S. commitments to self-determination. It would likely drive African nationalists to the Soviets or Chinese for support. Active American encouragement of majority rule, however, risked a disruption of European solidarity and might well result in weak, ungovernable nations ripe for subversion.

Rhodesia

Although Rhodesia's unilateral declaration of independence from Great Britain on 11 November 1965 focused international attention on its white government, the "Rhodesian problem" existed long before. White rule in Rhodesia grew out of aggressive British imperialism, in general, and the manipulations of Cecil Rhodes, in particular. After making his fortune in the diamond and gold mines of South Africa in the 1870s and 1880s, Rhodes devoted his life to promoting British expansion in Africa. He used his British South Africa Company as the vehicle to extend British control north from Cape Province and Natal in South Africa into what was to become Rhodesia. In 1888 Rhodes persuaded King Lobengula to grant exclusive mineral rights in his kingdom to the British South Africa Company. Two years later Rhodes sent a small band of whites north from the Transvaal into Mashonaland in search of gold and land. They established a capital for the new territory at Fort Salisbury in 1890. While the British high commissioner in Capetown had ultimate authority, the British government recognized the British South Africa Company as the de facto ruler.

Lobengula and his people fiercely resisted the "opening" of their territory to settlement. Continued wars between whites and blacks forced Great Britain to send regular troops to complete occupation of the area. Eventually, the new territory was divided into Southern and Northern Rhodesia. Southern Rhodesia, the area of most white settlement, received its own legislature and administration in 1898. Great Britain's victory in the Boer War in 1902 gave it control of South Africa and gradually led the Foreign Office to establish its rule in all of Rhodesia. The small cluster of white settlers welcomed British interest, as they were increasingly unhappy with the administration of the British South Africa Company. In 1922 they voted to become a direct British colony. The next year Southern Rhodesia became a "self-governing colony," and Northern Rhodesia, with a miniscule white population, became a British protectorate.

The 1923 agreement would become a source of conflict between white

Rhodesians and Great Britain in the 1950s. The document allowed the settlers control over their internal affairs but reserved foreign policy for the mother country. London also reserved the right to veto any action by the Rhodesian legislature and to repeal the constitution at any time.

Despite such paper provisions, Rhodesians had a large degree of autonomy. Whites used this power to insure their dominance over the black majority. In 1930 they divided land between the whites (5 percent of the population) and the blacks. Whites received half of the territory and more than 80 percent of the most fertile terrain. White Rhodesians developed a prosperous agricultural economy using black labor to produce high-quality tobacco and other export crops. Whites in Rhodesia eventually enjoyed the highest standard of living in Africa and established strict provisions to insure their privileged position. They suppressed political aspirations of the black majority with economic pressure and military force.

The growth of black nationalism in Africa after World War II terrified white Rhodesians. Outnumbered more than twenty to one, they feared England would abandon its African colonies to the black majority. White fears were intensified in 1953 when Great Britain combined its three Central African colonies (Nyasaland and Northern and Southern Rhodesia) into a common federation. Whites were reluctant to enter into an agreement with the two nearly all black nations but agreed when they became convinced that it was one way to avoid immediate pressure for majority rule.

The Central African Federation was never successful. The agreement called for a common defense and economic policies, but it reserved "local affairs" to each nation. To whites in Southern Rhodesia, this condoned racist policies. The whites intensified racial segregation, banned African labor and political organizations, and enlarged their police and army reserves. By 1960 England conceded that the federation was a failure and moved to dissolve it. It was clear that, with the end of the pact, Nyasaland and Northern Rhodesia would be granted independence. Southern Rhodesia argued that it, too, should start the process of decolonization. London rejected any plans for independence until there were provisions for African political participation. Rhodesia, in turn, pressed Great Britain to give up the right reserved in the 1923 constitution to intervene in Rhodesian affairs. Britain agreed to scrap the 1923 agreement in exchange for "safeguards" for the rights of black Africans. A new constitution in 1961 allowed limited black representation through a separate voting roll but kept white control of the legislature. Britain also retained the right to revoke the new pact.

Black Rhodesians were not consulted in the negotiations for the new constitution, and they protested the agreement. They denounced the token black representation as a ruse and demanded an end to white rule. The Rhodesian government responded by arresting black leaders, banning black organizations, and declaring a state of emergency. Extremist whites were convinced that the British would never grant Rhodesia independence without complete majority rule and the redistribution of land. They attacked the "sellout" of whites in Kenya and pointed to the chaos in the newly independent Belgian Congo as the inevitable result of black control. In December 1962, the new "Rhodesian Front" defeated the ruling government with a campaign calling for "getting tough" with both blacks and the British and for eventual, complete Rhodesian independence.

By 1963 the situation in Rhodesia was so chaotic and complex that many informed observers predicted racial war. In that summer Britain began discussions on the final dissolution of the Central African Federation. Rhodesian leader Winston Field demanded immediate freedom for all three members of the federation, while Britain's representatives insisted on an end to racial discrimination, a broadening of the franchise, and repeal of the Land Appropriation Act as prerequisites to self-rule. Finally, in December 1963, Great Britain buried the long-dead corpse of the federation. The controversial agreement transferred the bulk of the federation's military forces to the white government in Salisbury. Responding to the demands of the newly independent African nations, the United Nations passed a resolution calling on Great Britain to prevent the transfer of weapons to Southern Rhodesia since they would likely be used against the black majority. London exercised its first veto since the Suez crisis of 1956 and completed the arrangement.

The formation and breakup of the Central African Federation convinced whites in Rhodesia that Great Britain was totally under the control of the Afro-Asian nations of the British Commonwealth. Rhodesians felt surrounded by hostile black nations and abandoned by whites in London. They reacted by electing the most extreme opponent of black rights and most outspoken advocate of unilateral independence, Ian Smith, as prime minister.

When Nyasaland became the independent nation of Malawi and Northern Rhodesia became the sovereign state of Zambia in 1964, Southern Rhodesia remained a British colony. When Smith pressed again for independence, the Labour Government of Harold Wilson demanded not only an end to racial discrimination but also complete majority rule. Whites, convinced for over two decades that black rule would bring their destruction, defied Great Britain, black Africa, and the UN by announcing Rhodesia's Unilateral Declaration of Independence (UDI) on 11 November 1965.

With the announcement of UDI, a largely British problem became a global issue. Like other nations, the United States was forced to respond to Rhodesia's action. America weighed its relations with black Africa, its "special relationship" with Great Britain, the authority of the UN, and the entire Cold War strategy of avoiding communist influence in Africa. By 1965 America had committed itself to the support of majority rule in Africa. Washington also determined that it should follow Great Britain in a campaign against Smith's "illegal" action. The United States also wanted to rally the support of non-European nations for American intervention in Vietnam. Each of these considerations seemed to lead to strong, decisive action against Rhodesia.

Balanced against these influences, however, were serious concerns about the effects of black rule in Rhodesia, doubts about London's ability to handle the situation, and fear that the UN might embroil the United States in direct intervention in Africa. Not all Americans believed that Rhodesia had acted illegally. America had announced its own UDI in 1776. Others in the United States argued that the entire issue was an internal matter within the British empire and of no immediate concern for America. Some in Washington also feared that a strong action against Smith would set a precedent for international moves against the governments of South Africa and the Portuguese colonies. Finally, the Rhodesian Government was white, Christian, capitalist, and anticommunist on a continent that, to many Americans, was radical, undemocratic, and chaotic.

As in the other areas of "white Africa," the United States faced a difficult choice. Americans wanted to honor a historic commitment to self-determination, but they feared that implementating this doctrine might be more dangerous than continued white control.

South Africa

International opposition to South Africa's policy of apartheid (racial separatism) clearly symbolized the emergence of race as a foreign-policy issue in the post–World War II era. South Africa has defied the world by holding to the notion of white control, while the rest of the continent has moved toward majority rule. At the same time that most of the rest of the world has endorsed the principle of racial equality, South Africa has pursued an official policy of racial classification and separatism. If South Africa were a small or weak nation, its policies would remain repugnant to other nations, but its international importance would be minimal. Instead the country's size, wealth, and location have made it at once more offensive and less responsive to the international community.

South Africa is a multiracial rather than a biracial society. The broad distinction between white and black has been refined into more detailed categories. Approximately nineteen of its twenty-six million inhabitants are black and more than three million are either Asian or "colored" (of mixed racial background). Whites are divided between Afrikaners (60 percent) and English-speaking (40 percent). Although whites share a common color, they have separate languages, cultures, and heritages. Conflict between Afrikaner and Englishman has dominated the history of South Africa nearly as much as strife between white and black.

Few people are as guided by their past as are the Afrikaners. Their ancestors arrived in Africa in 1652 when the Dutch East India Company established Capetown as a stopover for the Asian trade. The Dutch persuaded Jan van Riebeeck to lead a group to settle at the Cape. They established an agricultural community based on slavery, developed a common language (Afrikaans), and embraced a theology that preached white supremacy, fundamentalism, and patriarchal rule. The Boers (a form of the Dutch word for farmer) were isolated from the intellectual and political changes in Europe in the seventeenth and eighteenth centuries. Like the Puritans in New England, they believed that they had been chosen by God to create the true New Testament society on a primitive continent.

Great Britain annexed the Cape Colony after the Napoleonic Wars and thus rudely ended Boer isolation. The clash between the Afrikaners and their new English rulers was immediate and protracted. Issues of race, religion, language, and economics separated them. Afrikaners proclaimed the inferiority of the African and endorsed slavery. The British, while making no claim for racial equality, abolished slavery in 1833 and sought minimal rights for the African. England also endorsed religious freedom and the spread of Christianity among the Africans. The Boers rejected religious pluralism and opposed missionary activity. To the Boers, the British were "Europeans," while the Boers had been in Africa for nearly two hundred years. The Afrikaners glorified agrarianism and rejected the British commitment to trade and manufacturing. With the abolition of slavery and support of a more complex economy, Great Britain seemed to threaten the very heart of Afrikaner society.

The conflict between Briton and Boer culminated in one of the most celebrated events in Afrikaner history: the Great Trek. Between 1835 and 1838 over one-fifth of the Boers abandoned Cape Colony and moved hundreds of miles to the north and east into the wilderness. Fighting skirmishes with the Africans, the Boers formed their wagons each night into tight circles or "laagers." The "laager" became a symbol of the need for the white Afrikaner to turn inward for support against a hostile world. The harshness of the Great Trek and the courage of the Boers have made the trek nearly a sacred event to the Afrikaners. The sacrifices of their ancestors to preserve their culture and identity have served as reminders to the Afrikaners of the need to resist erosion of their community.

The Boers eventually settled in what were to become the South African provinces of Natal, Transvaal, and the Orange Free State. For a brief period they were free from the British and other foreign influences, but their isolation was short-lived. With the discovery of diamonds in 1867 and, more important, gold in 1886, the Boers were inundated with speculators, engineers, and miners drawn by the lure of sudden wealth. Unable to stop the invasion of the "Uitlanders," or foreigners, the Boers were again threatened with the destruction of their society and the loss of their political independence. Foreign mining magnates were convinced that the backward Boer government and its out-dated agrarianism had to be eliminated if the region was to be developed. Foreign missionaries demanded the opportunity to spread the gospel among the Africans. Cecil Rhodes and the British government saw the chance to expand their influence to the north. In 1896 Rhodes, American mining engineers in the Transvaal, and, at least indirectly, the British government organized a military expedition to topple the Boer government of Paul Kruger. Kruger's "army of farmers" crushed the invasion, but the Jameson Raid served as a preview for the final conflict between Boer independence and British control three years later.

The Boer War finally broke out in 1899. Most observers assumed that the mighty British empire would easily crush a few thousand Boer farmers, but the war was not the rout most predicted. Early Boer victories and daring commando raids on British positions forced Great Britain into a major campaign that lasted over two years. England triumphed only after it adopted a policy of burning Boer farms and interning the civilian population in concentration camps. More Afrikaner women and children died in the British camps than did Boer troops in the field.

Despite Great Britain's victory, the Boers did not assimilate English culture. In 1910, the British merged the four colonies into the Union of South Africa, but unity existed only in the name. South Africa remained deeply split between English-speaking and Afrikaner whites. While moderate Boers participated in the government of the new Union, more obstinate Afrikaners rejected any cooperation with the hated British. Former Boer general James Hertzog, in particular, preached a fervent Afrikaner nationalism. Hertzog eventually formed the National party pledged to Afrikaner control of the politics and culture of the nation.

Past antagonisms surfaced again during World War I. The South African government's decision to support England provoked an armed rebellion by extremist Boers. The South African government crushed the revolt, but again the conflict between English-speaking and Afrikaner whites had been violent. During the war, South African troops captured German South West Africa—a victory that would later have international ramifications.

After the war, Afrikaner nationalists concentrated on private organizations, self-help societies, and cultural clubs to maintain their identity and to preserve their heritage. One of the most significant of these private groups was the Afrikaner Broederbond, a secret organization to promote Afrikaner culture, language, political power, and financial assistance. In small, secret cells the Broederbond taught the superiority of the Afrikaners and their destiny to rule the nation. It did and still does include many of the leaders of the National party.

The triumph of Adolf Hitler and National Socialism in Germany fueled Afrikaner nationalism in South Africa. Many national party leaders admired the discipline and direction of Nazi Germany and agreed that individualism and materialism should be secondary to the glory of the state. Hitler's definition of

Germany as a people rather than a territory limited by boundaries paralleled their own view of South Africa as a nation of Afrikaners united by language, culture, and history. Some nationalists also accepted Hitler's anti-Semitism and his idea of a "superior" race destined to rule over "inferior" peoples. Future prime ministers of South Africa, Johannes Strijdom, Hendrik Verwoerd, and B. J. Vorster all supported Nazi ideology in the 1930s. The South African government interned Vorster during World War II after he openly advocated a German victory.

As long as the national party remained a minority, its leaders' ideas were of little concern outside South Africa. The stunning victory of the Nationalists in 1948, however, transformed Afrikaner ideology into policy and made South African apartheid an international issue. Under Afrikaner rule, South Africa's traditional racial segregation was transformed into racial separatism. The adoption of apartheid brought not only continued white control but also the elimination of the few remaining rights for nonwhites, massive population relocation, racial classification, and suppression of dissent by persons of any color.

In 1948 South Africa lurched to the right, and over the next two decades it became even more extremist and rigid. As nations in black Africa gained independence and as international pressure on South Africa intensified, its rulers reverted to the "laager mentality." Afrikaners felt besieged by black nations in Africa and abandoned by whites in Europe and North America.

At first glance, it would seem that in South Africa American diplomats faced problems similar to those in the Portuguese colonies and Rhodesia: All were minority governments in violation of the principles of self-determination and human rights, and all were potential areas of racial conflict and communist influence. South Africa, however, raised a much more difficult issue for America than the other areas of white control. It was not a colony, and its white minority had no place to go. The Afrikaners considered themselves as "African" as the black majority. Thus, any solution to the racial situation in South Africa would have to provide for the millions of whites.

South Africa was also far more powerful than Portugal or Rhodesia. Its mineral and industrial wealth made it less vulnerable to international pressure than Portugal or Rhodesia. Foreign nations needed South Africa's gold more than South Africa needed their products. Unlike Rhodesia or Portugal, South Africa also developed a powerful military in the 1960s. Any black revolt would be lengthy and bloody.

South Africa was also strategically important to the United States. America needed its minerals for defense industries, its ports for the U.S. fleet, and its tracking stations for America's space program in the 1960s. Finally, South Africa was militantly anticommunist. It often supported Washington's Cold War policies.

In spite of differences, Rhodesia, South Africa, and the Portuguese colonies shared a fierce determination to perpetuate minority control. They looked to the United States to insure their continued existence as bastions of stability and anticommunism. To black Africa and much of the rest of the third world, the liberation of Africa was incomplete without majority rule in the Portuguese colonies, Rhodesia, and South Africa. They demanded that America aid in the destruction of these pockets of white supremacy as proof of the U.S. commitment to majority rule and human rights. Washington confronted problems of moderating white intransigence, restraining black militancy, and placing the entire problem of white Africa within Cold War priorities.

2. RACE AND CONTAINMENT | Truman and the Origins of Apartheid

Since its overthrow of British rule in 1783, the United States has repeatedly proclaimed its opposition to colonialism and its support for the self-determination of all peoples. While America has rarely hesitated to intervene in the domestic politics of other nations and even annexed its own colonial empire in 1899, it has traditionally denounced European imperialism and called for freely elected governments representative of ethnic majorities. The verbal encouragement of the European revolutions of the mid-nineteenth century, intervention in 1898 to "free Cuba" from Spain (and to gain the Philippines), and Woodrow Wilson's eloquent proclamation of self-determination as a war aim in 1917 all symbolize America's self-definition as an opponent of colonial rule and an advocate of political democracy.

America's anticolonialism and support of majority rule have not been merely altruistic idealism but often have served as means of securing its own international interests. Often the nation has been willing to set aside its opposition to imperialism and totalitarianism for political expediency. While the gap between rhetoric and action has often been large, America has generally acknowledged an obligation to serve as both a model and an active promoter of the broad principle of self-determination.

During World War II the United States repeated its anticolonial message. The speeches of President Franklin Roosevelt, Secretary of State Cordell Hull, and others during the war seemingly pledged America to the destruction of the European colonial empires and the support of majority rule. Roosevelt thought that colonies sparked international rivalry and would cause postwar conflict. While his commitment to decolonization has been exaggerated, the president's statements identified the United States with the cause of independence not only in nations occupied by Germany and Japan but in the colonies of the other European powers as well.

Wartime rhetoric not only supported self-determination but also introduced a second issue that would become increasingly important in the decades that followed: race. Allied propaganda emphasized the racism of both Nazi Germany and imperial Japan. Roosevelt and other leaders did not support racial equality at home or abroad, but their attacks on official racism worked to make the war appear to many non-Europeans partly as a struggle for their own aspirations. The war also aided the growth of black political power within the United States and, as a result, the development of civil rights as a domestic issue. Thousands of blacks migrated from the American south to jobs in defense plants to the north and west. Although the black vote had been important in elections prior to the war, it became more significant as a result of the wartime migration. Black soldiers fighting a war to destroy racism and to restore freedom found segregation in the armed forces and at home a cruel hypocrisy. They returned to the United States with a new militancy and with the votes to channel their frustrations into political power.

World War II thus served as a catalyst for the twin issues of self-determination and race that would shape American relations with much of the world in the period that followed. The conflict seemingly committed the Allies to decolonization, weakened the power of the imperial countries, and fired the imagination of Africans and Asians. Third-world leaders became convinced that the war would be the vehicle of their independence. They interpreted American generalities about freedom as endorsements of their liberation and thought that the United States would use its power to overwhelm opposition to independence from their enfeebled European rulers.

Roosevelts's encouragement of anticolonial sentiment had begun even before Pearl Harbor. The Atlantic Charter, which followed a meeting between the president and British prime minister, Winston Churchill, in August 1940, was hailed by some African and Asian leaders as a death warrant for imperialism. A press release rather than an official document, the Atlantic Charter contained only a vague reference in Article III to the right of all peoples to self-government and freedom to select the form of that government. Both Roosevelt and Churchill later stressed that this was aimed at nations occupied by Germany and Japan, but to the emerging educated elites in Asia and Africa the announcement seemed to be a declaration of eventual independence.[1] America's war aims further encouraged anticolonial nationalists. Secretary of State Cordell Hull argued that the European powers "should fix, at the earliest practicable moment, dates upon which the colonial peoples would be accorded the status of full independence." Even though Hull later claimed that Washington never pressed Europe for "an immediate grant of self-government" but only wanted plans for decolonization "after an adequate period," his statements alarmed imperialists in Europe and inspired leaders in the colonies.[2]

In addition to the Atlantic Charter and the assumed dedication of America to the dismantling of the European empires, the establishment of the United Nations created a climate of expectation among critics of colonialism. Afro-

---

1. An excellent discussion of the origins and impact of the Atlantic Charter and the entire subject of American anticolonialism during the war is William Roger Louis, *Imperialism at Bay*. See also Jean-Donald Miller, "The United States and Sub-Saharan Africa, 1939–1950: The Roots of American Policy toward Decolonization in Africa."

2. Cordell Hull, *Memoirs*, 2:1235, 1599.

Asian leaders were disappointed that the final agreement did not call for an immediate end to colonialism, but they were convinced that the organization would be the guiding force in the rapid transition to independence. The war had exhausted Europe both physically and psychologically, and the colonial powers found the "burden of empire" especially heavy. European rule seemed doomed, and the United States appeared to be the agent of its destruction.

America's image as an anticolonial advocate was inaccurate. At best, the nation's record during the war shows support only for long-range plans for eventual independence accompanied by continued strong European influence. Its tradition of anti-imperialism and support of majority rule, however, combined with its wartime oratory unwittingly to designate the United States as the champion of decolonization. America did not mind being perceived as a critic of imperialism, but it was not prepared to exert strong pressure on Europeans to divest themselves of colonies. Leaders in Washington welcomed the support of the Africans and Asians, but their major priority continued to be close cooperation with Europe. The postwar conflict between the United States and the Soviet Union rapidly destroyed even America's superficial commitment to decolonization.[3]

Initially, the Cold War served to solidify America's anti-imperialist position. President Harry Truman and other U.S. leaders justified the conflict with communism as a battle between freedom and slavery. Cold War rhetoric emphasized the American goals of self-determination, democracy, and human rights. By portraying the United States as dedicated to political freedom and national self-determination, its leaders seemingly endorsed decolonization. African and Asian nationalists pointed out that, like the nations under Soviet control, their countries lacked majority rule and political rights. They again interpreted American statements as universal and logically supportive of self-rule by colonial peoples.

As the Cold War intensified, however, the U.S. position on decolonization grew more conservative. Statements about freedom and self-determination focused on Eastern Europe, not Africa or Asia. Although American officials easily could denounce Soviet imperialism and call for self-determination in Poland, they did not extend such demands to the colonies of their allies. They saw rapid independence for Africa and Asia as dangerous to the Western alliance and to the colonial peoples. While they remained sympathetic to the aspirations of the Africans and Asians, American leaders feared rapid freedom would cripple European economic recovery (and Europe's ability to resist communism) and would create weak nations unable to resist penetration and subversion by Moscow.

3. Edward Baum, "The United States, Self-Government, and Africa: An Examination of the Nature of the American Policy on Self-Determination with Reference to Africa in the Postwar Era." See also James Roark, "American Black Leaders: The Response to Colonialism and the Cold War, 1943–1953."

As the Cold War dragged on, American leaders moved toward more active support of continued European colonialism. They submerged self-determination under the larger policy of global containment of communism. Increasingly, America tried to restrain the very nationalism it had helped to create during the war. The United States first encountered the problems of anticommunism, black liberation, and human rights in the Union of South Africa. American reaction to institutional racism and white minority rule in South Africa set the pattern for its later involvement in the Portuguese colonies and Rhodesia.

The surge of African nationalism unleashed by World War II created problems in South Africa. The government of Jan Christiaan Smuts feared that the economic and political weakness of Great Britain would force South Africa to stand alone against the demands of its black majority. Furthermore, the Labour government in London was far less sympathetic to the white regime in Pretoria than the wartime Tory administration had been. Britain's acceptance of independence for India, Pakistan, and Burma convinced many in South Africa that it would be only a short time before British Africa also succeeded in gaining freedom.[4] Smuts and other South Africans also doubted that they could turn to the United Nations for assistance. They feared the organization not only would become a lobbying force for decolonization and majority rule but also would try to tamper with South Africa's racial restrictions. By 1947, many whites in the nation believed they would have to "go it alone" in the impending conflict with the black majority at home and the anticipated independent black states in Africa. In 1948, South Africa responded to fears of potential threats to white rule by repudiating Smuts and by embracing a militant white supremacy.

Smuts had ruled South Africa since 1939 as the leader of the moderate United party. His cabinet included both Afrikaners and English-speaking South Africans. The domestic and international reputation of its leader strengthened the government. Smuts, a hero of the Boer War, later played a major role in the peace conference following World War I. He was recognized internationally as a skilled diplomat. To many outside Africa, Smuts and South Africa were nearly synonymous. When he called for elections in 1948, most of the rest of the world confidently assumed that Smuts would be returned for another term. While militant Afrikaners attacked the government for its support of England during the war and for its "betrayal" of Afrikaner culture, few observers felt they would have much impact.

Smuts's distinguished career and international acclaim, however, proved to be no match for the driving forces of Afrikaner nationalism and racial fear. The National party challenged Smuts in 1948 in an emotional campaign that attacked communism and demanded stronger protection of white supremacy. The

---

4. William K. Hancock, *Smuts*, 2:447–448.

Nationalists, led by Dr. Daniel Malan, represented a fervent strain of Afrikaner nationalism that few outside South Africa understood. Born in Cape Province, Malan attended Stellenbosch University, the intellectual center of militant Afrikaner sentiment. After graduate training in theology in Holland, Malan was recruited by Hertzog into the National party and edited the Nationalist newspaper *Die Burger*. In 1933 Malan broke with Hertzog and other party leaders. He condemned Nationalist officials for being too moderate in their demands for a true Afrikaner state and not sufficiently alarmed about "Jewish conspiracies." Malan formed the "purified" National party based on an extreme form of Afrikaner nationalism. It emphasized the mission of the Boers as God's elect and the need to withdraw from contact with non-Afrikaners to return to the close community of the Great Trek. Both critics and supporters dubbed Malan the "Boer Moses."

Malan's campaign confirmed impressions of him as a fanatic and his followers as extremists. The chief political issues in 1948 were liberalism, communism, and race. Nationalists accused Smuts of drifting toward liberalism, tolerating the Communist party, and, most important, being too sympathetic to the desires of nonwhites. Throughout the campaign the Nationalists played on white fears of the black majority. They argued that Great Britain had given in to Asian demands for independence, and Africa was the next target. Malan contended that South Africa faced a choice between destructive black rule or more strict racial segregation and suppression of dissent.

Malan's call for "separate development" of the races, or apartheid, however, provoked the most controversy during the election. The Nationalists made it clear that their racial policies were dedicated to more than continued white rule. A National party campaign pamphlet explained the objectives of apartheid:

> The guiding principle behind the policy is that the non-Whites of the country, especially the Blacks, should be guided by the Whites towards self-realization and self-government within their own communities and in their own areas. . . . The Black man's ambitions must be realized within the bosom of his own people and as he progresses he should not leave the masses of his people in the lurch by seeking to penetrate the White Man's society or to participate in the latter's institution of government. . . . White and Black must each seek their own future in every respect within their respective racial groups.[5]

Malan and his followers never explained the exact details of apartheid during the campaign, but it was certain that nonwhites would lose what few rights still existed and would be allowed in white areas only as temporary laborers.

Like most foreigners, American representatives in South Africa thought that the Nationalists were impractical extremists and could never defeat Smuts. American impressions of South Africa came largely from contact with English-

5. Quoted in William Vatcher, *White Laager*, 156.

speaking whites, and U.S. officials showed little understanding of the appeal of the Nationalists. They were enamored of the personality and internationalism of Smuts and disdainful of the leadership of Malan. Washington's minister in Pretoria reported to the State Department that the Nationalists were "narrow racialists and parochial in outlook." Malan was "clearly incapable of ruling" and "at a decided disadvantage in opposing a statesman of the calibre of General Smuts."[6]

Malan's pledge of apartheid further convinced American diplomats that the National party provided an outlet for protest votes and could never seriously challenge the ruling government. Apartheid "is so transparently unworkable," concluded one U.S. official, "that even Afrikaners recognize that it is folly." On the eve of the election, the American representative in Pretoria predicted that Smuts would win easily and reported that even National party workers had accepted "the inevitability of defeat in the General Election."[7]

Such estimates were logical given Smuts's reputation and the apparent extremism of his opponent, but they also show an inability to understand the intense fears of white South Africans in 1948 and the resultant appeal of the Nationalists. Afrikaner nationalism had not been abandoned despite British control. The threat of black liberation throughout Africa and within South Africa combined with Malan's call for a return to Afrikaner exclusiveness to create an emotional atmosphere more intense than most foreign observers could comprehend. Although they did not receive a majority of votes, the Nationalists controlled parliament when rural areas (the stronghold of the Afrikaners) gained disproportionately heavy representation. The National party won 70 seats to the United party's 65 and formed a government with the cooperation of the splinter Afrikaner party's 9 representatives.

Few people recognized the long-range effects of the "revolution of 1948." Malan's victory was not an aberration but the culmination of Afrikaner nationalism and white fear. Contrary to most expectations, the Nationalists not only ruled South Africa but also revised fundamentally the direction of the country. They did not just win an election but established a monopoly on political power that intensified throughout the next two decades. In 1948 the Boers won at the ballot box what they had lost on the battlefield five decades earlier.

Americans reacted to Malan's victory with a combination of shock and skepticism. Most U.S. journalists, diplomats, and politicians knew little about Afrikaner exclusiveness, the depths of racial prejudice, or the determination of Malan. Many observers were baffled by the election returns and by the cultural

6. Thomas Holcomb to the Department of State, Pretoria, 18 February 1948, 848a.00/2-1848 and 4 March 1948, 848a.00/3-148, General Records of the Department of State, Record Group 59, National Archives.
7. Holcomb to the Department of State, "Report on the General Election," 13 May 1948, RG59, SD848a.00/5-1348, National Archives.

chauvinism and religious emphasis of the Nationalists. The Council on Foreign Relations sent Whitney Shepardson of the Carnegie Endowment on a tour of South Africa to try to explain the election. His report, later passed on to the State Department and eventually to Truman, emphasized the "national shock" of the upset. Like many Americans, Shepardson predicted Malan's victory would be short-lived. He noted that the English-speaking population still controlled the economy and forecast that they would soon oust the "extremists" now ruling the nation.[8]

Liberal and religious groups in the United States were more pessimistic about South Africa's future, although they did not appreciate the full significance of the victory. The *Christian Century* labeled Malan "South Africa's Senator Bilbo" and claimed that, unless his government rapidly collapsed, he would provoke "a racial explosion in South Africa which is likely to be the most horrible in history." Other religious leaders expressed concern that the new regime would curtail missionary activity and further restrict educational opportunities for blacks.[9]

Black Americans, also dismayed by the victory and fearful of the effects of apartheid, issued a strong attack on Malan and his proposed racial policies. While the National Association for the Advancement of Colored People dismissed Smuts's reputation as a liberal on race as "phony," it conceded he was far better than "the Nazi-minded Dr. Malan." Unless he was checked by either domestic or foreign influences, Malan would "turn back the hand of the clock of civilization" to the naked exploitation of blacks in the earlier Boer republics.[10]

American business leaders feared that the new government might be incompetent to rule and, given traditional Afrikaner hostility to industrialism, might oppose foreign investment. Some corporate leaders urged American businessmen to suspend new investments until the Malan regime proved stable and it was clear apartheid would not threaten the black labor supply necessary for the mines. Pretoria's ambassador to the United States tried to calm businessmen's fears by publicly encouraging new investments and by assuring American executives that the Nationalists would not jeopardize economic stability. He explained that apartheid would not eliminate black workers but transform South Africa into "a great racial laboratory" with benefits for all races.[11]

The presidential election in the United States in 1948 generated keen interest in race, civil rights, and politics among Americans as well as South Africans. When the Dixiecrats bolted the Democratic party at the convention, some reporters sympathetic to black civil rights noted a similarity between the Nationalists in South Africa and the Democratic party in the South.

8. Whitney Shepardson, "Report on a Visit to the Union of South Africa," 25 October 1948, John Sumner Papers, box 5, Harry S. Truman Library. See also Edgar H. Brookes, "South African Swing-Over."
9. *Christian Century* 65 (June 1948): 563.
10. *Crisis* 55 (July 1948): 201.
11. *New York Times*, 9 April 1948, p. 14; 25 July 1948, p. 13.

Truman's call for a limited civil rights program in 1948 provoked a storm of protest in the American South. On the basis of southern opposition to civil rights in the United States, South Africa compared their racial situation with America's. The Nationalist government ridiculed Truman's calls for desegregation as a propaganda appeal for black votes. Though they favored his response to the Berlin crisis, they were also disturbed by one of Truman's campaign speeches, which called for self-government "for all peoples who are prepared" not only in Europe but "in Asia and Africa as well." To some Nationalists this oblique reference implied American support for black rule throughout Africa.[12]

While most Americans concentrated on the presidential election and the problems of the Cold War, U.S. officials in South Africa tried to forecast the effects of the new Nationalist government on American interests. Still smarting from their erroneous predictions of a Smuts landslide, they initially argued that Malan's government soon would collapse. His victory had served as a cathartic release for the frustrations and hate of the Afrikaners, they insisted, but would not survive to implement his extreme ideas.[13] Though it was clear by the fall of 1948 that Malan would endure and had begun the process of apartheid, Americans remained dubious. North Winship, the U.S. chargé d'affairs in Capetown, ridiculed early efforts to impose apartheid as "adventures in Blunderland." He concluded that the Nationalists "seem to be so blinded by racial bitterness that they are willing to sacrifice (or do not realize that they are sacrificing) the future of their nation to the altar of fear."[14]

Following Truman's election, the State Department began its first full assessment of the changed situation in South Africa. Malan sent a delegation to meet with officials in Washington to try to explain the need for and goals of apartheid. America agreed to South African suggestions that the two nations upgrade their missions to full embassies and exchange ambassadors rather than ministers. The State Department followed with an order for a complete review of U.S.–South African relations and an evaluation of the likely foreign and domestic policies of the new regime.[15]

The department's summary of U.S. interests in South Africa stressed the nation's economic and strategic importance and its zealous anticommunism. It concluded that the need for South African minerals, port facilities, and votes in

12. See the letter from M. G. de B. Epstein to Truman, 26 November 1948, and enclosures, President's Personal Files, box 4383, Truman Library, and *U.S. News and World Report* 24 (18 June 1948): 20–21. A copy of Truman's speech on self-determination is in the George Elsey Papers, box 33, Truman Library.

13. Holcomb to the Department of State, "Probable Policy of the Nationalist Government," 16 June 1948, RG59, SD848a.00/6–1648, National Archives.

14. North Winship to the Secretary of State, "Further Developments in the Implementation of Apartheid," 5 October 1948, RG59, SD848.4016/10–548, National Archives.

15. Robert A. Lovett, "Memorandum for the President," 23 November 1948; T. R. D. Muir to Matthew Connelly, 17 November 1948, White House Central Files: Official File, box 451, Truman Library.

the United Nations were sufficient to seek "the maintenance and development of friendly relations" regardless of the Nationalists' domestic policies. The report expressed fear that the racial attitudes of the new government might jeopardize the nation's stability. If apartheid were implemented, it might provoke racial war and destroy the South African economy. U.S. officials also were concerned about the "immaturity" of the Nationalists and their inexperience in foreign affairs. While the "ineptness" of South African leaders did not immediately threaten their support of the containment of Soviet aggression, their militant white supremacy either might lead them to "an expansionist policy" on the African continent or might drive them to "isolation" as they concentrated on domestic affairs.[16]

This early evaluation of the Nationalist regime showed assumptions and priorities that guided U.S. policy throughout the Truman administration. The major concern of American officials was, not surprisingly, the continuing global conflict with the Soviet Union. South Africa was an important source of gold and other raw materials for the free world and also a force for anticommunism on the African continent. The United States did not want to risk losing either the material or the diplomatic support of South Africa. However, South Africa's racism and particularly its intended policy of apartheid continued to threaten favorable relations. In 1948, Malan and his party made their first efforts toward racial separatism by abolishing Indian suffrage in Natal and by limiting the voting rights of the colored in Cape Province. As the Nationalists successfully pushed their program of apartheid through parliament, America recognized that its initial assumption that Malan would soon be turned out of office was wrong and that it would have to weigh the advantages of South African gold and anticommunism against the liability of American identification with institutional racism.

In the period immediately following his election, Malan moved slowly toward apartheid because the coalition between the National and Afrikaner parties was not secure. In 1951, the Nationalists succeeded in extending parliamentary representation to South West Africa, the former German colony seized during World War I. This move insured an absolute Nationalist majority. After 1951, the National party rather than parliament ruled South Africa, and the pace of racial separatism accelerated.

Even prior to gaining a clear majority in parliament, however, Malan had begun the process of physically separating the races and ending opposition to Afrikaner rule. In 1949, parliament declared mixed marriages illegal and excluded blacks from unemployment benefits. The next year the Nationalists passed three laws that clearly indicated their ultimate intentions. They forced mandatory classification of all South Africans as either white, "native," or colored. Many who had passed for white were reclassified as colored. Africans

16. Department of State Memorandum, "U.S. Relations with the Union of South Africa," 1 November 1948, RG59, SD711.48a/11-148, National Archives.

were issued passes and were obliged to produce them for inspection by officials. Malan also pushed through the Group Areas Act, the "kernel of apartheid." A complicated series of provisions, the bill extended residential segregation to all areas of the nation and restricted each of the three racial groups to certain areas. Blacks could work in white areas only as transients with no legal rights. Property could be leased or sold only to members of the same race. Blacks became aliens in white regions allowed entry only to work.

Perhaps the most ominous action of the government was the sweeping Suppression of Communism Act. The act not only outlawed the Communist party but also gave the government nearly unlimited powers to curtail all criticism of the government or the National party. The law, and later additions, allowed the government to muzzle the press, to intern all citizens without due process, and to ban "subversive" organizations.

The first significant apartheid legislation attracted the attention of the popular press in America as well as the earlier critics of the Nationalists. Most journalists were unsure of the exact nature of the new laws, and many believed they were temporary. Blacks and liberals, more alarmed by the measures, charged that the Nationalists were violating basic American notions of human rights and the UN Charter.[17]

South African violations of human rights also concerned officials in the Truman administration who feared that apartheid would jeopardize the nation's stability and usefulness in the Cold War. In 1949, the Central Intelligence Agency prepared a lengthy report on "The Political Situation in the Union of South Africa." Unlike other American observers, the CIA correctly predicted that the Nationalists were firmly in power. The report concluded that, although South Africa was militantly anticommunist and supported American foreign policy, it might well become a "propaganda liability to the U.S. and the Western bloc." Its racism provided the Soviets with evidence for American prejudice and hostility to decolonization. The document noted that racial fear united white South Africans but increasingly divided the world. South Africa embodied a dilemma Washington soon would have to face: support of white rule or alignment with the growing force of black nationalism as "black-white antagonisms are on the rise not only in the Union but in colonial Africa generally."[18]

The CIA made no policy recommendations, but it defined the choice facing America in southern Africa. Continued normal relations with South Africa might well insure support for U.S. objectives in the Cold War, but America risked identification with the white minority on a black continent. Washington

17. *New York Times*, 6 July 1949, p. 23; Thomas Sancton, "South Africa's Dixiecrats," *Nation* 168 (28 May 1949): 602–3; R. K. Cope, "White Skin in a Dark Continent," *Nation* 169 (8 October 1949): 347–48.
18. Central Intelligence Agency Memorandum, "The Political Situation in the Union of South Africa," 31 January 1949, President's Secretary's Files, box 256, Truman Library.

could well be mortgaging the future if the process of decolonization already underway in Asia extended to Africa. Pretoria would use force to control the black majority. Black-white conflict would put even more pressure on America to openly condemn the Nationalist regime.

Predictions of racial violence soon proved accurate. Blacks and police clashed in Johannesburg in February 1950 following protests against apartheid. The American consul general in Johannesburg argued that further bloodshed was inevitable as the Nationalists expanded apartheid. On May Day additional disturbances erupted. The U.S. representative in Capetown, Sydney Redecker, concluded that South Africa faced only three choices: "compromise, further riots, or a police state." He claimed that the government had decided on the latter and warned that blacks would be driven to communism and Soviet aid as all legitimate avenues of protest had been closed.[19]

The United States passively had observed developments in South Africa in the period immediately following the Nationalist victory until the UN forced Washington to make decisions about its continued relations with Pretoria. Two issues concerned the UN in the late 1940s: South Africa's racial laws and its continued control of South West Africa. More than thirty years later they remain annual items on the organization's agenda. As early as 1946, India protested South Africa's racial discrimination. With the adoption of apartheid, the UN began annual discussions of South Africa in 1948. The question of South West Africa had raised international concern even earlier. Formerly a German colony, it had been occupied by South Africa during World War I and had been placed under mandate to Pretoria by the League of Nations. With the collapse of the League, the legal status of the area was unclear. As the heir of the League, the UN argued that it retained jurisdiction over the territory. Pretoria contended that the death of the League meant the end of the mandate system. South Africa claimed sovereignty over the region and denied any responsibility to the UN or any other international agency.

Malan recognized that the UN would be hostile to apartheid and would continue to press its claim to South West Africa. As minister of foreign affairs as well as prime minister, he denounced the UN for meddling in South Africa's internal affairs and reminded the organization that his nation had joined the UN with the clear understanding that it had no rights "in our domestic affairs nor any tampering with our autonomous rights." He reluctantly agreed to make a report on conditions in South West Africa but repeated South Africa's assertions that the UN had no claims to the area.[20]

In July 1948 the UN debated Pretoria's report on its administration of South

19. Sydney Redecker to the Department of State, 17 February 1950, U.S. Department of State, *Foreign Relations of the United States, 1950*, 5:1809–13 (hereafter cited as *FRUS* followed by the year); Joseph Sweeney to the Secretary of State, 8 June 1950, *FRUS: 1950*, 5:1824–26.

20. Amry Vandenbosch, *South Africa and the World*, 130.

West Africa. U.S. delegate Francis B. Sayre offered some mild criticism of South African failures in education and health care but opposed a Soviet move to reject the report as it gave tacit acknowledgment of South African control. The following year, American officials again lobbied effectively to block a resolution critical of South African governance of the area.[21]

The Nationalist government ignored American efforts to prevent UN censure and responded instead to the rather gentle U.S. attacks on its failures in social programs. Pretoria claimed Washington did not recognize the importance of South Africa as an ally and that America's own racial record made it "scarcely qualified to throw the first stone." South African ambassador H. T. Andrews conveyed his government's annoyance directly to Secretary of State Dean Acheson.[22]

In December 1949 the UN asked the International Court of Justice to give an advisory opinion on the status of South West Africa. To the consternation of South Africa, the United States voted in favor of the resolution. On 17 February 1950, Assistant Secretary of State John D. Hickerson met with South Africa's ambassador and explained that the United States thought South Africa had been following "an incorrect and injudicious course" in South West Africa. He reminded Andrews that the United States "pursued the policy of endeavoring to be helpful to the Union in the sense of moderating extreme criticism," but wanted "some constructive action on South West Africa" before the world court's ruling. Hickerson explained that, given "the new and powerful forces now emerging in the world, the United States itself would find it extremely difficult in the future to take positions on this problem helpful to the Union." George McGhee, assistant secretary of state for Near Eastern, South Asian, and African affairs, met with the South African secretary for external affairs two weeks later to emphasize American concerns about the issue.[23]

Pretoria feared the United States was preparing to abandon South Africa in the UN and tried to use its anticommunism to maintain Washington's support. Malan repeatedly praised Truman's efforts to contain Soviet expansion. He supported NATO and even suggested South Africa be allowed to join the pact. When American officials tactfully pointed out that NATO was a strictly European organization, Malan proposed an "all African political and defense pact" to serve "as a bulwark against communism and to preserve Western European civilization in Africa." The United States, Great Britain, and South Africa would be the major members.[24]

21. *New York Times*, 24 July 1948, p. 3; 25 July 1948, p. 13.

22. "Memorandum of Conversation," 29 March 1949, Dean Acheson Papers, box 64, Truman Library.

23. Department of State, "Aide-Memoire to U.S. Embassy, Pretoria," 20 February 1950, *FRUS: 1950*, 5:1813–15; "Memorandum of Conversation by the Chargé in South Africa," 7 March 1950, *FRUS: 1950*, 5:1818–23.

24. *New York Times*, 7 May 1949, p. 19; "Memorandum of Conversation by the Chargé in South Africa," 6 March 1949, *FRUS: 1950*, 5:1815–17.

Washington refused to comment on Malan's proposal. The American ambassador in Pretoria cautioned that Malan was using anticommunism to lure the United States while his racial policies were actually "driving the natives to communism." The American chargé in Capetown agreed. John Erhardt argued South Africa used the fear of communism as an excuse to crush black nationalism and to stifle white criticism.[25]

In early 1950, officials in the State Department recognized that the South African situation served as a preview of larger problems for American diplomacy in Africa. Although no European colonies on the continent had gained freedom, pressure for independence mounted constantly. The department organized a conference of governmental officials, academics, and journalists to discuss future policy toward black nationalism and decolonization. Under-Secretary of State Durward Sandifer summarized the U.S. dilemma. He noted that America's "traditional policy" supported self-determination and majority rule but also upheld "an orderly and stable" transition of power and continued good relations with Europe. He concluded that America must find "a middle position" between direct support of rapid decolonization and outright defense of continued white control.[26]

The "middle position" was difficult to find in South Africa. Malan's government had eliminated any legitimate means of protest and peaceful change. Washington struggled to find a position between unequivocal endorsement of white supremacy and encouragement of black violence. The blatant racism of the South African government made American blacks and liberals critical of any official cooperation with Malan. They protested U.S. inaction at the UN and the refusal of the administration publicly to condemn apartheid. The Nationalists were equally adamant that any change in Washington's support of South Africa at the UN or public attacks on its racial policies jeopardized continued economic and political cooperation in the Cold War. Dr. T. E. Donges, Malan's minister of the interior, met with Acheson and criticized Truman for allowing private citizens openly to attack the Union.[27]

The North Korean invasion of South Korea in June 1950 effectively determined U.S. policy toward South Africa. The sudden need for immediate assistance in the battle against communism overwhelmed all other considerations. Administration officials concluded that they could not risk the loss of an

25. John Erhardt to Acheson, 3 October 1950, *FRUS: 1950*, 5:1834–37; Bernard Connelly to the Department of State, 12 May 1950, State Department Correspondence, box 37, Truman Library.
26. Department of State Memorandum, "Political and Economic Problems of Africa," *FRUS: 1950*, 5:1503–09.
27. "Memorandum of Conversation with Dr. T. E. Donges," 8 December 1950, Acheson Papers, box 65. See also "Memorandum of Conversation by the Chargé in South Africa," 7 March 1950, *FRUS: 1950*, 5:1818–23, for protests by the South African minister for external affairs. In response to criticism of U.S. policy by black leaders, Truman asked Walter White, executive director of the NAACP, to make a trip to South Africa and prepare a report for the president. White initially agreed but eventually dropped the idea. See White to Truman, 3 May 1950, President's Personal Files: NAACP, box 393, Truman Library.

ally as wealthy and powerful as South Africa at a time of international crisis even if its internal policies were repugnant to American ideals. South African military support in Korea, more symbolic than decisive, provided the Truman administration with evidence of a united, multilateral effort against communism. Prior to the North Korean attack, the South African minister of defense had promised Secretary of Defense Louis Johnson that his nation would send troops anywhere in the world "in the event of a war against communism." When war erupted, South Africa dispatched an air squadron to Korea, and in 1951, Acheson persuaded it to send ground forces as well.[28]

South Africa strongly backed U.S. efforts in Korea but tried to use the crisis to insure American support in the UN and to gain assistance in its atomic energy program. South Africa had great potential as a source of uranium, and, throughout 1950, Washington had negotiated with Pretoria for an agreement to sell the strategic material. Before the North Korean invasion, South African officials had mentioned to Great Britain that they wanted "a special position" in the development of atomic energy in exchange for their uranium. Britain passed the South African demands to American members of the Combined Policy Committee on Atomic Energy.[29]

Two weeks after the outbreak of hostilities in Korea, South African ambassador G. P. Jooste called on Acheson and repeated his nation's request for "a special position on atomic energy." He suggested that South Africa "associate itself with the 'inner circle' of Western countries" in return for an agreement on uranium. Acheson was mildly encouraging but made no commitments. Four months later, Minister of the Interior Donges bluntly argued that South Africa did not want "membership in the club," only some form of "associate membership." Acheson agreed that "something could be worked out" after they had arrived at an understanding on uranium.[30] In November 1950, Pretoria agreed to sell uranium to the United States. Acheson's special assistant wrote to the secretary of the British embassy requesting meetings to determine a mutual response to South African demands on atomic energy. He reported that America was willing to offer Pretoria assistance on nonmilitary uses of nuclear material in exchange for its agreement on uranium ore.[31]

South Africa's decision to sell uranium seemed to many in Washington yet another example of its loyalty in the Cold War. It had paid back its lend-lease debt

28. F. C. Erasmus to Johnson, 15 June 1950, *FRUS: 1950*, 5:1826–27; "Memorandum of Conversation with G. P. Jooste," 20 April 1951, Acheson Papers, box 66.
29. "Minutes of the Meeting of the American Members of the Combined Policy Committee," 25 April 1950, *FRUS: 1950*, 1:551–52.
30. "Memorandum of Conversation by Mr. Clarence A. Wendel of the Office of the Under Secretary of State," 12 July 1950; *FRUS: 1950*, 1:566–67; Acheson to Jooste, 24 August 1950, *FRUS: 1950*, 1:571; "Memorandum of Conversation with Dr. T. E. Donges," 8 December 1950, Acheson Papers, box 65, Truman Library.
31. Gordon Arneston to F. W. Marken, 4 December 1950, *FRUS: 1950*, 1:591–92.

and had provided a fighter squadron for the war in Korea. Even his critics acknowledged Malan's fierce anticommunism. The Suppression of Communism Act coincided with America's own "red scare" and the McCarran Act aimed at radicalism in the United States. Sen. Joseph McCarthy's attacks on the State Department for being "soft on Communism" made it difficult for officials to criticize a nation more militantly anticommunist than America. Most Americans knew little about apartheid and were far more impressed with South African support of containment than they were concerned about its racial laws. While South Africa was not a model of freedom, it served American foreign-policy objectives. One U.S. official candidly noted that Congress and the public were not interested in "promoting the general welfare of the 'hottentots' except to the extent that it contributes to the general welfare of the United States." Similarly, Acheson explained that Washington must judge a nation by its foreign policy rather than its domestic legislation. He denounced "purists" who wanted America to avoid cooperation with "any but the fairest of democratic states." Cold War "realists" judged communism as the ultimate international evil and the most dangerous threat to the United States. They were willing to restrain their criticism of South Africa to assure its continued support in the global struggle.[32]

As with the sale of uranium, South Africa tried to use its support of the war to its own advantage. In October 1950, the South African defense minister, F. C. Erasmus, met with Acheson and Secretary of Defense George Marshall in an effort to secure increased military aid from the United States. He argued that it had been a great burden for "a small state such as South Africa" to send troops to Korea. South Africa needed American help to maintain its own defenses and to control "communist subversion within the nation." Ambassador Jooste sent a personal letter to Acheson announcing that his country would consider "any military attack by a communist power or powers on the Continent of Africa" as a direct attack on South Africa. As a result of this self-proclaimed obligation, South Africa needed U.S. equipment and money to train an "expeditionary force" for deployment anywhere in Africa. Acheson commended South Africa's commitment to containment but agreed only to further discussions among military officials of the two nations.[33]

Despite South African aid in the war and its sale of strategic materials, some officials in the administration warned that South Africa was a potentially dangerous ally. They pointed out that the Soviets emphasized U.S. cooperation with Pretoria in propaganda broadcasts in Africa and Asia, as an example of American racism. Throughout the Korean War, U.S. officials refrained from any

32. Durward Sandifer oral history interview, Truman Library; Dean Acheson, *Present at the Creation*, 379.
33. "Memorandum of Conversation of the Secretary of State and the South African Defense Minister," 5 October 1950; "Memorandum of Conversation by the Director of Military Assistance" (Maj. Gen. L. L. Lemnitzer), 5 October 1950, *FRUS: 1950*, 5:1837–41; Jooste to Acheson, 9 October 1950, *FRUS: 1950*, 5:1841–42.

open criticism of Malan or apartheid. Prior to Korea, McGhee had spoken openly of the problems of racial discrimination in South Africa and the need for America to cooperate with the emerging leaders of black nationalism in Africa. A year later, however, during the war in Korea, the assistant secretary gave a speech labeling Africa "a fertile field for communism" and warning against "premature independence for primitive, underdeveloped peoples." McGhee argued that black governments would be "unprepared to meet aggression or subversion" and would thus be a threat to "the security of the free world." Although white rule may seem an evil to the black African, "the greatest danger . . . lies in the menace of Communist imperialism."[34] American liberals and blacks, while acknowledging South Africa's help in Korea, contended that indirect U.S. support of apartheid furthered communist aims by antagonizing African and Asian leaders and by paving the way for armed revolution in South Africa.[35] Although U.S. officials generally remained silent on South African racial policies, the American press regularly attacked apartheid.

In February 1951, Malan lashed out at his U.S. critics. He argued that if America had a black majority at the same "low civilization level" as in South Africa, it would recognize the necessity of racial separatism. If America believed in racial equality, Malan contended, it would rapidly "lose its authority and strength as a first rate world power and sink to the level of a first rate American Liberia."[36] Nonetheless, Malan's periodic outbursts were more for domestic consumption than signs of any serious split with Washington.

The United States quietly continued to support South Africa when heated debates over apartheid in the UN revealed the ferocity of racism among whites in South Africa. In 1949, the organization had asked India, Pakistan, and South Africa to discuss Pretoria's racial policies as a prelude to investigation of possible violations of the UN Charter and the Universal Declaration of Human Rights. South Africa reluctantly agreed, but the talks accomplished nothing, and the UN prepared for a full debate on apartheid in 1950.[37] Prior to the UN session, McGhee met with the ousted Smuts to discuss race discrimination in South Africa and possible UN actions. To McGhee's surprise, Smuts proved to be as vehement in his contempt for the UN and in his hatred of India as any member of the National party. He charged that India had a secret plan to export millions of

34. George McGhee, "United States' Interests in Africa," *U.S. Department of State Bulletin* 22 (19 June 1950): 999–1003 (hereafter cited as *SDB*); "Africa's Role in the Free World," *SDB* 25 (16 July 1961): 97–101.

35. Department of State Memorandum, "Soviet Propaganda in Africa," 14 August 1951, Sumner Papers, box 5, Truman Library. A. Phillip Randolph, president, American Brotherhood of Sleeping Car Porters, to Acheson, 13 April 1951, Acheson Papers, box 66, Truman Library.

36. *New York Times*, 10 February 1951, p. 3.

37. South Africa had joined the Soviet bloc and Saudi Arabia in opposing the Universal Declaration of Human Rights in 1947. This caused considerable outrage among the U.S. delegation to the UN, in particular Eleanor Roosevelt, who had been one of the major forces behind the document. See "U.S. Delegation's Position Paper," 24 November 1948, *FRUS: 1948*, 1:285–88.

its citizens to southern Africa, and its attacks on Pretoria were only a ruse to distract the world from its plot to relocate its surplus population. Smuts claimed that all white South Africans were united in their opposition to any UN interference in their racial policies. Governmental officials repeated the claim of an Indian conspiracy in conversations with McGhee in Capetown.[38]

As Malan accelerated his program of apartheid there were renewed demands for some UN action. In October 1952 Jooste met with Acheson to secure continued U.S. support of South Africa in the upcoming UN session. He made it clear that Pretoria expected America to use its influence to avoid an "acrimonious debate" on apartheid as well as to defeat any resolution condemning South Africa. Acheson replied that Washington could not avoid the debate but would oppose any formal resolution. The secretary of state explained that the United States would vote to allow the UN to discuss apartheid but would work to defeat any statement on the issue. He admitted that this strategy was "conditioned to an undetermined extent by complicating factors of our own domestic and public opinion situation."[39] Acheson clearly wanted to ward off liberal criticism of cooperation with South Africa while avoiding an open rift with Pretoria. American maneuvering at the UN managed to achieve both goals.

At the UN, American delegate Charles Sprague agreed that the organization could discuss "race conflict in South Africa," despite Pretoria's objections that it was purely a domestic matter. Sprague, however, reminded the group that the UN was "not a super government." While it could "proclaim" abstract ideals of human rights, it had "no power to impose standards." As a result of this position, the United States abstained on a resolution establishing a UN commission to study apartheid but voted in favor of a vague statement in support of racial equality that did not mention South Africa by name. This compromise did not fully satisfy American liberals or South Africa. Pretoria's new foreign minister, Eric Louw, attacked U.S. cooperation with "misguided liberals" at the UN whose naive support of racial equality only served India's policy of "*lebensraum* in Africa for her wretched, starving, millions."[40]

Washington also worked to postpone any direct UN action on South West Africa. Curtis Strong of the Office of Dependent Area Affairs, in a memo to the State Department's "Working Group on Colonial Problems," concluded that it was essential to maintain "the friendship and close cooperation" of South Africa because it was "strategically located," was actively supporting America in Korea, and "has minerals and other resources of great value to this country." These "political, security, and economic interests" compel the United States to

38. "Memorandum of Conversation between George McGhee and Jan Smuts," 7 March 1950, *FRUS: 1950*, 1:187–90; "Memorandum of Conversation by the Chargé in South Africa: George McGhee and D. D. Forsuth," 7 March 1950, *FRUS: 1950*, 5:1818–23.

39. "Memorandum of Conversation with G. P. Jooste," 14 October 1952, Acheson Papers, box 67, Truman Library.

40. *New York Times*, 16 November 1952, p. 1.

"show our solidarity with the Union." Conversely, America also was interested in "insuring the friendship and cooperation of the many 'anticolonial' nations . . . as well as the emerging colonial peoples." To avoid a clash with Pretoria, Washington would have to oppose action "favored by the majority of United Nations Members." The United States temporarily solved the problem by supporting a successful Brazilian resolution postponing consideration of South West Africa until the next session.[41]

The Truman administration's decision to continue its cooperation with South Africa despite objections to its racial policies was a logical expression of Cold War priorities. A forceful condemnation of apartheid and an end to normal diplomatic relations would have gained the approval of liberals, blacks, and third-world nationalists, but it risked the loss of South African strategic and military support. American blacks and African leaders had little influence on foreign-policy decisions. Africa still remained under European control, and most black Americans were far more concerned with Truman's domestic civil-rights program than with events in South Africa. Although many in the U.S. government admitted that South Africa was a potential problem for America, they realized that it was foremost an immediate Cold War ally.

Americans outside the administration criticized U.S. inaction on apartheid and predicted Washington would soon find its tacit support of Pretoria a diplomatic burden. In its 1952 report *Major Problems of U.S. Foreign Policy*, the Brookings Institute warned that South Africa's racial policies invited black uprisings and worked to disrupt the entire region. The report suggested that black unrest undercut South Africa's effectiveness as an anticommunist ally.[42]

In a similar analysis, columnist William White of the *New York Times* attacked Washington's preoccupation with Europe and the "low priority" given Africa. He argued that the administration saw no real alternative to the Nationalist regime and, as a result, the United States "is not doing much to stop Dr. Malan." White charged that American policy suffered from "unnecessary timidity" in its dealings with South Africa and its refusal verbally to condemn white supremacy.[43]

Officials in Washington justified their silence on apartheid by claiming that the United States had no right to intervene in domestic matters of a foreign power. Although South African racism violated American ideas of human rights, the force of world opinion, rather than either unilateral or UN action, would eventually work to moderate apartheid. Sprague summarized the American rationale for its policies in a debate on South Africa at the UN in November 1952.

41. Curtis S. Strong, "The Dilemma for the United States Presented by the South West Africa Question," 26 August 1952, *FRUS: United Nations' Affairs, 1952–1954*, 1146–47.

42. Brookings Institute, *Major Problems of United States' Foreign Policy, 1952–1953* (published in 1954), 264–73.

43. *New York Times*, 18 May 1952, p. 1.

He urged member nations to leave the issue of race discrimination to the "the conscience" of the South African people as "the power of world opinion" was far more influential than any UN resolution. Unfortunately, for American policymakers, Dr. Malan also succinctly summarized his nation's attitude when he remarked that "to do what world opinion demands would mean suicide by white South Africa."[44]

44. Ibid., 16 November 1952, p. 1; Malan as quoted in *Time* 59 (8 September 1952): 46.

3. "PREMATURE INDEPENDENCE" | Eisenhower, Dulles, and African Liberation

In 1953, Dwight Eisenhower inherited the problem of apartheid. He and his advisers continued the search for a "middle position" between support of white supremacy and endorsement of black rule begun by the Truman administration. There were few changes in America's UN policy or in direct diplomacy with Pretoria. It was clear to U.S. diplomats that the Nationalists would remain in power and that they would continue to impose their program of racial separatism. It was also obvious that criticism of South Africa would increase among American liberals and third-world leaders. American ambivalence toward black nationalism and white rule continued, with only minor adjustments, until pressure for African independence, the domestic civil-rights movement, and continued white defiance forced adjustments in policy in 1958. Pressure from opponents of apartheid by itself, however, was not powerful enough to alter official policy. While disgruntled liberals railed away at Washington's "Europe first" orientation and insensitivity to black nationalism, it was only when the international situation changed that there was a shift in U.S. policy. Even the Sharpeville massacre in 1960 resulted in symbolic changes in policy rather than a substantive reorientation of American diplomacy.

Although they generally continued Truman's approach to white Africa, officials in the Eisenhower administration did alter the appearance of American policy. In many ways the rhetoric, style, and personalities of these officials made the United States seem more conservative, more hostile to African aspirations, and more supportive of white rule than it actually was. While scholars may bemoan the confusion of style and substance, oratory and action, it is often difficult to distinguish between them. The subtleties of personality, international "image," and rhetoric are often as important as particular actions. African nationalists and their supporters perceived the Eisenhower administration as hostile to their interests not only because of diplomatic decisions but also as a result of apparent personal insensitivity, aloofness, and prejudice. Decades of colonialism and white control made Africans acutely aware of any hint of racism or paternalism in language and personal relations. They thought that oratory was important and accurately reflected attitudes that determined policy. The speeches and actions of American officials during the Eisenhower years seemed to the Africans to show only a perfunctory commitment to self-determination, racial equality, and majority rule. While Eisenhower did not significantly alter

U.S. policy, he and his aides often appeared to abandon black Africa completely for the short-term support of Europe and South Africa.

Both domestic and foreign critics of Eisenhower's approach to Africa focused as much on individual attitudes and "style" as official policy. His seeming lack of concern with racial inequality at home appalled them, and they concluded that he supported white supremacy abroad. Neither the president nor his administration wanted to use their power to attack segregation in the United States. Despite the Supreme Court's decision on school segregation in 1954 and the federal intervention in the Little Rock school crisis in 1957, the Eisenhower administration seemed indifferent to the emerging issue of race in both domestic and international politics.

Eisenhower and his aides contributed to this impression through their personal encounters with black Africans. The president rarely bothered to court African leaders either officially or socially. Eisenhower was a product of the American South and the segregated U.S. army. He reportedly objected to inviting "those niggers" to diplomatic receptions and regularly, if unwittingly, insulted African leaders by appearing uninterested in their problems and uninformed about their nations. Secretary of State John Foster Dulles also managed to alienate Africans with his seeming lack of concern for their objectives, his inability to accept their rejection of his Cold War bipolarity, and his preachy approach to personal as well as official relations.[1]

American diplomats, both in Washington and in Africa, also appeared to be indifferent to Africa. Often they seemed as arrogant and aloof as the European colonial administrators of an earlier period. U.S. representatives in Africa were usually political appointees with little knowledge of Africa and even less contact with Africans. Many maintained segregation within the American embassies and socialized with whites rather than with Africans. The "ugly American" was as conspicuous in Africa as in Asia. Blacks repeated stories of the wives of American diplomats trying surreptitiously to slip on their white gloves when Africans came through the receiving line. In Washington, African specialists remained second-class citizens in the bureaucracy of the State Department. Power and status rested in the more important European and Asian desks. Many diplomats viewed Africa only as a stepping-stone to more prestigious positions and rarely advocated forceful diplomacy toward the continent.

Dulles's periodic denunciations of neutralism and revolution further angered Africans. While he later tempered his rhetoric, his speeches and writings prior to 1957 showed a contempt for the idea of nonalignment and a tendency to identify reform with revolution and revolution with communism. As most Africans were

1. For Eisenhower's general attitude toward Africa and Africans, see William Attwood, *The Reds and the Blacks*, 14–16; Waldemar Nielsen, *The Great Powers and Africa*, 262–66; and Vernon McKay, *Africa in World Politics*, 320–23. On Dulles, see Donald Secrest, "American Policy toward Neutralism during the Truman and Eisenhower Administrations," 122–32, 229–46.

committed to neutralism in the conflict between the United States and Russia and to economic and social reform of the inequities of colonialism, they believed that Dulles opposed their basic goals. Africans wanted independence from white control, and they expected American support. Instead they were offered endless warnings of the dangers of "premature independence" and the need to guard against communist subversion. Dulles graphically portrayed the Cold War as an apocalyptic struggle between freedom and slavery. To black Africa, freedom meant majority rule, and colonialism was a contemporary form of slavery. They were not willing, as some American officials suggested, temporarily to abandon the black-liberation struggle for the more important battle with communism.

Africans quickly sensed that their goals were secondary to the defense of western Europe and the containment of communism in Asia among U.S. diplomatic priorities. Washington's rigid definition of the Cold War, inattention to racial equality, and offensive diplomatic style combined with its continued normal relations with South Africa and Portugal to convince most Africans that America's "middle position" was merely a disguise for supporting white supremacy.

Dulles and others in the new administration recognized that South Africa would continue to pose a diplomatic problem in the UN. In spite of the administration's disdain of the UN's ineffectiveness in Korea, it recognized the propaganda value of the organization and its importance to newer nations. The United States believed that multilateral defense pacts would preserve peace better than the "debating society" in New York. Nevertheless, the government ordered an exhaustive review of America's UN policies in the spring of 1953. The State Department's UN Planning Staff responded with a lengthy analysis of likely issues and alternative strategies.

The evaluation predicted that the UN would increasingly concentrate on the issues of decolonization and racial discrimination. A summary of "Principle Stresses and Strains Facing the United States in the UN," issued in July 1953, gave particular attention to Africa and the problem of apartheid. It noted that both the United States and the Soviet Union "claim to be champions of equality, self-determination, freedom from oppression, prosperity for all, human rights, and tolerance of other races." Washington, however, faced the problem of reconciling such ideals with the need for the continued cooperation of the colonial powers and South Africa. The report concluded that as demands for majority rule in Africa intensified, the United States would "find itself maneuvering on precarious middle ground," caught "as middle man" between "a global revolution against European pre-eminence" and its friendship with Europe and South Africa.[2]

The State Department reviewed past U.S. efforts at the UN to occupy "a

2. Department of State UN Planning Staff, "Principal Stresses and Strains Facing the U.S. in the UN," 27 July 1953, *FRUS: 1952–1954*, 3:82–90.

moderate, middle-ground position" but noted that on "important matters of principle and substance," such as race discrimination, self-determination, and decolonization, "the middle-ground position which we would have wished to occupy has been obliterated." By its "history and disposition," America favors political freedom and self-determination. It also has tried to give the appearance of supporting the third world to combat "Soviet efforts to lay successful claim to the title of 'champions of dependent peoples.'" American fears that majority rule might lead to unstable governments and communist influence, however, tempered this commitment. The United States wanted self-government at a pace "rapid enought to prevent extremists from seizing control" but slow enough to insure the new nations' stability and support for "basic U.S. objectives."[3]

The State Department's summary shows both the dilemma of the American position on self-determination and the accepted strategy to resolve it. The "moderate, middle-ground" was the approach followed by Truman prior to the war in Korea. It combined normal diplomatic cooperation with the white governments with open criticism of their racism and verbal support of the principle of majority rule. In 1950, Truman's advisers determined that such a compromise solution risked the loss of important strategic and military aid and curtailed any official attack on apartheid. In 1953, the new administration recognized that South Africa still represented the most immediate problem in maintaining the compromise between full cooperation with and active criticism of minority rule.

In a review of past policy toward South Africa, State Department analysts observed that the United States had succeeded in taking the middle position. It had used propaganda and public statements to reassure critics of apartheid while it had assisted South Africa on "substantive policies" at the UN: "We sought through our statements to soften Arab-Asian dissatisfaction with our failure to support condemnation of the Union." This approach had been effective, but officials predicted it would not work in the future. Non-Western nations no longer accepted statements but wanted some direct U.S. action against apartheid. The United States had created an image of "impartiality" but now faced "the problems of choice of audiences." It could either side with the international opponents of apartheid, firmly support the Nationalist government for reasons of immediate self-interest, or try "to walk an even more delicate rope" by continuing the "middle position."[4]

America also faced the problems of its Cold War rhetoric. Its repeated attacks on violations of human rights by the communists seemed to imply dissatisfaction with other nations that defied American ideals. State Department officials candidly admitted that "we have avoided condemning some of our friends (South Africa, e.g.) for deprivations for which we have unhesitatingly condemned the

3. "The Colonial Question in the United Nations," *FRUS: 1952–1954*, 3:96–115.
4. "Propaganda in the United Nations," *FRUS: 1952–1954*, 3:105–13.

Soviets." Such a dual standard smacked of hypocrisy. The room for American maneuvering and compromise was narrowing, and the issue of white control would become more pressing as additional colonies gained independence.[5]

The long and perceptive analysis of potential problems for America at the UN did not endorse specific policies, but Eisenhower decided to follow the ever-narrowing "middle road." When the UN considered three questions involving South Africa, the new administration had its chance to walk the diplomatic tightrope. India, with the support of the Soviet bloc, demanded that the UN continue to control South West Africa, to protect the nonwhite population, and to create a special UN commission to examine and report on apartheid. On each of these three issues, the Eisenhower administration tried to mediate between demands for direct UN action and the arguments of South Africa and Europe that the organization had no right to consider such "internal questions."

When the UN resumed its consideration of the tangled question of South West Africa in 1953, it met renewed South African opposition. Pretoria presented an elaborate justification for its refusal to accept UN supervision of the territory and rejected any further cooperation on the issue. The General Assembly, with U.S. support, responded by creating a committee on South West Africa to report on conditions in the area. In 1954, the committee presented its findings, and the UN immediately became embroiled in a complicated procedural fight over accept-ance of the document. The committee suggested that all actions on the issue require a two-thirds vote because it was "an important question" under the UN Charter. South Africa demanded a unanimous vote in accordance with provi-sions of the defunct League of Nations. Other nations argued that a majority could authorize action.

The United States tried to arrange a compromise by referring the voting issue to the World Court. American representatives refused to vote on acceptance of the report and rejected membership on the committee itself until the two-thirds voting question was decided. Faced with U.S. opposition to any further action, the UN finally agreed to send the issue to the court. America gained the victory by opposing South Africa and its strongest ally, Great Britain, as well as India and the other critics of Pretoria. By delaying consideration of the report, the United States avoided having to vote either for or against the South African administration.[6]

America found a similar moderate position on the treatment of the Asian minority in South Africa. America's representative to the General Assembly, Francis Bolton, angered South Africa, Great Britain, and members of the British Commonwealth by supporting the right of the UN to discuss the issue. He cautioned against direct outside pressure, because it "may cause more

5. "Bloc Politics in the United Nations," *FRUS: 1952–1954*, 3:118–26.
6. *SDB* 29 (7 December 1953): 805–6; 31 (22 November 1954): 783–85.

intolerance and more grief to those most deserving of help." The United States thus called for resumption of bilateral talks between India and South Africa but rejected any direct resolution as "harmful and inappropriate."[7]

The UN's creation of the special Commission on the Racial Situation in South Africa presented the most direct challenge to the African nation. Great Britain and South Africa bitterly attacked it as an illegal intrusion into the domestic affairs of a sovereign nation. Advocates of the commission claimed that apartheid was a threat to world peace and thus was not an internal issue. In its search for the "middle road," the United States voted to allow discussion of the commission on the UN agenda but abstained on the vote that created the body. When the group offered its first report, a number of states joined South Africa in dismissing it as biased. They declared that the commission was illegal and demanded that the UN seek an opinion from the World Court.

The United States again tried to avoid being identified with either camp. It rejected the argument that the commission was illegal, but it urged the group to disband because it was ineffective. When the commission presented a second report, debate followed a similar pattern. European and Commonwealth nations supported South Africa's claim that the commission had no right to report, while most other countries defended the duty of the UN to investigate apartheid. America argued that the UN could "concern itself" with apartheid yet opposed any resolution that singled out one nation for its violation of human rights. The United States abstained on the vote to accept the report and refused to vote for renewal of the commission's mandate. The special commission finally disbanded in 1955.[8]

U.S. policy at the UN was cautious but consistent. It tried to stake out and maintain a position between inaction and provocation. By supporting the right of the organization to discuss apartheid and South West Africa, it sought to identify with critics of South Africa. It refused to vote for specific resolutions, however, for fear of alienating Pretoria and its European allies. America's reaction to the UN's attempt to establish a Covenant on Human Rights in 1953 was more decisive and gave critics more evidence of its cooperation with white rule.

Dulles was extremely skeptical of the UN plan for an international conference to draft a document of common human rights because he feared it would become a propaganda forum for the Soviets. The secretary also doubted that such an abstract notion as human rights could be captured in any document. He ordered U.S. delegates to separate "civil and political rights" from "economic, social, and cultural rights" because the latter could never be legislated.[9] After numerous

7. *SDB* 39 (29 November 1953): 728–30. See also *New York Times*, 28 October 1953, p. 5.
8. *New York Times*, 20 October 1954, p. 12; *SDB* 32 (3 January 1955): 32–36; *Annual Review of UN Affairs, 1955–1956*, 5–6.
9. "Memorandum by the Assistant Secretary of State for United Nations' Affairs to the Secretary of State," 9 February 1953, "United States Policy Regarding Draft International Covenant on Human Rights," 17 February 1953, *FRUS: 1952–1954*, 3:1542–47, 1550–54.

State Department studies, reports, and recommendations, Dulles argued in a cabinet meeting on 20 February 1953 that America should reject any agreement on human rights as ineffective and vague. Eisenhower agreed, and Dulles instructed the U.S. representative at the conference to announce that while America was committed to human rights, it felt "there are more effective ways" to promote them than a written agreement. Dulles drafted a statement to be issued by Eisenhower affirming the administration's position.[10]

The rejection of the human-rights covenant created additional problems for the U.S. delegation to the UN. Some nations charged that it indicated an American acceptance of apartheid. The State Department's UN Planning Staff warned that "the perennial and ticklish question of South African treatment of its race conflict" persisted, and the refusal to sign the statement on human rights increased pressure on the United States to take some stance against apartheid. "South Africa shows no inclination to deviate from its race segregation," and other nations "show no inclination to desist in demanding that South Africa change those policies," so America's diplomatic dilemma remained.[11]

Washington's temporizing at the UN and its refusal to condemn the Nationalists provoked strong criticism from liberals and blacks at home. The "constitutional crisis" in South Africa in the early 1950s offered American opponents of apartheid a new issue. Critics charged that Malan's attempt to circumvent the law to protect his racial program demonstrated his government's immorality as well as its illegality.

This latest round of criticism came after Malan attempted to remove the names of colored voters in Cape Province from the common electoral roll. In 1936, South Africa put blacks on a separate voting roll to select white representatives in parliament. This had been done legally with the two-thirds vote required to amend the constitution. In 1951, Malan tried to shift the colored voters to a similar segregated list but tried to do so with a simple majority vote. White critics immediately charged that he was trying to wreck the constitution. Moderates mounted a campaign to oust Malan and the Nationalists. The United party, Labour party, and a spontaneous organization headed by World War II veterans, the Torch Commando, led demonstrations against the "illegal" government.[12]

In 1952, the courts declared the Separate Representation of Voters Act null and void. Malan's critics were overjoyed. Many Americans felt Malan would fall

10. "Memorandum by the Secretary of State," 20 February 1953, *FRUS: 1952–1954*, 3:1555; Dulles to Eisenhower, 7 April 1953, *FRUS: 1952–1954*, 3:1569; Dulles to the United States' Representative on the Commission on Human Rights (Mrs. Oswald Lord), 6 April 1953, *FRUS: 1952–1954*, 3:1564–67.

11. Department of State, UN Planning Staff, "Human Rights," no date, *FRUS: 1952–1954*, 3:127–33.

12. The best summary of the constitutional dispute is Gwendolen Carter, *The Politics of Inequality: South Africa Since 1948*, 119–44.

from office or at least would be forced to give up apartheid.[13] Far from losing power, the Nationalists acted to remove the last restraints to their rule. Malan rushed through parliament a provision declaring parliament the ultimate court with the right to overturn judicial decisions. When the courts declared this act illegal, Malan took his case to the people in a general election in 1953. The Nationalists won a smashing victory but still lacked the two-thirds majority necessary to amend the constitution. When Malan retired in 1954, his successor, J. C. Strijdom, resolved the crisis by increasing the size of both the Senate and the court and by appointing new members sympathetic to the Nationalist cause. Unlike Malan, Strijdom was unconcerned with the legality of his actions and made no apologies for his "Parliament-packing." He claimed that the National party represented the will of the people and would not be frustrated by "legal gimmicks" such as the constitution.

The legal crisis in South Africa showed Americans that the Nationalists were entrenched and would tolerate no effective restraints on their racial policies. Some Americans believed that apartheid was the personal creation of Malan and would be repudiated by his successor. Many U.S. observers predicted that a moderate would take over when Malan left. They were shocked when Strijdom, an open admirer of Hitler and a militant advocate of apartheid, was selected as his replacement. Similarly, many Americans greatly overestimated the opposition to the Nationalists and exaggerated the strength of the English minority. The American press was enamored of the colorful Torch Commando and the Black Sash, a women's group that stood silently with black emblems to mourn the death of the constitution. Although Strijdom scorned the Torch Commando and dismissed the Black Sash as "a bunch of foolish English virgins," U.S. critics saw such groups as powerful and as signs of possible peaceful change in South Africa. The Nationalist victory in the constitutional battle, however, dashed their roseate hopes.

Another result of the legal battle was a dramatic growth in American criticism of South Africa. Attacking apartheid became a rallying issue for U.S. liberals. Like support of civil rights or opposition to capital punishment, condemnation of South Africa emerged as a touchstone of liberalism in the 1950s. With the continued drive toward racial separatism by the now "illegal" Nationalist regime, those opposed to apartheid mobilized to pressure the Eisenhower administration to confront Pretoria. Throughout the 1950s, a variety of organizations developed to educate Americans to the horrors of apartheid and to demand U.S. opposition to South Africa. One of the earliest protest groups was the Council on African Affairs headed by Dr. Max Yergan, a black Marxist, and activist-entertainer Paul Robeson. The council included prominent black leaders

13. *Time* 59 (31 March 1952): 37–38; *Newsweek* 41 (27 April 1953): 56; E. Sachs, "South African Madness," *Nation* 174 (12 April 1952): 344–46.

such as Ralph Bunche but was labeled a subversive group by the House Un-American Activities Committee and dissolved in 1955. Yergan converted to conservatism and became a vocal defender of South Africa and later of Portugal and Rhodesia as well.[14]

George Shepherd, Jr., formed a more lasting and influential organization: the American Committee on Africa. It combined civil-rights leaders, church officials, and liberal Democrats in an effort to encourage "democratic, self-governing states free from the racialism, poverty, and ignorance under which the people of Africa suffer today." Its major concern was South Africa, and, through its journal, *Africa Today*, it became the most persistent critic of America's "support of apartheid."[15]

American labor leaders, church officials, and the liberal wing of the Democratic party also joined the campaign against South Africa. In response to pressure from black members, several unions took a public position against "normal" U.S. relations with Pretoria. Walter Reuther, president of the Congress of Industrial Organizations, was the most outspoken labor critic of U.S. policy in the 1950s. He demanded a shift in America's UN policy and official support of the right of black workers in South Africa to organize unions.[16]

Although many church officials ignored South Africa, leaders of major liberal Protestant denominations denounced apartheid as a violation of Christian love. They were particularly incensed by the Afrikaners' use of the Bible to justify discrimination and by their refusal to allow unrestricted missionary activity among the blacks. When U.S. missionaries formally protested South African restrictions on the curriculum and books in missionary schools, Hendrik Verwoerd, minister of native affairs and later prime minister, responded:

> The missionaries have hitherto preached the wrong gospel to the Africans—that they can be the equal of a white man. Anyone who preached this was doing a great disservice to the country and to the Africans. The African must realize that he can never be the equal of the white man. . . . The African needs only enough education to enable him to follow his employer's instructions.[17]

The Methodist Church Board of Missions protested South African interference in its activities directly to Eisenhower.[18]

Liberal Democrats argued that continued U.S. cooperation with South Africa

14. George W. Shepherd, *Anti-Apartheid*, is an exhaustive summary of the organizations, leaders, and tactics of groups both in the U.S. and Great Britain active in opposition to apartheid. On the Council on African Affairs, see 60–62.

15. *Africa Today* 1 (April 1954): 1.

16. *New York Times*, 5 April 1953, p. 22.

17. *Africa Today* 2 (March-April 1955): 11–13. See also Ned O'Gorman, "Darkness Over the Land," *Commonweal* 63 (13 January 1956): 374–75.

18. Mrs. Frank Brooks, Board of Missions of the Methodist Church, to Dwight D. Eisenhower, 24 October 1954, and Sherman Adams to Brooks, 8 November 1954, White House Central Files, Official File 116, box 571, Dwight D. Eisenhower Library.

exemplified the conservatism, rigidity, and cynicism of the Republican administration. The most vociferous critics were Chester Bowles, former governor of Connecticut and U.S. ambassador to India, and Adlai Stevenson, the defeated Democratic candidate for the presidency in 1952. Bowles adopted the role of spokesman for the "new Africa" and wrote numerous articles, speeches, and books calling for America to end its support of white rule and to align with black nationalism. Bowles argued for a shift in U.S. policy for both humanitarian and strategic reasons. He claimed that America had a moral obligation to support independence and majority rule. Eisenhower's refusal to commit the United States to decolonization and racial equality was "an abdication of leadership" and a cynical disregard of American idealism. His policy was "as outmoded as the Maginot Line." Bowles also claimed that a break with the colonial powers and South Africa was an effective form of anticommunism. By giving tacit support to white rule, the United States alienated black leaders and paved the way for communist gains. America should encourage UN efforts against apartheid and for an end of Pretoria's control of South West Africa because it was right and a necessary step in the struggle against Moscow.[19] Stevenson was less direct. He stopped short of specific policy recommendations but insisted that Eisenhower's refusal to speak out against apartheid helped maintain Nationalist rule. During a visit to South Africa in 1955, he criticized apartheid at a press conference, and charged that it aided communist propaganda and weakened the free world.[20]

The media also joined the mounting attack on apartheid in the 1950s. The *Nation*, the most persistent journalistic critic of South Africa, devoted its entire December 1953 issue to "Africa South of the Sahara." It recommended that America use its economic power to force South Africa to repeal apartheid. Even conservative *Life* magazine, in a special issue on Africa, ran an editorial calling apartheid "a mask for brutality and greed" and urged more "idealism" in American policy toward South Africa. John Gunther, author of the popular "Inside" books, wrote an article for the January 1954 *Reader's Digest* predicting the inevitable collapse of white rule in southern Africa unless whites compromised with the black majority.[21]

Obviously, not all of the American press or its political leaders opposed South Africa. Many still argued that the anticommunism of the Nationalists made them worthy of continued American support. Others claimed that apartheid maintained order and controlled radicalism, and they contended that blacks in South Africa had the highest income per capita on the continent. Many echoed the Nationalist position that racial separatism offered blacks the opportunity to

19. Chester Bowles, *Africa's Challenge to America*, 96–107. Bowles made a similar argument in an earlier book, *The New Dimensions of Peace*.

20. John Bartlow Martin, *Adlai Stevenson and the World*, 178–87.

21. *Nation* 177 (26 December 1953): 559–62; *Life* 34 (4 May 1953): 178; John Gunther, "Is the White Man Finished in Africa?" *Reader's Digest* 64 (January 1954): 91–96.

preserve their own culture and to develop their own forms of political organization. Nearly all those who defended South Africa stressed its consistent support of American foreign policy.[22]

The public debate over apartheid and U.S. policy had little immediate impact on Eisenhower and Dulles. Throughout their first term, both remained hostile to black nationalism and convinced that African independence would only foster communist expansionism. They thought that the Soviet Union was behind the agitation against colonialism and the demonstrations against white rule in South Africa.[23] Dulles feared that anticolonialism would culminate in violence, revolution, and anti-Western regimes. He greeted the surge of nationalism in the 1950s with "uneasiness and distaste" and attacked third-world neutralism as a "transitional stage to communism." Even as late as 1956, Dulles condemned nonalignment in the Cold War as "immoral and shortsighted" and warned that Soviet aggression posed a far greater danger than continued white control. Eisenhower shared this lack of sympathy for African aspirations. He observed that African nationalism "resembled a torrent overrunning everything in its path, including, frequently, the best interests of those concerned."[24]

The president and secretary of state remained committed to a "Europe first" policy that rejected any open criticism of NATO allies. Their frequent comments on the dangers of nationalism and the horrors of neutralism and their emphasis on "order" and "stability" convinced many Africans that the United States would not oppose white rule either by the Europeans or by the Afrikaners.

The administration's approach to South Africa reflected its uneasiness about nationalism and hatred of communism and its assessment of America's strategic needs. In 1953, the Senate, in cooperation with the White House, commissioned a survey of American mineral reserves and sources of supply. The study noted the diminished U.S. resources because of World War II, Korea, and the loss of Eastern European sources and emphasized the importance of South Africa as a current and future source of supplies for private industry and the military. It concluded that South Africa was the best source of strategic minerals in the free world. It not only provided gold but also supplied antimony ore (an alloying agent for steel and batteries), asbestos, chrome, manganese, industrial diamonds, and platinum. Any diplomatic conflict with Pretoria jeopardized the continued supply of these crucial items.[25]

22. See, for example, A. Desmond Burridge, "Some Racial Truths about South Africa," *American Mercury* 83 (December 1953): 5–14; "Where the White Man Is Rich and Scared," *U.S. News and World Report* 36 (21 May 1954): 42–46; and *Time* 66 (11 July 1955): 27–29.

23. In fact, the Soviet Union was not very active or effective in the African independence movement of the 1950s. See Christopher Stevens, *The Soviet Union and Black Africa*, 195–97.

24. John Foster Dulles, "The Cost of Peace," *SDB* 34 (18 June 1956): 1000. See also Townsend Hoopes, *The Devil and John Foster Dulles*, 315–16, 489; Dwight D. Eisenhower, *Waging Peace*, 572–74.

25. John Walton Cotman analyzes the report but somewhat overemphasizes its influence on policy in "South African Strategic Minerals and U.S. Foreign Policy, 1961–1968."

Despite their fear of the possible effects of nationalism and their desire to retain South Africa as an ally, Eisenhower and Dulles did not shift U.S. policy toward direct support of the Nationalists. As in their UN policy, the administration still sought a "middle" position. State Department officials continued to endorse self-determination but interjected continued warnings of the hazards of too rapid a shift to majority rule. A speech in late 1953 by Assistant Secretary of State Henry Byroade offers a good example of problems inherent in taking the "middle road." Byroade conceded that the independence movement was growing and the "clock of history cannot be turned back." He cited approvingly traditional American support of self-determination but cautioned against "premature independence" by peoples unprepared to resist the "new imperialism" of Moscow. Byroade stressed the need for continued U.S. cooperation with European allies and noted that Washington "cannot blindly disregard their side of the colonial question."[26]

Warnings of "premature independence" were sprinkled throughout the speeches of U.S. officials in the 1950s. Byroade's successor, George Allen, bluntly admitted that America's interests in Africa were strategic and not "idealistic." He asserted that "all of the so-called colonial powers . . . are our friends and allies in a world-wide contest between the Free and Communist worlds." Allen charged that the protests in South Africa against apartheid were headed by "extremists" who, did not care about racial equality but were "exploiting these tensions for ulterior purposes." The former American ambassador to Pretoria, W. J. Gallman, also warned of communist influence in the protest movement in South Africa. Gallman claimed that the U.S. press had overemphasized the harshness of apartheid. Malan had "a streak of reason-ableness," he insisted, but was forced to take a strong line against the African because of communist penetration of black groups and intense foreign criti-cism.[27]

American officials hesitated to speak out against the racial policies of Portugal in southern Africa. Washington's emphasis on NATO included the avoidance of public attacks on members of the alliance. By the early 1950s, the international community criticized Portugal for its exploitative colonial policies and its refusal to make any plans for independence. American diplomats, however, publicly endorsed the Portuguese dedication to a "civilizing mission" in Africa. In response to press attacks on conditions in Angola, Byroade defended Portuguese rule in language nearly identical to that of Salazar. He explained that Portugal had no policy of racial discrimination but recognized differences "between the

26. Henry Byroade, "The World's Colonies and Ex-Colonies: A Challenge to America," *SDB* 29 (16 November 1953): 655–60.
27. George Allen, "United States' Foreign Policy in Africa," *SDB* 34 (30 April 1956): 716–18; W. J. Gallman, "Some Thoughts on Foreign Affairs: From the Sidelines," April 1953, President's Personal File: Foreign Affairs, Truman Library.

civilized and non-civilized." When Africans "meet the standards of citizenship, they are automatically able to participate in the responsibilities of government." The *New York Times* also supported Portugal when it hailed Angola as "a triumph of assimilation" and "an example to the rest of Africa" of enlightened colonial rule.[28] Such assertions failed to mention that, after four hundred fifty years of "assimilation," fewer than 1 percent of the Africans in the Portuguese territories were considered "civilized" or had attended a school.

Despite American efforts to maintain normal relations with white Africa, embarrassing incidents involving apartheid occasionally arose. In 1953, U.S. tennis promoter Jack Kramer canceled an exhibition tour of South Africa when Pretoria objected to the inclusion of Ecuadoran pro Pancho Segura. Segura, who was part Indian, would have violated regulations against interracial sport in the Union.[29] South Africa also alienated many Americans with its strict censorship of books, magazines, and films. In the early 1950s, the Nationalists banned "all Negro American magazines." By 1955, it had excluded works by such prominent U.S. authors as Damon Runyon, Lillian Smith, Richard Wright, Erskine Caldwell, James Farrell, Zane Grey, and Mickey Spillane as either immoral or dangerous to "peaceful race relations." It even suppressed a comic book version of the life of Davy Crockett, because it showed cooperation between whites and Indians, and banned Mary Shelley's *Frankenstein*, because it portrayed the monster turning against his master.[30]

A report issued by the Commerce Department in 1953 prompted a miffed response from South Africa. Recognizing the potential dangers of racial conflict in South Africa, the American report on "Factors Limiting U.S. Investments Abroad" called South Africa "an area of concern" because of possible racial violence and instability. Eric Louw, soon to become foreign minister, denounced the report as "an unfriendly action" and demanded a formal U.S. apology for "meddling in the internal policy of another government." Commerce officials "expressed amazement" at Louw's remarks but refused additional comment.[31]

The most serious incident between America and South Africa in the mid-1950s occurred when the U.S. aircraft carrier *Midway* stopped in Capetown in 1955. The ship included eighty-six blacks and three hundred orientals, mostly Filipinos, in its crew. South Africa announced that non-white sailors would be governed by apartheid rules segregating theaters, bars, restaurants, and other facilities. The government did offer to arrange special entertainment for nonwhites, but only on a segregated basis.[32] The American consul in Capetown and the *Midway*'s captain announced that they were "fully satisfied" with this

28. Byroade, "The World's Colonies," 658; *New York Times*, 2 May 1954, p. 24.
29. *New York Times*, 2 August 1953, p. 1; 8 August 1953, p. 4.
30. *Africa Today* 3 (January-February 1956): 7.
31. *New York Times*, 26 November 1953, p. 11.
32. Ibid., 14 January 1955, p. 3.

compromise, but the NAACP and other groups protested cooperation with institutional racism. They complained to military officials and to the State Department but were told that the navy's policy was to obey all laws of foreign governments. When questioned at a news conference about the incident, Eisenhower referred the reporter to the Defense Department.[33]

South Africa's decision to apply apartheid to Americans was partly the result of a new aggressiveness by the government after 1953. Nationalist officials determined that they needed to defend apartheid abroad and to take the diplomatic offensive against critics of their policies. Pretoria's representatives abroad began a campaign to "educate" other nations of the need for apartheid. Government officials in South Africa granted interviews to foreign newsmen. Louw was given control of the Foreign Office with orders to breathe "fire and enthusiasm" into the bureaucracy.[34]

As a result of this new concern for world opinion, South Africa attempted to combat the criticism coming from the United States. Max Yergan, the former radical leader of the American Council on Africa, became the major spokesman for the Nationalist policies in the United States. He argued that Africa was "the next communist goal" and that South Africa "was completely justified" in its racial restrictions to control subversion.[35] More significant, in 1954, Malan agreed to an interview by the *U.S. News and World Report*. The prime minister stressed the growing threat of communism in Africa and pointed to the Mau Mau rebellion in Kenya as a consequence of weakening white control. He rejected any comparison of the racial situation in his country with that in America. The American "native" was far more civilized than the African; more important, the United States had a white majority and could allow blacks some political rights. Malan pledged continued support of the battle with the Soviet Union and concluded with a plea for more white immigration and increased U.S. investment.[36]

Malan's successor continued the public-relations effort by granting a lengthy interview in the same magazine. Strijdom also played heavily on the anticommunist theme. He attacked the "deliberate misrepresentation" of South Africa in the American press. He reaffirmed the Nationalist view that "the white man must remain supreme" in his nation because he has an obligation "to keep Western Civilization alive in Africa."[37]

Along with this new concern for foreign opinion, South Africa's "diplomatic

33. Ibid., 16 January 1955, p. 9; 17 January 1955, p. 22; 20 January 1955, p. 12.

34. James Barber, *South Africa's Foreign Policy*, 43–46. The Nationalists embarked on a similar "diplomatic offensive" in Africa. See Sam Nolutshungu, *South Africa in Africa*, 60–96.

35. *U.S. News and World Report* 34 (1 May 1953): 52–63.

36. Ibid. 36 (16 April 1954): 60–66. Malan even personally answered a letter from an American minister asking for an explanation of apartheid "to convince the American public" of its worth. See Malan to John Piersma, 12 February 1954, in Leo Kuper, *Passive Resistance in South Africa*, 217–32.

37. *U.S. News and World Report* 41 (14 September 1956): 46–50.

offensive" included a second attempt to involve the United States in a defense pact similar to NATO. When such an agreement did not materialize, South African military leaders began to refer to their nation as "an auxiliary of NATO." Pretoria also showed its new "toughness" by withdrawing from UNESCO in 1955 in response to criticism by "wooly-headed intellectuals" and by walking out of the UN whenever it discussed apartheid.[38]

South Africa's propaganda efforts in the United States were largely unnecessary because Washington had already determined that it could not risk offending Pretoria or its NATO allies. Administration leaders believed that African independence would lead to communist gains, that South Africa was vital to U.S. strategic needs, and that the foundation of American foreign policy was the Western alliance. Its approach to African issues reflected these assumptions. By 1956, Eisenhower's African policy was, in the slightly exaggerated phrase of one critic, "more royalist than the Queen."[39]

Beginning in late 1956, American attitudes toward Africa gradually changed. The United States never championed independence or challenged the South Africans directly, but Washington did reconsider its neglect of black Africa and its apparent acquiescence to apartheid. Both domestic politics and changes in the international situation accounted for the diplomatic reassessment. The split with Great Britain and France following the Suez crisis of 1956, the rush toward independence within Africa in the late 1950s, the emergence of civil rights as a more pressing domestic issue following the confrontation at Little Rock, and the presidential ambitions of Vice-President Richard Nixon all worked to alter the administration's approach to Africa.

American opposition to the Anglo-French invasion of Egypt in the fall of 1956 influenced its attitudes toward decolonization. The United States did not abandon its fears of "premature independence," but it no longer associated as closely with the two dominant colonial powers. The United States began to emphasize its lack of colonies in Africa and the resulting freedom of action in its diplomacy. Nixon, in a speech written by Dulles, declared that the United States would act independently of France and Great Britain in its dealings with Africa. He called for the two nations to prepare for the eventual freedom of all of their African possessions.[40]

Nixon's comments largely reflected Dulles's anger at the actions of the French and the British in Egypt, but they also were a practical response to the changing situation in Africa. With Ghana scheduled for independence in 1957, America

38. Barber, *South Africa's Foreign Policy*, 71–75, 82–86.
39. McKay, *Africa in World Politics*, 323. An excellent summary of third-world disillusionment with American policy in Africa and Asia during Eisenhower's first term is Harin Shah, *The Great Abdication*.
40. John Emmet Hughes, *The Ordeal of Power*, 209; Richard Goold-Adams, *John Foster Dulles*, 142.

belatedly recognized that freedom for the rest of Africa would soon follow. While many in the United States did not foresee that decolonization would occur as rapidly as it did, it was clear that colonialism in Africa was dying. Faced with the prospect of a sizable number of new nations in the immediate future, Washington accepted the inevitable. Even Dulles, although still hostile to neutralism, resigned himself, albeit reluctantly, to the end of European rule.

It was Nixon who led the push for a more active African policy. While representing the United States at the independence ceremonies for Ghana in March 1957, the vice-president publicly called for American support of decolonization and economic aid to the new nations. He also attacked racial discrimination within the United States as an obstacle to its diplomatic effectiveness in Africa.[41] When he returned to Washington from Africa, Nixon wrote a long report on his trip for Eisenhower. He called for a series of changes in U.S. policy. He again noted that segregation was fuel for communist propaganda in Africa and argued forcefully that equal rights was "in the national interest as well as for the moral issues involved." Nixon also lobbied for the creation of a separate Bureau of African Affairs within the State Department to deal with the continent that "could well prove to be the decisive factor" in the Cold War battle.[42]

Despite some opposition from Congress and within the State Department, Nixon and the administration succeeded in establishing the Bureau of African Affairs in 1958. The act was as much symbolic as substantive. The African Bureau was separate but not equal. The State Department favored the European section for promotion and prestige. Most senior officials in the African Bureau were European specialists who opposed American support of decolonization or any change in its policy toward South Africa. Even after a colony became independent, they routed all economic aid and much of the diplomatic correspondence through the former colonial power rather than directly to the new African nation. In 1958, the United States stationed more diplomats in West Germany than in all of black Africa.[43]

Despite the strong European orientation of the State Department and the rest of the administration, some officials in Washington began to argue for a shift of U.S. policy in favor of majority rule. Kenneth Young, of the Office of Defense

41. *New York Times*, 7 April 1957, p. 46.
42. "The Vice-President's Report to the President on his Trip to Africa," White House Central Files, OF 116, box 594, Eisenhower Library.
43. On the political problems of creating the Bureau of African Affairs, see Loy Henderson to Clarence Randall, 16 April 1958, and Randall to Sherman- Adams, 16 April 1958, White House Central Files, OF 8–S, box 172, Eisenhower Library. On the European orientation of the State Department and the African Bureau see U.S. Congress, Senate, Committee on Foreign Relations, *United States in the United Nations 1960: A Turning Point*, 39; and Russell Warren Howe, *Along the Afric Shore*, 114–15.

Mobilization, contended that colonialism was doomed and, before long, black Africa would unite to put pressure on South Africa. Without American influence, the leadership of opposition to apartheid would go "by default" to the communists. Julius Holmes, Dulles's personal assistant, returned from a tour of Africa to argue a similar position. Apartheid was a "dead-end policy," he insisted, that succeeded only in provoking "a burning hatred of whites and encouraging communist gains."[44]

The situation in South Africa seemed to confirm such pessimism. In late 1956, the government moved to silence the remaining active opponents of its racial policies. It arrested more than five hundred leaders of both black and white organizations including Chief Albert Luthuli, president of the African National Congress (ANC). The ANC had engaged in sporadic attempts at passive resistance throughout the period since 1948. The arrests, and the announcement that over one hundred fifty people would be tried for treason, contributed to U.S. fears that the only opposition in South Africa would be violent and Marxist. Sen. Francis Green of Rhode Island announced that America faced a clear choice between "friendship with South Africa and support of human rights, dignity, and freedom." He argued that Washington must press the Nationalists for immediate changes or face the possibility of a racial war. Adlai Stevenson also predicted that South Africa was approaching "a day of reckoning" and warned U.S. investors of impending violence in the area.[45]

The comments by Green and Stevenson indicate not only a new candor about apartheid but also the influence of domestic politics on foreign policy. Potential Democratic candidates for the presidency saw Republican opposition to decolonization and timidity on apartheid as possible election issues. Attacks on the administration's support of South Africa might gain black votes as well as help portray Eisenhower's foreign policy as outdated and harmful to American prestige. John Kennedy would use these themes effectively in the 1960 campaign against Nixon. He and his rivals for the Democratic nomination, however, focused on U.S. failures in Africa far earlier.

Kennedy received the most attention as a critic of American policy in a highly controversial speech in the Senate on 2 July 1957. Kennedy concentrated on U.S. opposition to the decolonization struggle against France in Algeria but broadened his attack to condemn Washington's refusal to back global self-determination. He argued that America could not "ride two horses" by trying to remain friendly with both Europe and its colonies. Kennedy called Eisenhower's approach to nationalism and decolonization "a head in the sand policy" that has

44. Kenneth T. Young, "Some Ideas and Proposals for Developing a Program for the Development of Leadership within the Free and Independent Nations of Asia, Africa, and the Arab World," 21 June 1957, Christian Herter Papers, box 19, Eisenhower Library. See also Howe, *Along the Afric Shore*, 116–19.

45. *New York Times*, 11 June 1957, p. 20; 13 June 1957, p. 4.

"earned the suspicion of all."[46] Kennedy's attack on a NATO ally provoked the condemnation of the State Department and the foreign policy establishment headed by Dean Acheson. Even Stevenson, the administration's most consistent critic, denounced the remarks and suggested "a six month moratorium on self-righteous moralizing and preaching." The speech did, however, have its intended effect of generating some liberal and black support for Kennedy.[47]

Sen. Hubert Humphrey of Minnesota, Kennedy's major rival for the nomination, also denounced Eisenhower's African policy. Unlike Kennedy, Humphrey raised the issue of U.S. support of apartheid. He ridiculed America's voting record in the UN and the reluctance of officials to speak out against South Africa. "Cultivating racism, whether under Hitler or *apartheid*, is an evil humanity will not tolerate," he concluded.[48]

The politicians' attention to Africa and race also resulted from the gradual growth of civil rights as an issue in America. Black leaders in the late 1950s became more vocal in their attacks on segregation at home and cooperation with South Africa and Portugal abroad. The NAACP contended that U.S. support of apartheid was costing it the friendship of new nations in Africa and Asia and their votes at the UN. The NAACP called on Washington to condemn apartheid and "press" Portugal for a plan for the independence of its African territories.[49] The NAACP joined with the American Committee on Africa and other liberal organizations for a "Day of Protest" on 10 December 1957 to commemorate the UN Declaration of Human Rights and to call attention to South Africa's refusal to sign it. Eleanor Roosevelt and Martin Luther King, fresh from his successful leadership of the Montgomery bus boycott, led the demonstration. The group circulated a "Declaration of Conscience" against apartheid signed by Roosevelt, King, Walter Reuther, the Reverend James Pike, John Gunther, and international celebrities such as Pablo Casals, Bertrand Russell, Arnold Toynbee, and Martin Buber.[50]

Blacks also tried to export their successful tactics of passive resistance and economic boycott from the American South to South Africa. American civil-rights workers helped Africans organize a boycott of the buses in Johannesburg in 1957. Mary-Louise Hopper, an American activist, was temporarily imprisoned and finally expelled for her activities. The boycott eventually lowered fares but failed to end discrimination.[51]

46. U.S. Congress, Senate, 85th Congress, 1st Session, *Congressional Record*, 2 July 1957, pt. 8: 10780-88.
47. Arthur M. Schlesinger, Jr., *A Thousand Days*, 553-54; Martin, *Adlai Stevenson*, 415-16.
48. Hubert Humphrey, "The U.S., Africa, and the UN," *Africa Today* 5 (January-February 1958): 9.
49. *Crisis* 64 (February 1957): 99.
50. *New York Times*, 15 October 1957, p. 25; *Africa Today* 4 (November-December 1957): 33-35.
51. Mary-Louise Hopper, "The Johannesburg Bus Boycott," *Africa Today* 4 (November-December 1957): 13-16.

The crisis over the integration of the Little Rock, Arkansas, high school in September 1957 most directly raised the issue of race and U.S. foreign policy. Reports by American representatives in Africa and Asia of the devastating propaganda impact of the opposition to integration finally influenced Eisenhower to reconsider his African policy. Although he felt no burning commitment to integration, he became convinced that discrimination hurt America's image abroad and particularly relations with the "new" Africa.[52]

Following the events at Little Rock and the creation of the African Bureau, some members of the administration attempted to push for a total change of African policy. Mason Sears, U.S. representative on the UN Trusteeship Council, prepared an "Estimate of the Next Five Years in Africa" for UN ambassador Henry Cabot Lodge. Sears concluded that the National party showed no signs of moderating apartheid and that the situation would "get progressively worse" as more African nations obtained independence. As it was unlikely that Washington could persuade Pretoria to change its racial policies, Sears suggested that America join the UN efforts against South Africa or risk being identified with white rule on an all-black continent.[53] In 1958, the State Department ordered a general review of policy toward Africa. It hired the Center for International Studies at the Massachusetts Institute of Technology to estimate future economic and political trends on the continent in preparation for a complete reappraisal of U.S. diplomacy and possible "new approaches."[54]

The first evidence of a "new approach" to African issues appeared at the UN. From 1953 to 1958 America had either abstained from or opposed all resolutions critical of South Africa. To the surprise of nations that annually had introduced resolutions condemning that country, the U.S. delegation made it known in 1958 that it would support a weakened version of a resolution mentioning South Africa. Sponsoring countries changed the language from "condemning" South Africa to "expressing regret and concern" over its racial policies, and America voted in their favor. The United States also reversed its opposition to resolutions that "call attention" to individual governments' violations of the UN Charter. American delegate George McGregor Harrison defended his vote in support of a resolution singling out South Africa by stating that apartheid "was inconsistent with U.S. principles and with the UN Charter."[55]

To many American officials this change in UN policy was significant, but by

---

52. Frederick Morrow oral history interview, Eisenhower Library; Hughes, *The Ordeal of Power*, 245. See also James Moss, "The Civil Rights Movement and American Foreign Policy"; and Alfred O. Hero, "The Negro Influence on U.S. Foreign Policy, 1937–1967," 222–23.

53. Sears to Lodge, 23 January 1958, U.S. Council on Foreign Economic Policy Files, box 1, Eisenhower Library.

54. "Africa Project: Outline for the First Phase of the Study," January 1958, White House Office, Office of the Special Assistant for National Security Affairs, box 57, Eisenhower Library. See also *SDB* 38 (26 May 1958): 857–62.

55. *New York Times*, 17 October 1958, p. 10; *SDB* 39 (24 November 1958): 843.

1958 it was clear that votes for weakened UN resolutions would not satisfy either domestic or foreign critics of apartheid. Although outraged by U.S. actions, South Africa was not influenced by the UN resolutions. The death of Strijdom in 1958 brought to power a more militant Nationalist, Dr. Hendrik Verwoerd, former minister of native affairs. Verwoerd, who had drafted much of the apartheid legislation, immediately announced plans for increased racial separatism. A White House staff report on "The African Revolution" in December 1958 was extremely pessimistic about the future of South Africa and warned of the "new troublespot," Rhodesia. Both nations were "pro-West," but the racial situation was growing worse, and the pressure for American action against the white governments would increase.[56]

African demands for U.S. support of the "liberation" of southern Africa intensified despite the votes in the UN. Ghana's delegate to the organization bluntly told America that it needed to do more than vote for resolutions. He argued that the United States must decide whether it favored the Africans or the "white exploiters" in Pretoria and Lisbon. Kenyan leader Tom Myboa, on a tour of the United States, repeatedly charged America with hypocrisy for condemning Chinese and Russian violations of freedom while "remaining silent on apartheid."[57]

Liberals also stepped up their attack on the administration. In 1959, the AFL-CIO passed a resolution calling for an end to white rule in Africa and urging the United States "to speak in a clear voice condemning the racism of South Africa." It organized an emergency defense fund to support political prisoners in South Africa. Michigan Gov. G. Mennen Williams, later Kennedy's assistant secretary of state for African affairs, told an African Freedom Day rally in New York that America "must exert leadership against the policy of apartheid." Black Rep. Charles Diggs of Michigan assailed Eisenhower for allowing NATO countries to dictate American policy in Africa. The Democratic National Committee issued a report on U.S. foreign policy charging that the administration was unconcerned about human rights abroad.[58]

Republicans also prodded Eisenhower for some action. Sen. Jacob Javits of New York criticized the U.S. embassy in South Africa for refusing to employ black foreign-service officers and for not inviting blacks to official functions. A month later, American ambassador Henry Byroade (author of the "premature independence" speech) broke precedent by asking a black American newsman to an embassy reception attended by South African officials.[59]

56. "The African Revolution," December 1958, White House Office, Office of the Staff Secretary, box 1, Eisenhower Library.

57. *New York Times*, 23 February 1959, p. 6; *Africa Today* 6 (May-June 1959): 3–6.

58. *New York Times*, 16 April 1957, p. 8; Charles Diggs, "U.S. Policy in Africa," *Africa Today* 6 (January-February 1959): 20–23; "A Vigorous and Sensible Economic Foreign Policy," Acheson Papers, box 93, Truman Library.

59. *New York Times*, 2 December 1958, p. 33; 24 January 1959, p. 4.

In 1959, the United States again voted for a UN resolution expressing "deep regret and concern that the Government of South Africa has not yet responded to appeals . . . to conform to the UN Charter." State Department officials generally endorsed the vote, but some worried that Washington was being "stampeded" toward a confrontation with South Africa. They recognized the need to gain influence with the new nations and to moderate domestic criticism, but they warned that South Africa remained strategically and economically important and was a bulwark against communism in Africa. If pushed too hard, Pretoria might close its ports to American ships, curtail its mineral exports, and perhaps place more restrictions on the black population. Bureaucratic fears of a clash with South Africa prompted one White House aide to note sarcastically, "Some officials at State are trying to carry on in the splendid British white dinner jacket tradition."[60]

The decisive event in U.S.–South African relations in the Eisenhower years was the massacre of black protesters at Sharpeville in March 1960. Several times in the 1950s, police in South Africa had attacked black demonstrators protesting apartheid. The confrontation near Johannesburg at Sharpeville, however, was so violent and seemingly so unprovoked that it drew instant and sustained international attention. As blacks marched on a police station in nonviolent protest of the pass laws, police opened fire, killing sixty-nine and wounding over two hundred. America's response to the massacre exposed the rift within the government over apartheid. The massacre provoked strong official criticism of Pretoria and also revealed the deep fear of many in Washington of challenging the Nationalists.

The State Department's response to the killings was swift and, as later became evident, independent of the White House. After hearing of the shootings, department officials, without consulting Secretary of State Christian Herter or Eisenhower, hurriedly drafted a statement. In a chaotic scene, Press Officer Lincoln White, his voice breaking with emotion, read the release to a hastily assembled group of reporters. White announced that "while the United States . . . does not ordinarily comment on the internal affairs of governments with which it enjoys normal relations," the severity of the incident at Sharpeville demanded a direct response. He declared that the United States "condemns violence in all forms" and supports the right "of the African people of South Africa . . . to obtain redress for legitimate grievances by peaceful means."[61]

White's statement was a weakened version of an earlier draft that had attacked the entire policy of apartheid as inevitably provoking violence. Even the milder comments that were released were far too strong for many in the administration.

---

60. Ibid., 3 November 1959, p. 8; Rupert Emerson, *Africa and United States' Policy*, 22–23; Frederic Fox to Karl Harr, 15 January 1960, White House Office, Office of the Special Assistant for National Security Affairs, box 57, Eisenhower Library.

61. *SDB* 42 (11 April 1960): 551; *New York Times*, 23 March 1960, p. 1; 27 March 1960, p. 1.

Herter was incensed that neither he nor Eisenhower had been consulted. As a result, an apparently official statement represented the sentiments of only a few middle-level State Department bureaucrats. Herter strongly objected to the phrase that seemed to pledge U.S. support for protests, however peaceful, in another nation. In an angry memo to Andrew Goodpaster, Eisenhower's staff secretary, Herter "disowned" the statement.[62]

Other senior officials at the State Department, the White House, and the Defense Department were equally livid. They feared that South Africa would respond to the seeming encouragement of black protest by ending the sale of strategic materials, by closing Capetown to the U.S. fleet, or by protesting American plans to fire a missile from Florida past South Africa to the Indian Ocean. Eisenhower refused to defend the State Department release. He called apartheid "a touchy thing" and claimed that many within South Africa were working for peaceful change and "human understanding."[63]

American fears of South African reprisals proved to be groundless. Pretoria was so inundated with protests that it responded to the American statement in relatively routine fashion. The government summoned U.S. ambassador Phillip Crowe for a fifteen-minute lecture on the dangers of meddling in South Africa's internal affairs. Louw attacked the U.S. comments in the press as incitement to violence. South Africa was more upset, however, with the American announcement that it would support a special session of the UN Security Council to investigate the incident. At the session, Lodge denounced apartheid by name for the first time and voted for a resolution that stated that, if continued, the policy "might endanger international peace and security." The statement called on South Africa "to abandon its policy of apartheid and racial discrimination."[64]

The Sharpeville tragedy led to an outpouring of public outrage. Nearly all American magazines and newspapers ran features on apartheid. Many contrasted the violence in South Africa with the relatively peaceful reaction to the sit-in demonstrations sweeping the American South. Celebrities ranging from Harlem Rep. Adam Clayton Powell to evangelist Billy Graham deplored the shootings, and, with varying intensity, apartheid. The American Committee on Africa announced plans for a "united front" to organize a boycott of all South African products.[65]

The South African government reacted with its usual mixture of bombast and public relations. Louw dismissed the State Department statement as "low level" but was incensed by U.S. television coverage of the incident. He told parliament

62. Herter to Goodpaster, 24 March 1960, White House Office, Office of the Staff Secretary, box 1, Eisenhower Library.
63. *New York Times*, 26 March 1960, p. 2; 31 March 1960, p. 14.
64. Ibid., 27 March 1960, p. 26; 2 April 1960, p. 1.
65. See, for example, Gwendolen Carter, "South Africa's Rubicon," *Nation* 190 (16 April 1960): 317–30; "Exploding South Africa," *Newsweek* 55 (11 April 1960): 49–55; "Sharpeville," *Africa Today* 7 (May 1960): 6–7.

that the South African ambassador in Washington had met with representatives of Caltex, a Texaco subsidiary and sponsor of the Huntley-Brinkley newscast, and "reminded them of the major business they were doing in this country." Louw reported: "The company said they would see what they could do and for a time Mr. Chet Huntley left us in peace." At home, the government banned the organizations responsible for the protest at Sharpeville, and Verwoerd assailed Great Britain and the United States for abandoning "their only true friend in Africa."[66]

Despite the Nationalists' aggressive rhetoric, the nearly unanimous criticism of South Africa did have some effect on them. Even the militant Afrikaner newspaper *Die Burger* conceded: "It is a bitter thing to be forced into the role of the skunk of the world."[67] After its initial defense of the violence at Sharpeville, the South African government began a more detailed analysis of the causes and effects of the affair. The Sharpeville massacre occurred in the "year of Africa" as sixteen new black nations gained independence. France, Great Britain, and Belgium had accepted the inevitability of decolonization, and South Africans realized that they stood with Portugal and Rhodesia as the last bastions of white rule. They believed that their European and American allies had abandoned them. British Prime Minister Harold Macmillan's famous "winds of change" speech in South Africa only a few weeks before Sharpeville convinced many Afrikaners that England soon would pressure them to grant political rights to the black majority. In fact, some militant Nationalists charged that the protests at Sharpeville were in response to Macmillan's public "sell-out" to black nationalism.[68]

South African leaders were also concerned about the expanding protests of segregation within the United States. The sit-in movement and other organized opposition to discrimination would, many concluded, increase pressure on Washington to denounce apartheid. It was an election year, and American politicians would vie for the black vote by assailing South Africa. The Nationalists decided that they must undertake a major effort to court America by explaining apartheid and reiterating South Africa's importance as a Cold War ally.

Pretoria's propaganda campaign following the Sharpeville massacre resembled its earlier public-relations efforts of the mid-1950s. Wentzel C. du Plessis, Pretoria's ambassador to the United States, wrote an article for *U.S. News* pointing out that all nations practice some form of discrimination. He compared his nation's racial policies with American treatment of women. Neither, he argued, was the result of prejudice but only "based on a fact of

66. Stanford D. Greenberg, "U.S. Policy toward the Republic of South Africa," 120; *New York Times*, 3 July 1960, p. 6.
67. Colin Legum and Margaret Legum, *South Africa*, 235.
68. Barber, *South Africa's Foreign Policy*, 121–25.

nature." Just as men and women have different talents, interests, and functions, so, too, do the races.[69] Typically, Foreign Minister Louw took the "hard" approach. In a speech to the National Press Club in Washington, he contended that America would follow a policy similar to apartheid if it were faced with the problem of a black majority. He emphasized that "South Africa's strategic position . . . is of the greatest importance to the Western countries as a bastion against Communist penetration." After a lengthy review of Pretoria's support in the Cold War, he concluded: "I suggest that the Union of South Africa is an ally worth having—and worth keeping."[70]

The Nationalists realized that speeches would not sufficiently counter the expanding criticism of their racial policies and decided on a more sophisticated propaganda campaign in America. The South African government hired the Hamilton Wright Organization, a New York public-relations firm, to coordinate a major effort to create a more favorable image of South Africa within the United States. The Wright group wrote and distributed pamphlets and articles on apartheid and produced several films showing the prosperity and diplomatic importance of South Africa.[71]

More influential in limiting American efforts against South Africa, however, was the explosive situation in the Congo in the summer of 1960. Following its independence from Belgium on 30 June, the Congo rapidly degenerated into separatism, tribalism, and violence. In early July, Congolese troops mutinied against their white officers. Moise Tshombe declared the mineral-rich province of Katanga in secession from the central government. President Joseph Kasavubu tried to dismiss Premier Patrice Lumumba, and Gen. Joseph Mobutu seized control in a military coup. The Congo rapidly divided into three rival governments: a central regime at Leopoldville headed by Kasavubu and Mobutu; another government led by Lumumba and Antoine Gizenga in Stanleyville; and the independent state of Katanga under Tshombe.

The UN intervened in the crisis in the Congo to preserve order and to restore a unified state. America supported efforts to crush the Katanga rebellion and tried to block radicalism by working against Lumumba. In January 1961, Lumumba was murdered, and Washington concentrated on forcing Tshombe to end his secession.[72]

The chaos in the Congo had a significant impact on America's African policy and indirectly influenced its dealings with Portugal, Rhodesia, and South

69. *U.S. News and World Report* 48 (20 June 1960): 138–39.

70. Ibid. 49 (7 November 1960): 108–9.

71. U.S. Congress, House, Committee on Foreign Affairs, *Hearings on U.S.–Southern African Relations*, 85–86. Over the next three years the Wright Organization was paid $274,000 for its efforts. In 1965 South Africa hired a Washington firm to continue the campaign and make a survey of U.S. public opinion.

72. On U.S. Congo policy see Stephen Weissman, *American Foreign Policy in the Congo, 1960–1964*; and Ernest Lefever, "U.S. Policy, the UN and the Congo."

Africa. Although most Americans could not keep track of the changing governments and leaders in the Congo, the savagery of the warfare and vivid descriptions of violence against whites seemed to confirm predictions of the disastrous results of "premature independence." Accounts of rapes of white nuns and mutilations of European missionaries did far more than South African propaganda to temper criticism of white rule in Africa. The Congo drove Sharpeville from the headlines and gave new credence to the claims of Lisbon, Salisbury, and Pretoria that they were the only safeguards against violence, tribal warfare, and radicalism.

Even before the turmoil in the Congo, the Eisenhower administration had begun to reconsider its "new" approach to Africa. Many within the government were upset over the "official" U.S. statement on Sharpeville and fearful of any rash attempt to confront the Nationalists. Assistant Secretary of State Francis Wilcox, in a speech on Africa immediately following Sharpeville, pointed out that America had divided loyalties in dealing with South Africa: "On the one hand, the sentiments of those who feel oppressed and discriminated against are easy to understand. On the other hand, one can appreciate the feeling of people . . . who now find themselves in a minority on a restless stirring continent." Although he doubted that apartheid "can very long endure," Wilcox cautioned against the demands of "political extremists" for "the premature withdrawal of white men from positions of responsibility." Too much pressure on South Africa would result in opportunities for communist penetration.[73]

Eisenhower also had limited any active encouragement of black liberation in Africa. On his way to the aborted summit conference with Nikita Khrushchev in 1960, he stopped in Lisbon for two days of discussions with Salazar. The president rejected suggestions from his aides that he raise the issue of decolonization of Portugal's African territories. Instead he publicly praised Lisbon's "civilizing mission" in Africa and claimed "there are no great problems between the United States and Portugal."[74]

The events of 1960, however, worked to introduce Africa into the presidential campaign. Nixon was forced to defend Eisenhower's African policy and to explain the complicated issues involved in the Congo. He cited his visit to Africa, support of the Bureau of African Affairs, and efforts to maintain Congolese unity as examples of the administration's interest in Africa. To Kennedy, Republican diplomacy in Africa was a prime example of the failure of leadership and the decline of American prestige during the Eisenhower years. He made nearly five hundred references to Africa in his campaign speeches. He attacked American reluctance to support independence and its neglect of the new African nations. Kennedy courted black voters by promising to post more black

73. Francis O. Wilcox, "The Challenge of Africa," *Vital Speeches* 26 (15 May 1960): 476–80.
74. "The President's Trip to Portugal, May 19–20, 1960," Papers of the President, Ann Whitman File, International Series, box 41, Eisenhower Library.

diplomats in Africa and by personally paying for the transportation of African students to the United States when the administration refused funds. During the campaign, he also sent veteran diplomat Averell Harriman on a "fact-finding" tour of the continent. Kennedy offered few specific new policies toward Africa, but he hammered away at the Republican's refusal to "accept the inevitable triumph of nationalism in Africa."[75]

Nixon's campaign advisers recognized that Kennedy effectively used the Africa issue to appeal to black voters. They urged Eisenhower to arrange a public meeting with African representatives at the UN to show the administration's concern and interest in the continent. The president obliged with a rather perfunctory reception at the White House on the eve of the election.[76]

Eisenhower and his aides supported Nixon's campaign and were sensitive to Kennedy's attack, but they cared more about U.S. strategic interests in Africa. In the middle of the campaign, South Africa announced that it would allow the United States to establish three missile-tracking stations in the Transvaal and to expand telecommunication facilities for American submarines patrolling the Indian Ocean. Democrat Sen. Wayne Morse of Oregon charged that Pretoria had agreed to the arrangement with the tacit understanding that America would soften its UN policies on apartheid. Although there is no evidence to support Morse's contention, the timing of South Africa's announcement seemed calculated to remind America of the importance of maintaining cooperation with the Nationalist regime.[77]

After Kennedy's victory, the administration reverted to its earlier cautious approach to black Africa. For example, when more than forty African and Asian nations sponsored a UN resolution denouncing colonialism in late 1960, Eisenhower refused to support it. U.S. delegate John Wadsworth urged the president to allow him to vote for the resolution, but Eisenhower, responding to a personal request from Macmillan for U.S. opposition, ordered Wadsworth to abstain. America joined Australia, Great Britain, the Dominican Republic, France, Portugal, Spain, and South Africa in abstaining as the resolution passed 89–0. Though one black member of the U.S. delegation rose to his feet and led the cheering when the motion passed, the United States continued to oppose premature independence. In fact, America sponsored Portugal for a seat on the Security Council despite emotional attacks on Lisbon for its refusal to consider independence for Angola and Mozambique.[78]

In his last weeks in office, Eisenhower made a final move that angered many

75. Schlesinger, *A Thousand Days*, 554; Nielsen, *The Great Powers and Africa*, 276–77.

76. Charles Rosenbaum to Eisenhower, 6 October 1960, White House Central Files, OF 328, box 936, Eisenhower Library; "Minutes of Cabinet Meeting, 7 October 1960," Ann Whitman Files, Cabinet Series, box 16, Eisenhower Library.

77. Greenberg, "U.S. Policy toward South Africa," 99–100.

78. *SDB* 44 (2 January 1961): 21–28; George Houser, "US at the UN: Cause for Concern," *Africa Today* 8 (January 1961): 5–6.

African sympathizers. He attempted to appoint a group of aging career foreign-service officers to ambassadorships in new African states. Many of these diplomats, near retirement age, wanted the prestige of the rank of ambassador before they left governmental service. Only the loud protests of Robert Kennedy and Chester Bowles blocked the move.[79]

Eisenhower's policies toward white rule in Africa show essential continuity with Truman's "middle road" position. While the administration made some adjustments after 1957 in its voting at the UN and in its public statements, it was slow to adapt to the changed situation in Africa and within the United States. By the late 1950s, all of Africa, with the exception of the Portuguese territories, Rhodesia, and South Africa, was on the road to independence, and the new nations that emerged would concentrate on the complete liberation of the continent by forcing the end of white rule. They expected all friendly nations to support this objective. The growth of black protest within America also indicated that race would become an important issue in domestic politics and in foreign affairs. By continuing a "Europe first" approach at the expense of alienating the newly independent countries, Eisenhower may have insured immediate support for America's Cold War efforts, but he identified Washington with the dwindling pockets of white rule.

Both blacks and whites in Africa assumed Kennedy's victory would result in a new approach to the problem of white Africa. During the campaign, he had championed civil rights at home and had promised bold departures from the tired, conservative diplomacy of the 1950s. When he assumed office, Kennedy immediately tried to restructure U.S. policy in favor of black liberation. He soon found, however, that any new approach to white rule in Africa threatened other American Cold War objectives.

79. G. Mennen Williams oral history interview, John F. Kennedy Library; Schlesinger, *A Thousand Days*, 510–11.

4. NEW FRONTIERS AND OLD PRIORITIES

America and the Angolan Revolution, 1961–1962

It is difficult to predict accurately the foreign policies of a new administration, because changes in the international situation often force adjustment of even the most sincere campaign pledges. Advocates of a more active American involvement in Africa, however, were certain that John Kennedy would align the United States with the inevitable force of black nationalism. Kennedy's campaign, personality, and appointments created a climate of eager anticipation among domestic liberals and Africans, who believed he would eliminate the deference of African issues to European sensitivities and would moderate the emphasis on a bipolar world struggle that had characterized the Eisenhower years.

In his campaigns for the Democratic nomination and the presidency, Kennedy stressed his support of the civil-rights movement at home and called for bold initiatives abroad to regain American power and prestige. His apparent acceptance of third-world nationalism, his frequent campaign references to Africa, and the appointment of Chester Bowles as a campaign adviser on foreign policy all implied strong support of decolonization and majority rule and a willingness to use American power to secure them. Those in favor of the liberation of white Africa assumed Kennedy's election marked a major shift in both the objectives and the tactics of U.S. diplomacy. With the rapid decolonization of Africa and, many assumed, a forthcoming clear commitment of American political and economic power to self-rule, African nations would rapidly obtain independence.

America's response to the Angolan revolution in 1961 and 1962, however, forced Africanists to reassess their optimism in Kennedy's leadership. The situation in Portugal's colonies reminded the Kennedy administration of old strategic priorities that set boundaries on the New Frontier. As the events in Angola unfolded, some people in the State Department sensed that the president and his advisers had decided to place no further demands on Portugal, to adopt a more conservative position in the UN, and to relegate Africa to its traditional secondary role in American diplomacy. Chester Bowles attributed the shift to the fact that "the people Kennedy listened to most on foreign affairs had a European-oriented view." G. Mennen Williams offered a more accurate conclusion: "The

Africans had much higher hopes and expectations for us than we had any ability to deliver."[1]

When Kennedy first took office, his personal diplomacy and early appointments gave Africans reason for high hopes. In contrast to Eisenhower, Kennedy courted African leaders through private meetings and personal correspondence. He appeared genuinely interested in Africa and successfully used his considerable charm on Africans of all political persuasions. Accustomed to the paternalism and homilies of the previous eight years, Africans welcomed Kennedy's attention. He established a personal rapport with many leaders that later helped mitigate their disappointment with some of his policies.[2] Kennedy's youth, and that of many of his advisers, further impressed the new nations of Africa and their leaders. Africans easily identified when Kennedy spoke of a "new generation" of leaders. They assumed that the "tired policies of old men" had given way to bold innovations by young, tough-minded liberals.

Africans were also pleased by the new president's statements on race and discrimination. Kennedy repeatedly had pointed out the burden that segregation created for U.S. diplomacy. He had castigated the Republicans for their failure to enact significant civil-rights legislation and their reluctance to recruit black diplomats. Africans were well aware of the importance of the black vote in Kennedy's narrow victory and expected him to use foreign policy as well as domestic legislation to retain their support.

Perhaps nothing did more to give the impression of a shift in America's African policy than did Kennedy's appointments. Partly to appease liberal Democrats who had supported Humphrey or Stevenson, Kennedy named a number of prominent liberals to positions in the foreign-policy bureaucracy. Immediately after his election, he appointed Michigan Governor G. Mennen Williams to the position of assistant secretary of state for Africa. Williams had wanted to head the Department of Health, Education, and Welfare, but Kennedy consoled him by announcing that this first appointment emphasized the importance of Africa in his administration and by promising that Williams would have direct access to the president.

To many Americans, the selection of the flamboyant "Soapy" Williams to head the African Bureau seemed to be mere repayment for the governor's early support of Kennedy's nomination. Williams had no experience in foreign affairs and was known primarily for his early and outspoken advocacy of civil rights—a trait quite useful in his dealings with Africans. The new assistant secretary exhibited boundless enthusiasm and idealism and advocated strong American support of African independence. To many liberals, his appointment signaled a

1. Bowles oral history interview; Williams oral history interview, Kennedy Library.
2. Many studies of Kennedy note his successful use of personal diplomacy. The best illustrations of his effectiveness with Africans are Schlesinger, *A Thousand Days*, 557–60, and Ibezim Chukwumerije, "The New Frontier and Africa, 1961–1963."

break from the "cold war perspective" of Dulles and the "stuffed shirtedness" of the State Department. Although some feared his "galloping liberalism," the nomination did have the effect of both soothing liberals and assuring Africans.[3]

Although Williams somewhat surprisingly proved to be the most effective and durable defender of a new approach to Africa, Kennedy's selection of Chester Bowles as under-secretary of state and Adlai Stevenson as ambassador to the UN seemed to be the clearest signal of a vigorous new African policy. Bowles, the darling of many liberal Democrats, had been one of the first prominent liberals to support Kennedy. During the campaign, he had served as an informal adviser on foreign affairs. As a particularly outspoken supporter of African liberation, Bowles had long advocated a third-world emphasis in U.S. policy. Throughout the 1950s, Stevenson also had called for increased American attention to Africa. Like Bowles and Williams, Stevenson pushed strongly for U.S. support of black rule in Africa.

Williams, Bowles, and Stevenson, all faced conflicts with career diplomats in the State Department. Williams clashed with the bureaucracy over his strong advocacy of an American commitment to black liberation both at home and abroad and over his independence, colorfulness, and outspokenness. Advocates of somber, quiet diplomacy did not appreciate his numerous trips and tactics such as holding a square dance for African diplomats with himself as the caller. Williams conceded that he was too liberal for most in the State Department and that in style he was "more a John the Baptist than a disciple." Bowles's liberalism and personality, like Williams's, soon proved incompatible with Kennedy's emphasis on precision, pragmatism, and "toughness" on the New Frontier.[4] His arrogance, inattention to detail, and inability to work with Secretary of State Dean Rusk eroded his effectiveness, and, in less than a year, he was removed from his position and given the vague title of special adviser. Stevenson eventually earned a reputation among some foreign policy officials for softness and laziness. George Ball, Kennedy's under-secretary of state for economic affairs, noted that some people in the White House felt Stevenson "had gone to seed," did not do his homework at the UN, and was more interested in socializing than in diplomacy.[5] Dean Acheson, titular head of the Democratic party "establishment," thought Stevenson was "soupy" on Africa and that Bowles and Williams were idealistic utopians.

Many of Kennedy's lower-level appointments also seemed to point to a new concern with Africa. He picked Wayne Fredericks, a former Ford Foundation executive with extensive knowledge of and contacts in Africa, as Williams's

3. Helen Kitchen, "Africa and the Kennedy Era," *New Republic* 143 (19 December 1961): 17–19.

4. Williams oral history interview, Kennedy Library; David Halberstam, *The Best and the Brightest*, contains sketches of nearly all of the influential foreign-policy advisers under Kennedy and effectively shows the problems Bowles had with other officials.

5. Martin, *Adlai Stevenson*, 579–81, 588.

deputy in the African Bureau. The nomination of a group of young, aggressive ambassadors to the new African nations was hailed as another sign of the increased importance of the continent. Although the new U.S. representatives generally supported stronger American efforts to gain African independence, they also believed that the continent remained primarily a battleground in the Cold War. Unlike Bowles, Stevenson, and Williams, they were in tune with the administration's emphasis on power politics and view of diplomacy as a weapon in the global contest with communism. To the "new crew," as they were dubbed by the State Department, Africa was important because it was an area of potential communist infiltration and thus offered a chance for American victories. These diplomats were not "idealists," almost a perjorative term in the Kennedy administration, but were considered "practical" and, most important, "tough."[6]

Most analysts of Kennedy's African policies have praised his appointments, personal diplomacy, and obvious interest in the continent. They argue that he made major innovations in U.S. policy, reversed Washington's opposition to black rule, and scored some of his most dramatic diplomatic triumphs on the dark continent. Arthur Schlesinger, Jr., spoke for most when he concluded: "In no part of the third world did Kennedy pioneer more effectively than in Africa." Schlesinger and others favorable to Kennedy contend the president greatly sympathized with African nationalism and committed America to its support. Even those highly critical of his diplomacy elsewhere agree Kennedy had a sustained interest in Africa and reversed many previous policies.[7]

There is no doubt that the Kennedy administration was much more interested and active in Africa than were the Truman and Eisenhower administrations, but it does not follow that his policies represent major, new departures. Given the substantial changes in Africa in the early 1960s, especially the revolts in the Portuguese colonies, it was inevitable that the United States would be more involved. It is less clear that the objectives of American diplomacy changed as much as Kennedy's early interpreters contend. Not all in Washington shared the goals articulated by Bowles, Stevenson, Williams, and even Kennedy. There remained a large, vocal, and skilled group of "Europeanists" who were extremely effective in questioning the wisdom of an American commitment to black rule, tempering U.S. criticism of the white governments, and pushing for the continued subjugation of African issues to European priorities.

6. See Attwood, *The Reds and the Blacks,* and the oral history interviews of Attwood, Charles Darlington, Thomas Estes, Philip Kaiser, and the other ambassadors to Africa in the Kennedy Library.

7. Schlesinger, *A Thousand Days,* 551–84, is the best of the numerous favorable assessments of Kennedy's African policies, but even those generally harsh on Kennedy's diplomacy elsewhere, such as Richard Walton, *Cold War and Counterrevolution,* are generally impressed with his efforts in Africa. Some recent studies have been more critical of Kennedy's effectiveness in Africa and less convinced of his innovations. See Melvin Gurtov, *The United States Against the Third World,* 41–81; Weissman, *American Foreign Policy in the Congo;* and Chukwumerije, "The New Frontier and Africa."

The "Europe first" perspective was not as clearly associated with specific individuals as was the "African" point of view. The most obvious spokesman for "Europe first" was George Ball, who later replaced Bowles as under-secretary. Ball, a protegé of Acheson, recalled, "Acheson cared nothing for Africa. Acheson was a Europeanist. I'm considered one too." Those who shared Ball's skepticism about the importance of Africa included Roger Hilsman, the director of intelligence and research in the State Department, John McCone, director of the CIA, and, to a lesser degree, Dean Rusk. Many Defense Department officials and military officers, deeply committed to NATO, also held the Europeanist view, as did many of the State Department bureaucrats. Several key ambassadors, particularly C. Burke Elbrick and Robert Anderson in Lisbon and Joseph Satterthwaite in Pretoria, were also critical of any significant realignment of America's African policies.[8]

Additional support of the European orientation came from leaders of the "foreign-policy establishment," such as Robert Lovett, Paul Nitze, John McCloy, and Acheson. These "in-and-outers" alternated between private corporations and public service throughout the Cold War and remained influential whether in or out of office. Most had helped shape U.S. policy under Truman and Eisenhower and were dedicated to a strong Atlantic community centered around NATO. They favored continuation of existing priorities and were convinced that relations with Africa were less important than maintaining close ties with Europe. When consulted, or, in the case of Acheson, even when not consulted, they were quick to oppose any adjustment of policy that risked dissension within the Western alliance.

Although this lack of consensus of foreign policy was not unique to African issues, the splits within the administration did perhaps have a larger impact on African questions than on questions involving other geographic areas. A new approach to Africa involved substantial changes in prevailing policies. The area did not have the benefit of traditional U.S. interest or an active domestic constituency. As a result, nearly every American action, UN vote, speech, or response involving Africa producd a bureaucratic battle. African diplomacy was the product of paper warfare as Europeanists and Africanists both inside and outside the government fought a war of memos. Williams, Bowles, Stevenson, and others argued the symbolic and practical importance of boldly aligning with the forces of liberation in the Portuguese colonies and taking a tough stance against continued white oppression in South Africa and Rhodesia. Their opponents minimized the strategic importance of Africa and cautioned against any hasty commitment to black rule that might jeopardize U.S. interests in more

---

8. Ball is quoted in Martin, *Adlai Stevenson*, 588–89. Important statements of the "Europeanist" perspective are George Ball, *The Discipline of Power*, 221–59; Roger Hilsman, *To Move a Nation*, 240–48; and William S. White, "Which Friends Come First?" *Harpers* 224 (March 1962): 100–105.

significant areas. Often personal antagonisms and rivalries shaped the debate as much as real policy disagreements.

To make matters more complicated, both sides were certain that the president shared their objectives in Africa. Liberals, mindful of Kennedy's speeches attacking colonialism and accepting international diversity and enamored with his appointments, expected an immediate reversal of America's tacit acceptance of white rule and open support of black liberation. Traditionalists remained convinced that Kennedy's criticism of previous African policy was largely campaign rhetoric. They believed that, while the president might make some adjustments of policy and style, he would not pursue any action that would threaten the primacy of Europe or lead to the creation of weak, potentially communist nations in the third world.

Kennedy did have a strong affinity for Africa and a hatred of the racism of the white regimes, but he never allowed these to interfere with his view of international politics as a continuing struggle between America and Russia. Anticommunism was at the heart of Kennedy's diplomacy, and he viewed Africa primarily as an area of East-West competition. His support of decolonization was as much for strategic as for idealistic reasons. He was willing to alter his position on minority rule whenever the international situation shifted. While he clearly deplored continued Portuguese colonialism and white exploitation in Rhodesia and South Africa, like his two predecessors he also feared that violent overthrow of white control might lead to communist gains and grave threats to America's strategic interests. Kennedy's approach to Africa was shaped in part by Nikita Khrushchev's apparent redefinition of the Cold War in his famous 6 January 1961 speech. Although the Russian leader rejected nuclear war, he argued that the socialist revolution would continue through "wars of national liberation" supported by Moscow. To Kennedy and his advisers, this indicated that the liberation movements in Africa and the rest of the underdeveloped world were in constant danger of communist infiltration. Thus America must guard against too rapid or radical change. Khrushchev's belligerency also led to a stronger emphasis in Washington on the importance of military preparedness and, as a result, of NATO and Europe. Although some of his aides tried to separate Africa from Europe in American diplomacy, Kennedy saw the two as part of a single elaborate communist offensive. As a result, his actions in Africa were often controlled directly by events in Europe.

Other issues also influenced Kennedy's handling of African questions. Despite the assumptions of some Africanists, the continent remained secondary to the dramatic crises of the Kennedy years. The conflict with Cuba leading to the Bay of Pigs invasion and eventually to the missile crisis, the constant tension over Berlin, the escalating U.S. involvement in Laos and Vietnam, and the efforts to limit nuclear testing all affected American diplomacy in Africa. These immediate crises shifted attention from all other foreign issues and forced changes in African policy to meet the new international balance. Washington adjusted its position on the rebellion in Angola, for example, in response to the situation in Berlin, the need to gain Senate approval of the test-ban treaty, and other pressing priorities.

Kennedy's personality and approach to decisionmaking also dictated his reaction to African issues. His early impatience with the bloated bureaucracy of the State Department rapidly turned to disdain. He was appalled by imprecision, impatient with idealists, and scornful of perceived weakness. He demanded clear presentation of policy alternatives with practical suggestions for maximum use of American power. Faced with a series of foreign crises immediately after assuming office, he quickly abandoned long-range planning for immediate action. The traits the president found most appealing (clarity, toughness, and a recognition of the dangers of communist expansion) were often lacking among the Africanists. Their justifications for U.S. support of black liberation were often abstract and usually emphasized long-term gains. They were forced to try to convince Kennedy of the need for new approaches and priorities at a time of crisis and tension. They soon recognized that the only way to gain a response was to couch their arguments in the prevailing Cold War rhetoric and present black Africa as a strategic battleground between communism and freedom rather than as a moral issue involving worthy but abstract notions of self-determination and racial equality.

The first test of Kennedy's "new approach" to Africa was the rebellion in Angola in early 1961. Because Salazar had steadfastly refused to prepare Portugal's African possessions for independence, blacks in Angola and Mozambique organized resistance movements to duplicate the policies that had been successful in other colonies. The liberation movements in Angola and Mozambique were fragmented into dozens of groups and wracked by tribal differences. By 1961 two major organizations vied for control of the independence struggle in Angola. The União das Populações de Angola (UPA) headed by Holden Roberto and the Movimento Popular de Libertação de Angola (MPLA) under Dr. Agostinho Neto and Mario de Andrade both claimed to represent the Angolan people in their struggle with Portugal.[9]

To most American observers, Roberto's UPA seemed the dominant group. The nephew of nationalist leader Barros Necaca, Roberto had grown up amid the emerging independence movement and its leaders. Named after the British missionary who baptized him, Roberto was educated at missionary schools in the Belgian Congo. He eventually became an accountant for the Belgian

9. Indispensable to an understanding of the Angolan liberation movement are the exhaustive accounts of John Marcum, *The Angolan Revolution: The Anatomy of an Explosion, 1950–1962* and *The Angolan Revolution: Exile Politics and Guerrilla Warfare, 1962–1976*. Marcum had extensive personal contacts within the various factions of the Angolan movement and documents in great detail the continuing rivalries and politics of the struggle for independence. For a shorter summary, see Richard Gibson, *African Liberation Movements*, 187–242.

government in Leopoldville, where he met Patrice Lumumba, Cyril Adoula, and other Congolese nationalists. He returned to Angola in 1951 at the age of twenty-eight to work for its independence. In 1958 he formed the UPA and went to Ghana to solicit the aid of its leader, Kwame Nkrumah. While in Ghana he made additional contacts among African leaders and became a fervent admirer of the Algerian revolution and the writings of Franz Fanon. In 1959 Roberto came to New York with the Guinean mission to the UN to work for international support of Angolan freedom. While in New York, he made important contacts among American academics and within the U.S. government. By late 1960, Roberto was convinced that Portugal would never accept peaceful decolonization of its African empire. He and the UPA decided that only an armed revolt would force Lisbon to yield. Nonetheless, Roberto was careful to emphasize that he was not a Marxist. His knowledge of America, his understanding of U.S. opinion, and, most important, his rejection of communism eventually earned him diplomatic and economic support from the United States. Roberto became "America's man" in Angola.

Roberto's major rival, the MPLA, was weaker and more radical. Neto and Andrade had both studied in Portugal and long been involved in anti-Salazar activities. Both were Marxists who saw revolution and socialism as the only sources of Angolan freedom. While Roberto and the UPA initially secured international support, ultimately the more radical MPLA gained the backing of most nations.

The liberation movement in Mozambique was more embryonic and divided than that in Angola. In 1959 Dr. Eduardo Mondlane tried to unite the various factions in the Frente de Libertação de Moçambique (FRELIMO). Mondlane had studied and taught in the United States and, like Roberto, impressed Americans with his anticommunism. Until his assassination in 1969, he kept FRELIMO "acceptable" to U.S. officials.

America first confronted Angolan nationalism two days after Kennedy took office. Capt. Henrique Galvao, a leader of anti-Salazar efforts in Portugal, hijacked the Portuguese luxury liner *Santa Maria* on 22 January 1960 in the hope of precipitating a coup against the dictator. Galvao was an opponent of Salazar but was not motivated by a desire to gain independence for the colonies. Africans, however, saw his brazen move as an indication that the time was ripe for direct action against Lisbon. On 4 February, the day after Galvao abandoned the *Santa Maria* off the coast of Brazil, several hundred Angolans stormed the main prison in Luanda, Angola's capital. Seven Portuguese police and about forty Africans were killed. Although this was not an organized rebellion, the incident did provoke Liberia, in response to the urgings of Roberto, to introduce a resolution in the UN Security Council calling on Portugal to end colonialism and demanding an international inquiry into the 4 February conflict.

Africanists in Washington saw the UN resolution as a chance to signal a realignment of U.S. policy. Even before this time, the new administration had made several gestures to show its new concern for Africa. Prior to his inauguration, Kennedy's Task Force on Africa recommended that the United States support future UN resolutions against Portuguese rule and that American officials speak out against continued white domination of southern Africa. Kennedy also had ended the previous practice of channeling foreign aid to Africa through Portugal. Bowles, in one of his first memos, wrote Rusk demanding that Washington stop its "appeasement" of Salazar. He argued that America should try to prevent a violent revolution against Portugal but, failing that, should "place ourselves in the most advantageous possible footing" by establishing contacts with the liberation movements.[10]

Officials in the Kennedy administration also broke immediately with Eisenhower's policy of avoiding public criticism of Portugal and the other white governments. In the most memorable incident, Williams in a speech in Nairobi declared, "Africa is for the Africans." The phrase produced sharp criticism from Europe and from Congress. Williams tried to explain to Rusk that he had been misquoted and had not implied that whites had no place on the continent, but the secretary cabled him to avoid additional public statements on his tour and to submit additional speeches to the department for prior approval.[11]

Kennedy was surprised by the vociferous attacks on Williams's talk. Even though he publicly supported his new adviser and even kidded about the incident, privately he was upset by the remark. He telephoned Bowles and ordered him to talk to Williams about the incident and to have the brash assistant secretary clear all future comments with either Bowles or Rusk.[12] Part of the reason for the overreaction to Williams's remarks was the timing. His speech occurred during the height of the debate in the UN on the Liberian resolution on Angola. There were rumors that the new administration was preparing to reverse traditional U.S. policy and support the statement. Many thought Williams's comments were a "trial balloon" testing reaction to a shift in policy. In reality, Washington was still unsure of its response in the UN at the time of the talk.

Of major concern to the administration were the U.S. bases in the Portuguese Azores. Any action at the UN would obviously be only symbolic, yet even the gesture of a favorable U.S. vote threatened American use of these air and naval facilities. American air bases on Techeira and Santa Maria islands in the Azores were designed to handle long-range flights and troop deployment. They represented an investment of approximately $100 million. George Kennan, the U.S. chargé in Portugal, had negotiated American use of the Azores during

10. "Report to the Honorable John F. Kennedy by the Task Force on Africa," 31 December 1960, James Thompson Papers, box 1, Kennedy Library; Bowles to Rusk, 9 February 1961, box 300, Chester Bowles Papers, Yale University.

11. Rusk to Williams, 25 February 1961, National Security Files: Africa, box 2, Kennedy Library (hereafter cited as *NSF:* followed by the subject).

12. Bowles to Kennedy, 3 March 1961, Bowles Papers, box 297, Yale University.

World War II, in spite of Lisbon's fears that once America occupied the islands it would never leave. After a confusing series of instructions, Kennan finally flew to Washington and gained Roosevelt's personal assurances that the United States would not remain in the Azores or demand their independence. Portugal believed that this agreement committed Washington to support of continued Portuguese colonialism in all its overseas possessions. The United States repeatedly denied that the wartime agreement was a pledge to maintain Lisbon's empire, but Portuguese officials were adamant that Kennan had assured them that Washington "would respect Portuguese sovereignty in all Portuguese colonies."[13] Thus, although Portugal had agreed the United States could use the facilities until the end of 1962, a vote against Lisbon in the UN might jeopardize renewal of the arrangement and the loss of a crucial military base.

Aside from its control of the Azores, Portugal was also a member of NATO. There had been some opposition to Portugal's inclusion in the alliance because of its neutrality during World War II and the undemocratic rule of Salazar, but it gained admittance on 4 April 1949. As a result, any action against Portugal threatened the near-sacred notion of Western unity and the fundamental Cold War axiom of avoiding public disputes with a NATO ally.

Although some in Washington raised the issues of the Azores and NATO in early 1961, the first bureaucratic victory belonged to the Africanists. On 4 March, Rusk instructed the U.S. ambassador in Lisbon, C. Burke Elbrick, to inform Salazar that America would vote in favor of the Liberian resolution on Angola. Rusk explained that the Kennedy administration was finding it "increasingly difficult and disadvantageous to Western interests . . . to support or remain silent on Portuguese African policies." America's "close association with Portugal" had caused African nations "to hold us responsible for Portuguese actions . . . which clash with America's traditional position in regards to colonialism and self-determination." He ordered Elbrick to take a tough line and tell Salazar that his policies "are so totally out of step with political and diplomatic advancements elsewhere in black Africa" that they would lead to a major revolt and possible communist gains. Elbrick was to urge Portugal to develop an immediate plan for "full self-determination within a realistic timetable." Rusk added that he was "fully aware of the distasteful nature of the above line to the Salazar regime." He instructed Elbrick to hint that the United States might be prepared "to help economically" in the transition of the African colonies to independence but would not tolerate continued Portuguese "inaction."[14]

Having informed Portugal in advance, the United States voted on 15 March

13. George Kennan, *Memoirs*, 146–63, and *FRUS: 1943*, 2:527–76.
14. Rusk to Elbrick, 4 March 1961, NSF: Portugal, box 154, Kennedy Library. When making direct quotations, I have inserted the articles (a, an, of, the, it, etc.) usually dropped from diplomatic cables.

1961 in favor of the Liberian resolution. France, Great Britain, and four other nations abstained, and the motion failed. The same day a major revolt began in northern Angola as hundreds of Africans attacked white farms, police stations, and army bases. What had begun as an isolated incident in February became a full-scale rebellion by late March.

The Kennedy administration had made its decision to support the UN resolution long before the revolt on 15 March. Public reaction to the vote, however, linked the UN statement with the later violence. Acheson and Robert Murphy, former under-secretary of state and a leader of the American Council on NATO, led the assault on the U.S. action at the UN. Acheson called the vote "a public and humiliating attack upon an ally's governmental conduct." It was, he explained, the product of "misguided idealism" and "the crumbling of America to the pressures of the new nations." The move threatened to disrupt NATO and risked the loss of the Azores, "the most important U.S. base in Europe."[15] Murphy claimed Kennedy was "kicking a friendly government in public" and wrote to Stevenson that such actions threatened to destroy NATO. *New York Times* columnist Arthur Krock raged against reversal of the "fundamental past policy" of NATO unity, while Republican leaders Everett Dirkson of Illinois and Charles Halleck of Indiana issued a statement calling the vote "hardly a proud moment for Uncle Sam."[16] Conservative James Burnham summed up much of the criticism in an article in *National Review*. He noted that Portugal had been "a faithful ally and a charter member of NATO." It had granted the United States the use of the Azores and supported the containment of communism. In return, it had been betrayed by those such as Stevenson, Williams, and Bowles who held "the illusion that the primitive jungles of Africa are more important than the advanced men, ideas, and machines of Europe."[17]

Not surprisingly, Portugal was outraged by the vote. With the government's encouragement, anti-American demonstrators stormed the U.S. embassy in Lisbon. Foreign Minister Franco Nogueira warned that Washington's new position encouraged violence and communism in Africa.[18]

Just as predictably, the decision won Kennedy support from liberals and Africans. Liberal journals interpreted the vote as evidence of a significant change in America's approach to African nationalism. The NAACP was overjoyed. Kennedy mentioned the vote in remarks to African diplomats at an African Freedom Day reception and promised to continue U.S. support of the drive "toward political freedom" on the continent. Rusk defended U.S. actions in an interview in *Business Week* by arguing that Washington must risk offending

15. Dean Acheson, "Fifty Years Later"; *New York Times*, 17 March 1961, p. 1. Acheson had been a great admirer of Salazar since they first met in 1952. In his memoirs he compared the Portuguese leader to Plato's philosopher-king. See *Present at the Creation*, 627–28.

16. Martin, *Adlai Stevenson*, 616–17; *New York Times*, 21 March 1961, p. 4; 22 March 1961, p. 11.

17. James Burnham, "Image in What Mirror?" *National Review* 11 (15 July 1961): 15.

18. *New York Times*, 21 March 1961, p. 1.

traditional allies if it wanted to be an effective power in a changing world.[19] Despite the criticisms from Acheson and others both in America and in Europe, the administration concluded that the vote had served its purpose, and a month later the United States supported another UN resolution calling on Portugal to accept a "Declaration of Independence" for Angola.

American diplomats were fully aware of the ineffectiveness of UN actions and also sought other means to influence events in Africa. As the war in Angola widened in the spring of 1961, Washington tried to assure its influence among the rebels by establishing stronger contacts with Roberto. In late March 1961, Roberto met secretly with State Department officials. They cautioned him against violence and warned of the lure of communism. Roberto responded that while he personally favored nonviolence, it had proved ineffective. He claimed he would lose control of the liberation movement to extremists if he abandoned the use of force. Roberto successfully played to U.S. anticommunism by repudiating Marxism and emphasizing the radicalism of his opponents. He welcomed America's "moral support" but claimed he needed direct economic and military aid to avoid losing power to Marxist rivals.[20]

The administration made no commitments to Roberto, but he had made a strong impression. The State Department continued talks with the Angolan leader through the American embassy in the Congo. When Lisbon complained that the United States was encouraging "Portugal's enemies," Washington ordered officials in Leopoldville not "to initiate" discussions with Roberto but to see him if he made the request.[21] By the fall of 1961, U.S. diplomats had become convinced of Roberto's worth and power and increasingly fearful of the radicalism of his rivals. Late in 1961 the CIA began supplying Roberto's UPA with nonmilitary materiel. It also placed Roberto on the CIA payroll, where he remained until 1969.[22]

Several of its European allies were uneasy about the seeming shift of America toward active support of black liberation in the Portuguese colonies. Great Britain and France had abstained on both UN resolutions on Angola, and the

19. Marcum, *The Angolan Revolution*, 1:182; *New Republic* 144 (27 March 1961): 6–8; *Africa Today* 8 (May 1961): 4–5; *Commonweal* 74 (23 June 1961): 317; *Crisis* 68 (April 1961): 226; Schlesinger, *A Thousand Days*, 226; Dean Rusk, "Coping with a World Plunged in Revolution," *Business Week* (25 March 1961): 104–109.

20. Martin, *Adlai Stevenson*, 617–18.

21. Elbrick to the Department of State, 1 May 1961, NSF: Portugal, box 154, Kennedy Library; Department of State to American Embassy, Leopoldville, 10 May 1961, NSF: Africa, box 2, Kennedy Library.

22. U.S. Congress, Senate, Subcommittee on African Affairs, *Angola*, 174; *New York Times*, 25 September 1975, p. 1. The U.S. stopped direct aid to Roberto's organization in 1969, but he continued to receive $10,000 a year "look-in money." When it became clear that Marxist forces were close to victory in Angola in 1975, America resumed large-scale aid to Roberto. See *New York Times*, 19 February 1977, p. 9, and Stephen Weissman, "The CIA and U.S. Policy in Zaire and Angola," 381–432.

British even increased arms sales to Lisbon to help quell the rebellion. Both cautioned Kennedy against too strong a stance against a NATO ally. French leader Charles de Gaulle warned that U.S. assistance to an armed rebellion in Angola would only encourage violence and radicalism throughout Africa.[23] Despite the disapproval of its allies, the administration continued to press Portugal. The State Department defied Lisbon by organizing a scholarship fund for Angolan students who had fled Portugal and by setting up a program for Portuguese-speaking Africans at Lincoln University in Pennsylvania. Washington also cut military aid to Lisbon from a promised $25 million for 1961 to less than $3 million and eventually banned private arms sales to Portugal.[24]

Portuguese officials continued to denounce America's "betrayal." They claimed they had abandoned planned reforms in Angola because of "foreign pressures" and inflammatory statements by "high United States' officials." The real indication of Lisbon's rage was the reaction of Salazar. Initially he remained silent on U.S. actions and refused to even acknowledge Rusk's suggestion that Portugal prepare for the eventual independence of its empire. Then, in April, he fired his minister of defense, Botelho Moníz, for "plotting with the United States." Moníz had been meeting unofficially with Elbrick to discuss possible American assistance in the transition of Angola to independence. Salazar announced he would personally take control of the Defense Ministry.[25]

The Portuguese press, under heavy censorship, berated the United States daily. After white mobs in Alabama attacked the integrated buses of the freedom riders, Lisbon's newspapers ran front-page photos of Southern whites beating blacks next to pictures of black Angolans saluting the Portuguese flag. When Rusk attended a NATO meeting in Oslo, the Portuguese delegate delivered a diatribe against Washington's "interference in Portugal's internal affairs."[26]

The administration expected such criticism but was disappointed that not all African leaders seemed appreciative of U.S. actions. Nkrumah dismissed the American votes in the UN as "propaganda." He argued that Portugal was using NATO weapons supplied by the United States to kill African nationalists. If Washington was sincere in its commitment to black freedom, he contended, it would expel Lisbon from NATO, and "Portugal's colonial rule would collapse the day after." Similar comments from other Africans caused deep resentment within the State Department. U.S. officials felt they had made a significant effort

23. *New York Times*, 16 April 1961, p. 19; Rostow to Bundy, "De Gaulle, Africa, and Southeast Asia," 13 May 1961, NSF: Africa, box 2, Kennedy Library.

24. Marcum, *The Angolan Revolution*, 1:184; *New York Times*, 18 April 1961, p. 6.

25. Elbrick to Rusk, 28 and 29 March, 13 and 14 April 1961, NSF: Portugal, box 154, Kennedy Library; *New York Times*, 6 April 1961, p. 4.

26. *New York Times*, 28 May 1961, p. 38; Rusk to American Embassy Paris, 23 May 1961, NSF: Angola, box 5, Kennedy Library.

to accommodate black nationalism and that African complaints were "unreasonable and unwarranted."[27]

In the face of continued Portuguese obstinacy and growing African pressures for stronger action, the Department of State Policy and Planning Council circulated a pessimistic "Status Report on Portuguese Africa" in May 1961. It concluded that America's "diplomatic offensive" had failed to alter Portugal and had not produced as favorable a reaction in Africa as expected, and it noted that Great Britain and France were "not very optimistic about the prospects of persuading Portugal to change its policies." The report concluded, "At this juncture it is doubtful any useful purpose would be served by the United States applying further pressure against Portugal."[28]

One of the reasons for such a discouraging assessment was the shift in U.S. public opinion in response to a massive propaganda campaign by Portugal. Following America's vote against Portugal in the UN in March, the Portuguese hired the New York public-relations firm of Selvage & Lee at an annual fee of $100,000 plus expenses to coordinate a campaign to sway American opinion and influence congressional leaders.[29] The firm concentrated on journalists, politicians, and other selected "opinion-makers." It emphasized the communist issue and Portugal's strategic importance to America. It also tried to use Southern opposition to the domestic civil-rights movement to Portugal's benefit. The major effort was to portray the Angolan revolt as directed from Moscow and its leaders as communists. Selvage & Lee provided material to newspapers, magazines, and congressional leaders "documenting" the Portuguese charge that the revolt was "an invasion from the Congo" in response to "orders from Moscow." The agency included forged letters provided by Portugal quoting Roberto on the glories of communism and false "secret Russian documents" in "educational kits" sent to American newsmen.

Partly as a result of this effort, numerous articles and books appeared in the spring and summer of 1961 condemning the revolt as a communist plot and attacking America for "serving the cause of communism." Most were based on materials provided by Selvage & Lee, but some, such as the pamphlets *The Communists and Angola* and *On the Morning of March 15*, were written directly

27. Bahram Farzanegan, "United States' Response and Reaction to the Emergence of Arab and African States in International Politics," 241–42.

28. Department of State Policy and Planning Council to Bundy, "Status Report on Portuguese Africa," 25 May 1961, NSF: Portugal, box 154, Kennedy Library.

29. The first detailed account of the activities of Selvage & Lee was Daniel M. Friedenberg, "The Public Relations of Colonialism: Salazar's Mouthpiece in the U.S.," *Africa Today* 9 (April 1962): 4–6, 15–16. In the spring of 1963 the Senate Foreign Relations Committee investigated the firm's activities and published many of the details of the campaign. See U.S. Congress, Senate, Committee on Foreign Relations, *Activities of Non-Diplomatic Representatives of Foreign Powers in the U.S.* See also Russell Warren Howe and Sarah Hays Trott, *The Power Peddlers*, 170–224. Unless otherwise noted, material in this section is from the Senate hearings.

by the firm. Many included vivid photos of alleged atrocities committed by blacks against innocent whites.

The agency also wooed newspaper columnists and editors and was particularly effective in approaching black journalists. With special funds from Portugal and using the Moss H. Kendrix Organization, a black public-relations firm, as a cover, Selvage & Lee paid for visits to Angola by writers, editors, and publishers of a number of black publications, including *Jet*, *Ebony*, and the *Pittsburgh Courier*. While in Africa, the journalists heard lectures on the success of Portugal's assimilation policies and the lack of racial discrimination. Selvage & Lee also paid for special supplements in black newspapers and even provided employment for the relatives of some black editors in its New York office. James Selvage, president of the firm, also claimed to have influenced such white columnists as Walter Trojan of the *Chicago Tribune* and George Peck of the *New York Times* to write in favor of Portugal and in opposition to U.S. policy.

To lobby political leaders, the company formed the Portuguese-American Committee on Foreign Affairs, nominally headed by Martin Comacho, a Massachusetts lawyer with a Ph.D. from Harvard in political science. Comacho received a retainer of $400 a month and expenses to coordinate letter-writing campaigns to key congressmen and to speak before various organizations. His major success was persuading Speaker of the House John McCormick and prominent House leader Thomas "Tip" O'Neill of Massachusetts to make speeches in Congress praising Portugal. Selvage & Lee compiled McCormick's and O'Neill's remarks into a pamphlet called *Friendly Relations between America and Portugal* for mass distribution. Comacho also offered the political support of the Portuguese-American Committee on Foreign Affairs to politicians who spoke out against U.S. policy, such as Sen. Thomas Dodd of Connecticut.

Through its American agents, Portugal also approached conservative groups, especially those opposed to black protest in the South. Comacho provided free copies of Selvage & Lee's publications and films to organizations including the Young Americans for Freedom, the Young Republicans, the American Friends of Katanga, the National States Rights party, and the John Birch Society. He attended meetings of fundamentalist groups such as Billy James Hargis's Christian Crusade to speak on Portugal's "Christian mission" in Africa and the communist threat to missionary activity. Comacho was convinced that Southern hatred of the civil-rights movement could be used effectively to create opposition to U.S. policy in Africa. He wrote to Kenneth Downs, vice-president of Selvage & Lee, "The entire South could be persuaded to side with Portugal." By mobilizing the South, conservatives, and Congress, Comacho argued, the firm could shift U.S. opinion away from the ideas "of such men as Chester Bowles, Williams, and Adlai Stevenson."

The campaign also tried to counteract adverse television coverage of the Angolan revolt. Selvage & Lee vehemently protested a planned NBC "White Paper" on Angola. The agency called the rebellion "a communist plot" and charged that the program "would only help create a new trouble spot for the United States' government while the Kremlin rejoices." The firm enclosed a fake letter from Roberto describing a master plan for the communist takeover of Africa and concluding, "LONG LIVE COMMUNISM!"[30]

Executives at the firm as well as officials at the State Department were convinced of the success of these efforts. On 31 May 1961, Selvage wrote to Portuguese officials that he had been able to present "Portugal's side of the Angolan story to the American people." He enumerated the firm's successes and announced that *Reader's Digest* would soon publish an article by retired Brig. Gen. Frank Howley called "Reversion to Savagery" and ghostwritten by the agency. Others in the firm were feeding articles to Southern newspapers. He suggested Portugal appropriate additional funds for trips to Angola by "big names" such as Acheson. The State Department, meanwhile, closely monitored the efforts of Selvage & Lee, and many were disturbed by its results. Department public-opinion analysts concluded that while "the line they took was pure Salazar," the agency had been extremely successful both with the general public and with Congress.[31]

Portugal aided its propaganda efforts by announcing a much-publicized plan for major reforms in Angola under a new minister of overseas provinces. The reforms soon proved to be cosmetic, but Lisbon and its U.S. representatives repeatedly pointed to efforts to improve conditions in the colonies as signs of Portugal's good intentions.[32]

By the summer of 1961, when the activities of Selvage & Lee were most intense, U.S. policy toward Angola was in a state of flux. The spring "diplomatic offensive" had failed. Portugal showed no interest in receiving American aid in exchange for a timetable for independence. Administration efforts in the UN had alienated Lisbon with little corresponding growth of influence among the Africans. As Kennedy prepared to leave for consultation with his European allies prior to his summit meeting with Khrushchev in Vienna, Salazar finally reacted publicly to American actions. On 30 May he granted an exclusive interview to

30. The firm also tried to discredit organizations critical of Portugal, especially the American Committee on Africa. When Comacho demanded Congress investigate the ACOA as a "subversive group," one member of the Committee sued for slander, and Selvage & Lee settled out of court by paying $7827.96 in damages. See Marcum, *The Angolan Revolution*, 1:132.

31. Department of State to Bundy, "Updating of Portuguese-U.S. Relations," 24 August 1961, NSF: Portugal, box 154, Kennedy Library. See also same to same, "Selvage & Lee," 25 September 1961, ibid., and the summary of the campaign enclosed in Fredericks to Bowles, 14 July 1962, Bowles Papers, box 299, Yale University.

32. McKay, *Africa in World Politics*, 4. For an attack on the "reforms," see the devastating evaluation by American missionary E. Edwin LeMaster, "I Saw the Horror in Angola," *Saturday Evening Post* (12 May 1962): 50.

Benjamin Welles of the *New York Times*. Even though Portugal's foreign minister told Elbrick that the interview was "extremely important" and "an official expression of Portuguese Government policy,"[33] Salazar was remarkably restrained. He told Welles he was "confused" by Williams's "Africa for the Africans" statement and "perplexed" by America's UN votes. He affirmed his nation's dedication to remaining in Africa and reminded the United States of the need for Western unity in the face of Russian threats on Berlin.[34]

The rather moderate tone of the Portuguese leader was in part attributable to yet another UN vote scheduled for early June. The Portuguese clearly hoped America would oppose the measure, which called on Portugal "to account" for its actions in Angola and was considered by many diplomats to be a prelude to calls for economic sanctions. Two days after the Salazar interview, Foreign Minister Nogueira wrote Rusk of plans to expand the rights of Africans in Angola and of the dangers additional UN pressure posed to such reforms. Rusk replied that he was "encouraged" by Portugal's actions. He promised that the United States would work "to delete or alter the most objectionable features" of the pending resolution, but would support it if it did not demand sanctions. Rusk concluded that he realized that America's position "is not one which you will like."[35]

Shortly before Rusk told Lisbon of America's decision to continue its support of decolonization, Kennedy raised the question of Angola in his meetings with de Gaulle and Khrushchev. De Gaulle agreed that Portugal was "inflexible" on the issue but again warned the president that pushing Salazar too hard might lead "to a revolution in Portugal" and perhaps even to a communist regime in Lisbon. De Gaulle did agree to try to use his influence with the Portuguese dictator to soften his position but rejected Kennedy's suggestion that France join the United States in supporting the pending UN resolution.[36] During his stormy confrontation with Khrushchev in Vienna two days later, Kennedy again discussed the revolt in Angola. In response to the Russian leader's attack on American opposition to decolonization, the president replied that he had supported freedom for Angola even at the risk of angering his NATO allies. Kennedy, in turn, questioned Khrushchev about his "wars of national liberation" speech and asked if this included Angola. Khrushchev denied Soviet involvement in the revolt but declared that all wars of liberation were "sacred" and the U.S. should refrain from intervention.[37]

A week after the exchange in Vienna, America cast its promised vote against

33. Elbrick to Rusk, 2 June 1961, NSF: Portugal, box 154, Kennedy Library.

34. *New York Times*, 31 May 1961, p. 1.

35. Nogueira to Rusk, 2 June 1961; Rusk to Nogueira, 7 June 1961, NSF: Angola, box 5, Kennedy Library.

36. Schlesinger, *A Thousand Days*, 352–53.

37. Department of State Memorandum for Mr. Walter Rostow, "Talking Points on the Vienna Conversations," undated, Bowles Papers, box 300, Yale University.

Portugal. Like the votes in March and April, the action provoked wide criticism. Columnist Thomas Hamilton charged that Kennedy had abandoned an important ally "to court the Asian-African group," and Arthur Krock described U.S. foreign policy as "a popularity contest" designed to win the favor of "anti-colonial extremists." Salazar returned to his more typical aggressiveness. In a nationwide speech, he claimed that the vote "had served communist subversion in Africa"; the world had "gone topsy-turvy" with America's rejection of its European ally. Portugal's new ambassador, Pedro Pereira, followed by disrupting the normally routine procedure of presenting his credentials to Kennedy with a speech deploring foreign interference in Portuguese affairs and the encouragement of communist "extermination" of the Angolan people. Kennedy responded by blandly noting, "There are diverse ways of interpreting what is taking place in Africa."[38]

Africanists in the administration were increasingly concerned by Portugal's refusal to compromise, the growth of public opposition to U.S. policies, and the expanding guerrilla war in Angola. Led by Williams, Bowles, and Stevenson, they made a push for a stronger effort to force Salazar to agree to self-determination even at the risk of losing the Azores bases and NATO unity.

In June, Williams organized the Task Force on the Portuguese Territories in Africa, which soon produced an eighty-three-page report on the background of the revolt, the American response, and suggestions for future policy. The document stressed the need for immediate U.S. initiatives before public opinion and the mounting violence in Angola destroyed American leverage. The report stated that America's objective in Angola should be "a realistically phased program of reform . . . leading to specific political options including independence, within a specified time period." To obtain this goal, America should work with France and Great Britain to establish "a timetable" for Angolan freedom and use sources in the Vatican and Brazil to help convince Salazar to accept it. This should be accompanied by "a most serious demarche to the Portuguese" threatening an end to all U.S. arms sales. In addition, Washington should begin "a massive propaganda campaign" to pressure Lisbon. The report recommended that the State Department prepare a "white paper" for distribution to African nations showing "our continuing efforts to induce Portugal to liberalize her colonial policies" and that the Defense Department prepare contingency plans for the possible loss of the Azores facility and American bases in Spain and even the withdrawal of Portugal from NATO. The group concluded that "the situation in Angola is explosive and deteriorating steadily," and the violence might soon spread to Mozambique. There was even the possibility that South Africa and Rhodesia would intervene to aid Portugal. Washington was "faced with a true dilemma in which our policy posture toward

38. *New York Times*, 11 June 1961, p. 11; 13 June 1961, p. 34; 1 July 1961, p. 1; "Remarks by Ambassador Pedro Pereira and the President," July 1961, President's Office Files, box 123b, Kennedy Library.

newly emerging nations will bring a conflict with our policy posture toward our NATO allies." The task force made it clear that it was willing to accept such a confrontation when it recommended "a massive effort of persuasion and coercion" designed to force Lisbon to yield.[39]

Such recommendations were exactly the bold initiatives that many liberals had expected. Stevenson wrote from New York in support of the plan. He warned that if America wanted influence in the third world, it would have to move away from its preoccupation with NATO and military power. Bowles was even more enthusiastic. In a personal letter to the president, he concluded, "It is fantastic that the weakest and most backward nation in Europe should continue to stress its 'rights' to govern 10 million Africans. . . . Even more fantastic are its demands for American support in this impossible enterprise." Bowles predicted that Salazar would threaten to expel America from the Azores and would complain of the betrayal of a NATO ally, but Kennedy must accept such risks if he wanted to show the Africans and Asians that they were as important to the U.S. as Europe.[40]

Adverse reaction to the recommendations of the task force was equally swift. The Defense Department was appalled that anyone would seriously consider the loss of the Azores, particularly with the growing crisis over Berlin. Sam Belk, executive secretary of the National Security Council, reported to McGeorge Bundy, Kennedy's special assistant for national security affairs, that the U.S. military considered retention of the Azores "vital" and that "any action which would jeopardize retention of the Azores or bases in Spain would be unacceptable." Kenneth Hansen, assistant director of the Bureau of the Budget, circulated the task force's report among officials at the Departments of Treasury, Defense, and State. He wrote a long sarcastic commentary to Bundy opposing the document and suggesting that "we get down to brass tacks with Governor Williams" and make it clear that the report was unacceptable and the entire task force was "badly run."[41]

Williams tried to justify the need for a "tough" stance. He described Angola as "a test case of America's commitment to freedom." "Like Berlin," it was "the center of the great battle between freedom and oppression." On 6 July, he met with Henry Fowler of the Treasury Department, Paul Nitze of Defense, and Bundy to convince them of the need for increased pressure on Portugal. Williams observed that "Fowler saw things our way" and Bundy "is in essential agreement," but Nitze "is generally in opposition to doing anything."[42]

39. "Report of the Task Force on the Portuguese Territories in Africa," undated, NSF: Angola, box 5, Kennedy Library.

40. Stevenson to Rostow, "U.S. Foreign Policy as Seen from New York," 26 June 1961, ibid.; Bowles to Kennedy, "Some Requirements of American Foreign Policy," 1 July 1961, Bowles Papers, box 297, Yale University.

41. Belk to Bundy, 29 June 1961; Hansen to Bundy, 28 June 1961, NSF: Angola, box 5, Kennedy Library.

42. Williams to Fredericks, 6 July 1961, G. Mennen Williams Papers, box 1, National Archives.

On 14 July, Kennedy met with the National Security Council to discuss the Angolan situation and Williams's recommendations. Walt Rostow, Bundy's deputy, argued that the recent votes in the UN had "taken the pressure off" the United States to stand up to Lisbon. Because of the crisis in Berlin, it was not a good time to disturb NATO or jeopardize America's military capabilities. The group agreed with Rostow's argument. It decided to renew the U.S. offer of economic aid to Portugal in exchange for acceptance of the idea of self-determination, but also to increase covert support to Roberto. Kennedy and his advisers rejected any additional steps such as demands for a firm "timetable" for independence or a complete end of military aid to Lisbon.[43]

The next day, the State Department launched its second "diplomatic offensive." Elbrick met with Salazar and explained that a commitment to self-determination did not necessarily require immediate independence for the colonies. The Portuguese leader was unconvinced. He charged that U.S. policy had "only served to encourage terrorists" and refused to accept the notion of self-determination. Two weeks later, Rusk ordered Elbrick to approach other Portuguese officials with the U.S. plan for massive economic aid to offset any hardship resulting from the independence of Angola and Mozambique. Following Salazar's lead, they totally rejected the idea. Rusk finally contacted the Vatican to ask if the Papal Nuncio in Lisbon would talk with Salazar about the American plan.[44]

Washington's efforts were designed only to get Portugal to agree to the idea of self-determination. Elbrick and Rusk repeatedly tried to make the point that self-determination would not require total Portuguese withdrawal from Africa but was only a way of assessing the sentiments of the Africans. Salazar countered with his oft-proclaimed idea that the people of Angola and Mozambique were Portuguese citizens and had already determined to remain a part of Portugal. According to Salazar, only a handful of "communist terrorists" were unhappy with Lisbon's rule. Faced with Salazar's rigid definition of the status of the "overseas provinces," Washington's attempts to get him to accept self-determination failed completely.

Portugal's refusal to yield on Africa led Williams and others to again demand more decisive U.S. action. After his second trip to Africa, in August 1961, Williams reported that the war in Angola would continue indefinitely and the rebels would inevitably become more violent and more radical. America was running out of time to assure the transition of Angola to an independent, noncommunist nation. He ordered the U.S. chargé in Mozambique, William Taft, to tour Angola and make a report on the war and prospects for settlement.

43. Rostow to Kennedy, 14 July 1961; National Security Council "Action Memorandum," 14 July 1961, NSF: Angola, box 5, Kennedy Library.
44. Elbrick to Rusk, 15 July 1961; Rusk to Elbrick, 28 July 1961; Elbrick to Rusk, 5 August 1961; Rusk to Elbrick, 11 August 1961, ibid.

Taft echoed Williams's pessimism. He argued that while African nationalism was unstoppable, the Portuguese leader was intractable. "It is the case of irresistible force meeting immovable body," he concluded.[45]

America was in the uncomfortable position of being caught in the middle. It had incurred the wrath of Portugal for trying to work for self-determination and was under attack from Africans for being allied with an oppressor. African nations were particularly incensed when Angolans charged that U.S. weapons provided to Portugal through NATO were being used in Angola. Since the first uprising in March there had been rumors that Portugal was using American military equipment in Africa, in violation of an agreement that U.S. military aid to Portugal be used only in Europe. In July, Rusk formally protested Portugal's actions, and, in August, Elbrick again raised the issue with Nogueira. The foreign minister vowed that his nation would defy the agreement "as long as there is any fighting in Angola." He asked why Washington was not equally concerned about U.S. weapons being used by the rebels. It was, he concluded, "extraordinary" that America would threaten Portugal "when the crisis over Berlin demands even greater unity than before." Elbrick reported that the weapons problem was "the latest nail in the coffin of U.S.-Portuguese relations."[46]

When East European officials publicly accused America of supplying Portugal in its war in Angola, Kennedy ordered Rusk and Secretary of Defense Robert McNamara to make a full study of U.S. equipment being used in Africa but to avoid direct protests to Lisbon. McNamara reported that Washington had provided Portugal with nearly $300 million in military aid since 1949, but it was impossible to know how much of this was being used in Angola. He noted that the Defense Department previously had cabled Lisbon to tell officials that they were breaking the NATO agreement and had informed Portuguese military leaders of cuts in future aid. McNamara cautioned Kennedy "that any further public pressure on the Portuguese regarding the use of U.S. military materiel in Angola should be avoided" as it might jeopardize the use of the Azores. Accordingly, American representatives at the UN repeatedly denied that any U.S. weapons were being used in Africa.[47]

The tension between the United States and the Soviet Union over Berlin, culminating in the construction of the Berlin Wall on 13 August, had a direct effect on American policy toward the Angolan rebellion. The crisis in Europe increased the significance of the Azores as a base for U.S. aircraft and as a staging area for troop deployment in any military conflict. It also reaffirmed the

45. Williams, "Report on Second Trip to Africa," 9 September 1961, NSF: Africa, box 2; William Taft to Rusk (for Williams), 16 August 1961, NSF: Angola, box 5, Kennedy Library.
46. Rusk to American Embassy Lisbon, 28 July 1961, NSF: Angola, box 5; Elbrick to Rusk, 16 August 1961, NSF: Portugal, box 154, Kennedy Library.
47. McNamara to Kennedy, 25 August 1961, NSF: Angola, box 5, Kennedy Library; see also Williams to Rusk, 14 September 1961, Williams Papers, box 1, National Archives.

importance of NATO as a barrier against Soviet aggression. Finally, Berlin riveted public and administration attention on Europe and buttressed the arguments of those who advocated a "Europe first" policy.

Africanists were also hurt by the diminished power and eventual ouster of Bowles from his post as under-secretary of state. In July 1961, Kennedy became convinced that the State Department was ineffective and Bowles was one of the major reasons. The president owed considerable political debts to Bowles but determined that Bowles lacked the organizational and management skills to run the department effectively. In mid-July, Kennedy decided to ease Bowles out. Many in the administration sympathetic to Bowles were convinced he was not being removed for his style or lack of ability but for championing increased U.S. attention to the third world. Bowles encouraged this interpretation. He wrote Stevenson that he was being forced out by "the Achesons" in the State Department and White House who opposed his demands for an American commitment to African freedom. He warned Stevenson that he and Williams would be the next to go.[48]

The rumors of Bowles's removal led to efforts by liberals to save him. Williams and Stevenson wrote to Kennedy on Bowles's behalf. Harris Wofford, a close associate of Bowles and special assistant to the president for civil rights, argued in a note to Kennedy that it was the "old school, Europe-first policy-makers" who were after the under-secretary. Wofford reported one official in the State Department chanting, "One down and Williams to go," while another observed, "The trouble with Bowles and Williams was that when they saw a band of black baboons beating tom-toms they saw George Washingtons." It was Bowles and Williams, Wofford argued, who were responsible for "our new policy on Angola," and their removal would severely damage America's image in Africa.[49] The liberal campaign to "save Bowles" won him only a short reprieve, however. He retained his position as under-secretary until November, when Kennedy made him a special adviser for African, Asian, and Latin American affairs with few clear duties and little power. Although he continued to circulate memos and reports pushing for stronger policies in Africa, Bowles's influence was diminished. George Ball, a fervent admirer of Acheson and a self-proclaimed "Europeanist," replaced Bowles as under-secretary.

Ball's appointment illustrated the dominance of Berlin and Europe in American diplomacy in late 1961. Policymakers reacted to African issues largely as they affected the European situation. Bundy and the National Security Council were increasingly upset with Stevenson's private and public statements criticizing Portugal, and Bundy informed Deputy Under-Secretary of State Alexis Johnson that such comments were inappropriate given the growing

48. Bowles to Stevenson, 23 July 1961, Bowles Papers, box 301, Yale University.
49. Wofford to Kennedy, 15 July 1961, ibid. For other efforts to save Bowles see Schlesinger, *A Thousand Days*, 437–42, and *New York Times*, 17 July 1961, p. 1.

tension in Europe. Stevenson "must be kept fully informed as to the military importance of the Azores" and explain their significance to the Africans. Similarly, Rostow met with the Portuguese ambassador to try to reach an accommodation on African issues that would preserve NATO unity. He had little success and predicted to Kennedy that relations with Lisbon were "going to be very difficult in the forthcoming period" because Portugal, through the efforts of Selvage & Lee, was "pulling out all stops" to reverse U.S. opposition to its policies in Africa.[50]

The Portuguese tried to take advantage of the chill in U.S.-Soviet relations by again emphasizing the communist influence in the liberation movement. Ambassador Pereira, in an article for the *U.S. News and World Report* on "Wars of National Liberation in Africa," claimed Angola was the first example of the Kremlin's new strategy as outlined in Khrushchev's January 1961 speech.[51]

Williams responded to Washington's new emphasis on Europe by "going public" in a series of speeches in the fall of 1961. He called for a continued U.S. commitment to African freedom and tried to show the importance of the continent in the Cold War. In an address in Boston, he argued that America "must manifest our commitment to freedom and independence" in all of Africa. He complained that U.S. policy was too often "slow in action . . . and cautious in moving." It must "measure up in action to the dynamism of the times." In a talk to the Overseas Press Club he was more specific. He admitted that the Portuguese saw the Kennedy administration as "hostile to their interests" but warned that Washington could not revoke its support of self-determination to appease Europe. On 2 November, Williams called for an American pledge to help achieve the complete independence of all Africa by 1970. He even protested that Kennedy's proposed address to the UN was overly concerned with Berlin and "white man's freedom" and ignored Angola and other African issues. He suggested the president rewrite the speech to endorse "self-determination everywhere," not just in Europe.[52]

Just as his earlier "Africa for the Africans" remark had provoked criticism, Williams's efforts in the fall of 1961 caused consternation among many U.S. diplomats. Elbrick, in particular, was upset. He returned to Washington in November to meet with Kennedy and blasted Williams's speeches, America's UN policy, and the steady deterioration of U.S.-Portuguese relations. Kennedy agreed that America had been pushing Salazar hard on Angola and suggested, "It

50. Bundy to Johnson, "Additional Guidance Relating to the Portuguese Territories," 28 July 1961, NSF: Africa, box 2; Rostow to Kennedy, 14 September 1961, NSF: Portugal, box 154, Kennedy Library.

51. Pedro Theotonio Pereira, "Wars of Liberation in Africa: What do They Mean?" *U.S. News and World Report* 51 (30 October 1961): 74–76.

52. *SDB* 45 (20 November 1961): 864–65; *SDB* 45 (27 November 1961): 885–88; *New York Times*, 3 November 1961, p. 11; Williams to Harlan Cleveland, 14 September 1961, Williams Papers, box 1, National Archives.

might be wise for the U.S. to abstain on some of the votes affecting Portugal in the UN." Even Stevenson expressed some doubts about how much had been gained by opposing Portugal. He was angered by the Africans' lack of appreciation for American efforts and felt the UN was becoming obsessed with Angola and other colonial issues. He complained to John Steele of *Time* magazine that he was impatiently waiting for the time "when the last black-faced comedian has quit preaching about colonialism so the UN could move on to the more crucial issues like disarmament."[53]

The debate within the government over the future of its Angolan policy continued into the end of 1961. Africanists solicited liberal John Kenneth Galbraith, U.S. ambassador to India, to use his influence. Never one to avoid a skirmish, Galbraith wrote Rusk that America was "too apologetic" to Portugal. In reference to the Azores, he denounced those who would trade Africa "for a few acres of asphalt in the Atlantic." Bowles also attacked the U.S. fascination with the base. He wrote Rostow that Washington "must push the Portuguese more vigorously" even if they threatened to expel U.S. forces from the Azores. "Would it not even be preferable as a last resort to plan to hold the Azores by force if they are as vital to our security as our military insist?" he asked.[54]

Few others suggested the possibility of using force to retain the Azores, but many in the administration were convinced that the United States had made a pledge to support African independence and could not retreat without alienating the entire third world. In his "Year End Report" to Rusk, Williams lavishly praised the "new posture and new spirit" of America's African policy but warned that the good will gained on the continent would be destroyed if Washington relaxed its pressure on Salazar.[55]

Although Williams, Bowles, Galbraith, and other liberals were clearly willing to challenge Portugal even at the risk of losing the Azores, events in late 1961 and early 1962 made others in the administration more reluctant to maintain a "tough" stance. In December 1961, India invaded and conquered Portuguese Goa, infuriating even the most ardent U.S. critics of Portugal. India had been one of the leaders of the international campaign against Portugal and South Africa. Its use of force to seize Goa made it seem hypocritical and lent support to administration critics of American efforts to court the Afro-Asian bloc. Stevenson was especially outraged by India's action, as he had been fending off Europeanist attacks of his "appeasement" of the third world at the UN.[56]

Of even greater impact on U.S. policy was the growing split within the

53. "Memorandum of Conversation between the President and C. Burke Elbrick," 27 November 1961, NSF: Portugal, box 154, Kennedy Library; Martin, *Adlai Stevenson*, 711.
54. Galbraith to Rusk, 18 December 1961, NSF: Portugal, box 154, Kennedy Library; Bowles to Rostow, 21 December 1961, Bowles Papers, box 300, Yale University.
55. Williams to Rusk, "Year-End Report," 6 January 1962, Williams Papers, box 2, National Archives.
56. Schlesinger, *A Thousand Days*, 527–31; Martin, *Adlai Stevenson*, 687.

liberation movement in Angola. Africans were well aware of U.S. support of Roberto and the UPA. His opponents accused Roberto of being an American "puppet" and dismissed his organization as a "NATO front." MPLA leaders denounced U.S. votes at the UN as "shams" and charged Washington with providing weapons to murder Angolans.[57] For their part, Americans feared the MPLA was increasingly under the control of communists and would pose an ever-stronger challenge to Roberto. The civil war in the Congo was a continuing reminder to the administration of the instability of many new African nations and the possibility that freedom for Angola might lead to a battle for leadership that could involve the major powers. Unless Angolans united, the nation had the potential to become "another Congo," and, as Rusk warned Williams in early 1962, "One or two more Congos—and we've had it!"[58]

To try to insure Roberto's success in his struggle with his more radical rivals, the United States increased its covert assistance to the UPA in early 1962. The Congo and its new leader, Cyril Adoula, became the conduit for American aid. Adoula was a veteran of the labor movement in the Congo and had served as vice-president under Lumumba. He had rejected Lumumba's radicalism and, with U.S. encouragement, had become prime minister of the Congo in August 1961. In close cooperation with American officials, Adoula provided vital political and economic support for Roberto in his battle with the MPLA.[59]

Washington also established contacts with Mondlane to try to retain influence in the emerging liberation struggle in Mozambique. When Mondlane visited the United States in early 1962 seeking support, Williams's deputy, Wayne Fredericks, suggested to Attorney General Robert Kennedy that he meet with the African leader. Fredericks told Kennedy it was inevitable that Portugal would be forced out of Mozambique as well as Angola, and the administration should work with nationalist leaders to prevent them from turning to the communists for aid. The attorney general met with Mondlane and was greatly impressed with his leadership and anticommunism. He arranged for CIA funds to cover the cost of Mondlane's trip to the United States and urged increased covert assistance to Roberto as well.[60]

Portuguese intelligence sources quickly learned of the expanded U.S. aid to Roberto and Mondlane. Elbrick reported Portugal was "outraged" and seemed "to have a fixation about U.S. support for Roberto." He warned that assistance to

57. Marcum, *The Angolan Revolution*, 1:200–220.
58. Rusk to Williams, 8 January 1962, Williams Papers, box 29, National Archives. See also Belk to Ralph Dungan, Special Assistant to the President, "Portuguese Africa," 9 January 1962, NSF: Africa, box 2, Kennedy Library.
59. "Cyrille Adoula," undated biographical summary, NSF: Congo, box 4, Kennedy Library. On Adoula's support of Roberto, see Marcum, *The Angolan Revolution*, 1:258–61, and Weissman, "The CIA and U.S. Policy in Zaire and Angola," 399–400.
60. Arthur M. Schlesinger, Jr., *Robert Kennedy*, 562.

Roberto had led to "extreme bitterness, suspicion, and a general lack of confidence over U.S. intentions in Africa." The Portuguese ambassador in Washington also condemned American aid to "murderers, arsonists, and torturers" in Angola and the mistaken impression in the United States that Roberto "was a distinguished political leader."[61]

The decision to use the CIA to assist Roberto and the UPA was an example of Kennedy's new definition of the agency's role. Following the dismal planning and disastrous predictions that led to the Bay of Pigs invasion in 1961, Kennedy ordered a study and reorientation of the CIA. He gave Gen. Maxwell Taylor control over covert activities. Taylor was convinced that the agency should concentrate its clandestine efforts in critical third-world countries to prevent wars of national liberation from becoming vehicles for communism. Both he and the president were still worried about Khrushchev's earlier speech on the new direction of the Cold War.[62]

Some within the government felt America must go beyond merely increasing payments to Roberto. They argued that Salazar's rejection of America's approaches and the growing challenge to Roberto from the left demanded the direct use of U.S. power to force a rapid settlement. In late 1961, Richard Bissell, head of CIA Clandestine Services, assigned Paul Sakwa to study insurgency and subversion in the emerging nations. Sakwa had just completed two years as chief of the Vietnam covert action section of the CIA. He was convinced that "Vietnam was going to hell" and that only decisive U.S. action would avoid a similar setback in Angola. On 17 January 1962 he wrote a long "think-piece" advocating an ambitious program of U.S. covert actions designed to force Portugal to grant independence to Angola and Mozambique and to insure anticommunist regimes in the new nations.[63] Sakwa's memo, "U.S. Policy towards Portugal," demonstrated America's diplomatic dilemma. He argued that the Indian takeover of Goa demonstrated "the sterility of last minute pressure by the U.S. on two seemingly irreconcilable opponents." The situation in Angola was similar but "with more serious and far-reaching consequences." Portugal was doomed to a long war it could never win that would weaken NATO and alienate the Africans from Lisbon's allies. America, therefore, must force a rapid solution to the Angolan problem, or the country would "drift into a Congo-type situation" with the possibility of South African intervention.[64]

Sakwa recommended a nine-point plan to insure the independence of Angola

---

61. Elbrick to Rusk, 21 February 1962, NSF: Portugal, box 154, Kennedy Library. Elbrick suggested the United States end all support for Roberto and cease any contacts with the Angolan rebels. Elbrick to Rusk, 7 April 1961, ibid.; Pedro Pereira, "The Distorted Image of Angola," *Vital Speeches* 28 (1 May 1962): 431–34.

62. Schlesinger, *Robert Kennedy*, 454–62.

63. Paul Sakwa, Letter to the author, 24 September 1979.

64. Paul Sakwa, "U.S. Policy towards Portugal," 17 January 1962, NSF: Portugal, box 154, Kennedy Library.

and Mozambique by 1970. The United States would finance a massive educational program to prepare the two countries for freedom. Roberto would be given "a salaried consultative status and groomed for the Premiership of Angola," while Mondlane would "be offered a similar post in Mozambique." Political parties would be formed in 1965, elections held in 1967, and independence achieved three years later. Sakwa conceded that "an aged potentate like Salazar is not likely to accept the above plan without benefit of a frontal lobotomy," but he argued that America had "tacit responsibility" for Portuguese security and "a moral right to act firmly" and must not allow Portugal "to commit suicide" by continuing the war. Thus he suggested ways to persuade Lisbon to accept the plan. The major inducement was a massive economic-aid package for Portugal that included an agreement to double the per-capita income of the nation within five years. Sakwa maintained that the economic incentive must be so large "as to capture the imagination of the average literate Portuguese to whom it will be leaked if turned down by Salazar. It should be a document of breathtaking appeal."

If Salazar rejected the offer, Sakwa suggested that Washington turn to "Phase Two—an overthrow of the Salazar regime by pro-American officers of a younger generation with whom friendly contacts would have been established." It was likely, Sakwa predicted, that the Portuguese people would topple the government even without direct American encouragement once they were aware of the U.S. financial offer. Sakwa estimated the entire plan would cost about $500 million per year for eight years. This, he concluded, was "a cheap way to avoid a disaster." He defended the possible coup against Salazar by claiming the dictator "was not a legitimate spokesman for the Portuguese nation." His threats over the Azores justified direct U.S. action. "A vigorous counter-response to blackmail has never been regarded as a positive criminal act," Sakwa explained.

Sakwa sent copies of his evaluation and suggestions to James Thompson, a member of Bundy's staff, Arthur M. Schlesinger, Jr., a special assistant to the president, and to Bowles. Although many in Washington shared Sakwa's pessimistic analysis of the stalemate in Africa, most were not prepared to endorse the possible overthrow of Salazar. They preferred his idea of using the promise of massive economic assistance as an inducement to Portugal to yield. The administration accepted Sakwa's economic "carrot" but rejected the "stick" of a coup. The tension in Europe and the unsettled situation in Angola made it difficult to endorse the covert overthrow of an allied government, albeit one reactionary and harmful to American interests in Africa.

In March 1962, the National Security Council adopted a modified version of Sakwa's recommendations. It ignored the suggestion of toppling Salazar but supported the strategy of using economic aid as an incentive. Kennedy ordered Elbrick to tell Salazar: "The United States is prepared to extend bilateral assistance to Portugal . . . and to explore the possibilities of multilateral aid with selected NATO countries in order to minimize the economic consequences for Portugal" of independence for its African possessions. Kennedy and Ball later agreed on a figure of $70 million in direct assistance to be gathered from a variety of governmental sources. Rusk met with Brazilian officials in an attempt to get them to back the plan and to use their influence with Salazar to convince him to accept it.[65]

American attempts to "buy" African independence were not new. Elbrick several times had made vague suggestions that Washington would aid Portugal if it agreed to decolonization. The new approach was more specific and showed the U.S. desire for a quick solution to the problem. The lease for the Azores was to expire at the end of 1962, and Salazar had refused to enter into serious negotiations for its renewal. The U.S. military had made clear its opinion of the absolute importance of the facility, and Kennedy faced the problem of acting rapidly to secure Angolan freedom while preserving Portuguese cooperation.

While the State Department waited for Salazar's reply to its economic offer, Kennedy ordered a full review of U.S. policy on Angola and the importance of the Azores. He solicited the views of a variety of persons both inside and outside the government on future actions. The splits between Africanists and Europeanists became more pronounced as each side tried to impress the president with its foreign-policy priorities.

Williams responded immediately to the request for opinions and options. On 15 April he met with Kennedy and his special assistant, Ralph Dungan. Williams made an emotional appeal for continued pressure on Portugal. He claimed that the Azores were not as crucial as the military contended and could easily be replaced by expanding other facilities. He also warned that any retreat on the commitment to African independence might lead to the loss of U.S. bases in Morocco, Libya, and Ethiopia. Later, Williams noted that, while Kennedy was attentive, he was still "very concerned about the Azores." Williams complained to Fredericks that "the Azores side seems to be the one receiving disproportionately, if not exclusive consideration in some quarters." In response to the president's obvious worries about the base, Williams later shifted his argument and claimed that Salazar was bluffing and would never actually order U.S. forces off the base.[66]

Other Africanists followed Williams's lead in pressing for action against Portugal. William Attwood, the U.S. ambassador to Guinea, met with Kennedy to lobby for a showdown with Salazar. He reported that Kennedy mentioned "the

65. National Security Council, "Financial Assistance to Portugal," 23 March 1962, ibid., box 155; Department of State "Memorandum of Conversation between the Secretary, the Brazilian Ambassador, and the Brazilian Foreign Minister," 3 April 1962, NSF: Angola, box 5, Kennedy Library.

66. Williams to Fredericks, 16 April 1962, Williams Papers, box 2, National Archives; Williams oral history interview, Kennedy Library.

problem he had with the European Bureau," but Attwood was convinced that the president intended to continue strong U.S. support of freedom for Angola. Kennedy ended the conversation by asking Attwood: "What would they say if there was a tidal wave, and the Azores just disappeared under the sea? Are they all that vital?"[67]

To many Americans, the answer to Kennedy's query was that the base was vital. Acheson, who had called the facilities "the single most important we have anywhere," wrote the president recommending he do "absolutely nothing" to offend Portugal. He attacked the administration's voting record in the UN and particularly Stevenson's work with third-world nations in drafting resolutions aimed at Portugal. Acheson urged Kennedy to order the U.S. delegation to abstain on all motions dealing with Portugal and to stop helping to write them.

Stevenson and Bowles both responded to Acheson's attack. Stevenson argued that his efforts were designed to "moderate" the resolutions and that Acheson had no understanding of the issues involved or the procedures of the organization.[68] Bowles tried to counter Acheson with a memo to Kennedy proposing a seemingly simple solution to the entire Azores problem. He admitted that the administration faced "a harsh squeeze by the Portuguese" to alter its policies but stated, "It would be unthinkable to modify an effective policy in a key continent to fit the 18th century views of the Lisbon Government." Instead, Bowles suggested transforming the Azores base "from that of an exclusively U.S. facility to that of a NATO base for which all NATO members are responsible." This would allow Washington to separate the Azores from its African policy and would bring all members of the pact involved into the negotiations with Portugal.[69]

Congressional leaders also tried to influence the president. Rep. Porter Hardy of Virginia, chairman of the House Foreign Operations Subcommittee, met with NATO officials in Paris in April and publicly accused the State Department of contributing to the breakup of NATO and risking the loss of the Azores by offending Portugal. Selvage & Lee flooded Congress with letters opposing the "anti-Portuguese" policies of the United States and sent each member a copy of the pamphlet by Speaker McCormick and Congressman O'Neill, *Friendly Relations between America and Portugal*.[70]

By May, Kennedy was inundated with conflicting memos and finally asked Rusk for specific suggestions on Angola and the Azores. The secretary

67. Attwood oral history interview, Kennedy Library.

68. Stevenson to Rusk, 10 May 1962, NSF: Portugal, box 155, Kennedy Library.

69. Bowles to Kennedy, "The Azores," 4 June 1962, Bowles Papers, box 297, Yale University.

70. James Gavin, U.S. ambassador to France, to the Department of State, 27 April 1962, NSF: Portugal, box 154; Kennedy to Porter Hardy, 5 June 1962, ibid., box 155, Kennedy Library; U.S. Congress, Senate, Committee on Foreign Relations, *Activities of Non-diplomatic Representatives of Foreign Powers in the U.S.*, 1186.

responded that the Department of State was still working on its recommendations and was trying to incorporate "the useful thoughts of Acheson and Stevenson."[71] To reconcile their diametrically opposed positions was beyond the ability of the most skilled diplomat, and the department never gained enough consensus among its factions to write even one memo on the issue.

On 29 May, during the height of U.S. debate on future policy toward Portugal, Salazar made one of his infrequent but telling public pronouncements. In a speech in Lisbon, he charged Washington with supporting "armed revolution" in Africa. He contrasted America's aid to the rebels in Angola with its "inaction" when India seized Goa. He complained that Portugal was "fighting not without alliances, but without allies." State Department officials extrapolated that this was an implied threat not to renew the Azores lease.[72]

A month later, Rusk flew to Lisbon to solicit Portuguese reaction to the earlier economic-aid proposal and to try to determine Salazar's intentions on the Azores. After a two-hour meeting with Salazar and three hours with Nogueira, Rusk had gained little new information. Both officials spent most of their time haranguing the secretary for U.S. actions, particularly Williams's speeches in support of an independent Angola. Salazar did finally agree to resume negotiations on the Azores but made it clear that "greater restraint" by America was the minimum price for a new agreement.[73]

A week after Rusk's visit, Salazar again "went public." In an interview in *U.S. News and World Report*, he delivered his sharpest attack on the U.S. He labeled American diplomacy "diluted and self-contradictory" and "divorced from reality." He charged that Washington assumed that the "terrorists" in Angola were "an authentic expression of Angolan nationalism," while they were really revolutionaries trained in Moscow. Angola was the first example of Khrushchev's "wars of national liberation." Salazar gave his standard defense of Portugal's assimilation policy in Africa but soon returned to the offensive. He denounced "certain intellectual circles" in America that assumed the United States had the right to interfere in Portugal's internal affairs and the duty to spread "freedom to the world." Salazar's rhetoric contained nothing new. However, his response to a question about the Azores lease was significant. When asked if Portugal would renew the agreement, he paused and finally asked "to be excused from replying to that question."[74] It seemed clear that the Portuguese leader wanted to keep America dangling a bit longer. The lease expired in less than six months, and he recognized that the closer it came to ending the more effectively he could use it as leverage.

His evaluation proved to be correct. Immediately following publication of the

71. Rusk to Kennedy, 23 May 1962, NSF: Portugal, box 155, Kennedy Library.
72. *New York Times*, 29 May 1962, p. 10.
73. Ibid., 29 June 1962, p. 3.
74. *U.S. News and World Report* 53 (9 July 1962): 78–81.

interview, the administration tried to downplay its identification with Roberto and the Angolan rebels. U.S. diplomats at the UN had engaged in informal talks with UPA representatives for nearly a year, often through the arrangements of the American Committee on Africa. Suddenly American officials in New York and Washington refused all contacts with Roberto's envoys. Similarly, the State Department seriously considered eliminating the program at Lincoln University for Angolan students. Portugal had regularly protested that the program was a training ground for guerrillas. The Portuguese were particularly upset that its director, John Marcum, had made an unauthorized visit to Angola to meet with the rebels and had been an outspoken advocate of liberation. After "a very bloody struggle" between representatives of the African and European bureaus, the State Department agreed to continue funding the program out of fear that the students would go to Moscow if it were closed. The department did successfully demand Marcum's removal as the price of continued governmental support.[75]

Such diplomatic signals did not escape Lisbon, but the Portuguese remained in no hurry to decide on the Azores. They rejected an American effort to use de Gaulle as a mediator on the issue. A State Department intelligence report concluded that the rebels in Angola were nowhere near victory and the strains of the war on the Portuguese economy were not as great as had been anticipated. Lisbon was convinced it could win the conflict if no foreign power intervened. The Portuguese thus were determined to resist any imposed settlement or negotiations with the Nationalists.[76]

By August 1962, U.S. diplomacy had become somewhat frantic. Elbrick asked the Portuguese Foreign Office for a list of its complaints about American actions as a basis for negotiations to "clear the air" and resume discussions on the Azores lease. Nogueira responded with a lengthy summary of "Causes of Friction in Portuguese-American relations." The list included the activities of the American Committee on Africa (particularly statements by its director, George Houser); "pro-terrorist" remarks by Williams, Bowles, Stevenson, and U.S. church and labor leaders; aid to the rebels by "American agents" in Africa; State Department funding for the program for students at Lincoln University; America's UN policy; and the cuts in military aid to Portugal.[77]

Kennedy met with Elbrick and Ball to review the Portuguese grievances, and then invited Nogueira to the White House on 24 October to discuss his list. After

75. Marcum, *The Angolan Revolution*, 1:273–74; Department of State, "Memorandum for McGeorge Bundy: Report on Lincoln University African Student Center at the Conclusion of its First Year," 16 July 1962, NSF: Angola, box 2, Kennedy Library. Marcum and George Houser of the American Committee on Africa secretly entered Angola on 5 January 1962 using forged passports and spent two weeks studying the rebellion. Marcum sent an account of his findings to James Thompson, an aide to Bowles. A copy is in the Thompson Papers, box 28, Kennedy Library.
76. Gavin to Rusk, 10 July 1962, NSF: Africa, box 2; Roger Hilsman, Bureau of Intelligence and Research, to Rusk, 12 September 1962, NSF: Angola, box 5, Kennedy Library.
77. Elbrick to Rusk, 17 August 1962, NSF: Portugal, box 154, Kennedy Library.

listening to the foreign minister's recitation of U.S. "outrages," Kennedy pressed for the continuing American goal of acceptance of "the principle of self-determination." Nogueira replied that he was "not opposed to the principle" but could not say so publicly as the UN would instantly demand immediate independence for the Portuguese territories. Kennedy repeated the U.S. position that self-determination did not imply automatic independence, but the discussion reached no agreement.[78]

Following the president's unsuccessful meeting with Nogueira, Washington made one final attempt to reconcile African nationalism and Portuguese inflexibility. The administration suggested that the UN appoint an individual to act as a "rapporteur" to meet with the rebels and the Portuguese, evaluate the situation in Angola, and establish points of difference as a prelude to serious negotiations. Elbrick presented the plan to the Portuguese while Stevenson approached the Angolans and their African allies at the UN. Like the other American initiatives, the "rapporteur" proposal failed dismally. Portugal rejected any effort sponsored by the UN as a ploy for immediate independence. Stevenson found some initial enthusiam among African diplomats, but they "suddenly became chilly" when Roberto announced his opposition. Roberto claimed that Portugal would only use the arrangement for delay and argued that the issue would have to be decided on the battlefield.[79]

With the specter of the Azores hanging over the United States, many Africanists were convinced that they had lost the fight for continued pressure on Portugal. Williams was especially fearful that the military-strategic arguments of the Europeanists would cause Kennedy to pull back from his early commitment to African liberation. In a long and rambling memo to Rusk titled "The U.S., Europe, and Africa," he tried to show "that a strong U.S. European policy is complete only in conjunction with a strong U.S. African policy." He repeated the rationale for support of African independence as an expression of "traditional American concerns for liberty and independence," but he also emphasized the strategic and economic importance of Africa. Williams showed he had learned the lessons of past bureaucratic battles. Most of his paper dealt with "hard" interests in Africa such as raw materials, potential military bases, and support of U.S. policies in the UN.[80] Thus, having failed to sustain American interest in the continent with appeals to abstract notions of freedom and majority rule, the Africanists shifted their emphasis to more traditional

78. Department of State, "Memorandum of Conversation: the President and C. Burke Elbrick," 5 September 1962; Ball to Kennedy, 29 September 1962; "Memorandum of Conversation," 24 October 1962, ibid.

79. Francis Plimpton, USUN Delegation, to Rusk, 13 November 1962; "Memorandum of Conversation between C. Burke Elbrick and Franco Nogueira, 29 November 1962," enclosed in Elbrick to Rusk, 4 December 1962; Stevenson to Rusk, 18 December 1962, ibid.

80. Williams to Rusk, "The U.S., Europe, and Africa," 30 October 1962, Williams Papers, box 2, National Archives.

interests such as trade, bases, and anticommunism. They also tried to use the fear of possible domestic political reaction to a softening of the administration's African policy.

In late 1962, prominent black leaders, including Martin Luther King, James Farmer, Roy Wilkins, and Whitney Young, formed the Negro Leadership Conference on Africa. They met and issued a statement calling for continued U.S. encouragement of African liberation and specifically for increased support of "the Nationalists in Angola and Mozambique in their struggle for freedom and independence." Williams passed their recommendations along to Rusk with a warning that blacks would lose confidence in the government unless it maintained an "African emphasis" in its foreign policy.[81]

Bowles, also, tried to rally support for a strong American effort in Africa. After a trip to the continent, he proposed a revival of the Sakwa plan for economic aid to Portugal. Bowles suggested that, unlike the unanswered initiative of March, a new offer be made publicly in hopes it would "dramatize to Africa and the world" American concern. If Salazar rejected the package, the leak would "create healthy political pressures within Portugal" that might lead to the dictator's downfall. Since Kennedy and the National Security Council had already rejected any public announcement of the economic incentive, it was not surprising that Bowles's memo went unanswered.[82]

On Thanksgiving weekend, Kennedy finally dismissed Bowles from his job at the State Department. In a bitter twelve-page, single-spaced letter to the president written the day after his "reassignment," Bowles attacked "the heavy European orientation" of the Kennedy administration. He warned the president, "No one at a high level, closely associated with you, has been giving priority attention to what are frequently referred to as the 'outlying areas,' in other words, to the rest of the world where most of the human race lives."[83]

American policy in the UN in late 1962 seemed to confirm the fears of Bowles and other liberals that pressure on Portugal would be relaxed. Since its vote in favor of the 15 March 1961 statement on Angola, the United States had supported all resolutions critical of Portugal's continued colonialism. In December 1962, however, as the Azores lease neared expiration, America voted against two Security Council resolutions condemning Lisbon and demanding economic sanctions against Portugal.[84]

81. "American Negro Leadership Conference on Africa Resolutions," enclosed in Williams to Rusk, 3 December 1962, ibid.

82. Bowles to Kennedy, "Report of Mission to Africa," 13 November 1962, Bowles Papers, box 311, Yale University.

83. Bowles to Kennedy, 1 December 1962, ibid., box 297.

84. The resolution on 14 December called for "immediate independence" for Angola and an embargo on arms to Portugal. It passed 82-7 with 13 abstentions. On 18 December the General Assembly passed by a vote of 57-14 (with 18 abstentions) a motion condemning "mass extermination" in Angola and again calling for an arms embargo. A summary of the votes and American rationale is "US, UN, and Portugal," undated, NSF: Portugal, box 154, Kennedy Library.

Many Africans saw these votes as a blatant attempt to appease Salazar and insure retention of the Azores, and U.S. officials explained that their action was prompted by the language of the resolutions rather than their intent. Both resolutions described the situation in Angola as "a threat to world peace and security." This wording reflected the language in chapter 7 of the UN Charter and, if accepted, called for members to adopt sanctions and possibly even military force to deal with the crisis. The United States had repeatedly made it clear that it opposed any statement that invoked chapter 7. American officials feared that such resolutions would set a precedent for direct UN intervention in international disputes and leave nations in the difficult position of either automatically imposing sanctions and sending troops or being in defiance of the organization. Such language should be reserved for the most serious acts of aggression or it would become meaningless. In a press conference following the votes, Stevenson tried to make it clear that America supported the "spirit" and "intent" of the resolutions but opposed the mandatory language. He declared that there was no change in the U.S. commitment to Angolan independence. Bowles, in a speech to the Phelps-Stokes Fund the evening of the second vote, reiterated administration support of self-determination in Africa and argued that the United States agreed with the UN on colonial issues "in most cases." The recent votes were based on concern about the inflammatory language and were not a serious shift in policy.[85]

To many Africans, however, America's position at the UN was just another indication of its "softening" on the Angolan issue. On 19 December, Roberto wrote a personal note to Kennedy complaining that the United States had abandoned "its courageous position" on Africa and asking for an immediate meeting with administration officials to explain the need for a return to a more active policy. Neither the White House nor the State Department acknowledged his letter.[86]

If Washington hoped its abstentions at the UN would prompt Portugal to come to terms on the Azores, it was disappointed. At the end of 1962 the issue remained unresolved. Salazar did not oust America from the base, but he also refused to sign a new lease. The United States continued to use the facility after the 31 December 1962 expiration date, but without any formal agreement. Portugal refused to play its "trump card," preferring to retain it for later use.

By late 1962, Africanists privately spoke of a "retreat" in American policy, even though there were few formal changes in diplomacy. The United States had moderated its public criticism of Portugal and had eliminated informal meetings

85. "Remarks of Ambassador Stevenson to the Press, December 21, 1962," *SDB* 48 (28 January 1963): 147–52; Bowles, "A Close Look at Africa," ibid. 47 (31 December 1962): 1002–7. American opposition to the use of chapter 7 was traditional and remained consistent until the Rhodesian crisis of 1965. It became especially important in later debates on resolutions dealing with South Africa. See Chapter 6.

86. Marcum, *The Angolan Revolution*, 2:131.

with rebel leaders. Its opposition to the December 1962 UN resolutions, although perceived as a shift in policy, was consistent with the American position throughout the Kennedy administration. Kennedy retained the traditional American emphasis on NATO and, with the deepening crisis in U.S.-Soviet relations in 1961 and 1962, became even more preoccupied with defense and military preparedness. The president and his top aides also had far more misgivings about the Angolan revolt than did the Africanists. Kennedy supported African independence but wanted it to result in stable, pro-Western governments. Even though he accepted the inevitability of African nationalism and the necessity of U.S. support of decolonization for its long-term influence in the third world, other issues were of more immediate importance. America remained involved in the Angolan situation, but, during his last year in office, Kennedy implemented the diplomatic "retreat" that many Africanists feared.

5. THE PURSUIT OF MODERATION | America and the Portuguese Colonies, 1963–1968

Nineteen sixty-three began with the evident need for a new approach to the problems of Portugal and its colonies in Africa. To secure both independence and stability, America had pressured Lisbon to accept self-determination and had assisted moderates like Roberto and Mondlane in their conflict with Marxist rivals for control of the nationalist movement. Washington had used the speeches of its officials and its votes in the UN to signal its dissatisfaction with Portugal's policies. Eventually it adopted stronger measures such as the cutback in military aid and the promise of economic assistance in an effort to force some concessions. The State Department had repeatedly tried to promote a dialogue between the combatants in hopes of facilitating a political solution. The aid offer, the rapporteur proposal, and the attempts to use Brazil and France as mediators were all designed to resolve the issue rapidly enough to guarantee that the new nations would remain closely tied to the West. The assurances to Portugal that it would still play an active role in Africa and that self-determination would not bring immediate independence were additional indications of the search for an arrangement that would lead to eventual independence but would avoid humiliating a NATO ally.

Pursuit of the twin goals of decolonization and continued good relations with Portugal had made the United States vulnerable to attacks both from traditional allies and third-world nations and from liberals and conservatives at home. The decision to adopt an active campaign for a moderate solution led to criticism of both the activism and the moderate objectives. Many Europeans, conservatives, and Europeanists in the government questioned the wisdom of any direct involvement in the situation. Although few favored active support of Portugal, most argued that Africa was not vital to U.S. interests. The administration's "diplomatic offensives" had only antagonized allies and distracted America from more crucial issues. Africans and Africanists had generally welcomed Washington's initiatives in 1961 and 1962 but worried that the dedication to preserving Portuguese honor, maintaining the Azores base, and assuring moderate leadership in the struggle had diluted U.S. efforts and would eventually diminish its ability to force a settlement. On the one hand, Bowles denounced America's "appeasement of Portugal," while Ball ridiculed the same policies as signs of unwarranted attention to insignificant countries with "names like a typographical error." Portugal could accuse Washington of encouraging revolu-

96

tion and communism at the same time that Africans charged the United States with actively supporting continued European imperialism.

Unless Kennedy either unhesitatingly backed Salazar or totally committed America to immediate independence, such criticism was inevitable. However, what caused the president and his advisers to reevaluate their policy in late 1962 and early 1963 was not the criticism but the fact that two years of efforts had failed to produce any solution. America had been unable to force concessions from Salazar or generate much good will among the Africans. The war in Angola continued, and a guerrilla movement in Mozambique seemed inevitable. By 1963, Kennedy faced the options of increasing pressure on Portugal, which would likely result in the loss of the Azores and a severe domestic reaction from conservatives; abandoning the "new approach" to Africa and risking loss of third-world support and the possible Marxist control of the liberation movements; or continuing the seemingly ineffective policies of his first two years. Although he did not completely discard his previous positions, the president was reluctant to undertake any new initiatives toward Africa and was increasingly skeptical of the benefits of continuing the U.S. confrontation with Portugal.

Those within the administration who had pushed for a firm commitment to decolonization shared Kennedy's concern that U.S. actions, while well intended, had not been successful. To Bowles, the answer was not a "retreat" but even bolder efforts. In January 1963, he sent the president a plan for "a real breakthrough in the near future on the whole Portuguese-African problem." His "radical solution," however, was merely another version of the old Sakwa plan for U.S. economic aid in return for a Portuguese pledge to accept self-determination. Kennedy and Rusk ignored the suggestion, and even Williams felt the proposal was unlikely to produce any results.[1] In contrast, Elbrick argued that the time was ripe for "easing-off" on Lisbon. He urged Rusk to force the Angolans to accept a ceasefire, resume U.S. military aid to Portugal, and restore "normal relations" between the two powers. Elbrick's proposals were also rejected.[2]

Williams was aware that the mood in Washington was unreceptive to any bold diplomatic departures, but he did try to maintain American interest in the situation and at least preserve existing commitments. In early 1963, after one of his numerous trips to Africa, he reported to Rusk that America's "weakness of action" on the issue of white rule was forcing Africans to turn to Moscow for support in the liberation effort. The Soviets "are standing in the wings ready to enter the drama whenever we fumble our lines." Williams had no major

1. Bowles to Kennedy, "Proposal for a Breakthrough in U.S.-Portuguese Relations in Regard to Africa," 10 January 1963, NSF: Portugal, box 154a, Kennedy Library; Williams to Bowles, 4 March 1963, Bowles Papers, box 297, Yale University. See also Bowles to Bundy, 11 January 1963, ibid.
2. Elbrick to Rusk, 13 March 1963, Bowles Papers, box 297, Yale University.

suggestions beyond the need to "develop much more effective policies vis-à-vis Portuguese Africa."[3]

Williams was also quick to recognize shifts in the bureaucratic power structure, in particular the emergence of Averell Harriman as the dominant individual in the State Department. Kennedy had offered the veteran diplomat the position of "roving ambassador" in 1961 largely as an act of courtesy in recognition of his past services. Following the "Thanksgiving massacre" in November 1961, Harriman became assistant secretary for Far East affairs. By 1963 he had become under-secretary of state and was influential in nearly all areas of diplomacy. Thus, Williams tried to enlist Harriman's support for continued U.S. involvement in the liberation battle. He wrote to Harriman that, because of the Azores, "we have softened our approach to GOP [the Government of Portugal] during the past year," which had only confirmed Salazar's interpretation of America as weak and convinced Africans that, despite its rhetoric, the administration really favored continued colonialism. Williams urged Harriman to try to convince Rusk and Kennedy to continue American demands on Salazar and, even more important, to increase contacts with the nationalists in Angola and Mozambique. He warned that, unless the United States retained its influence in the independence movements, it would have no control over the governments that followed decolonization. "When the crisis in Portuguese Africa comes to a head," he concluded, "we must not be cut off from nationalist leadership."[4]

America had good reason to be concerned about its influence with the nationalists. Roberto was bitter over what he saw as the Kennedy administration's "retreat," and Mondlane was publicly skeptical of the sincerity of the U.S. commitment to decolonization. On 2 May 1963, Mondlane asked Robert Kennedy for direct military aid to FRELIMO. He claimed that independence for Mozambique was inevitable and Washington's efforts "to placate Portugal" to keep the Azores were preventing Mozambique from "moving to the forefront of this struggle for freedom." When he received no reply, Mondlane charged that America had "abandoned" Africa to save its good relations with Lisbon.[5]

One reason the administration ignored the FRELIMO leader was its belief that Angola was the key to the Portuguese territories. A CIA memo issued three days before Mondlane's request for aid concluded that the liberation movement in Mozambique was weak, divided, and not likely to attract "an effective political following." The memo argued that Angola, in which there existed a strong political organization and sustained military action, should be America's major

3. Williams to Rusk, "Major Conclusions of Williams' African Trip," 25 February 1963, Williams Papers, box 3, National Archives.
4. Williams to Harriman, "Progress for Portuguese Africa," 2 May 1963, ibid., box 29.
5. John Marcum, "The Politics of Indifference: Portugal and Africa, a Case Study in American Foreign Policy," pp. 8–9.

concern rather than "sleepy Mozambique." The outcome in Angola would determine the settlement in Mozambique.[6]

A part of the reassessment of U.S. policy was an attempt to find a unified approach to all areas of white rule. Rostow had criticized the administration for concentrating on the Portuguese territories rather than creating a regional policy to deal with the entire "white redoubt" of southern Africa, and he was well aware of the splits within the bureaucracy on Africa and especially concerning Angola.[7] In May 1963 his Policy Planning Council issued a lengthy report on "Problems of Southern Africa" that tried to combine Rhodesia, South Africa, and the Portuguese colonies into a single policy problem with a unified U.S. response. He noted that the State Department must "reconcile the somewhat divergent views and approaches of AF [the African Bureau] and EUR [the European bureau] and others." After a review of the conflicting priorities of the two groups, Rostow concluded, "The divergence between the two Bureaus seems less a matter of substance than of methods and tactics." He reminded both factions that the area had the potential for a major race war that would "enhance Sino-Soviet bloc opportunities in Africa." China and Russia were "looking for opportunities to increase their influence" and wanted to use the black nationalist movements "to gain a foothold in Southern Africa." America must be actively involved in the region to assure stability and to block communist penetration. "If events are allowed to drift in these dangerous directions, it is apparent that they would have a profound effect on the overall balance of forces in the world," he summarized. Not only would the West lose the "credit gained by the wise decolonization policy of most Western nations," but the United States would be shut out of trade and investment opportunities and compromise its strategic interests.[8]

The need for U.S. interest and action was clear, but, Rostow noted, America was "caught between competing interests in maintaining the good will of the new nations of Africa and our direct security interests in Southern Africa." Washington was dedicated to self-determination but also to avoiding violent conflicts "which would open avenues of exploitation by the [communist] bloc." Thus, the document effectively made a case for continued U.S. involvement, but it contained few recommendations for new policies. America should "deal reasonably" with Salazar but continue to point out "the dangers of intransigence." Washington should work with its European allies to give "a strong impression of Western concern" while assuring Lisbon that it would have "a con-

6. CIA Memorandum, "Prospects for Nationalism and Revolt in Mozambique," 30 April 1963, NSF: Africa, box 3. See also CIA Report, "The Angolan Rebellion and White Unrest," NSF: Angola, box 5, Kennedy Library.

7. Department of State Policy Planning Council, "The White Redoubt," 28 June 1962, ibid., box 2.

8. Department of State Policy Planning Council, "Problems of Southern Africa," 6 May 1963, ibid., box 3.

tinuing role to play in Africa." Only an active, but moderate, policy would insure pro-Western governments and prevent communist inroads.

By the spring of 1963, there was mounting criticism of Kennedy's African diplomacy by lobbyists and Congress. Some American conservatives argued that by opposing Portugal and aiding Roberto the administration was encouraging rather than resisting communist influence. The State Department was under almost daily attack for its support of UN efforts to preserve the central government in the Congo. The "Katanga lobby," often working out of the Senate offices of Thomas Dodd (the "Senator from Katanga"), was most vocal. Sen. Barry Goldwater, in turn, led the fight against U.S. encouragement of Angolan independence. Goldwater accused the State Department of "anti-European sentiment" and charged it was helping Adoula arm "Angolan terrorists." Williams arranged a hurried meeting with the senator to explain that Adoula and Roberto were both "moderate, anticommunists" and to deny that U.S. policy was "anti-white." He assured Goldwater, "We do not seek immediate independence in Angola" but only "realistic steps toward self-determination" with "guarantees of a continued Portuguese presence."[9]

In 1962, Roberto had broadened the base of the UPA by creating the National Liberation Front and persuading rival nationalist leader Jonas Savimbi to join it. He followed by announcing that he had formed the Government of the Republic of Angola in Exile (GRAE) in Leopoldville. GRAE was unable to gain diplomatic recognition until, on 29 June 1963, the Congo became the first nation to grant it official status. Portugal was outraged and withdrew its chargé from Leopoldville. The rival MPLA and its African supporters were also angry. Williams had recently completed talks with Adoula, and the MPLA was convinced Washington had engineered the recognition. Although Roberto was the obvious American favorite, Williams insisted that recognition "was up to the Africans" and denied he had any role in Adoula's decision.[10]

Of even greater significance to Roberto was the support he gained a month later from the Organization of African Unity, established in May 1963 by independent African states to help resolve disputes among members and to aid in the complete decolonization of the continent. In July the group's Liberation Committee met in Dar Es Salaam to decide which Angolan faction it should support. Roberto and other representatives of GRAE were well organized and emphasized that they were the only force actually fighting in Angola. MPLA officials claimed their lack of military activity was the result of opposition by

9. G. Mennen Williams, Letter to the author, 15 January 1980; "Talking Points for Governor Williams's Meeting with Senator Goldwater," undated, Williams Papers, box 17, National Archives.

10. Marcum, *The Angolan Revolution*, 2:78–80, 93–99. In support of Williams's denial is a circular from Rusk to all American embassies in Africa that claimed the MPLA had shown signs of moderation and the United States should encourage this "move toward the West" by not officially choosing between the liberation movements. Rusk to All American Posts in Africa, 16 July 1963, NSF: Africa, box 3, Kennedy Library.

Adoula. The Congolese leader produced documents showing that he had offered aid to both factions. As a result, on 18 July, the OAU acknowledged GRAE as the official vehicle of Angolan liberation. By early 1964, eighteen African nations had formally recognized Roberto's exile government. Roberto had scored a major diplomatic triumph.

Americans were pleased with Roberto's victory but somewhat concerned about OAU demands for the immediate liberation of Africa and endorsement of force to achieve it. State Department intelligence concluded that the OAU was relatively weak, deeply divided, and its resolutions "contain no real surprises." The CIA, in a more detailed evaluation, was impressed with the OAU's depth of commitment to ending white rule and particularly with the group's determination to drive Portugal from Africa. It predicted that the organization would not be an immediate force, however, as most African leaders were "free wheelers . . . unprepared to give up freedom of action for the sake of an intangible concept no matter how worthy."[11]

Despite the diplomatic developments in Africa, American attention was still largely fixed on Europe. Even with the "thaw" in U.S.-Soviet relations following the Cuban missile crisis, Kennedy still worried about the unsettled status of the Azores and its effect on U.S. military preparedness. In July 1963, he made it clear he wanted to decide permanently on the importance of the facility and its role in any future policy toward Portugal. The UN Security Council was considering another resolution on Angola, and Kennedy had to again weigh U.S. action and the Portuguese response.

The president approached this problem in the same way he had approached his earlier decisions. Again he solicited opinions from both liberals and conservatives and various governmental agencies. Stevenson wrote a long personal letter pleading with Kennedy for permission to support the pending resolution and another aimed at South Africa. "We are approaching a decisive situation from which the Africans will draw conclusions about the longrun nature of our policies," he argued. "In *over-simplified* terms, they [the Africans] want to know whether, if it comes to that, we will stand for self-determination and human rights . . . or whether we will give our Azores base and the tracking stations in South Africa priority."[12] Arthur Schlesinger and Robert Kennedy suggested that the president make another study of the Azores to see if they "are so indispensable to us that they must determine our African policy." On the other hand, the Joint Chiefs of Staff and McNamara remained convinced that the base was crucial to U.S. defense. Maxwell Taylor, chairman of the joint chiefs, claimed that loss of the Azores and the possible refusal of Portugal to cooperate

11. Department of State Memorandum for the President, "Addis Ababa Meeting and Related African Developments," 1 June 1963; CIA Memorandum, "The Addis Ababa Conference and Its Aftermath," 11 July 1963, NSF: Africa, box 3, Kennedy Library.
12. Stevenson to Kennedy, 26 June 1963, ibid.

with Washington "could dangerously weaken our efforts to revitalize NATO." (McNamara urged Rusk to avoid any action in the UN that would antagonize Portugal or South Africa as both were essential to America's strategic interests.) As a result, the State Department recommended to Kennedy that "any position involving serious risk of the loss of the Azores is unacceptable."[13]

Likewise, the CIA also pushed for a relaxation of pressure on Portugal. Although it predicted that Salazar would not "play his trump card" by expelling the United States from the Azores regardless of any vote in the UN, it questioned the benefits of continued demands on Lisbon. It was clear that Portugal would not compromise until Salazar died. The Portuguese leader was totally committed to preserving the empire and was so unreasonable that continued demands for self-determination would only result in the further alienation of a NATO ally.[14]

On 18 July, Kennedy met with Stevenson and his UN staff, Rusk, McNamara, William Bundy of the Defense Department, Schlesinger, Williams, and other State Department and White House aides to discuss the UN resolutions and long-range policy toward Portugal. The president was influenced not only by the military's demands for the Azores but also by fear Congress might reject the pending nuclear test ban treaty if the administration lost the base. He asked Stevenson what would happen if "we hung back, did nothing, and let nature take its course" at the UN. Stevenson claimed that such inaction would lead to "an extreme resolution" that the United States would be forced to oppose. As a result, America would lose all credibility among the African nations. McNamara mentioned the joint chiefs' fear of losing the Azores and argued that the United States should "not take the lead" on any proposal aimed at Portugal. Stevenson's deputy, Charles Yost, protested the lack of concern for the sensitivities of the Africans and the disregard of traditional American commitments to self-determination. Stevenson followed by trying to convince the president that the resolution could be supported without a disastrous Portuguese reaction. Kennedy cut him off by bluntly stating his "desire to avoid a conspicuous American initiative" on the matter. Stevenson was "so far as possible to sit back and let others take the lead."[15]

The Africanists had lost a crucial battle, yet Stevenson still tried to salvage something to preserve influence with the Africans. In defiance of Kennedy's instructions, he worked with the Norwegian delegation to arrange a compromise resolution that did not include the dreaded chapter 7 language of "a threat to international peace." When he cabled the State Department of his efforts, officials were impressed. They reported to Kennedy that "the draft is now

13. Schlesinger, *Robert Kennedy*, 561; Maxwell Taylor to McNamara, 10 July 1963, NSF: Portugal, box 154a; McNamara to Rusk, 11 July 1963, NSF: South Africa, box 159; Department of State to the President, 18 July 1963, NSF: Portugal, box 154a, Kennedy Library.
14. CIA Memorandum, "Significance of Portuguese and Spanish Colonial Problems for the U.S.," 11 July 1963, NSF: Portugal, box 154a, Kennedy Library.
15. "Memorandum for the Record: Meeting with the President on Portuguese Africa, 18 July 1963," ibid.

explicitly *not* Chapter 7 language" but "is as close as you can come without adopting Chapter 7 language."[16]

Stevenson's success only infuriated both Kennedy and the Portuguese. Clearly the ambassador had not followed the president's orders to "sit back and let others take the lead." The Portuguese Foreign Office protested to Elbrick that "the objectionable resolution before the UN was the work of the U.S." Jose Fragoso, director of political affairs at the Foreign Ministry, charged that Stevenson was "responsible for the resolution" and Lisbon would "hold the United States responsible for the results." Elbrick immediately phoned Rusk, and the secretary sent Harriman to explain the U.S. position to the Portuguese ambassador in Washington. When the amended resolution came up for a vote in New York, Kennedy issued last-minute orders for Stevenson to abstain on the resolution that he had helped to write.[17]

The abstention was a major setback for advocates of an "Africa-first" policy. Stevenson and others at the UN had repeatedly argued that, unlike the December 1962 votes, this was a "crucial" resolution of tremendous symbolic importance. Those directly involved in the UN were under constant pressure to take a strong position on racial and colonial questions, and they obviously placed more significance on America's voting record than did officials in Washington. These differences often caused UN officials to function as "the other State Department."[18] Stevenson's disregard of Kennedy's instructions was an example not only of conflicting international priorities but also of a fundamental disagreement over the importance of the UN. To Stevenson, Williams, and others closely involved with representatives of the nonaligned nations, UN policy was essential to America's international prestige and continued influence among the third-world countries. As the organization was important to Africans and Asians, the United States had to take the rhetoric and essentially powerless resolutions of the UN seriously.

Kennedy, in contrast, was distrustful of UN resolutions "which promised big things that could not be carried out." He was not impressed with "hortatory rhetoric against colonialism" but favored "realistic resolutions" that would be effective.[19] In addition, many conservatives were scornful of the UN's use of force to preserve Congolese unity. The continuing financial crisis of the body, its increased "anti-American" oratory, and the control of the General Assembly by non-Western states had seriously eroded U.S. confidence in the UN by the summer of 1963.

Although many Americans saw the UN as "toothless" and its resolutions as only

16. Department of State Memorandum for the President, "Portuguese African Problems," 30 July 1963, ibid.
17. "Memorandum of Telephone Conversation between C. Burke Elbrick and Francis E. Maloy," 31 July 1963, ibid.; see *SDB* 49 (19 August 1963): 303–9, for Stevenson's rather awkward explanation of his abstention and Martin, *Adlai Stevenson*, 767–68, for his anger with Kennedy.
18. See Arnold Beichman, *The "Other" State Department*, 143–207.
19. Schlesinger, *A Thousand Days*, 562–63.

propaganda, Portugal was still sensitive to its actions. Despite Stevenson's abstention, Lisbon still blamed him for the resolution condemning its actions in Africa. It seemed that even by abstaining the United States had again risked the loss of the Azores. In response to Portuguese attacks on Washington, Kennedy ordered the Defense Department to prepare a contingency plan for the loss of the base. McNamara responded that evacuation of the facility would pose massive problems of communication and supply for both planes and ships and greatly weaken America's ability to respond to a sudden crisis in Europe or the Middle East.[20]

Kennedy's concern over possible loss of the base was prompted by the extreme Portuguese reaction to the 31 July resolution and America's help in drafting it. Salazar finally expressed Lisbon's rage directly in a ninety-minute speech on 12 August. He condemned the UN as "an oppressive majority" acting in violation of its own charter and charged Kennedy with "trying to defend the interests of the West in Europe while subverting them in Africa." The most significant statement in Salazar's oration was a reference to the U.S. proposal for economic aid in exchange for self-determination. He accused America of working for African independence out of narrow, economic self-interest. The United States wanted Portugal out of Angola and Mozambique so it could dominate the weak new nations. America's greed had led it to offer Portugal "compensation for the loss of Africa," but, Salazar vowed, "Portugal overseas is not for sale." The Portuguese were "the trustees of a sacred heritage" that could not be purchased by American dollars. Salazar concluded by promising to retain the provinces even if it led to war with all of Africa.[21]

Salazar's rejection of American economic incentives and his claim that greed rather than principle directed U.S. policy provoked a rare display of public anger from Rusk, who called a news conference to rebut Salazar's interpretation of America's actions. Rusk defended U.S. policy as based on "the simple notion that governments derive their just power from the consent of the governed." He totally repudiated the charge that the United States wanted an independent Angola only so it could be exploited by American corporations.[22]

Portugal's refusal of the aid offer and pledge to continue the war in Africa were painful illustrations of the failure of U.S. policy. After more than two years of notes, threats, offers, and discussions, Washington had accomplished little. Salazar continued to define the "overseas provinces" as integral parts of Portugal and to dismiss self-determination as synonymous with a humiliating abandonment of the empire.

In an attempt to soothe Salazar and convince him of the sincerity of American

20. Kennedy to McNamara, 31 July 1963; McNamara to Kennedy, 14 August 1963, NSF: Portugal, box 155, Kennedy Library.

21. A copy of the speech was enclosed in Elbrick to Rusk, 13 August 1963, ibid., box 154a, and most of it was published in the *New York Times*, 13 August 1963, p. 1.

22. *New York Times*, 17 August 1963, p. 1.

intentions, Kennedy decided to send George Ball to Lisbon. As the most forceful of the Europeanists in the administration, Ball seemed to be the least offensive U.S. official to approach Portugal. The State Department prepared detailed instructions for Ball's negotiations with Salazar. He was to reassure the Portuguese leader of America's appreciation for Lisbon's "civilizing mission" in Africa and of U.S. support for "a continued Portuguese presence" in the colonies. The department admitted that Washington's position was weakened by the need to retain the Azores, by the fact that military aid had already been cut, and by Salazar's recent rejection of economic aid in return for self-determination. Despite these handicaps, Ball was to press for an agreement on the "principle of self-determination even if couched in Portuguese phraseology" and for acceptance of a special visit by the secretary-general of the UN as a prelude to "quiet talks" between Portugal and the rebels. If he was successful, he was to raise the possibility of a plebiscite in Angola and Mozambique in the near future.[23]

This was an ambitious program given Portugal's position and the lack of American leverage. Prior to his trip, Ball asked Williams if the United States could force Roberto to accept a ceasefire if Salazar agreed to "a minimum program" of discussions and eventual self-determination. Williams replied that Roberto would never halt guerrilla activity unless Ball could guarantee an absolute Portuguese commitment "to independence within five years."[24] Ball was left with little to offer Salazar in exchange for the hoped-for concessions. After his first talks it was clear that there was no hope of gaining agreement to any of the State Department's suggestions. Ball complimented Portugal on its civilizing efforts in Africa and made the traditional U.S. claim that "self-determination does not mean independence." Salazar and Nogueira remained unconvinced. When Ball pointed to the friendly relations that France and Britain maintained with their former African possessions as a model for "a continued Portuguese presence," Salazar responded that real influence could only be maintained by direct political control.[25]

Ball returned to Washington to meet with Kennedy, the National Security Council, and new U.S. ambassador to Lisbon George Anderson. Ball was blunt and pessimistic. Salazar was "a man of charm and urbanity" but was "extremely conservative." There was "little hope of satisfactory negotiation with the Africans," and Ball doubted that Portugal would take any "new initiatives" to reform the colonies.[26]

Although he was personally impatient with the administration's attention to

23. Department of State, "Scope Paper: Visit of the Under-Secretary to Lisbon, August 29–30, 1963," NSF: Portugal, box 154a, Kennedy Library.

24. Williams to Ball, 27 August 1963, Williams Papers, box 29, National Archives.

25. "Summary of Conversation between Under-Secretary Ball and Portuguese Officials, August 29–30, 1963," ibid., box 155. See also Ball, *The Discipline of Power*, 245–52.

26. "Meeting with the President on Under-Secretary Ball's Debriefing on His Lisbon Meeting with Salazar," 9 September 1963, Williams Papers, box 154a, National Archives.

colonial questions, Ball agreed to follow up his meeting with a personal letter to Salazar urging some concessions. Ball appealed to Portuguese honor and self-interest. He cited de Gaulle's courageous decision to withdraw from Algeria rather than continue to weaken France through an unwinnable war. Lisbon must also recognize that it could not halt nationalism through force. Continued violence would only lead to "communist penetration" of the liberation movements and the eventual loss of all Portuguese influence in Africa. Although it was unable to "block the tide" of independence, Portugal could "build canals and conduits to direct its flow." To preserve its honor, it must prepare for "an orderly and peaceful" transition to freedom. The key to such progress, Ball contended, was self-determination: "From it flow other considerations such as timing and programs."[27]

In response to Ball's letter, Portugal agreed to preliminary talks with Angolan leaders that would not include the issue of independence. Roberto and others in the movement rejected negotiations without prior Portuguese acknowledgment of eventual independence.[28]

In November 1963, when President Kennedy was shot in Dallas, the war continued unabated. The Kennedy administration ended with few tangible results from its sustained diplomatic activity. The succession of Lyndon Johnson to the presidency had little immediate impact on America's African policies. Although most African leaders were deeply affected by Kennedy's assassination and expressed their admiration for his personal interest in their continent, official American policy was essentially unchanged by his death. Johnson kept Kennedy's foreign-policy advisers and made no major alterations in the U.S. position. He phoned Williams to assure him that Africa remained as important as it had been under Kennedy and to promise the assistant secretary that he would have direct access to the White House whenever he wished.[29]

What did change with Kennedy's death was the style of American diplomacy and the degree of direct presidential involvement. Johnson saw himself as a domestic president. Unlike Kennedy, he claimed no great expertise on international relations and initially allowed his advisers a large degree of latitude on policy matters. Johnson's reluctance actively to intervene in foreign policy was a detriment to U.S. relations with Africa. African leaders were convinced that Kennedy had a strong interest in their problems. Although they often disagreed with his actions, they were flattered that the president seemed to consider Africa an important area of American diplomacy. Johnson did not have

27. Ball to Salazar, 21 October 1963, ibid.
28. Department of State Circular 888, "Suspension of Portuguese-African Talks," 9 November 1963, ibid.
29. G. Mennen Williams, Letter to the author, 15 January 1980. The Africans' praise of Kennedy following his death has led some to exaggerate the impact of his assassination on America's African policy. Perhaps most extreme is the comment by W. Scott Thompson that "Buried with Kennedy was America's African policy." See his *Ghana's Foreign Policy, 1957–1966*, 300.

this tradition of interest, and his lack of direct involvement in African policy was taken as a sign of unconcern. Johnson was also handicapped by being a Southerner. Even though Johnson had at least as deep a commitment to civil rights and racial equality as did Kennedy, Africans were convinced that a Texan in the White House could only harm their cause. Despite Johnson's efforts on behalf of the civil-rights and voting-rights bills, African leaders remained skeptical of his ideas on race. Finally, the new president was unable to match Kennedy's effective use of personal diplomacy. Johnson repeatedly tried to duplicate Kennedy's direct approach to African leaders, but his style was far more effective with domestic politicians than with third-world diplomats. His "hands on, grab the lapels" lobbying of Congress was in marked contrast to his stiff and often ineffective dealings with foreign leaders.

Johnson inherited the issue of Portuguese decolonization and immediately faced the enduring problems of UN policy and Lisbon's use of American weapons in Africa. Characteristically, he largely remained out of the discussions and let the factions in the State Department decide policy. Prior to Kennedy's death, Elbrick had reported that, despite repeated denials, Portugal was using American F-86 aircraft in Africa. Rusk protested, and Lisbon agreed to withdraw the planes. In December 1963, African delegates to the UN charged that Portugal was still using U.S. planes to attack rebel positions in Angola. Stevenson was embarrassed, and Rusk was furious. The secretary cabled the new American ambassador in Lisbon, George Anderson, that it was "increasingly difficult to defend the U.S. position" that no American arms were being used in Africa when it seemed clear that they were. Anderson was to "make an immediate formal approach" to Nogueira and remind him of past promises to use U.S. equipment only in Europe and to demand "an early return" of the F-86s. Rusk also ordered U.S. officials in Bonn to protest Portuguese use in Angola of American materiel provided to West Germany.[30]

Once again the Portuguese promised to withdraw the aircraft. They claimed they needed time to disassemble the planes and ship them by sea to Lisbon. Despite this pledge, it soon became obvious that Portugal had kept the aircraft in Africa. The issue continued to surface periodically throughout Johnson's administration as Washington's protests were followed by Lisbon's promises to remove the materiel.[31]

At the same time that Rusk was protesting Portugal's violations of the Military Assistance Pact, the two nations again became embroiled in the murky and tangled question of UN resolutions. As before, the issues were language and American attempts to remain friendly with both Africa and Portugal. In

30. Elbrick to Rusk, 2 August 1963, NSF: Portugal, box 154a; Rusk to Anderson, 3 December 1963; Rusk to American Embassy, West Germany, 3 December 1963, NSF: Portugal, box 1, Lyndon B. Johnson Library.
31. Anderson to Rusk, 6 December 1963; Rusk to Anderson, 3 May 1964, ibid.

December 1963, the UN debated yet another condemnation of Portugal and South Africa. During the session American officials secretly met with Roberto in New York to discuss the resolutions and the progress of the war in Angola. Portuguese intelligence quickly relayed word of the meetings to Lisbon. Nogueira complained to Anderson that the United States had "betrayed previous official USG [United States Government] assurances that he [Roberto] would not be received at the State Department or USUN." American representatives in New York suspended the talks after Rusk warned that they should undertake "no action at this time that threatened possible new negotiations on the Azores."[32]

Even though the United States avoided further contacts with Roberto, it was not clear if Stevenson would be allowed to vote for the pending resolution. Stevenson had again managed to modify the language to avoid committing members to economic sanctions. He reported to Rusk that he had been able to change the word *affirms* to *recalling* in reference to the 31 July Security Council resolution that America had not supported. He also had "softened the first operative paragraph" to make it less offensive to Portugal. He argued that such changes made the statement acceptable and asked for permission to vote for it.[33]

The next day a subcommittee of the National Security Council met to consider the issue. It agreed with Stevenson's evaluation and recommended a favorable vote. Deputy Assistant Secretary of State Joseph Sisco summoned the Portuguese chargé and notified him that America would vote in support of the amended resolution. Portugal claimed that this was "a reversal of policy" from the U.S. position in July. Sisco explained in laborious detail that the present statement did not include sanctions, did not invoke chapter 7 of the charter, and contained "no words such as 'condemnation' to describe Portuguese policy." He reminded the Portuguese diplomat that "the U.S. worked extremely hard for this moderate resolution." Sisco "stressed that the present RES [resolution] represents a triumph of moderate African states over extremism. A U.S. affirmative vote is not a change in policy . . . because it [the resolution] recognizes a range of options for self-determination."[34] The key phrase in Sisco's explanation was "range of options." The UN motion did not call for immediate independence but only for the long-sought American goal of "self-determination" as a prelude to any further action. Despite a last-minute appeal from de Gaulle for Washington to abstain, Stevenson partly avenged his defeat in July when he voted for the resolution on 11 December.[35]

Portugal responded with the usual orchestrated anti-American demonstrations in Lisbon. Nogueira cornered William Tyler, the American delegate to a NATO meeting, and railed against the United States and the vote. Tyler reported: "I

32. Anderson to Rusk, 6 December 1963; Rusk to USUN Delegation, 6 December 1963, ibid.
33. Stevenson to Rusk, 9 December 1963, ibid.
34. A summary of Sisco's conversation with Rosa is in Rusk to Anderson, 11 December 1963, ibid.
35. Stevenson to Rusk, 12 December 1963, ibid.

have never known Nogueira to speak more bitterly than he did to me." Nogueira immediately rejected a "low key" but obviously ill-timed suggestion by Anderson to resume talks on the expired Azores lease. Portuguese officials also protested a speech by Williams that defended Roberto and Mondlane as "nationalists" driven to violence by "the rigidity of Portugal." The Portuguese claimed that "the opening of Communist consulates in Angola and Mozambique could not be as harmful to freedom as Mr. Williams."[36]

More important to American officials than Portuguese protests were the alarming actions of Roberto in early 1964. Throughout 1963 the Angolan leader had become more and more impatient with Washington's inability to influence Portugal and its refusal to provide him with weapons. On 30 December 1963, the U.S. embassy in Leopoldville sent an urgent cable to Rusk claiming that Roberto was "turning left." Intelligence sources in the Congo reported that, following the recent UN session and the cancellation of his talks with American officials, Roberto was "a changed man." He was "completely disillusioned with Western, and specifically U.S. policy on Angola" and was "convinced that the U.S. would never jeopardize its military ties with Portugal and . . . it was U.S. military aid to Portugal that enabled them to hold Angola." The report noted that the Chinese had offered GRAE "large scale military aid with no questions asked" and that Roberto felt he carried "the reputation of an American stooge without receiving any of the material benefits that a real stooge would expect." It suggested: "If we wish to pull Roberto back from the edge of the abyss, we must be able to convince him that our relationship with the Portuguese, far from damaging his interests, offers him the best hope of avoiding an Angolan bloodbath and achieving a negotiated settlement."[37]

On 4 January 1964, Roberto confirmed the rumors by announcing he would accept aid from China "and other communist countries" in his fight for freedom. He attacked the Western nations, particularly the United States, for selling arms to Lisbon "while paying lip-service to self-determination." Another indication of "American hypocrisy" was its refusal to help GRAE in its search for international recognition and assistance. "Only the communists can give us what we need," he concluded.[38]

Although the Congolese government immediately declared that it would not permit Chinese supplies to enter its country, Roberto's statement rocked the American bureaucracy. His announcement of Chinese aid came on the eve of a

36. "Memorandum of Conversation between Mr. Tyler and Foreign Minister Nogueira," 16 December 1963; Memorandum of Conversation, "Azore Base Rights," enclosed in Anderson to Rusk, 21 December 1963; Memorandum of Conversation, "Dr. Jose Manuel Fragoso and Theodore A. Xanthaky," 5 February 1964, enclosed in Anderson to Rusk, 13 February 1964, ibid. Xanthaky was Counselor of the U.S. Embassy in Portugal.
37. American Embassy Leopoldville to the Department of State, 30 December 1963, NSF: Angola, box 1, Johnson Library.
38. *New York Times*, 4 January 1964, p. 15.

tour of Africa by Peking's Chou En-lai. To a great number of U.S. officials and journalists, Chou's visit marked the beginning of a massive Chinese effort to infiltrate Africa and take control of the liberation struggle. They were convinced that China was planning to export revolution by stressing their affinities with the Africans as fellow nonwhites breaking away from European exploitation.[39]

No one was more alarmed by Chou's trip and Roberto's announcement than Dean Rusk. As former assistant secretary of state for the Far East, Rusk was haunted by the specter of China. He repeatedly had warned of the danger Peking presented to international stability. Usually moderate, cool, and self-controlled, Rusk was extreme and passionate when it came to the Chinese. Roberto's declaration of Chinese support provoked an instantaneous reaction. In an almost hysterical cable to all U.S. ambassadors in Africa and to Anderson in Lisbon, Rusk announced, "It is clear from the growing Chicom [Chinese Communist] presence and Chou En-Lai's visits that Red China is embarking on a major political offensive in Africa." He predicted that the Chinese would try to subvert African nationalism and take over the liberation movements. "The recent reports of GRAE leader Roberto's intention to accept these offers show that the Chicom offensive cannot fail to affect the situation in the Portuguese territories." To Rusk, the conflict in Angola was "made to order" for Peking. The Chinese could pit "non-whites against Europeans and NATO in a 'liberation struggle' which offers glittering opportunities to deal a blow to the West" and could also "assert the superiority of the Chicom revolutionary ideology over that of the USSR."[40]

In addition to his fear that the Chinese would gain control of Roberto, Rusk also feared that the Chinese would use their influence with the Angolans to try to topple Adoula's government in the Congo. Given the dire Chinese threat, he felt it was urgent that America make a new attempt to force Portugal to accept some form of self-determination. If Washington gained some concessions from Lisbon, it could still salvage a negotiated settlement and prevent Roberto from falling under Chinese domination.

As the secretary brooded over the "Chicom offensive" in Africa, he received another stunning blow: on 17 January the *New York Times* reported that, in response to French urgings, Portugal was considering formal recognition of China in an effort to end its dependence on America. Anderson confirmed the rumor in a dispatch three days later.[41] A rapprochement between reactionary

39. Chou visited seven African countries in early 1964. Examples of the American interpretation of his journey are Robert Scalapino, "Sino-Soviet Competition in Africa," 640–54, and Colin Legum, "Peking's Strategic Priorities," *Africa Report* 10 (January 1964): 19–21. In retrospect, it seems Chou's trip was not intended to gain control of liberation movements but was limited primarily to unsuccessful attempts to gain trade agreements. See Alaba Ogunsanwo, *China's Policy in Africa, 1958–1971,* 112–79.

40. Secretary of State to all American embassies, Africa and the American embassy, Lisbon, 17 January 1964, NSF: Portugal, box 1, Johnson Library.

41. *New York Times,* 17 January 1964, p. 1; Anderson to Rusk, 20 January 1964, NSF: Portugal, box 1, Johnson Library.

Portugal and revolutionary China seemed absurd to some officials in Washington, but Rusk was convinced that Lisbon was serious. He ordered Anderson to meet "immediately" with Salazar and to tell him that any move to recognize mainland China would be "dangerous" to Portugal and the entire free world. It would encourage "extremist elements" in Angola. Anderson was to make it clear that "the effect of such a move on Portuguese-U.S. relations would be adverse and profound."[42] Lisbon immediately dropped its contacts with China.

Not all American diplomats agreed with Rusk on the importance of the Chinese threat in Africa. The American ambassador in Tunisia, Francis Russell, reported that his sources in the nationalist movement indicated that "Roberto will not accept arms from the Red Chinese." According to Russell, Roberto remained strongly anticommunist, and his threat to take Chinese aid was "merely a tactical move" to generate leftist support in Africa and to pressure Washington for more assistance. U.S. representatives in the Congo sent a similar assessment. After meeting with Adoula, they quoted the Congolese leader as saying, "I can set your mind at ease on Holden [Roberto]." Adoula interpreted Roberto's announcement as a tactic to force the United States to press its demands on Salazar and to step up economic aid to GRAE. Adoula had agreed to meet with Roberto and "speak severely re the CHICOMS."[43]

If Roberto had planned his public "tilt to the left" to provoke American interest and action, he succeeded. In response to Rusk's urgings, the National Security Council met to consider the new situation in Angola. The group noted that Defense Department war games had predicted that Roberto might eventually turn to the communists for aid, but his actions enhanced the "current Chicom offensive in Africa" and threatened "the future political orientation of the Angolan nationalist movement." Ball's personal approach to Salazar had failed, and the war in Angola showed every sign of continuing indefinitely and becoming "more violent, racist, and communist-infiltrated." The liberation organizations would become increasingly "radical and anti-western."[44]

The NSC reviewed past American efforts and concluded that all had failed. Portugal had been prodded into some reforms, but they were "too little, too late." Exploratory talks between Portugal and the rebels had amounted to "nothing more than skillful delaying tactics on the part of the Portuguese." The United States had "sought to promote moderate resolutions" at the UN but had only "irritated the Portuguese" and angered the Africans with its "refusal to go

42. Rusk to Anderson, 4 February 1964, NSF: Portugal, box 1, Johnson Library.
43. Francis Russell to the Department of State, 20 January 1964, NSF: Angola, box 1; U.S. embassy Congo to Department of State, 6 January 1964, NSF: Congo, box 1; G. McMutrie Godley to Rusk, 10 March 1964, ibid., Johnson Library.
44. National Security Council Memorandum, "Portuguese African Territories," 15 February 1964, NSF: Portugal, box 1, Johnson Library.

farther and support sanctions." The use of American weapons remained "an embarrassing issue."

The group considered a variety of possible responses to the Angolan crisis ranging from "no new significant action" to "increased direct pressure on Portugal," weighing each possible course of action in terms of "the importance of maintaining U.S.-Portuguese military cooperation." Finally, the NSC endorsed another attempt to use America's European allies to work on Salazar for compromise, but admitted, "France will not touch the issue with a ten-foot pole" and "the UK [United Kingdom] is not very enthusiastic." The report concluded that, "for the lack of anything better," Washington should try to revive direct talks between Roberto and Lisbon, possibly with the mediation of Ivory Coast leader Felix Houphouet-Boigny. It rejected any direct action against Portugal such as cancelling food shipments, ending all foreign aid, or suspending loans, as they might "undermine our tenancy of the Azores facilities."

The NSC's suggestions showed the weakness of the American position. As long as the Azores were deemed absolutely necessary, the United States was unwilling to force Salazar to accept a settlement. As long as Salazar did not have to fear significant American actions, he could remain obstinate, and in a lengthy letter to Ball on 3 March, written in response to Ball's personal note of 21 October 1963, the Portuguese leader showed just how inflexible and defiant he was. Although most diplomats used instantaneous communication, Salazar had delayed responding to Ball because he felt serious issues could not be handled in haste. Thus, his letter was more of a philosophical treatise written in the florid style of the nineteenth century than a direct response to Ball's suggestions. The former professor lectured Ball on European history, past Portuguese glories, and the evils of American materialism. He spent five pages explaining his interpretation of the territories as a part of Portugal and its inhabitants as Portuguese citizens. He finally turned to Ball's suggested swap of U.S. aid for self-determination. He questioned how self-determination could "be imposed . . . by force of arms" and argued that America advocated self-determination not out of principle but only as "political pragmatism." Washington wanted to drive Portugal out of Africa in order to create weak states that could be easily dominated by the United States. Lisbon would never agree to economic assistance tied to decolonization: "The Portuguese have found it repugnant to accept aid which . . . is indissolubly linked with the demantling of the Nation." He concluded his critique of American diplomacy by judging it to have "political shortcomings and sociological gaps."[45]

This fresh evidence of Salazar's rigidity and arrogance, coming immediately after Chou's trip and Roberto's "turn to the left," led Johnson to become directly involved in the Angolan issue for the first time. He ordered Harriman to Africa to

45. Salazar to Ball, 3 March 1964, ibid.

counteract Chou's visit and to evaluate the situation in Angola. When the president announced Harriman's mission, some protested that it would be interpreted as undercutting Williams. Johnson quickly revised the press release to include a paragraph praising the assistant secretary and declaring that Harriman would "continue to rely heavily on Mennen Williams."[46] Nonetheless, Johnson's selection of Harriman for this mission indicates the power Harriman had gained within the administration.

Throughout his weeklong tour of Africa, Harriman raised the Angolan issue. On 23-24 March, he discussed the question with Kwame Nkrumah in Accra. In response to Nkrumah's demands for stronger U.S. efforts to gain "freedom for all of Africa," Harriman asked what Ghana had done to help freedom in East Europe. The veteran diplomat described efforts "to get Salazar to recognize the principle of self-determination" but mentioned America's concern that Angola and Mozambique "were not yet prepared for freedom, just as the Congolese were so thoroughly unprepared."[47]

Harriman next met with Adoula to discuss Chinese influence with Roberto. Adoula explained that Roberto was desperate because "time is running out, and Holden is under attack as an agent of the imperialists." He warned that GRAE could not hold forever "to a moderate position." Washington needed to force Salazar to negotiate soon or risk the complete collapse of anticommunist leadership of the liberation movement.[48]

While in Leopoldville, Harriman also talked with Algerian officials sympathetic to the more radical MPLA. They protested American aid to Roberto and reminded the under-secretary that the OAU had declared that all aid to African independence movements must go through its liberation committee. Harriman made it clear that the United States would continue to act independently and avoid any connection with the OAU "lest our bargaining position with Portugal disappear." When the Algerians persisted in their attack on America's policy and its failure to force Salazar to yield, Harriman announced that he had another appointment and left the room.[49]

Harriman did not meet with Holden Roberto, despite pleas from the Angolan leader. He explained that any contact with Roberto would immediately be noticed by Portuguese agents and "would completely destroy our usefulness vis-à-vis Salazar." Privately, Harriman offered another explanation. He cabled Rusk that "Holden is slipping" and might soon be forced out of leadership of the Angolan movement.[50]

Harriman's trip did little to reassure Africans of Washington's commitment to

46. Belk to Bundy, 13 March 1964, NSF: International Meetings and Trips: Harriman's Trip to Africa, box 2, Johnson Library.
47. Harriman to Rusk, 23 March 1964, ibid.
48. Ibid., 27 March 1964.
49. Ibid., 28 March 1964.
50. Ibid.

the immediate independence of the Portuguese territories. In his report to Johnson on 3 April, Harriman observed that the Africans were united in their determination to expel Portugal but argued that the guerrillas in Angola were not very powerful. He urged Johnson to continue efforts to convince Salazar to compromise but did not suggest any departures from existing policies.[51]

Harriman's African tour coincided with a thaw in U.S.-Portuguese relations largely resulting from the appointment of Admiral George Anderson as ambassador in Lisbon. Anderson was fervently dedicated to NATO and not overly concerned with African demands for independence. While he dutifully conveyed Washington's protests and suggestions for compromise, he personally was sympathetic to Portugal's position. Immediately prior to Harriman's trip, Anderson also toured Angola. In Africa he lavishly praised Portugal's lack of racial prejudice and advances in health and education. He denounced the rebels as "communists" and predicted a Portuguese military victory. He was rebuked by Rusk for his statements but remained strongly opposed to any American demands on Portugal for rapid decolonization.[52]

Anderson's statements were particularly galling to Mennen Williams, who had opposed Anderson's appointment and was repeatedly forced to explain the ambassador's comments to outraged Africans. Williams was also upset by Harriman's apparent refusal to push Johnson for a tougher approach toward Salazar. The American consul general in Mozambique informed Williams that the Africans were convinced that the United States had become "more favorable toward Portugal" and America was doomed to a total loss of influence in the liberation struggle unless it took immediate action to revitalize Roberto and stand up to Portugal.[53]

Roberto's flirtation with China and Salazar's refusal to agree to even minimum concessions convinced Williams that America finally must use its power to impose a settlement; otherwise, the United States would have to accept inevitable communist control of the liberation movement. On 29 April 1964, the African Bureau circulated an "Action Memo" on the Portuguese territories prepared largely by Williams, who sent copies to Rusk, McNamara, Bundy, Robert Kennedy, and the CIA in preparation for a full discussion on 4 May.[54] The memo argued that the conflict in Angola had reached a stalemate and that the rebels "have just admitted extremist and pro-Communist elements into the organiza-tion." America must act immediately and decisively, argued Williams, in order

51. "Meeting with the President RE Governor Harriman's Report on His Trip to Ghana, Nigeria, and the Congo," 13 April 1964, ibid.
52. For a detailed description of Anderson's attitudes, see "Memorandum of Conversation between Ambassador Anderson and President Salazar," 17 April 1964, NSF: Portugal, box 1, Johnson Library.
53. Thomas Wright to Williams, 1 April 1964, Williams Papers, box 28, National Archives.
54. Bureau of African Affairs, "Action Memorandum: Portuguese African Territories," 29 April 1964, NSF: Portugal, box 1, Johnson Library.

"to prevent the nationalists from mortgaging their future to the Communists and from reaching a stage where they will no longer be disposed to negotiate a moderate and evolutionary settlement."

Williams, however, rejected any new approach to Portugal as ineffective. He advocated an alternative strategy of a massive U.S. effort to convince the nationalists in Angola "to alter their tactics and develop a political action program" that would gain "broad-based support" by bringing new groups into the liberation movement. Convinced that Roberto and his followers could not win a military victory, Williams argued that they must fight a political battle similar to the decolonization efforts of the French and British possessions in the late 1950s. If the conflict remained essentially military, there was a good chance that Roberto "might soon be ousted by extremists" and replaced by "a pro Chicom leader." If the Angolans agreed to a shift in tactics, "the United States would be prepared to provide clandestine assistance" in helping GRAE in "setting up an extensive political organization within and outside the Territories" that would be "capable of bringing pressures to bear on Portugal to change its policies." A broad coalition of white, black, and mixed-race Angolans, united in a peaceful effort to gain independence, would, Williams asserted, "evoke significant international sympathy and impress on world opinion the need for a solution. . . . Even the Portuguese might feel obligated to face up to realities."

Williams admitted that the problem with the plan was to compel the rebels to accept nonviolence when "their whole strategy is based on guerrilla warfare." America could not expect Roberto to "keep his army 'on ice' indefinitely." Therefore, the project would have to be "massive and decisive" yet avoid being directly identified with the United States. All contacts should "avoid carrying a U.S. label, but rather seem to originate . . . by the leading African states." Washington should use Adoula, Tanzanian leader Julius Nyerere, "other selected African leaders and possibly Jawaharlal Nehru" to "sell the idea to the nationalists." The African intermediaries were to convince Roberto that "the issue can never be won militarily on the field" and that Portugal would resist any direct pressure from foreign nations. Only an extensive political movement within the colonies would bring independence. Such arguments must "overcome the insistence of extremist and pro-Communist elements to step up the terrorism." Once Roberto accepted the necessity of a political struggle, the U.S. would secretly provide money and advisers to make it work. American agents would help "organize an effective, resourceful, secret and extensive underground network" that could "undertake strikes and other public demonstrations."

Williams acknowledged that the operation would face the problem of "the ubiquitous and ruthless Portuguese secret police," but he felt it was worth the risk. If the United States could shift the battle from violence to peaceful protest, the rebels would gain "political and practical support from the American people.

The possibilities of private fund raising alone in the U.S. are almost limitless." American covert assistance would include "administrative support" for expanding the political base of GRAE. Specifically, Williams suggested that the United States supervise and finance

> a greatly expanded public relations program for outside consumption; clandestine radio stations, . . . printing presses and widespread circulation of leaflets, newspapers, etc.; nationalist cells in every village, industry, and large farm; penetration of the police and other Portuguese services . . . ; winning the support and cooperation of the tribal leaders; direct or indirect contacts with the white and mulatto elements in the territories, giving assurances of their continued presence . . . ; organization of peaceful demonstrations, ideally, leading up to a general strike.

What Williams and the African Bureau advocated was a major shift in strategy away from bilateral dealings with Portugal toward direct intervention in Angola. Overt protest would give way to covert use of American money and advisers. If Washington could make it appear as if Roberto had massive support, demonstrated by his ability to call strikes, mobilize mass rallies, and control disciplined cells of supporters, it could eventually still obtain its objective of African independence under moderate governments. Portugal would have to yield in face of such a united and broad movement. Roberto would be not just the head of a small band of guerrillas but the recognized leader of the Angolan people.

Administration reactions to Williams's suggestions recognized that they involved a major shift in policy. The U.S. consul in Mozambique hailed the plan as the only alternative to becoming "a helpless spectator" in the conflict. Senior officials in Washington, however, were not convinced of the proposal's effectiveness and were fearful of its risks. A brief note by Rusk prior to discussion of the document reminded the recipients "that consideration also needs to be given to the effects on our NATO relationships with and our military interest in Portuguese territory, as well as the place of Portugal in the NATO alliance."[55] Unlike Williams, the secretary of state doubted that a large commitment of American funds and agents to Angola would go undetected by Portugal. The plan would thus revive the possibility of losing the Azores and disrupting NATO. It was also unlikely that the United States could, in Williams's words, "reorient the whole strategy and tactics of an organization which until now . . . has concentrated primarily on violence." It would be nearly impossible for Roberto, already under attack as "an American stooge," to suddenly halt guerrilla warfare in favor of a lengthy political action program.

55. Wright to Williams, 23 May 1964, Williams Papers, box 28; Rusk is quoted in U. Alexis Johnson to the Attorney General, the Secretary of Defense, the Director, Central Intelligence Agency, and Mr. McGeorge Bundy, 3 May 1964, ibid., National Archives.

A major problem with Williams's plan was that it ignored the dynamics and politics of the revolution in Angola. It did not recognize that, while political action programs had been successful in the British and French colonies in the 1950s, they seemed obsolete in the Portuguese territories in 1964. The model for third-world decolonization was no longer the nonviolence of Gandhi but the guerrilla war in Algeria. Once a nationalist movement accepted force, it was difficult for it to return to passive resistance. When Wayne Fredericks met with Nyerere to discuss Angola, the African leader chided America for dealing with the situation as if it were 1960 not 1964. The uprising of 1961 had determined that Angola would be liberated by arms rather than through negotiations.[56] Williams's fascination with political organization and nonviolence shows his almost nostalgic vision of African politics. It indicates his great admiration for the American civil-rights movement more than an understanding of the independence struggle in Africa.

The Africa Bureau's recommendations were not vetoed directly but were allowed to die the slow bureaucratic death of postponement and inaction. Aside from strong reservations in the State Department and White House about the viability of the plan and its effect on the Azores and NATO, American intelligence reports also worked against the proposal. The CIA concluded that the independence movement in Angola did not have widespread support and that the war was not as disabling to Portugal as many in the African Bureau contended. Regardless of any change in the rebels' tactics, there was "little prospect for a change in Portuguese policies" until Salazar was removed and, "barring divine intervention, the good doctor will remain in office." Such an evaluation might have been used to support Williams's call for broadening the base of GRAE and abandoning violence, but the agency also was skeptical of the leadership ability of Roberto and unconvinced that Angola was ready for independence. It contended that the nation was still woefully unprepared for freedom. If it gained independence in the immediate future, it would revert to tribalism and chaos.[57]

The aborted call for an American-supported political action program was the last significant suggestion for direct U.S. intervention in Angola for over a decade. Washington continued its modest support of Roberto and its occasional prodding of Salazar but adopted no major new policies in the remaining Johnson years. When Moise Tshombe, the former leader of Katanga with strong ties to Europe, took control of the Congo in July 1964, America persuaded him to permit Roberto and the GRAE to remain in Leopoldville. In response to U.S. pressure, Tshombe allowed GRAE to continue its operations, but he limited

56. Fredericks to Williams, 29 May 1964, NSF: Angola, box 1, Johnson Library.
57. CIA Special Report, "Portuguese Economic Outlook and its Political Implications," 22 May 1964; CIA Special Memorandum No. 9–64, "Salazar's Current Prospects," 8 June 1964, NSF: Portugal, box 1, Johnson Library.

GRAE's ability to conduct direct military campaigns across the border into Angola.[58]

Portugal appreciated Tshombe's efforts to restrain Roberto. The U.S. consul in Luanda reported that Lisbon had "a good working relationship with Tshombe," and together they were effectively destroying Roberto's organization. "GRAE is virtually eliminated as an effective force," he concluded, "Roberto is a pathetic figure as a leader and has lost the respect of his troops as well as of other African leaders."[59]

Roberto's decline was accompanied by another Portuguese attempt to use America's strategic needs to convince it to limit pressure on Portugal concerning Angola. The foreign crises of the early Kennedy years had led Pentagon officials to demand more sophisticated weapons and equipment for U.S. military facilities abroad. They were especially insistent that America install long-range navigational aids (LORAN-C) in the Azores to help ships and planes establish their exact positions. As the United States remained a "guest" in the Azores, any additions to the base would have to be negotiated with Lisbon. On 5 January 1965, Rusk made his first direct approach to Portugal on the issue. He told Anderson to contact Portuguese officials with an offer to sell them American naval cannon and fire-control systems. He was to "use this to maximum effect vis-à-vis LORAN-C." Rusk mentioned that he had kept the offer from Portuguese representatives in Washington "in order to give you the opportunity to use it to the greatest advantage in Lisbon."[60]

Portugal rejected Anderson's overture, citing the continued criticism of the war in Angola by U.S. officials. The Portuguese were particularly upset with a "most unfriendly and ill-timed" speech by Williams that predicted the inevitable triumph of the nationalists in Angola and Mozambique. Anderson told Rusk that the talk was "unnecessarily offensive" and had destroyed "months of hard work" on the LORAN-C issue.[61]

After his rebuff on the naval deal, Anderson contended that the only way to secure permission for the new equipment in the Azores was to restore the military aid to Portugal that had been cut in response to the war in Angola. Rusk agreed that this was an option, but only if Portugal withdrew all U.S. equipment from Africa and gave firm assurances that any future supplies would "remain in the North Atlantic Treaty area." He added that "an agreement on LORAN-C would help," as the Defense Department and the State Department were both adamant that any aid be "conditional on a favorable response to LORAN-C sites." Ball later confirmed that Washington likely would be able to provide both weapons

58. Godley to Rusk, 11 July 1964, 17 July 1964, NSF: Congo, box 1, Johnson Library. See also Department of State Intelligence Note, "Moise Tshombe and the Angolan Nationalists," 17 July 1964, ibid.
59. Henry Reed to the Secretary of State, 27 July 1964, ibid.
60. Rusk to Anderson, 5 January 1964, NSF: Portugal, box 1, Johnson Library.
61. Anderson to Rusk, 6 February 1964, ibid.

and funds to Portugal if Lisbon guaranteed that the arms would not be used in Africa and agreed to the new radar system in the Azores.[62]

After further fruitless negotiations in Lisbon, Anderson, a career military man dedicated to the concepts of NATO and a strong defense, finally expressed his rage over the continued interference of African concerns on military necessities. He informed Rusk that he was "highly dubious as to the merit or net advantage to USG [United States Government] of continuing to hammer away at a theme at once unacceptable and unpalatable to GOP [Government of Portugal]." American support of the liberation of Angola and Mozambique had been not only "unproductive," but also "progressively erodes our good will, credit, and our ability to influence the Portuguese on other matters of importance to us." To Anderson, Washington had been "undesirably far out in front of practically all countries" on the issue. "While we continue to press and irritate the Portuguese on the matter of Africa and independence, other nations through a more passive role are picking up points and advantages."[63]

Many in Washington shared Anderson's opinion that continued demands for self-determination in Africa were too costly to American interests. The CIA, in an analysis of the LORAN-C question and African policy, predicted that Salazar would not force the United States out of the Azores unless there was "outright U.S. support for the nationalists." It did warn that Portugal would continue to stall any agreement on LORAN-C and would refuse a new lease for the Azores unless Washington agreed to provide weapons and to end its demands for self-determination.[64] Lisbon confirmed this interpretation. Anderson reported that the Portuguese wanted "a straight quid pro quo deal": a new lease for the Azores and permission to install the radar equipment in exchange for arms sales and an end of U.S. pressure for African independence. Portugal would agree not to use any new American equipment in Africa but would not remove weapons already in Angola.[65]

During its negotiations with Lisbon on LORAN-C and arms sales, the United States avoided any flare-up of hostilities by abstaining on a UN resolution directed at Portugal. Rusk cabled Stevenson that the motion would "not hasten the fundamental improvement in these territories that all of us hope for" but

62. Ibid., 2 March 1964; Rusk to Anderson, 3 May 1964; Ball to Anderson, 9 May 1964.
63. Anderson to Rusk, 6 May 1964, ibid.
64. CIA Special Memorandum No. 9-64, "Salazar's Current Prospects," 8 June 1964, ibid.
65. Anderson to Rusk, 10 July 1964, ibid. This became the basis for the eventual settlement of the Azores issue seven years later. In December 1971, Portugal agreed to a new lease for the base in exchange for $30 million in agricultural assistance, $5 million in "nonmilitary equipment" from the Defense Department, and up to $400 million in loans from the Export-Import Bank. Lisbon did not agree to remove U.S. weapons from Africa, and the Nixon administration had already curtailed public criticism of Portugal. See Ted Szulc, "Letter from the Azores," *New Yorker* 47 (January 1972): 54–58. Although telecommunication satellites had slightly diminished the importance of the Azores' navigational equipment, it became a crucial area for the massive American airlift of supplies to Israel during the Yom Kippur War in 1973.

would only encourage more violence. Fredericks explained in a speech following the vote that America was dedicated to "peaceful progress on the question of the Portuguese territories instead of further conflict."[66]

"Peaceful progress" still depended on some concessions by Portugal. Anderson reiterated his opinion that Lisbon was "in no mood to yield or . . . work towards possible compromise." Continued American demands would have no effect. To Anderson, the U.S. objectives in Africa were to "block communist penetration," keep the continent "Western-orientated," and insure "access to African markets for our commerce." Washington had two options for gaining these goals: sever relations with Portugal and back the rebels or end all contacts with the nationalists and all demands on Lisbon. Although Anderson clearly favored the latter, he argued that, "if we must stay in the poker game," the United States should separate African issues from European problems. Self-determination was an admirable goal but not worth the continued disruption of normal relations with a NATO ally. He advocated a retreat to the "middle ground" of total neutrality. Washington should stop "harassing" Portugal, end all aid to Roberto, and work with Lisbon for the reform of the colonies. If Portugal could be guaranteed a cease fire in Angola, it could shift its resources from military equipment to educational and social programs for the Africans.[67]

Anderson's recommendation for neutrality in the hope that long-range reforms would prepare the colonies for eventual freedom was a major departure from the early commitment of the Kennedy administration to immediate self-determination. His suggestions indicate the gradual shift of American diplomacy away from direct confrontation with Portugal and active support of the liberation movements.

Partly as a result of this "softening" of American policy, Roberto was in an increasingly untenable position. By late 1964, his GRAE was near collapse. Tshombe effectively blocked the promised aid from China and greatly limited U.S. assistance. The military campaign in Angola was nearly nonexistent. Roberto's followers attacked him for corruption, absolutism, and favoring his own Bakongo countrymen. At the OAU meeting in late 1964, Nkrumah dismissed him as "an agent of American imperialism." The OAU did reaffirm its recognition of GRAE but moved toward granting the rival MPLA equal status. Jonas Savimbi finally broke completely with Roberto and formed his own liberation organization.[68] Only the triumph of Joseph Mobutu in the Congo in 1965 saved Roberto from total collapse. Mobutu was a personal friend of

66. Rusk to USUN Delegation, 2 July 1964, NSF: Portugal, box 1, Johnson Library. Wayne Fredericks, "American Policy in Africa," *SDB* 51 (10 August 1964): 197–204.
67. Anderson to Rusk, 5 November 1964, NSF: Congo, box 2, Johnson Library.
68. Marcum, *The Angolan Revolution*, 2:169–72 discusses the problems of Roberto and the growth of the MPLA. Savimbi's new organization was União Nacional para a Independência Total de Angola (UNITA). It received some support from China to counter Soviet influence in the MPLA.

Roberto. He arrested Angolan critics of GRAE and restored the channels of foreign aid. Even though Roberto remained the nominal leader of Angolan liberation, his movement was in disarray. In contrast, the MPLA, aided directly by Cuba and the Soviet Union, flourished. In January 1966 a conference of nonaligned nations acknowledged MPLA as the sole representative of Angolan nationalism.

The decline of "America's man" in Angola coincided with the beginnings of guerrilla activity in Mozambique. America had maintained contacts with FRELIMO leader Mondlane and provided some economic assistance but had concentrated its efforts in Angola. In 1963 American intelligence sources were still unconvinced of the strength of the rebel movement in Mozambique. They predicted that FRELIMO could not mount an effective military operation against the Portuguese for several years. In the summer of 1964, Mondlane visited Washington to lobby for weapons. He met with Fredericks and other midlevel State Department officials who encouraged him to concentrate on political organizing rather than on violence. Denied American arms, Mondlane appealed to the OAU, China, and Russia for assistance. Peter Weiss, president of the American Committee on Africa, urged direct U.S. support to Mondlane as he was the only alternative to radical leadership in the nationalist movement. Washington responded that its policy was to provide arms only to official governments.[69]

In September 1964 FRELIMO, using weapons provided by the OAU, began terrorist attacks in Mozambique. Portugal now faced armed resistance in two colonies, and the United States effectively had been removed from influence in both. A year earlier the CIA had argued that there was little need to be concerned with "sleepy Mozambique." In late 1964 it concluded that FRELIMO had launched an effective guerrilla war and that Mondlane, under the influence of radical elements, was convinced that only warfare could ever force Salazar to negotiate.[70]

Mondlane's decision to use violence in Mozambique, Roberto's problems in maintaining leadership in Angola, and the apparent dominance of military considerations in U.S. diplomacy confirmed the worst fears of the Africanists. They had warned that an easing of American demands on Portugal would lead to radical control of the independence organizations and an end to any prospects for a peaceful solution. Fred Hadsel of the African Bureau admitted that advocates of an Africa-first policy had failed to keep the United States committed to

69. Weiss to Eric Goldman, Special Assistant to the President, 26 June 1964, White House Central Files, Country File: Mozambique, box 56, Johnson Library. [Hereafter cited as CF followed by the country.]
70. CIA Special Report, "Anti-Portuguese Campaign in Africa Shifts to Mozambique," 18 December 1964, NSF: Mozambique, box 1, Johnson Library.

African liberation and to sustained pressure on Lisbon. In a long memo to Williams on "Africa and the United States," he summarized the frustrations of his colleagues in the African Bureau, arguing that the Africanists had been unable to clearly define U.S. interests in Africa and persuade others of the need to back the liberation struggle. They had emphasized "self-determination, racial equality, and other general principles" judged less important than defense or European alliances. America's African policy had been eroded by "military needs and political imperatives." Africa did not have "established politico-military commitments (as in Europe), a threshold crisis (as in Cuba), or a sustained military expenditure (as in Asia)." As a result, a policy that was clearly dedicated to black liberation in 1961 had degenerated to "a collage of uncoordinated practices" three years later. Washington did not recognize that the end of white rule was "a 'manifest destiny' type of aspiration" for the Africans. Its support "is the touchstone whereby Africa measures attitudes of nations outside the continent." America's inability to force Salazar to yield and its refusal firmly to back the rebels had caused the Africans to dismiss the United States as "neo-colonial." America was now powerless to prevent a Marxist takeover of the independence struggle and the eventual creation of communist governments in Angola and Mozambique.[71]

Hadsel's predictions were prophetic. America continued to work with Roberto to revitalize his organization but refused to provide weapons or increased economic support. The CIA remained alarmed by the growing appeal of Marxism to the Angolans yet did not recommend any major efforts to strengthen Roberto in response.[72]

Williams, in particular, was frustrated as he observed the United States abandon its interest in the Portuguese territories. In early 1965 he had a bitter confrontation with Anderson over the relaxation of American demands on Portugal and the question of arms sales to Lisbon. Williams noted that Anderson "continuously interrupted" him and ridiculed suggestions that Washington again press Portugal to accept self-determination. Williams wrote Vice-President Hubert Humphrey and Robert Kennedy warning of the decline of American credibility in Africa and his "concern" that U.S. inaction would lead to radical control of the liberation movements.[73]

Williams's concern did not produce any action, because there were two major obstacles to the attempt to revive U.S. involvement. First, Portugal remained as intransigent in 1965 as it had been in 1961. Its officials still warned of the disasters of self-determination and claimed that communists controlled the African

71. Fred Hadsel, "Africa and the United States," June 1964, Williams Papers, box 29, National Archives.
72. On American attempts to help Roberto see Godley to Rusk, 24 March 1965, NSF: Congo, box 4, Johnson Library. For CIA concern about radicalism in the liberation movements see CIA Special Memorandum No. 14-65, "Prospects in Brazzaville," 17 May 1965, ibid.
73. "Memorandum for the Files," 16 January 1965, Williams Papers, box 5, National Archives.

rebellions. They reiterated their determination to fight forever to retain the "overseas provinces."[74] Second, direct U.S. military intervention in Vietnam in 1965 crushed any remaining possibility for renewed efforts to force Portugal to compromise. Even more than Berlin or Cuba, Vietnam shifted American attention from all other global issues. Diplomacy in Africa became largely concerned with trying to rally support for the war in Asia. Except for the crisis following Rhodesia's break with Great Britain in November 1965, Vietnam effectively subjugated all African issues, including the struggle in the Portuguese territories.[75] On 19 August 1965, Williams met for the final time with Johnson to try to revive interest in African liberation. He urged the president to take some "action on self-determination to improve our position in Africa." Williams found Johnson preoccupied with Vietnam and unwilling to risk the Azores or any loss of European support for the war.[76]

Portugal immediately capitalized on U.S. involvement in Asia. It gave strong verbal support to the war and tried to draw an analogy betwen America's attempt to contain communism in Vietnam and its own battle against "communist aggression" in Africa. Lisbon even announced that, in appreciation of U.S. efforts to preserve freedom in Asia, it would open Angola and Mozambique to U.S. trade and investment—after it had crushed the rebels in the territories.[77]

Whereas the U.S. had previously given covert support to Roberto and Mondlane, in 1965 it refused even to acknowledge a desperate appeal from the FRELIMO leader. In contrast, in May 1965 the CIA began "Operation Sparrow" to provide Lisbon with American aircraft for use in Africa. A CIA front company, Intermountain Aviation, sold seven B-26 bombers to Portugal to attack rebel positions in Angola and Mozambique, directly violating the long-standing pledge not to sell any weapons that would be used outside Europe. In September 1965, the Hungarian delegate to the UN exposed the arrangement. American ambassador Arthur Goldberg conceded that the planes had been flown from the United States to Lisbon, but he denied that the U.S. government had any knowledge of the deal.[78]

74. See, for example, Nogueira's speech "Guiding Principles of Portuguese Policy in Africa," 17 May 1965, in *Portuguese Foreign Policy*, 21–22.

75. G. Mennen Williams, Letter to the author, 15 January 1980. Johnson was also influenced by the recommendation of Edward Korry, former U.S. ambassador to Ethiopia, that America concentrate its efforts in Africa on the large, powerful states such as Nigeria and Zaire (the Congo).

76. "Resumé of Luncheon Meeting with the President," 19 August 1965, Williams Papers, box 5, National Archives. Williams resigned in March 1966 to run for the Senate from Michigan.

77. *New York Times*, 1 January 1966, p. 67.

78. Benjamin Read, Executive Secretary, Department of State, to Bundy, 8 October 1965, CF: Mozambique, box 56, Johnson Library; David Welch, "Flyboys of the CIA," *Ramparts* 5 (December 1966): 11–18; Victor Marchetti and John Marks, *The CIA and the Cult of Intelligence*, 243–45. See also Williams's protests of the scheme in his letter to Jeffrey Kitchen, Deputy Assistant Secretary of State, 15 September 1965, Williams Papers, box 5, National Archives.

The Justice Department prosecuted officials of Intermountain Aviation for violating the Munitions Control Act. They were acquitted when testimony disclosed that they were under contract to the CIA, that State Department officials had approved the sale, and that American military personnel had assisted in the transfer of the planes.[79] Goldberg's apparent ignorance of the project and the Justice Department's decision to prosecute indicate that "Operation Sparrow" was most likely a "rogue" initiative rather than an elaborate plot to aid Portugal. It does show, however, the willingness of at least some in the administration to actively support Lisbon in its battle with African nationalism.

Most U.S. officials simply adopted a policy of inaction. As Anderson had recommended, America abandoned any active involvement in the conflict. It continued to pay a retainer to Roberto but refused significant economic or diplomatic support of his organization. Washington rejected Portugal's demands for the massive sale of military equipment but did not push Lisbon for any compromise on decolonization or negotiations with the Africans.

Portugal was delighted with the shift in U.S. policy. After consultation with State Department officials in the summer of 1965, Nogueira announced that Washington had "adopted a more realistic attitude" on decolonization. He noted approvingly that Americans had finally recognized that the "same forces at work in Vietnam" were behind the violence in Angola and Mozambique.[80]

African leaders, on the other hand, denounced America's "retreat" as a cynical attempt to generate European support for the war in Vietnam. James Farmer, leader of the Congress of Racial Equality, toured Africa in 1965 and found its leaders nearly unanimous in their belief that the United States had abandoned black liberation to appease Portugal, preserve NATO, and concentrate on Vietnam. An article in *Foreign Affairs* in the fall of 1965 concluded that "Africa now has the lowest priority of any area" of American diplomacy. Decisions on African policy "are determined, not in the African Bureau of the State Department, but in the European Bureau."[81] When Under-Secretary of State Nicholas Katzenbach toured Africa to explain the war, he was confronted with near total opposition. Students argued that America was fighting "to make the Far East safe for Coca Cola." When Katzenbach tried to defend Vietnam as "a fight to preserve freedom," African leaders charged that Washington was providing weapons to prevent freedom in the Portuguese territories.[82]

As the war in Asia continued, America became even more cautious in its

79. *New York Times*, 7 October 1966, p. 14; 15 October 1966, p. 10.
80. *New York Times*, 26 June 1965, p. 5.
81. James Farmer, "An American Negro's View of African Unity," 70–77; Arnold Rivkin, "Lost Goals in Africa," 111–26.
82. Ibid., 19 May 1967, p. 2; 27 June 1967, p. 3.

relations with Portugal. Typical of the new concern for Portuguese sensitivities was a remark in 1967 by the new U.S. ambassador in Lisbon, Tapley Bennett. After de Gaulle withdrew France from NATO's military operations in 1966, the alliance shifted its naval facilities to Lisbon, giving Portugal even more leverage with Washington. When Scandinavian officials attacked Portugal for its continued refusal to grant independence to its colonies, Bennett urged the United States to remain silent rather than risk any further disruption of NATO. "If there is a Donnybrook," he wrote, "let us leave it to the Danes."[83] The policy of inaction had triumphed over the pursuit of moderation.

83. Bennett to Rusk, 20 May 1967, NSF: Portugal, box 2, Johnson Library.

6. "NO EASY SOLUTIONS" | Kennedy and South Africa

The interaction between domestic issues and foreign policy is complex. Diplomatic decisions can have a clear impact on domestic legislation or affect large and vocal segments of the population. Less often, internal matters can directly influence foreign affairs. The American civil-rights movement of the early 1960s was such an internal matter. It affected the nation's international relations generally, and especially its policy toward Africa. Because of its support of desegregation and legal equality at home, the Kennedy administration was at least verbally committed to similar objectives abroad. Thus, the pursuit of equality in the American South and in southern Africa created a rare case of reciprocity between domestic and foreign policy. Just as the internal "red scare" of the early 1950s and the global Cold War reinforced each other in their common battle against communism, the civil-rights movement and the demand for black rights in Africa became two aspects of the objective of ending racism. It was not coincidence that Kennedy's "new approach" to Africa directly followed the rise in black activism in the United States.

For a number of reasons, the commitment to equality was not unequivocal in either the South or Africa. Political considerations and conflicting priorities forced compromise and hesitation. Just as Kennedy had to overcome resistance to the use of federal power to enforce desegregation and needed to maintain Southern congressional support for his legislative program, so, too, did he confront strong opposition to a direct challenge to discrimination abroad. In both cases, the results were far short of what many liberals wanted. Kennedy and his aides were unwilling to take an uncompromising position in favor of immediate racial justice. Rather, they accepted equality as a long-term goal and tried to pursue pragmatic programs that would move them toward the objective. Often their tactics were cautious and their victories largely symbolic because they were reluctant to engage in confrontation for its own sake or to encourage expectations they could never meet.

South Africa was the most obvious target of the diplomacy of equality. Any foreign policy dedicated to human rights and an end to discrimination inevitably had to confront the problem of apartheid. Just as the state of Mississippi symbolized Southern intransigence, South Africa epitomized the defiant white regimes in Africa. The Portuguese at least claimed racial equality in their possessions (although their policies hardly supported it), and Rhodesia remained largely a British problem until 1965. Both areas were colonies, and America could pursue the difficult but clear goal of peaceful transition to independence and majority rule. South Africa was a far different case. It was independent of any effective foreign control, as illustrated by its withdrawal from the British Commonwealth in 1961. Whites did not have the option of leaving Africa for "home." To most whites in South Africa, equal rights meant majority rule and eventual economic and political suicide. They based their entire social, economic, and political systems on racial separation, in direct opposition to the growing American acceptance of legal equality. Apartheid made South Africa the most visible example of legal racism and invited at least symbolic assault by the new administration.

Kennedy was, however, limited in what he could do about apartheid. There was no significant guerrilla movement in South Africa as in Angola and no "mother country" to pressure. South Africa was far more important to the U.S. economy than any other nation in Africa and was of considerable strategic significance to the West. The whites were firmly entrenched and seemingly immune to outside criticism. The limits on U.S. actions in South Africa were at least equal to those restricting its pressure on Portugal over Angola. Even though South Africa did not have an Azores base, it provided crucial minerals, allowed America to operate important missile-tracking stations, and made its ports available to the U.S. fleet. It was anticommunist and supported American foreign policy on non-African issues. As a result, the Africanist-Europeanist split was again evident as humanitarianism and the need for third-world friendship clashed with more immediate interests.

To many American liberals, the obvious option for dealing with South Africa was to impose economic sanctions. Ending trade and withdrawing investments would be a dramatic gesture of America's fundamental disagreement with apartheid and would force the Nationalists to alter their policies. To Kennedy and most of his advisers, however, sanctions were both impractical and dangerous. They doubted a trade embargo would have sufficient impact to force whites to yield. Any hardships resulting from sanctions would likely be borne largely by the black majority rather than by the white minority. In addition, unless there was an effective global boycott, any number of other nations eager to deal profitably with the white government would rapidly replace U.S. firms. Many in Washington also feared that sanctions might cause Afrikaners to become even more fanatical in their fear of black unrest and more determined to maintain absolute control. A trade embargo or withdrawal of investments might deepen their isolation and encourage more militant suppression of the majority. Finally, effective sanctions would have to come from the UN and would be a dangerous precedent for the organization. Reprehensible as it was, apartheid was a domestic policy, and the UN was committed by its charter to intervene only in cases of an imminent "threat to world peace."

While some in Kennedy's administration would push hard for sanctions, the consensus in Washington was steadfastly against them. This left the United States with restricted options for effective action. It could and did verbally denounce apartheid and the Nationalist government with a vehemence rare for a country that enjoyed "normal relations" with America. It attempted to "disassociate" the United States from the South African government by desegregating American facilities in South Africa, protesting discrimination against its citizens, and supporting limited resolutions in the UN. Ultimately, it declared a limited arms embargo.

In determining his approach to South Africa, Kennedy also had to consider American economic interests, although American economic involvement in South Africa in the early 1960s was not extemely large when compared with other areas of the world or even with the rest of Africa. The nation absorbed less than 2 percent of U.S. exports from 1960 to 1965, and trade with South Africa declined steadily relative to the rest of the continent throughout the period. American investments amounted to slightly less than 1 percent of its overseas total and yielded about 1.5 percent of foreign returns. South African exports to the U.S. were more significant. From 1960 to 1965 they averaged a bit less than 9 percent of Pretoria's total.[1]

The recent debate over institutional and corporate divestiture of holdings in South Africa has led to an exaggerated emphasis on the influence of economics on past U.S. policy. It is true that American business leaders generally opposed any moves that might limit their trade and investment in the area. Kennedy also realized that the favorable trade exchange with South Africa was helpful to the U.S. balance of payments. Concern about possible loss of profits for American corporations, however, was rarely a crucial determinant in policy decisions. Strategic, military, and other interests were generally far more important. Obviously, certain American industries were heavily dependent on continued good relations with South Africa. Pretoria also provided the United States with gold and other essential materials. Direct economic interests, however, remained only one of a number of considerations in shaping policy. Fears of adverse effects on the U.S. economy were not crucial in the choice to reject sanctions or other diplomatic decisions.

In addition to America's economic interest, Kennedy also had to take into account the ramifications of domestic black protest, although the civil-rights movement was also less important on specific policy matters than some have argued. Certainly black protest was essential in making racial equality a goal of American diplomacy. The violent reaction to peaceful demonstrations against segregation generated indignation and idealism that naturally led to a concern about discrimination abroad. Blacks were less effective in influencing precise

1. U.S. Congress, *Hearings, U.S.–South African Relations*, pt. 1, 44–45.

diplomatic actions. Although black leaders regularly pushed for a stronger stance against apartheid, they never created a powerful lobby in international issues. Blacks never had the influence on African policy that the small but organized Jewish community had on U.S. relations with Israel or even that the old "China lobby" had on American policy in Asia. Most blacks were naturally more concerned about domestic race relations and legislation than with foreign affairs. Prior to 1965, their major effort was in the fight for desegregation in the South with only occasional attention to diplomacy. The administration soon found that it could compromise in its specific dealings with the white regimes without fear of massive black reaction as long as it maintained its rhetorical dedication to the larger but more abstract goal of equality.

The decolonization of Africa and the domestic civil-rights movement led to an American determination to show opposition to continued minority rule, but the same two forces made the Nationalists in South Africa even more fanatical in its defense. Events in Africa, the UN, and the American South in the late 1950s and early 1960s created a seige mentality in South Africa and led to political and military preparation for the suppression of any challenge to apartheid.

By 1960 France, Britain, and Belgium were largely resigned to the end of colonization. The uprising in Angola in 1961 indicated that eventually Portugal also would be pushed off the continent. Macmillan's "winds of change" speech calling for an accommodation with black nationalism and the Sharpeville incident a month later were further indications of the growing isolation of South Africa and the likelihood of increased internal resistance to white rule. In April 1960 there was an assassination attempt on Prime Minister Hendrik Verwoerd. Three months later, the Congo disintegrated into factionalism, civil war, and, most disturbing to South Africans, black attacks on the remaining Europeans. Accompanying these incidents were growing attacks on the Union in the UN and from African and Asian nations in the British Commonwealth. UN Secretary General Dag Hammarskjöld conferred with South African officials in January 1961 on their violations of UN principles and bluntly warned that the organization would increase its demands on Pretoria.

Black protest in the United States (and its endorsement by a large number of whites), Washington's "abandonment" of South Africa in the UN after Sharpeville, and the election of a president favoring desegregation forecast growing pressure for change from South Africa's most powerful ally. It seemed to the white Nationalists that they were going to have to confront an angry black continent and a restless black majority without support from either Britain or America. They faced the choice of accepting the "winds of change" or preparing for a protracted struggle to preserve their racial system. Few even mentioned the first option, and Pretoria mobilized for the defense of white rule. In a national referendum in 1960, whites voted to establish an independent republic. In March 1961, Verwoerd walked out of a meeting of Commonwealth nations, and on

31 May 1961, fifty-nine years after the end of the Boer War, South Africa became a republic free of British or Commonwealth ties.

Accompanying the political change was a military buildup in the early 1960s. South Africa poured its wealth into arms, troops, and police. The defense budget jumped from 43,500,000 Rand in 1960–1961 to 120,000,000 Rand two years later and over 250,000,000 Rand by 1966. Expenditures for the police and the police reserves showed similar growth. The nation also undertook a crash program to manufacture its own weapons, more than doubling munitions appropriations each year from 1960 to 1966. Military preparedness also extended to the private sector, as shooting clubs became one of the most popular forms of recreation in the early 1960s. South Africa grimly prepared for the ultimate battle with black nationalism.[2]

Kennedy thus faced an armed, isolated, and increasingly militant South Africa when he took office. The Nationalists expected Kennedy to reverse Eisenhower's tacit cooperation with white governments. His appointments of Williams, Bowles, and Stevenson, so pleasing to American liberals, heightened South African fears of immediate problems with Washington. Likewise, many Americans also expected the new administration to "get tough" with Pretoria. Democratic Sen. Frank Moss of Utah predicted a dramatic change in policy toward apartheid under Kennedy. He forecast a clear U.S. commitment to "freedom" in South Africa, active encouragement of "believers in self-determination" in the Union, and an immediate end to "temporalizing" in the UN on racial issues. The *New Republic* contended that, although other areas of the continent were important, South Africa was "the real touchstone of American intentions in Africa." Kennedy would be judged on his willingness to stand up to the Nationalists.[3]

Most liberals were not clear on what specifically they expected the government to do about South Africa. While black students published an "Open Letter to President Kennedy" demanding that he break diplomatic relations with Pretoria and impose immediate economic sanctions, most interested Americans called only for "new approaches" and official disapproval of apartheid.[4] Some diplomats feared that liberal and black demands for a major "new approach" toward South Africa would push Kennedy into a hasty and fruitless confrontation. Attacking South Africa had become "some kind of liberal 'loyalty test,'" and diplomats feared that frequent attacks on South Africa might force a rash action that would threaten American strategic interests. Harlan Cleveland,

2. Vernon McKay, "South Africa and Its Implications for American Policy," 1–32. See also Elizabeth Landis, "The New Order in South Africa," *Africa Today* 8 (October 1961): 4–6. One Rand was equal to about $1.40 in 1960.

3. *New York Times*, 24 December 1960, p. 1; Patrick Duncan, "South Africa: America Can Help," *New Republic* 145 (3 July 1961): 19–21.

4. *New York Times*, 22 June 1961, p. 14; Peter Ritner, *The Death of Africa*, 274–300, is a good summary of liberal expectations.

assistant secretary of state for international organization, was worried that a correct and sincere commitment to desegregation at home would produce an overreaction to South Africa's domestic racial laws. George Ball was equally upset with the rising demands for some decisive action against apartheid. To Ball, apartheid was "a plague of the mind" that could only be cured by "healing ideas." Rather than driving the country deeper into isolation, the United States should retain all economic, political, and cultural contact with South Africa to expose the Afrikaners to "the evolving social ideas of the West." According to Ball, the liberals' belief that Washington could force the Nationalists to accept equality was "pie in the sky." Too aggressive a policy would only feed Afrikaner paranoia and endanger vital U.S. interests.[5]

The Europeanists' apprehension about South Africa was caused, in part, by the vitriolic attacks on South Africa in the speeches of many New Frontiersmen. Upon taking office, Kennedy immediately ended the official silence on apartheid that, with the brief exception of the period immediately following Sharpeville, had characterized the Eisenhower administration. Throughout 1961, Williams, Bowles, and American representatives at the UN assailed South African racism. Bowles was the strongest advocate of a verbal offensive against apartheid. In response to a suggestion by Cleveland that the tough speeches by U.S. officials might alienate the Nationalists to the extent of destroying America's ability to work for peaceful change, Bowles defended "opening-up" on apartheid. "We must keep our position with the South Africans clear on the basic moral question," he argued. American rhetoric must be so strong that the Afrikaners would realize that Washington's dedication to equal rights was absolute.[6]

Mennen Williams became the "point man" in the administration's public criticism. In his tours of Africa and in speeches across the United States, he denounced apartheid and promised strong American efforts to change it. Apartheid was "a wrongheaded policy, fraught with dangers not alone to the peoples of South Africa, but to international peace," he concluded. He pledged that the United States would "stand up and be counted" at the UN and elsewhere on issues of self-determination and racial equality.[7]

Stevenson and his staff continued the campaign in New York. In April, Francis Plimpton declared, "The United States is squarely, utterly, and irreversibly opposed to the policy of racial discrimination epitomized in the term apartheid." Later he implied support of the resistance movement in South Africa when he stated that America "rejoices in the bravery of the men and women of South Africa who . . . fight day-by-day for racial justice." He predicted apartheid was

5. Peter Duigan and Lewis Gann, "White and Black in Africa," *National Review* 10 (28 January 1961): 47–49; Harlan Cleveland, *The Obligations of Power*, 126–34; Ball, *The Discipline of Power*, 255.

6. Bowles to Stevenson, 6 March 1961, Bowles papers, box 299, Yale University.

7. Williams, "South Africa in Transition," *SDB* 45 (16 October 1961): 638–42; "The Three 'A's' of Africa: Algeria, Angola, and Apartheid," ibid. (27 November 1961): 280–88.

doomed to failure: "How and when the South African Government will abandon its hateful racial policies one cannot know, but abandon them it will."[8]

Such language was a major departure from the timidity of earlier American diplomats, but the strength of the language was not matched by the policy. The African Bureau launched an early campaign for decisive actions to show American opposition to apartheid. It suggested an end to International Monetary Fund loans to South Africa, as they "subsidize apartheid," a cutback in U.S. arms sales, and active "discouragement" of new American investments. When these ideas were rejected, Bowles chided Kennedy for a reluctance to use American power to force the Nationalists to alter their policies. To Bowles, only direct U.S. pressure for change could save South Africa from a race war. Without rapid modification of apartheid, South Africa would "blow-up." He asked the president, "When this occurs, will we be able to say that we took every practical measure to prevent or temper the holocaust?"[9]

Most influential in resisting an immediate "get-tough" policy were Dean Rusk and the U.S. ambassador to South Africa, Joseph Satterthwaite. Rusk was as dedicated to civil rights and racial equality as anyone in the administration, as his eloquent testimony in favor of the civil-rights bill illustrated. As secretary of state, however, he tried to separate domestic and foreign issues. Although he deplored apartheid, he was not convinced that anything beyond verbal attack was practical in 1961. He was overwhelmed by the problems resulting from the Bay of Pigs invasion of Cuba and did not feel the United States was ready for any additional international crises. Satterthwaite agreed. As head of the Bureau of African Afffairs under Eisenhower, he had generally agreed with the Africanists' perspective. He was, however, a conservative career diplomat, unimpressed by "idealists" such as Williams and Bowles. He opposed any dramatic or sudden diplomatic initiatives and hesitated to intervene in the domestic matters of a foreign nation. He also was surrounded by a consular staff in South Africa that, in the words of one White House aide, was "as far right as any one in the U.S. Government on the subject of South Africa." Like Anderson in Lisbon, Satterthwaite worked to smooth over differences between the United States and the country in which he was posted. While he disapproved of discrimination, he did not feel Washington should push the Nationalists too hard and risk other important American interests.[10]

In response to Rusk's insistence, the United States deferred a "get-tough" policy in favor of preparing a carefully worded statement of the new administration's position on South Africa. Eventually, Foreign Minister Louw,

8. Ibid. 44 (24 April 1961): 602; Vernon McKay, *Africa in World Politics*, 352.

9. Williams to Fredericks, 23 June 1961, Williams papers, box 1, National Archives; Bowles papers, box 297, Yale University.

10. Satterthwaite oral history interview, Kennedy Library; William Brubeck, Executive Secretary, Department of State, to Bundy, undated, NSF: South Africa, box 159, Kennedy Library.

alarmed by the speeches of Williams and others, asked Satterthwaite if Kennedy was planning any abrupt changes in U.S. policy that threatened the "future cooperation" between the two powers. Rusk responded with an aide-mémoire setting forth official American policy. The secretary denied Kennedy was preparing any sudden shift in Washington's position but expressed America's "concern at evidence of increased racial tensions in South Africa and the country's drift toward international isolation." Rusk warned, "The U.S. can only view the continuance of South Africa's official policy of apartheid in terms of ultimate disaster to South Africa." Even those in Washington "who wish to retain close friendship with South Africa find themselves unable to accept a governmental policy which compels and perpetuates a system which denies fundamental human rights to the vast majority of the country's population." Rusk rejected Pretoria's assertion that its racial policies were a domestic matter. Apartheid violated the UN Charter and weakened the free world's ability "to resist Communist influence and penetration in the newly emerged Afro-Asian nations"; it was an international issue of grave concern to the United States.[11]

Rusk's statement, delivered by Satterthwaite to Louw, was an official presentation of the administration's position. The document reassured Pretoria that, despite some press reports, Washington did "not regard the white population as being expendable" and did not demand immediate majority rule. The United States did expect gradual relaxation of restrictions on nonwhites and preparation for their "full participation" in the political system. Until the Nationalists made such changes, America would continue to cooperate on matters of "mutual benefit to both countries," but "the U.S. could not be expected to cooperate in matters which . . . support South Africa's present racial policies." Rusk avoided elaborating on the distinction between "matters of mutual benefit" and "matters" that support apartheid, since he was announcing a broad policy rather than its exact details.

Military cooperation seemed to fall within the "mutual benefit" category. In late 1960 Pretoria had agreed to the establishment of U.S. missile-tracking facilities on its territory. However, as in the case of the Azores, Washington faced a deadline for renewal, since the one-year contract was to expire on 31 December 1961. Kennedy's dedication to the space program and the military's need for uninterrupted missile testing led to discussions with South Africa in the summer of 1961 for extension of the lease. South Africa made it clear it would renew the agreement only if the United States assisted in its arms buildup. Stevenson strongly opposed any new sales of military equipment given the opposition to South Africa at the UN and the official American position rejecting cooperation with apartheid. Rusk was sympathetic but reminded Stevenson that the missile stations were necessary for U.S. security. The UN ambassador replied,

11. Rusk to Satterthwaite, 25 August 1961, NSF: Africa, box 2, Kennedy Library.

"Relations with the rest of Africa, and especially the new states, are important to our security too."[12]

Bowles also lobbied against any arms deal. He argued that third-world demands for action against apartheid compelled Washington to end any formal cooperation with the Nationalists. The missile-tracking stations already kept America from acting as a "free agent" in its dealings with Pretoria. He noted that South Africa already had prodded the United States to agree to joint naval maneuvers in the fall. The South Africans were now demanding $100 million in airplanes and parts, $37.5 million from the International Monetary Fund, and American support for membership in the UN Outer Space Committee, "although they do not have a chance of being elected." Bowles contended, "If it were not for the leverage provided to the South African Government by the tracking stations," Washington could end all military aid, follow an "aggressive" policy at the UN, and gain valuable influence among the African nations. The United States would "probably have to pay a heavy political price" if Kennedy agreed to any additional arms sales. Bowles questioned whether the tracking stations were crucial to American defense and important enough to allow South Africa to use them to force agreement on other areas. The African Bureau followed Bowles's note with a strong memo urging abandonment of the satellite facilities on the grounds that they restricted freedom of action against apartheid.[13]

As in the Azores decision, strategic considerations triumphed. Kennedy ordered Jerome Wiesner, his special assistant on space and technology, to survey the military on the future need for the tracking stations. Wiesner reported that their loss "would be painful, but not fatal." Therefore, he urged that the United States not "be deliberately provocative" toward South Africa "nor permit the need for the site to be the reason for compromise on issues which the State Department regards as fundamental in the conduct of its foreign policy."[14] Washington agreed to sell limited arms for South African defense, rather than for internal use, in exchange for continued use of the tracking sites.

As the Africanists predicted, the arms deal weakened the impact of the rhetorical attacks on South Africa. The speeches by Williams, Plimpton, Stevenson, and others implied a frontal assault on apartheid, but American actions in the UN and elsewhere showed a continued refusal to accept an open confrontation with the Nationalists. Despite the verbal crusade against apartheid, the United States remained opposed to economic sanctions or an arms embargo. Throughout 1961, America blocked efforts at the UN to impose mandatory sanctions. Its lobbying finally forced a weak resolution that left it to

12. Martin, *Adlai Stevenson*, 641.
13. Bowles to Bundy, 21 September 1961, NSF: Africa, box 2, Kennedy Library.
14. Wiesner to Bundy, 18 October 1961, ibid.

the discretion of individual nations whether they would trade with South Africa.[15]

The decision to provide South Africa with weapons and to oppose sanctions contrasted with the continued symbolic attack on the National government. When Chief Albert Luthuli, confined by South Africa for his activities in the African National Congress, was awarded the 1960 Nobel Peace Prize, Williams strongly urged Kennedy to publicly congratulate him. American officials in Pretoria, however, warned that such a move would be a direct affront to the South African government. After lengthy discussions within the State Department over wording and timing, Kennedy sent a congratulatory telegram, but he avoided the lengthy tribute that the African Bureau had wanted. He also sent identical telegrams to other Nobel winners to make the response look more routine.[16]

By the end of 1961, Kennedy's middle course had alienated both Africanists and Europeanists. Bowles and Williams fumed about the reluctance to firmly oppose the white regime and pointed out the gap between the administration's oratory and its actions. In contrast, former ambassador to South Africa Phillip Crowe blasted the State Department for its public attacks on a nation "strategically important and anti-communist." Crowe predicted Kennedy and his advisers were preparing to abandon a loyal ally that had made a great deal of progress in improving the economic and educational opportunities for its black population. He argued: "We should keep her [South Africa] as a friend—even as a friend with whom we cannot possibly agree on internal policies, but with whom we very definitely do have an enemy in common in the cold war."[17]

The rhetoric that so worried Crowe did not have much impact on either white or black Africans. What did infuriate the new African states was America's rejection of sanctions, continued sale of weapons, and "normal" diplomatic relations with Pretoria, the very things that reassured whites in South Africa. Verwoerd told parliament that the speeches of Williams and others showed that the United States and South Africa "have differences regarding our color problem" but actual policy indicated America "is a safe and sure and permanent friend of the Union."[18]

In May 1962, in response to the continued internal battle over the correct policy toward apartheid, the State Department circulated an official "Guidelines for Policy and Operations." Based largely on Rusk's earlier aide mémoire, the

15. Nielsen, *The Great Powers and Africa*, 288–92. See also Moses E. Akpan, *African Goals and Diplomatic Strategies at the United Nations*, 90–93.

16. Williams to Kennedy, 3 November 1961; Department of State to Bundy, 13 November 1961; Kennedy to Luthuli, 15 November 1961, NSF: Africa, box 2, Kennedy Library.

17. Bowles to Rostow, 21 December 1961, Bowles papers, box 300, Yale University; Phillip Crowe, "A Diplomat's Advise: Keep South Africa as a Friend," *U.S. News and World Report* 51 (18 December 1961): 86–88.

18. American Committee on Africa, *The South African Crisis and U.S. Policy*, 6.

guidelines repeated the need to "distinguish between noncooperation in matters directly or indirectly related to apartheid policy, and cooperation in all other fields." The document showed the continued splits within the administration. It deplored apartheid as a violation of basic freedoms but observed that the United States also had "important military and economic interests in South Africa" that prevented too aggressive a policy. It rejected sanctions and other direct moves as "excessive pressure" that "could result in internal disintegration and anarchy in South Africa which would not be in our interest." It accepted a long-range goal of "gradual integration of the non-white population into the fabric of one nation" while simultaneously urging caution to avoid a race war that would lead to "communist infiltration and possible eventual control." America should work for relaxation of apartheid and the growth of "moderate political elements" yet resist UN pressure for direct international action. The report recommended "no public demonstration of our disagreement with apartheid" but urged private suggestions to U.S. business leaders "to be cautious, particularly with regard to long-term investments." It advocated maintaining the missile stations but encouraged the Defense Department to look for alternative sites.[19]

The African Bureau and some White House aides criticized the official "Guidelines" for being too cautious. In June, Williams organized an "Advisory Council on Africa" of academic, business, labor, and black leaders to advise the department on policy. As he expected, the council came out in favor of stronger efforts to show U.S. opposition to apartheid. Rostow's Policy Planning Group also issued its own evaluation of South Africa. Unlike the formal "Guidelines," this evaluation called for an arms embargo, continued verbal attacks, and support of UN resolutions against apartheid and against South African control of South West Africa (Namibia).[20]

Despite such dissension, Washington continued its dual policy of normal relations with "noncooperation" on apartheid. It repeated its condemnations of Pretoria's racial laws in the UN but opposed direct motions against the South African government. When African states introduced resolutions calling on member nations to end political and economic relations with Pretoria and asking the Security Council to consider expelling South Africa, Kennedy ordered Stevenson to oppose both moves. The president considered the resolutions "grandiose and ineffectual" and commissioned Schlesinger to work with Plimpton on a speech explaining the American position. Williams tried to point out that voting against the resolutions would "undermine our credibility in the Afro-Asian world," but he was opposed by most others in the State Department.[21]

19. "Republic of South Africa: Department of State Guidelines for Policy and Operations," May 1961, NSF: Africa, box 2, Kennedy Library.

20. "Report of the Advisory Council on African Affairs," undated; Department of State Policy Planning Council, "The White Redoubt," 28 June 1962, ibid.

21. Schlesinger, *A Thousand Days*, 579–81; Williams to Rusk, "UN Resolution on Apartheid," 1 November 1962, Williams papers, box 2, National Archives.

On 19 October 1962, Plimpton told the General Assembly that expulsion of South Africa would remove it "from the one place where the full weight of world opinion can be brought to bear on it." While sanctions offered "a means for a discharge of our own emotions," they would be unworkable and thus "weaken the authority of the United Nations, debase the effectiveness of its resolutions and generally impair its reputation." They would turn the UN into a meaningless organization like the old League of Nations. He tried to retain some good will among third-world nations by announcing that the United States would end the sale of weapons that could be used to enforce apartheid.[22]

American actions in the UN provoked a rare display of black protest over foreign policy. The American Negro Leadership Conference adopted a resolution deploring "our government's opposition to the United Nations' resolution calling for sanctions against South Africa." Martin Luther King declared that blacks demanded more than just "wordy condemnation" of apartheid and announced that he had joined with Chief Luthuli in an international campaign to force Kennedy to adopt economic sanctions.[23]

Aside from the traditional arguments that sanctions would not work, would be a precedent for future UN intervention, and would likely make the Nationalists even more intractable, there was growing concern in Washington that outside pressure on South Africa was encouraging blacks to use violent protest. Satterthwaite was particularly fearful of what he saw as rising communist influence in the nation. He told Rusk that radicals within South Africa were using the attacks on apartheid by foreign leaders and the repeated UN resolutions to entice blacks to sabotage and terrorism. The South African Communist party, although banned for over a decade, was "an old, well-trained, well-disciplined party" that "exercises an influence far greater than would be expected." Satterthwaite called for expanded American military aid for "counter-insurgency" by the white regime in response to the new threat.[24]

Those outside the government also worried about a potential communist influence in southern Africa. An influential book edited by Zbigniew Brzezinski of Columbia University on *Africa and the Communist World* warned that southern Africa was the target of a massive effort by the Soviets and Chinese to subvert black nationalism for their own gains. By supporting the black majority against white rule, the communists could infiltrate African liberation groups that would later be turned "into serviceable instruments of communism."[25] Although it did not see such a clear communist plot, the Policy Planning Council also was concerned that too strong a Western stance against South Africa might

22. *SDB* 47 (19 November 1962): 791–94.

23. *New York Times*, 24 November 1962, p. 2; 2 December 1962, p. 24. See also E. Eric Lincoln, "The Race Problem and International Relations," 39–59.

24. Satterthwaite to Rusk, "U.S. Overseas Internal Defense Policy—South Africa," 18 December 1962, NSF: Africa, box 3, Kennedy Library.

25. Zbigniew Brzezinski, ed., *Africa and the Communist World*, 13–14.

either provoke a major outbreak of racial violence, which "would enhance Sino-Soviet Block opportunities," or unite Portugal, Rhodesia, and South Africa into a "common front against black Africa." It recommended continued American efforts to promote peaceful reform rather than "a frontal assault on South African apartheid."[26]

These sudden American worries about communism were promoted by incidents of sabotage and other forms of violence in South Africa in 1962 and 1963. "Spear of the Nation," the "action arm" of the African National Congress, and Poqo, a splinter group of the Pan-Africanist Congress, both undertook sporadic attacks on police stations and other symbols of the white government. These acts of terrorism convinced some Americans that blacks were moving toward a new form of violent resistance in South Africa. Satterthwaite met with Luthuli to discuss the bombings and sabotage and reported that, while Luthuli remained dedicated to nonviolence, other blacks were convinced of the need for a terrorist campaign.[27] In a special report on "Subversive Movements in South Africa," the CIA downplayed the violence and concluded that neither "Spear of the Nation" nor Poqo had broad support. Despite this assessment, fear of possible communist inroads in a violent liberation struggle in South Africa worked against any major change in U.S. policy. Even Williams expressed fear that "hard core communists" were gaining influence in the resistance movements in white Africa.[28]

American reaction to the specter of communism in South Africa can best be understood as part of a rising concern about radicalism throughout the continent. In particular, the continuing crisis in the Congo had a major impact on Kennedy's perception of Africa. The president was convinced that the chaos in the Congo would pave the way for communist gains. Unless stability was achieved in the former Belgian colony, Democrats might be accused of "losing" the Congo just as they had been charged with "losing" China in 1949.[29] Kennedy generally maintained Eisenhower's policy of supporting the UN in its efforts to maintain stability and unity in the Congo, while working to keep former Prime Minister Patrice Lumumba from any position of power. To American officials, Lumumba was a dangerous radical. CIA head Allen Dulles was convinced Lumumba was "a Castro or worse," and his agency had prepared several plans, including assassination with a special poison, to deal with him. In January 1961, Congolese troops murdered Lumumba. Although there is no direct evidence that the United States ordered Lumumba's murder, when his death was announced in February, African leaders quickly blamed Washington. Ghana's leader, Kwame Nkrumah,

26. Department of State Policy Planning Council, "Problems of Southern Africa," 6 May 1963, NSF: Africa, box 3, Kennedy Library.
27. Satterthwaite to Rusk, 6 May 1963, ibid.
28. CIA Special Report, "Subversive Movements in South Africa," 10 May 1963, ibid.; *New York Times*, 8 June 1963, p. 8.
29. Weissman, *American Foreign Policy in the Congo, 1960–1964*, 136–51, 191–94.

spoke for many when he charged that Kennedy had arranged the murder to shore up "American puppets" in the Congo.[30] The virulent attacks on America following the death of Lumumba dampened enthusiasm for a new policy of closer cooperation with black African leaders. The continued turmoil in the Congo also gave support to those in the United States (and in South Africa) who argued that black Africa was not prepared for immediate majority rule.

Kennedy's actions in the Congo also provoked the condemnation of American conservatives, who accused him of being too supportive of the UN and of betraying a stable, pro-Western, anticommunist regime in Katanga. The American Congo lobby, a loose coalition of conservatives headed by Sen. Thomas Dodd of Connecticut and by the *National Review* magazine, railed against the administration's commitment to the central government. Even within the administration, there were major splits over policy toward the Congo. Caught between the anger of the Africans and the vocal criticism of conservatives at home, Kennedy's approach to the Congo became, in the words of one scholar of American policy, "the product of pure caution." Dismayed by the controversy over his actions in the Congo, it is not surprising that Kennedy exhibited the same caution in his dealings with South Africa.[31]

Aside from the fear of instability and communism, other forces worked to limit any significant U.S. efforts against Pretoria. Most American business leaders were strongly opposed to economic sanctions, an arms embargo, or any other direct pressure on South Africa. A survey of American executives active in South Africa found that an overwhelming majority considered apartheid an internal affair. They were convinced that statements by U.S. officials attacking South Africa hurt their businesses and that Kennedy was too sensitive to black Americans in his dealings with Pretoria. Clarence Randall, former president of Inland Steel, visited South Africa in 1962 and wrote that Washington had "no stauncher ally in the struggle against communism." He suggested that the administration "drop the tough talk" and recognize that "the white people of South Africa are charged with a great responsibility toward the black people, and they know it. At heart they are our kind of folk. In the end they will do right."[32]

Opponents of the civil-rights movement also criticized any American action against the white regime in South Africa. Segregationists repeatedly ridiculed Washington's assault on apartheid. Typical were the remarks by Rep. Clarence Cannon of Missouri, who denounced the United States for siding with "the jungle Bantu and against the white man, who was there before the native

30. For details of U.S. plots against Lumumba and the reaction to his death, see Madeleine G. Kalb, *The Congo Cables*, 128–96. Nkrumah's statement and the reactions of other African leaders are summarized in Francis H. Russell (U.S. ambassador to Ghana) to Rusk, 15 February 1961, NSF: Ghana, box 99, Kennedy Library.

31. Weissman, *American Foreign Policy*, 192.

32. Greenberg, "U.S. Policy toward the Republic of South Africa, 1945–1964," 104–7; Clarence Randall, "South Africa Needs Time," *Atlantic* 211 (May 1963): 78–80.

African." He equated America telling South Africa to give blacks equal rights with Pretoria "telling us to give the nation back to the Indians."[33] The most celebrated case of the interference of a Southern politician was the visit of Sen. Allen Ellender of Louisiana to Africa. An avowed segregationist, Ellender made a series of diplomatically embarrassing remarks culminating in the statement that black Africans were "incapable of self-rule" and "will need the whites for another 50 years." He also pledged U.S. support for "the civilizing whites" on the continent. The senator's comments provoked a storm of black criticism, formal protests from six African nations, and public repudiation by the State Department.[34]

In attacking America's African policy, Southern politicians were partly hoping to retain the support of their constituents angered by the administration's campaign for desegregation of the South. The violent opposition to black protest, peaking with the confrontations in Birmingham, Alabama, in the summer of 1963, heightened administration fears that black Africans would focus on America's internal racial problems rather than its foreign policy. The African Bureau carefully monitored the African press and prepared special summaries for Kennedy after each major demonstration in the South. Williams and his aides repeatedly urged more decisive action on domestic civil rights to aid effective foreign policy.[35]

In fact, South Africans were interested in the battles in Mississippi, Alabama, and the rest of the South. Even though they feared the rise in black militancy in the United States, they also tried to use it as proof of the need for strict white control. Verwoerd cited the violence in America in a speech to parliament defending racial separatism and white political dominance. South African ambassador William Naude met with Williams immediately following the violence in Birmingham and suggested that the "recent problems" in the South might help the United States be more understanding of the racial situation in Africa and the wisdom of apartheid. Williams strongly defended integration and racial equality. He reminded Naude that America had been dedicated to self-determination ever since Woodrow Wilson. The South African replied that "Wilson had never contemplated self-determination except for homogenous peoples."[36]

33. *New York Times*, 4 March 1963, p. 5.
34. Ibid., 6 December 1962, p. 9; Rusk to American Embassay Accra, 6 December 1962; Department of State Circular 1032, 4 December 1962, NSF: Africa, box 3, Kennedy Library. When he returned to the United States, Ellender repeated his statements and issued an 830-page account of his trip. See *New York Times*, 8 March 1963, p. 2, and Collin Gonze, "With Ellender in Africa," *Africa Today* 10 (May 1963): 4–6.
35. See the folder "Civil Rights" in the Williams papers, box 3, National Archives; and Carl Brauer, *John F. Kennedy and the Second Reconstruction*, 240–41.
36. Nielsen, *African Battleline*, 62; "Memorandum of Conversation between Mennen Williams and South African Ambassador William C. Naude," 3 June 1963, Williams papers, box 3, National Archives.

The growing white support for legal equality in America convinced many in South Africa that Kennedy would be forced into a tougher stance against apartheid. Well aware of the successful public relations efforts of Portugal, the Nationalists launched their own effort to sway U.S. opinion. Like the firm of Selvage & Lee hired by the Portuguese, they concentrated on key individuals as well as the general public. The South Africans not only hired private advertising agencies to create "a true picture of South Africa" but also used the semi-official South Africa Foundation to finance trips by business, religious, and political leaders to South Africa for "man-to-man" talks with individuals in their own fields. One of the most successful sponsors of the exchange program was Charles Englehard of Newark, New Jersey, the chairman of Rand Mines and a major contributor to the Democratic party. Others active in recruiting American visitors were Clarence Randall and former Secretary of the Treasury John Snyder. The foundation also made use of the old "China lobby," the "Friends of Katanga," and other conservative groups.[37]

In 1963, South African efforts to retain American support took on a new urgency as the nation became increasingly isolated in international affairs. In July, the UN moved to exclude both South Africa and Portugal from its Economic Commission for Africa. In August, a conference on International Trade and Tourism asked both nations to withdraw, and the next month the World Health Organizaion and the International Labor Organization both refused to seat delegates from South Africa. Washington was caught in the middle by such actions. It had argued that South Africa should remain in the UN, but the administration was under Afro-Asian pressure to help bar Pretoria from specific committees and meetings. The U.S. delegation did vote to deny South Africa admission to the International Labor Organization meeting, but it was not clear if this was a general policy. Cleveland wrote Satterthwaite that the South African issue was going to come up in every international conference and urged the ambassador to persuade Pretoria to "exercise restraint in its future participation in international organizations." When Satterthwaite failed to respond, Rusk cabled similar instructions. He told Satterthwaite that if South Africa declined to attend such conferences, the United States would work for a statement of noncooperation rather than for actual expulsion. The plan worked. Unlike Portugal, South Africa either withdrew or refused to send delegates to most international meetings. America responded by blocking efforts to expel the absent nation but did push through resolutions urging noncooperation instead.[38]

Such cosmetic compromises were the result of the middle-of-the-road policy in Washington. The administration found it increasingly difficult to maintain

---

37. Colin Legum and Margaret Legum, *South Africa*, 243–55.
38. Cleveland to Satterthwaite, 1 July 1963; Rusk to Satterthwaite, 5 July 1963; Department of State Memo for Mr. Bundy, "Addis Ababa Conference of African Heads of State," 27 May 1963, Williams papers, box 3, National Archives.

such tortuous diplomacy in the face of united African pressure. The establishment of the OAU and its call for the immediate liberation of the continent forced Kennedy to make clearer policy choices. The organizational meeting of the OAU in May 1963 coincided with the violence in Birmingham. Washington feared a strong resolution attacking U.S. segregation as well as apartheid. Milton Obote of Uganda did issue a statement condemning white violence in the American South. He noted that blacks in Alabama, "who, even while the conference was in session, have been blasted with fire hoses" and attacked by "snarling dogs," are "our own kith and kin." Their only offense "is that they are black." Obote noted that "nothing is more paradoxical" than such violent opposition to equal rights at a time when Washington was trying to "project its image before the world screen as the archetype of democracy and the champion of freedom." Strong lobbying by Rusk, Williams, and "friendly" African nations avoided an OAU resolution linking the United States with South Africa and Portugal. A substitute statement passed expressing "deep concern" but offering "appreciation for U.S. efforts" to end discrimination.[39]

The blocking of the direct OAU condemnation of American racial policies still left the problem of the organization's call for the liberation of white Africa and the demand that all nations break relations and end trade with Pretoria. While it soon became apparent that many OAU members were themselves ignoring such advice, State Department officials acknowledged that it would become increasingly difficult to continue to oppose sanctions without infuriating nearly all of black Africa.[40]

Williams was the most concerned with the OAU resolutions and the continued burden that segregation placed on American effectiveness in Africa. He had long urged passage of a civil-rights bill for international as well as domestic purposes. He warned Kennedy that discrimination and the violent southern response to black protest aided communist propaganda and encouraged the white minority regimes. He noted that South Africa took "comfort in U.S. troubles" and had used Birmingham as an example of American duplicity in opposing apartheid but not enforcing equality in the South. Williams gained Rusk's permission to form a special "working group" on civil rights and foreign policy headed by Rollie White, deputy special assistant for psychological strategy, to counteract communist propaganda. The group recommended that the U.S. Information Agency make "honest presentations" of American racial problems but put more emphasis on "constructive steps" by the government. It also urged the USIA and other agencies to highlight "racism in the Soviet bloc and Red China." It

39. Edward Korry, U.S. ambassador to Ethiopia, to Rusk, 23 May 1963; Department of State Memo for Mr. Bundy, "Addis Ababa Conference of African Heads of State," 27 May 1963, ibid.
40. Department of State Memorandum for the President, "Addis Ababa Meeting and Related African Developments," 1 June 1963, ibid. See also Colin Legum, "The West at Bay," *Nation* 197 (10 August 1963): 72.

suggested passing information on communist racial problems gathered by U.S. intelligence agencies to "selected newsmen" in America and Africa.[41]

Rusk shared Williams's conviction that segregation was morally wrong and harmful to U.S. foreign policy, but he feared that the racial struggle at home might provoke a major incident with the white governments abroad. When he heard that the UN Special Committee on Apartheid had invited Martin Luther King to testify, he wrote Kennedy of his "serious reservations" about the move. King had "no special knowledge about South Africa," and his appearance would focus on American rather than South African racial problems. Rusk reported that the Costa Rican chairman of the committee had "consistently cooperated with the United States" and had agreed to make King "confine his public testimony entirely to South Africa," but the press was expected to "blow up" the incident. The secretary suggested Kennedy use his scheduled meeting with King to ask the civil-rights leader to plead "the pressure of other duties" to cancel. If he insisted on speaking, Kennedy should mention "the serious implications" of his appearance for U.S. foreign policy.[42]

Partly in response to the black protests at home and the OAU resolutions in the summer of 1963, the administration decided to risk a minor confrontation with South Africa. Prior to his election, Kennedy had joined others in criticizing the exclusion of blacks from official receptions at American facilities in South Africa. In 1960, the U.S. embassy had finally integrated some social affairs, but all official functions still were limited to whites. In 1963, Rusk ordered Satterthwaite to integrate the traditional Fourth of July reception in Pretoria. Satterthwaite protested that the order put him "in a real dilemma." The Fourth of July party was the most important social event of the year for Americans abroad and, if it was multiracial, would lead to a boycott by all South African officials and possibly result in the arrest of nonwhites who attended. The issue was even more difficult because the affair was to be in Pretoria, the center of Afrikaner nationalism, rather than in Capetown, where there was "a more tolerant attitude towards such gatherings." Finally, there was a law against serving alcoholic beverages to Africans, and the party would have to be either dry or illegal. Satterthwaite suggested cancelling the entire affair and substituting private parties hosted by U.S. officials in their homes.[43] Despite such protests, Rusk was adamant. On 13 June, Satterthwaite announced that blacks would be invited to the party, but there would be a separate informal reception for governmental officials. Integrated gatherings were held in all U.S. consulates, but South

41. Williams to Kennedy, "Civil Rights," 15 June 1963, Williams papers, box 3, National Archives; African Bureau, "Status Report on Civil Rights in the United States and American Missions in Africa," 5 July 1963, ibid., box 16; Rollie White, "Race Relations and U.S. Foreign Policy," 19 July 1963, ibid. |

42. Rusk to Kennedy, 21 June 1962, NSF: South Africa, box 159, Kennedy Library. King eventually cancelled his appearance before the UN to prepare for the march on Washington in August.

43. Satterthwaite to Rusk, 16 May 1963, NSF: Africa, box 3, Kennedy Library.

African officials and American business leaders boycotted them. The U.S. representative at Port Elizabeth reported his embarrassment when none of the leading American businessmen showed up. The snub by his own countrymen was "shocking" and "the talk of the town."[44]

The integration of social functions did not ease the growing pressure for economic sanctions against South Africa. Even conservative African leaders such as Houphouet-Boigny of the Ivory Coast warned Washington that it could no longer avoid deciding between black Africa and the whites in Pretoria. Alex Quaison-Sackey of Ghana, the new president of the General Assembly, announced that America must "take a stand one way or another" on South Africa and "we will know who our friends are" following the vote on sanctions.[45]

Kennedy and most of his aides still rejected sanctions but recognized the need for some action to preserve American influence with the new nations. Almost inadvertently, Williams provided the answer. In a memo on U.S. policy and South Africa on 12 June, he advocated "a more vigorous stance against apartheid" in response to the OAU resolutions. He argued, "There are no 'moderates' on the colonization issue and apartheid is looked upon by Africans as another facet of colonialism." Williams knew the president opposed economic sanctions. Instead, he suggested America announce an embargo on the sale of arms to South Africa.[46]

The idea of a unilateral end to shipment of military equipment was not new. Stevenson had suggested it in January 1963, and Rusk had opposed additional South African purchases of weapons in March.[47] To Williams and Stevenson, an arms embargo was a first step toward economic sanctions. They saw it as the initial escalation of pressure on the Nationalists to moderate apartheid. To Kennedy, however, the idea offered an immediate solution to a difficult situation. An embargo would be a dramatic gesture of opposition to racism that would not involve complete economic sanctions. A sudden announcement of a ban on weapons sales would deflate criticism of Washington's refusal to accept sanctions and win the approval of the nonaligned nations. The United States already had banned the sale of small arms and other weapons that could be used against the black population. A total embargo was the type of practical and decisive move that so appealed to Kennedy.

The president immediately began preparations for the announcement. He ordered the Defense Department to study the impact of a total ban on weapons and to compile information on what was already scheduled to be delivered to Pretoria. Harold Brown of Defense registered his opposition to the plan but

44. *New York Times*, 14 June 1963, p. 12; H. F. Byrne to the Department of State, 5 July 1963, Williams papers, box 16, National Archives.
45. *New York Times*, 17 June 1963, p. 13; 27 June 1963, p. 5. See also Akpan, *African Goals*, 95–98.
46. Williams to Rusk, "U.S. Policy towards South Africa," 12 June 1963, NSF: Africa, box 3, Kennedy Library.
47. Stevenson to the Department of State, 23 January 1963; Rusk to Kennedy, 16 March 1963, ibid.

dutifully provided the figures on present commitments. Ralph Dungan, one of Kennedy's special assistants, surveyed the various factions in the government on the embargo issue. He found six distinct groups ranging from the "partisan view" of the African Bureau, which supported the move as the first step toward a total break with South Africa, to the "businessman's view" of "don't rock the boat" and the "global strategist's view" of keeping close relations with Pretoria "at all costs." Dungan advocated the "activist view" of a bold approach to show distaste for apartheid while avoiding mandatory sanctions.[48] Williams was encouraged by Kennedy's obvious interest in his suggestion and, in July, sent a more detailed rationale for the plan to Rusk. He argued, "A complete arms ban is the least the U.S. can do to maintain our position of influence with the Africans and our ability to prevent more radical and violent action on their part."[49]

Although Williams and others in the African Bureau thought the arms embargo a conservative measure and "the least the U.S. can do," there was considerable opposition to the idea. Ball feared it was a preliminary step toward sanctions. Alexis Johnson, under-secretary for political affairs, attacked the proposal as ineffective because other nations would still sell weapons. He reminded Rusk that the current policy of not providing materials that could be used against the black population gave Washington "flexibility and room to maneuver." A complete embargo, however, risked loss of the missile-tracking stations and the use of South African ports.[50] Rusk also had strong reservations. He observed that there were "many other states where obnoxious practices of one sort or another exist" aside from South Africa, particularly "the violation of human rights within the communist bloc." He cautioned that the United States "is not the self-elected gendarmes for the political and social problems of other states."[51]

Despite Rusk's concerns, it was clear by the middle of July that Kennedy had accepted the notion of an arms embargo combined with continued opposition to economic sanctions. He ordered Bundy to prepare an analysis of the possible effects of the action on the missile sites and other areas of cooperation with South Africa. Bundy reported that the tracking stations represented a $50 million investment but were not of great strategic importance, as "nothing we have there is vital." He took the opportunity to offer his own support of the embargo: "I myself remain quite favorable to the Black African position, in spite of this possible dollar cost."[52]

48. Harold Brown, "U.S. Policy towards Portugal and the Republic of South Africa," 8 July 1963, ibid.; Ralph Dungan, "Background of the South African Problem," 9 July 1963, Arthur M. Schlesinger papers, box 1, Kennedy Library.
49. Williams to Rusk, 12 July 1963, "Arms Policy and South Africa," Williams papers, box 3, National Archives.
50. Ball to the American embassy, Algiers, 2 July 1963; Johnson to Rusk, "U.S. Policy towards South Africa," 14 June 1963, NSF: South Africa, box 159, Kennedy Library.
51. Rusk to Johnson, 15 June 1963, ibid.
52. Bundy to Kennedy, "Missile Tracking Stations in South Africa," 13 July 1963, NSF: South Africa, box 159, Kennedy Library.

On 16 July, Ball reluctantly agreed to the plan as long as it was clearly understood that it did not imply further actions. He told Kennedy that he and the State Department were "anxious to avoid political and economic sanctions, but are ready to support a total arms embargo provision in a Security Council resolution."[53]

Kennedy, however, wanted the embargo to be an independent American action, not dependent on the UN. On 16 July, he met with Tanganyikan leader Nyerere in the White House. The two clashed on the sanctions issue, but Kennedy leaked the news of an impending American arms ban. He asked Nyerere "to hold what was said in confidence for the time being." At a press conference, the two leaders quipped that they "had agreed to disagree" on sanctions but avoided any mention of weapons.[54]

Stevenson and his staff in New York were worried that the president might make a premature public statement of the embargo and urged Kennedy to keep the move secret so they could make the announcement in the UN and soften criticism of their forthcoming vote against mandatory sanctions. The arms embargo gave them a chance to balance their negative votes with a positive step against apartheid.[55] On 17 July, Rusk met with ambassador Naude and told him that, while Stevenson would resist efforts to expel South Africa from the UN and would vote against binding sanctions, he would verbally condemn apartheid and announce an American ban on weapon sales.

Three days later, Naude, having received instructions from his government, called on Rusk. He read a long defense of apartheid and explained that "the Negro in America was far different from the Bantu" as he "has lost his African character, except possibly for music." Rusk was polite and even interested when Naude expounded on a possible future South African confederation of black and white states, but he refused to yield on the arms embargo issue.[56] Undeterred, Naude returned four days later and went down the hall to Alexis Johnson's office, with whom he was much more belligerent than he had been with Rusk. He accused Kennedy of giving in to Asian and African "blackmail" and sarcastically asked Johnson to present the "logic behind an arms embargo." He also threatened retaliation: "Is full weight given to South Africa's gold supply? . . . the Free World would be in a bad way without gold . . . And what about uranium?" He demanded that Johnson convince the administration "to rethink

53. Ball to Kennedy, "Next Steps with South Africa," 16 July 1963, ibid.

54. A summary of the conversation is in a memorandum "Proposed Lockheed Sale to South Africa," 22 September 1964, NSF: South Africa, box 2, Johnson Library; *New York Times*, 18 July 1963, p. 6.

55. Charles Yost, USUN Delegation, to Rusk, 17 July 1963; Memorandum of Conversation, "South Africa and the Security Council Meeting," 17 July 1963, NSF: South Africa, box 159, Kennedy Library.

56. Memorandum of Conversation, "The Secretary and Ambassador Naude of South Africa," 20 July 1963, ibid.

its position." Johnson took the diplomatic tack and stressed the "common interests" of the two countries in containing communism, but Naude returned immediately to the embargo. The meeting ended on a frosty note as "Mr. Johnson concluded the conversation by saying we are deeply distressed over the present state of our relations with South Africa."[57]

While the decision for an arms ban had been made, its secrecy caused problems for U.S. representatives at the UN. On 22 July, blacks occupied Stevenson's office protesting American inaction on apartheid and opposition to sanctions. Stevenson told the demonstraters that he "was trying like hell" to end apartheid, but he became irritated when they charged him with having abandoned morality for profits and strategic interests. "I will not be lectured to about moral issues," he shouted and left the room.[58]

Kennedy's approval of an arms embargo left to Rusk and Stevenson the problems of working out the details. It soon became obvious that the president did not want a permanent ban on all weapons but rather a qualified statement that would allow the United States to meet existing contracts and to review the situation in the future. The administration's position was to work for a UN resolution that was "recommendatory not mandatory" and with language that made clear the embargo was "without prejudice to requirements which may arise for maintaining international peace." If Stevenson could not convince a majority to accept this "escape clause," he was to announce a unilateral embargo but make clear its limitations.[59]

Rusk ordered Stevenson to tell sponsors of the resolutions aimed at South Africa of the decision to end weapon sales in hopes of getting them to soften the language "to assure that the resolution itself explicitly leaves us the flexibility for making future deliveries of strategic items such as submarines or anti-submarine weaponry if we concluded our national interest . . . makes this desirable." The United States had contracts with Pretoria "which we must honor," and "at some future time" Washington might want to provide equipment necessary for "the overall security interests of the free world community." Rusk assured Stevenson that this was "not an effort in any way on our part to hedge or delimit our support for the concept of an arms embargo" but was necessary to maintain some latitude in case of communist aggression.[60]

The State Department also objected to a statement in the pending resolution regretting "that some member states are indirectly providing encouragement in various ways to the Government of South Africa to perpetuate by force its policy of apartheid." Rusk felt this was aimed at the United States and "we do not feel

57. Memorandum of Conversation, "United States Embargo of Arms to South Africa," 24 July 1963, ibid.

58. *New York Times*, 23 July 1963, p. 6.

59. Department of State "Memorandum for the President," 2 August 1963, NSF: South Africa, box 159, Kennedy Library.

60. Rusk to Stevenson, 1 August 1963, ibid.

vulnerable on this . . . but we do think the resolution would be open to misunderstanding."[61]

Stevenson and his aides found it difficult to convince the Africans and Asians of the wisdom of the complex U.S. position. America opposed sanctions but favored a "recommendatory" arms embargo. The resolution, even though not binding, must be worded to allow America to provide weapons in the future. At the same time, the United States was working against an arms embargo on Portugal. As one observer concluded, the United States was "straddling the fence, with an ear to the ground, an eye to the future, and a finger in the dyke."[62]

During a week of hurried cables and calls between New York and Washington, Stevenson tried to implement the complicated American position. He abstained on the 31 July resolution banning arms for Portugal. On 2 August, unable to gain support for a weakened "recommendatory" arms embargo for South Africa, he announced his "bombshell." First he attacked the idea of mandatory sanctions as "both bad law and bad policy." He cited the wisdom of the founders of the UN in reserving chapter 7 for situations in which "there was the actuality of international violence," which did not apply to the situation in South Africa. The resolution would only encourage violence by "stifling the emerging voices of reason" in the nation. "We cannot accept the proposition that the only alternative to apartheid is bloodshed," he stated. "We cannot accept the conclusion that there is no way out."[63] Having made clear the continued U.S. opposition to sanctions, Stevenson paused and announced the unilateral American weapons ban, but with the required qualifications: "We expect to bring to an end the sale of all military equipment to the Government of South Africa by the end of this calendar year. . . . There are existing contracts which provide for limited quantities of strategic equipment for defense against external threats. . . . We must honor these contracts." He next added the "escape clause":

> The Council should be aware that in announcing this policy the United States as a nation with many responsibilities in many parts of the world would naturally reserve the right in the future to interpret this policy in the light of requirements, for assuring the maintenance of international peace and security. If the interests of the world community require, we would naturally feel able to do so without violating the spirit or the intent of this resolve.[64]

Five days later, the United States voted in favor of a UN resolution for an end of weapons sales to South Africa, but only after Stevenson had again explained American commitments to existing agreements and possible future alterations.

The arms embargo was the major effort of the Kennedy administration to show

61. Ibid.
62. Nielsen, *The Great Powers and Africa*, 297.
63. *SDB* 49 (17 August 1963): 7.
64. Ibid.

its hatred of apartheid and its sympathy with the frustrations of black Africa. It was intended to serve a number of purposes: to recoup losses from the abstention on the 31 July Angolan resolution; to moderate African rage at the failure to support sanctions; and to show clear American opposition to apartheid while preserving "flexibility" in future arms policy. It was neither total nor irreversible. While Kennedy and some of his advisers saw it as a dramatic new step, it was also a conservative gambit to avoid more radical measures. Having ruled out economic sanctions, Kennedy was left with only the arms issue. Fearing that a UN resolution would lock America into a complete weapons ban, he moved to a unilateral statement of policy that left considerable room for manuevering but would still generate third-world support.

The action only partly achieved its intended results. Some liberals and blacks were impressed that principle had apparently triumphed over profits. Others pointed out that South Africa was nearly self-sufficient in arms production and that Stevenson's promises to deliver weapons already agreed to and his desire to reserve the right to sell arms in the future severely diluted the move. The *New Republic* acknowledged the announcement was "a sort of psychological victory for the black African nations," but one with "little practical significance." It contended that if Kennedy really wanted to express his opposition to apartheid, he should have agreed to sanctions that would have a major impact on Pretoria.[65]

Foreigners saw more significance in the arms embargo than did most Americans. A British official argued the move signaled a general American abandonment of whites in Africa for the pursuit of black votes at home. He found it "curious that there is only one area of foreign policy in which America and Russia completely agree, and that is demanding the immediate freedom of all the African races and self-determination." C. W. De Kiewiet, a South African historian and president of the University of Rochester, claimed the move only further isolated liberals in South Africa and heightened Nationalist fears of foreign hostility. He described a meeting of academics at the University of Capetown that degenerated into "animal anger" at the American "stab in the back."[66]

The official South African reaction was predictable. Louw made the U.S. action the major topic of an address to a Nationalist party rally. He blamed the embargo on Williams, Stevenson, and Robert Kennedy, who were "blinded by hatred for South Africa." He exempted Rusk, calling him "one of the moderate members of the Kennedy Administration" who was unable to block the liberal vendetta against Pretoria. He told the cheering crowd that the government was considering retaliating by banning American ships from South African ports or ending gold sales to the United States. In Washington, Naude attacked Kennedy

65. *New Republic* 149 (17 August 1963): 7.
66. O. B. Bennett, "Where Negroes have the Whites on the Run," *U.S. News and World Report* 55 (9 September 1963): 69–70; C. W. De Kiewiet, "Loneliness in the Beloved Country," 413–28.

for trying to "buy black votes" and vowed nothing could deter South Africa from completing its plans for total separatism of the races.[67]

Despite its limitations, the embargo did represent a shift in U.S. policy that encouraged those in the government favoring stronger measures against South Africa. Stevenson reported that it was hard to continue to oppose sanctions against South Africa and Portugal while working for an economic embargo against Castro's Cuba. He urged additional steps to "disassociate" America from South Africa, including a ban on the sale of oil, a reduction of the U.S. diplomatic and consular staff, a boycott of selected South African goods, and cutbacks in commercial flights and tourism.[68]

Such suggestions were exactly what many in the administration had feared. Once the United States announced the arms embargo, there would be pressure to adopt further actions. Having won one battle, liberals and Africanists would demand additional curbs on normal relations. William Attwood, former ambassador to Guinea and now part of the American UN delegation, supported this interpretation when he sent a memo to the State Department urging an end to any new American investments in South Africa and a downgrading of the U.S. representative in Pretoria from ambassador to chargé d'affaires.[69]

While they lobbied for adjustments in policy such as those advanced by Stevenson and Attwood, the Africanists' real objective remained economic sanctions. They were unable, however, to overcome executive and State Department opposition. The State Department's Bureau of Intelligence and Research concluded that sanctions "would have little economic impact on South Africa" because America sold few items vital for the nation. In contrast, Pretoria had significant "economic leverage" with its control of gold, since a cutback on the sale of gold would cause a severe drain on American reserves already depleted by the U.S. trade deficit.[70]

Others opposed the move for political reasons. For example, Ball reiterated the argument that sanctions would only drive the Nationalists deeper into isolation and result in new oppression of the black majority. A boycott would harm the American economy and threaten strategic interests, while "the options of the beleaguered party are too broad, and the psychology of the besieged is too perverse" for sanctions to really alter apartheid.[71]

The push for action beyond the limited arms embargo failed in the fall of 1963. Increasingly, U.S. officials found it difficult to enforce the announced arms ban. Stevenson's statements that America would meet existing contracts created a

67. *New York Times*, 11 September 1963, p. 6; Williams to Naude, 14 September 1963, Williams papers, box 3, National Archives.

68. Stevenson to Rusk, 21 August 1963, NSF: South Africa, box 159, Kennedy Library.

69. Attwood, *The Reds and the Blacks*, 139–40.

70. Department of State Bureau of Intelligence and Research, "Research Memorandum: U.S. and South African Economic Leverage on Each Other," 12 August 1963, NSF: South Africa, box 159, Kennedy Library.

71. Ball, *The Discipline of Power*, 245.

major problem in defining *existing* and in dealing with long-term agreements to provide parts and maintenance materials. Stevenson reported that African delegates at the UN were pressing him on "exactly what we mean." He predicted that, if Washington supplied material beyond the announced 31 December cutoff date, third-world nations "could only conclude our arms policy is a phony." He urged immediate delivery of all weapons that had been contracted for so he could announce "unequivocally" that all sales had been stopped by the end of 1963.[72]

The major source of dispute was a promise to sell South Africa submarines and airplane parts. Lockheed Corporation had a long-term contract for the parts and was negotiating for submarines that could not be shipped until well after the end of the year. Delivery of these materials, while technically within the "escape clause" of Stevenson's statement, would, in the words of the State Department, create "problems of public opinion." However, discussions between Lockheed and Pretoria had begun prior to the announcement, and the sale would provide badly needed revenue to help the balance of payments.[73]

On 9 September, the president told Stevenson that he was leaning toward permitting the sale of the submarines. Stevenson pointed out that this would pose problems with the Africans who were convinced that the embargo was total as of 31 December. Kennedy claimed that the deal would mean nearly $100 million for the United States and "if the Africans are going to be mad for three days we can take it. If they are going to stay mad, it may not be worth $100 million." The president's remarks appeared in the next morning's *New York Times*, and Africans seized on the comments as an example of the cynical maneuverings of America. Kennedy was infuriated by the leak. He suspected Stevenson of having passed on his remarks to block the sale, but it was later proved that Schlesinger had lunched with James Reston of the *Times* and mentioned the conversation.[74]

A few days later, Stevenson was again upset when he heard the administration was considering selling antisubmarine airplanes to South Africa. He cabled Rusk that his interpretation of the embargo was that there would be "no further contracts undertaken" unless there was a direct threat to international peace. The airplane deal indicated that the United States was "in fact not changing our previous policy at all" and "put in question the sincerity of our public utterances and the sincerity of our opposition to apartheid." South Africa would quickly recognize that the arms embargo was "simply pandering to black Africans" and of no real importance.[75] Rusk and McNamara considered the problem and finally recommended that Kennedy approve the sale of submarines, planes, and parts as they would earn America between $75 and $90 million. The arrangement should be done "quietly" to minimize African and liberal attacks.

72. Stevenson to Rusk, 9 August 1963, NSF: South Africa, box 159, Kennedy Library.
73. Memorandum for the President, "Sale to South Africa of Submarines and Spare Parts for C–130's," 28 August 1963, ibid.
74. Martin, *Adlai Stevenson*, 771–72.
75. Stevenson to Rusk, 13 September 1963, NSF: South Africa, box 2, Johnson Library.

They noted that Stevenson was "not too happy with this position," but it was not a direct violation of his 2 August announcement because it was still before the 31 December cutoff date.[76]

Williams also was "not too happy." He had told African leaders that the embargo was a significant change in U.S. policy and that America "would cease all cooperation with the South African military." His inaccurate interpretation provoked an enraged response from Satterthwaite in Pretoria. South African officials demanded to know if Williams's statements belied the administration's assurances that it would fulfill existing contracts and consider future security needs. Satterthwaite asked Rusk if South Africa, "a valuable ally in three wars, has lost all strategic, military, and scientific importance? Are we prepared to abandon all efforts to block direct Soviet and CHICOM penetration into South Africa?" An end to all technical and military aid to the South African army and police would only encourage insurrection and communism and would have no effect on its racial policies. He added: "In view of recent events in Alabama, perhaps we would be a little less enthusiastic in condemning the South African Government."[77]

Kennedy finally decided to compromise. He approved the sale of spare parts and agreed to continue discussions of the submarine and airplane deals with the understanding that they "are to be strictly confidential and involve no implied commitment to sell." A decision would be made by the end of the year to meet the timetable of the embargo.[78]

The death of the president in November, before the issue had been resolved, created a major diplomatic problem. Johnson and the State Department were frantically trying to adjust to the assassination and the transfer of power and had less than six weeks in which to decide on the arms question. South Africa claimed Kennedy and Satterthwaite had implied the deal would be approved and pressed for an immediate agreement. Only four days after Kennedy's death, Pretoria offered to send a delegation to America to complete arrangements for the sale. Rusk "discouraged" the visit until the situation in Washington was more stable.[79]

On 10 December, Rusk told South Africa that the United States would honor all "existing contracts" and consider additional requests "in light of requirements for assuring the maintenance of international peace and security." The vagueness of Rusk's statement did not satisfy Pretoria. Three days later, Ball clarified U.S. policy when he informed Satterthwaite that oil was not covered by the embargo, that America would sell torpedoes, air-to-air missiles, and

76. McNamara and Rusk to Kennedy, "Sale of Submarines to South Africa," 16 September 1963, NSF: South Africa, box 159, Kennedy Library.

77. Satterthwaite to Rusk, 18 September 1963, ibid. See also Satterthwaite oral history interview, Kennedy Library.

78. Bundy to Rusk and McNamara, 23 September 1963, ibid.

79. Rusk to American embassy, Pretoria, 26 November 1963, NSF: South Africa, box 2, Johnson Library.

commercial airplanes, but would not provide military aircraft. The submarine issue would be subject to future negotiation.[80]

With the new year, the arms embargo was theoretically in effect, but the two nations continued discussions on submarines. To Stevenson this was a violation of stated policy. He told Rusk: "We would have a most difficult time defending the sale of submarines to South Africa now even under the possible exception 'in the future' for Western defense which I announced." He recommended that, if the vessels were really necessary for South African security, the United States should arrange their purchase from France or Britain to avoid "political embarrassment."[81]

America's willingness to discuss weapons sales after the 31 December cutoff date encouraged South African military officials. They promptly asked for other equipment. Rusk finally told them that, while Washington would consider all requests, it would not respond to "a shopping list" of military supplies. Negotiations returned to the submarine issue.[82]

The problems of the arms embargo and its loopholes continued to plague the United States throughout 1964. What had seemed a practical compromise between inaction and sanctions proved to be a complex web of legalistic interpretations and a continuing embarrassment to American officials. A moderate solution to a difficult problem, the arms embargo provoked African charges of U.S. hypocrisy and claims from South Africans that they had been misled.

Washington had fewer problems maintaining its symbolic protests against apartheid. Shortly before Kennedy's death, Pretoria denied a visa to a black State Department official, Ulrich Haynes, for a proposed visit to the three British High Commission territories adjacent to South Africa. Rusk raged against Verwoerd, the Nationalists, and apartheid. He demanded an immediate visa, an apology, and transport for Haynes on South African commercial flights. One State Department official reported that he had never seen Rusk so livid and warned, "Unless South Africa backs down, given the position the Secretary has taken, we may find ourselves in a minor diplomatic war." When Pretoria finally agreed to a visa, Rusk summoned its ambassador and Mennen Williams to his office. Williams recalled that the secretary was furious. He paced the room and slammed his hand on his desk as he denounced South Africa's actions as "insulting" to the United States. When Naude left, Rusk turned to Williams and asked: "Did I really give it to him tough enough? If not, I'll follow him downstairs and finish the job."[83]

Rusk's anger was real, and so was the Kennedy administration's abhorrence of

80. Ibid., 10 December 1963; Ball to Satterthwaite, 13 December 1963, ibid.
81. Stevenson to Rusk, 22 January 1964, ibid.
82. Satterthwaite to Rusk, 23 January 1964, ibid.
83. Rusk to American embassy, Pretoria, 5 December 1963; Brubeck to Bundy, 5 December 1963, ibid.; Williams oral history interview, Kennedy Library.

apartheid. It was much easier, however, to rail away at the South African ambassador than it was to implement official policy. American speeches remained uncompromising, but the policies were not. Global strategic, economic, and political interests moderated the somewhat unrealistic expectations of a dramatic confrontation with Pretoria over apartheid. America's ability to force improvements in South Africa's racial situation was limited. Even if Kennedy endorsed suggestions for stronger actions, there was no assurance that any U.S. effort could provoke significant change. Uncertain that a direct diplomatic assault on apartheid would succeed (in fact, convinced it might lead to a worsening of the situation), Kennedy fell back on rhetoric and compromise in the hope of a gradual improvement of the plight of the black African. As Stevenson summarized two weeks after Kennedy's death: "It is difficult, I know, to speak of long-range approaches when the pain and the provocation are so present and so intense. But in dealing with so intractable an issue as apartheid there are no easy solutions."[84]

84. *SDB* 50 (20 January 1964): 92–96.

7. DISTRACTED DIPLOMACY | Johnson and Apartheid, 1964–1968

From 1961 on, official American policy toward South Africa was based on a distinction between "matters of mutual benefit" and those supportive of apartheid, but this diplomatic dichotomy was never clear. U.S. policy was obvious in its intent but left great latitude in its application. In addition, exactly what constituted aid to apartheid was subject to changing interpretations and conditions, with domestic pressure and the international situation being the major determinants in the periodic reassessment of what fit within the general policy parameters.

In the period immediately following Kennedy's death, the two dominant influences on America's African diplomacy, the Cold War and internal black protest, were greatly altered. Kennedy had been primarily concerned with Soviet pressure on Berlin and the problems of Castro's Cuba. Johnson was increasingly preoccupied with direct military confrontation with communism in Vietnam. Prior to 1964, the American civil-rights movement was confined largely to the South, was generally dedicated to integration and the right to vote, and its tactics (if not the white reaction) were usually peaceful. Demonstrations after 1964 were increasingly concentrated in the North and were directed at more difficult and subtle targets such as jobs, political power, and white racism. They were also much more violent. The cry of black power and the ghetto riots in major Northern cities dramatically altered the earlier movement usually associated with Martin Luther King. Whites who supported the integration of the South often found themselves the object of black anger. The more militant phase of the movement alienated many whites who had sympathized with the peaceful demonstrations in the South.

Vietnam and the changed nature of the black movement caused Johnson and his administration to move even further from any direct clash with South Africa. There was no sudden "retreat" in the U.S. diplomacy or abandonment of the hope for racial equality. Rather, there was a gradual drift toward inaction based on a reluctant acceptance of the intractability of white rule. Burdened with an ever-expanding and increasingly unpopular war in Asia and uprisings in the ghettos of most American cities, Washington relegated Africa to its traditional peripheral position in U.S. diplomacy. The distractions of more pressing global and internal problems diluted American dedication to the diplomacy of equality. Johnson and his advisers did not repudiate the existing policy guidelines but interpreted them in a way that made America more conservative on the broad issue of apartheid.

There were few indications of the eventual "tilt" in U.S. policy in the first few months of the Johnson presidency. Vietnam was already an area of deep concern but not yet the dominant issue it would soon become. The first major black riots were nearly two years away. There were, however, signs of a general reassessment of the American approach to South Africa in late 1963 and early 1964. On 6 December 1963, the State Department "Country Team" for South Africa suggested that on the eve of the arms embargo it was time to consider long-range proposals to influence Pretoria to moderate its racial laws. The arms ban seemed to indicate a commitment to sustained pressure for change, and the new administration should evaluate additional actions and what their risks would be for other U.S. interests.[1]

Four days later the "Standing Group" on southern Africa of the National Security Council met to review American policy. It decided to solicit suggestions from various factions within the government on general diplomacy toward both the Portuguese territories and South Africa. Predictably, Williams and the African Bureau used the opportunity to lobby for stronger measures against apartheid. Their major suggestion was official "discouragement" of new American investments in South Africa as a prelude to possible full economic sanctions.[2]

Although opposition to sanctions remained widespread, there was some sympathy with the idea of restraining future U.S. investments. Satterthwaite responded to the push for "selective economic sanctions" in a series of lengthy dispatches. He agreed that it was an opportune time to approach South Africa because "it may well be too late when events have pushed us beyond the point of no return in race relations." He argued, however, that any immediate action would be premature. Washington should try "to reach a reasonable agreement" with the Nationalists "before considering sterner measures." Satterthwaite recommended that the United States officially assure the whites that they would retain their power if they relaxed the racial restrictions. South Africa was, he contended, willing to compromise if its critics would accept "less than universal franchise" and if "the U.S. and U.K. would guarantee that if South Africa made a policy change they would back her up against Pan-African pressures for 'one man, one vote.' " With a clear American commitment to the security of the white minority, the South African government might well be willing to make "concessions to educated, urban Africans . . . with vested interest in stability." Only such gradual reforms were possible, because the Afrikaners feared

1. Department of State, "Long-range Proposals on South Africa," 6 December 1963, NSF: South Africa, box 2, Johnson Library.
2. National Security Council, "Memorandum for Mr. Bundy," 10 December 1963, ibid.

"designs on the area by communists and ambitious Pan-African politicians to the North."[3]

Satterthwaite recognized that the idea of an American "guarantee" of white security in exchange for limited rights for some blacks would be opposed by both Africanists and Europeanists. He predicted that the African Bureau would claim the action did "not go far enough, and that the U.S. should not put its good faith on the line for anything less than equal rights for all South Africans." Others in the administration would likely argue that the plan was "too big a pill for South Africa to swallow." To Satterthwaite, the proposal was "a compromise that will put the country on a constructive path and avoid bloodshed and possible communist domination." A joint American-British "guarantee that Europeans and other non-Africans would not be swamped by external African pressures" was the only way to convince the Nationalists that compromise on apartheid would not lead to their destruction.

While proposing to officially assure whites of their survival, Satterthwaite rejected completely the idea of curtailing U.S. investments. Not only was there "no legal basis" for the move; it would also be unproductive. Regardless of outside pressure, the white government had "the capacity to maintain social order and it's expected to sustain this capacity into the foreseeable future." Satterthwaite believed American investors were well aware of the possibility of "social strife," but they remained convinced that the risk was "justified by the unrestricted repatriation of high profits which of course assist the U.S. balance of payments problems."[4] Satterthwaite's evaluation of U.S. business leaders was accurate. American corporations felt the risks in investing in South Africa were outweighed by the high returns. In 1964 and 1965 there was a surge of direct American economic activity in the area. *Business Week* reported, "Despite its touchy racial and political problems, South Africa is caught in a business boom." Over two hundred U.S. firms were directly involved in the nation, and their profits were "the highest in Africa . . . an average of 14 to 15 per cent."[5]

Given the consistent U.S. position against sanctions and the rapid growth of business activity in South Africa, the suggestion of "discouraging" new investments failed to gain support outside the African Bureau. Satterthwaite's novel idea that Britain and the United States formally guarantee the security of the white minority was also rejected. There is no evidence that it was seriously considered. The problems of the arrangement were immense, and it certainly would have produced strong international criticism. In addition, Satterthwaite had only a vague indication from South African officials that they would respond with significant reforms of apartheid. The "reassessment" of U.S. policy in 1964

3. Satterthwaite to Rusk, 14 December 1963, ibid.
4. Ibid., 22 December 1963.
5. "Where the Cash Grows in Africa," *Business Week* (19 June 1965): 134–38.

led to no departures from previous positions. Instead, there was a lull in diplomatic activity involving South Africa.

There were several reasons for U.S. inaction in 1964. Although Johnson had pledged to continue Kennedy's African policies, many in Washington hesitated to undertake any initiatives until they were certain of the diplomatic direction of the new administration. Johnson was embroiled in the fight for the passage of the civil-rights bill and in his election campaign. Clearly, he would undertake no major foreign-policy departures that would jeopardize his election. With Barry Goldwater likely to be nominated by the Republicans, there was concern that any stronger U.S. opposition to the white regimes might become an election issue. Goldwater was one of the most outspoken critics of American policy toward Angola, the Congo, and South Africa. By 1964 many other conservatives openly questioned Washington's support of black rule. The main targets of conservative complaints were Williams and the African Bureau. Williams contacted Goldwater and other critics to try to explain the U.S. position but could not defuse the attacks. On 20 February 1964, he met with Sen. Bourke Hickenlooper of Iowa, a leading opponent of American policy toward South Africa. According to Williams, the two had barely sat down before Hickenlooper "began to blow off steam." He defended South Africa as "the only stable pro-Western area on the continent" and demanded that Williams explain "why we have to trouble them?" Although the assistant secretary gave his usual vigorous defense of the U.S. position, others in the administration worried that African policy would become part of Goldwater's attack on the Democrats' "softness" in foreign affairs.[6]

The South Africans quickly sensed the administration's somewhat reduced attention to apartheid. Pretoria's chargé in Washington remarked to a State Department official, "You haven't been too horrible to us recently," and asked if Johnson might reconsider the arms embargo. Ambassador Naude called on Williams to inquire if the lack of verbal attack on his government indicated a change in official policy. Williams emphatically denied any relaxation of U.S. opposition to apartheid.[7]

Williams's statement that U.S. policy had not changed was technically correct. The Johnson administration continued to oppose UN demands for sanctions and the use of chapter 7 language. In June 1964, Stevenson argued that, although the situation in South Africa was "charged with somber and dangerous implications," it was not a threat to world peace. Therefore, America would not support sanctions or any "ultimatum" to the South African government.

6. "Memorandum for the Files," 20 February 1964, Williams papers, box 4, National Archives.
7. "Memorandum of Conversation between Gardner Dunn and Jeffrey Kitchen," 29 April 1964, NSF: South Africa, box 2, Johnson Library. "Notes on Conversation," 19 April 1964, Williams papers, box 4, National Archives.

Washington also rejected an OAU demand for a boycott of South African exports and the elimination of tourism and cultural exchanges. The CIA dismissed the recommendation as propaganda by "leftist-inclined" governments. In talks with the new British foreign secretary, Gordon Walker, in the fall of 1964, State Department officials reaffirmed U.S. opposition to sanctions or any UN resolutions that invoked chapter 7. Walker confirmed that the new Labour government in London was in agreement with the American position.[8]

Although the administration refused to endorse economic sanctions, many outside the government felt the United States must use its economic power to force South Africa to change its racial system. Leaders of the American Committee on Africa and other liberal groups encouraged Williams to continue to work for a phased reduction of U.S. investments and an extension of the arms embargo to include oil. In the spring of 1964, the *New Republic* called for immediate sanctions. Phillip Mason, director of the Institute for Race Relations in London, urged a joint U.S.-British naval blockade of South Africa. Phillip Quigg, managing editor of *Foreign Affairs*, stopped short of endorsing sanctions but suggested that Johnson announce that investments in South Africa "are not in the national interest."[9]

A part of the moderation of U.S. policy in 1964 was a toning down of official rhetoric against apartheid. For over three years, Williams had led the verbal campaign against South Africa. In March 1964 he submitted a draft of a speech he proposed to give at the Harvard Law School on apartheid for routine State Department approval. To his shock, it was killed by his superiors as "too provocative." Specifically, it implied that the United States was considering economic sanctions. Williams dropped the issue and gave a different speech but clashed with the department again in June when Satterthwaite protested that another of his proposed speeches would "only strengthen Nationalist propaganda" by supporting the Nationalists' claim that South Africa was besieged by hostile governments. The ambassador accused Williams of being too concerned with preserving his reputation among American liberals to use "quiet diplomacy" to moderate the situation in South Africa.[10]

The issue that broke U.S. silence on South Africa was the much-publicized

8. *SDB* 51 (6 July 1964): 29–33; Central Intelligence Agency, "Current Intelligence Memorandum: OAU Boycott Action Against South Africa," 7 August 1964, NSF: South Africa, box 2; Department of State, "Visit of Foreign Secretary Gordon Walker, October 26–27, 1964: Talking Points," NSF: United Kingdom, box 4, Johnson Library.
9. "USG Policy Re South Africa," 19 February 1964, Williams papers, box 7, National Archives; "Stop South Africa Now," *New Republic* 150 (16 May 1964): 2–4; Phillip Mason, "Some Maxims and Axioms," 150–64; Phillip Quigg, "South African Problems and Prospects," *African Report* 10 (January 1965): 9–14.
10. Satterthwaite to Rusk, 16 March 1964, NSF: South Africa, box 2, Johnson Library; Satterthwaite to Williams, 17 June 1964, Williams papers, box 28, National Archives; Williams to Satterthwaite, 30 June 1964, ibid., box 4.

Rivonia trial in the summer of 1964. On 11 July 1963, South African agents raided a farmhouse at Rivonia, near Johannesburg, and arrested a group of white and black activists. They claimed to have found documents linking the group with "Spear of the Nation" and plans for a major terrorist campaign known as "Operation Mayibuye." Eventually, thirteen people were arrested, including Nelson Mandela, a leading black opponent of apartheid already serving a jail sentence. Two of those indicted escaped by bribing a prison guard, and another agreed to testify for the state in exchange for immunity. The remaining ten were charged with treason and went on trial in June 1964.[11] No incident in South Africa since Sharpeville generated as much international interest and protest as did the trial and eventual conviction of the Rivonia group. Many outside South Africa were convinced there could never be a fair trial given the emotional atmosphere following the bombings in 1962 and 1963. There were demonstrations, petitions, and other demands for international action to gain the release of the defendants or at least insure a fair trial.

The American press joined the attack on the South African government and its draconian legal codes adopted to suppress terrorism. Verwoerd finally lashed out at the American media, charging that U.S. newspapers were "blindly partisan" and "slanted." Their coverage of South Africa was "sensationalized" and designed to "proselytize for non-whites." He singled out the *New York Times*, *New York Herald-Tribune*, *Christian Science Monitor*, and *Baltimore Sun* as the worst offenders. Verwoerd reported that his government had a file "three feet thick" documenting distortions in the *New York Times* alone.[12] In Great Britain, there was even greater public agitation over the trial. On 2 April 1964, the British Foreign Office appealed to Washington to join in efforts to assure a fair trial and moderate the expected severe sentences. To symbolize its concern, America agreed to send Judge Charles Fahy, former U.S. solicitor general, as an official observer of the proceedings. The State Department also told African nations it would support a "cautious appeal" by the UN Security Council on the matter.[13]

South Africa eventually found five of the defendants, including Mandela, guilty of treason and sentenced them to life imprisonment on Robben Island. Fahy returned to Washington to brief Williams, Rusk, and other U.S. officials on the trial. He concluded that the proceedings had been fair and that those convicted were guilty of "revolutionary activity." Rusk noted that "granting

11. Department of State Memorandum for Mr. McGeorge Bundy, "The Apartheid Trials in South Africa," undated, NSF: South Africa, box 2, Johnson Library. For the South African interpretation of the affair, see Lauritz Strydom, *Rivonia Unmasked*, and H. H. W. De Villiers, *Rivonia: Operation Mayibuye*.

12. *New York Times*, 12 May 1964, p. 4. Verwoerd did praise the *U.S. News and World Report* as "factual and fair."

13. R. A. Butler, Secretary of State for Foreign Affairs, to Bundy, 2 April 1964; Brubeck to Bundy, 16 April 1964, NSF: South Africa, box 2, Johnson Library.

greater status to blacks is not all that revolutionary," but Washington did not formally protest the convictions as many African nations demanded. Williams did condemn the severe sentences in a speech in Cleveland, and Stevenson told the UN that the defendants were driven to desperate means by South Africa's suppression of all legitimate protest.[14]

Despite the obvious determination of South Africa to continue apartheid and to crush its opponents, there was some cautious optimism about Africa in Washington in the summer of 1964. Many believed that the passage of the civil-rights bill in July would convince Africans of America's dedication to equality and support of black Africa. However, Carl Rowan, head of the USIA, told Johnson that, while Africans were "greatly pleased" with the civil-rights bill, they assumed it would be followed by a hard line against white rule in South Africa.[15]

Johnson became more "visible" on African issues after the passage of the civil-rights legislation, meeting with businessmen to discuss the problem of apartheid. On 29 July, he met with Lewis Douglas, an American business leader who had recently talked with Verwoerd. Douglas reported the Nationalists were "unyielding on apartheid" and convinced that "the United States is the only country that can crush South Africa." Johnson sent Douglas to talk with Harriman about how best to use American business leaders as agents to force moderation of apartheid. Johnson later talked with Harry Oppenheimer, a wealthy diamond magnate and member of South Africa's Progressive party, to ask for his assessment of the chances for peaceful reform of apartheid. The president congratulated Oppenheimer for maintaining a "dialogue" on the racial issue.[16] Johnson's discussions with both American and South African businessmen were designed to explore the possible use of private channels to work for peaceful changes in Pretoria's racial laws. Rather than withdrawing investments and imposing sanctions to force the Nationalists to yield, the president accepted the strategy of using U.S. corporations to work within the system for progress. Although this approach did not succeed, it illustrated Johnson's opinion that cutting economic ties with South Africa would be ineffective. Like most in the administration, he wanted to keep as much foreign interaction with South Africa as possible, believing that normal cultural, political, and economic relations would expose South Africans to more enlightened ideas and gradually convince them that a relaxation of apartheid would not be disastrous.

14. Department of State "Memorandum of Conversation," 17 June 1964, ibid.; *SDB* 51 (6 July 1964): 29–33; (13 July 1964): 51–54.
15. Carl Rowan to Johnson, "African Reaction to Recent U.S. Civil Rights Developments," 21 July 1964, CF: Africa, box 6, Johnson Library.
16. "Memorandum for the President: Meeting with Mr. Lewis Douglas," 29 July 1964, "Memorandum for the President: Harry Oppenheimer," 25 September 1964, NSF: South Africa, box 2, Johnson Library.

By August 1964, the feeble push for sanctions was over. The press rapidly abandoned the Rivonia trial and South Africa to cover the U.S. election campaign. Black Americans concentrated on passage of additional civil-rights legislation. Congress, never overly concerned with Africa, remained unconvinced of the need for any new demands on Pretoria. Those in the House or Senate most interested in Africa tended to be conservatives highly critical of existing policy as too radical rather than too cautious and thus not interested in forcing new demands.[17]

Johnson did face a problem in continuing Kennedy's announced arms embargo. The U.S. statement that it would honor existing commitments and consider future sales left open the possibility of supplying weapons even after the 1 January 1964 official start of the embargo. Kennedy's postponement of a decision on the sale of submarines and planes left the question for his successor. South Africa made several appeals to Johnson for additional weapons. One week after the embargo went into effect, military officials approached the U.S. naval attaché in Pretoria with an offer to "stretch-out" American payments for uranium in exchange for an agreement to provide military equipment. Two months later, Pretoria's chargé in Washington asked Jeffrey Kitchen, deputy assistant secretary of state, if Washington had considered "a reappraisal of the reservations of Ambassador Stevenson's speech of last August."[18]

The administration postponed clarifying its position throughout the spring and summer of 1964, as internal disagreements developed over a specific case involving the Lockheed Corporation. On 31 August, South African air-force officials told Lockheed, with whom they had contracted for anti-submarine planes, that they would buy French Brequet Atlantique aircraft unless the U.S. government swiftly approved the earlier deal with Lockheed. Kitchen informed Lockheed executives that permission for the sale was "extremely doubtful."[19] Lockheed then appealed to the White House for immediate approval of the deal. It cited Stevenson's statement that the United States would fulfill existing contracts and pointed out that the transaction would bring in $64 million immediately, and $20–40 million in the sale of parts over the next five years. The corporation mobilized support from the Defense, Commerce, and Treasury departments and Congress. Secretary of the Treasury Douglas Dillon was a strong advocate of the purchase. He told Rusk, "The South African payments alone of about $85–100 million in 1965–66 would be a major step toward achieving the sales targets set for the military component of our balance of

17. Stanley Meisler, "The U.S. Congress and Africa," *Africa Report* 9 (August 1964): 3–7.
18. Satterthwaite to Rusk, 8 January 1964; Department of State, "Memorandum of Conversation between Gardner Dunn and Jeffrey Kitchen," 29 April 1964, NSF: South Africa, box 2, Johnson Library.
19. Memorandum for Mr. Bundy, "Proposed Lockheed Sale to South Africa," 22 September 1964, ibid.

payments program." Dillon argued that failure to sell the planes would not only be a severe blow to Lockheed but also jeopardize the ability of other U.S. corporations to compete in the international arms market. Luther Hodges, secretary of commerce, agreed. He predicted, "If we do not allow sale of the Lockheed aircraft the French and British will pick up the business" and increase the attractiveness of their weapons to other nations.[20]

Others in the administration stressed the links between military equipment and other foreign-trade products. They contended that the South African deal was clearly within Stevenson's exemptions from the embargo since it was "in the interests of common defense to maintain international peace and security." The deal would help the immediate balance of payments and encourage South Africa to buy commercial planes and other nonmilitary goods from American firms. One Commerce Department official noted, "The U.S. faces increasingly aggressive competition in the South African market from European suppliers." Rejection of the aircraft sale would cause Pretoria to turn elsewhere for industrial and consumer goods. The contract was also crucial to the "well-being of the Lockheed Company and its employees as well as the economic health of California."[21] Congress, particularly the California delegation, also lobbied for administration approval of the purchase. They contended that the planes could only be used for defense against a foreign power and thus did not provide any assistance to apartheid. Johnson must agree to the sale quickly, as it was obvious France was eager to sign a contract.[22]

Other U.S. corporations watched the debate over the Lockheed deal with great interest. The State Department received "informal inquiries" from North American Aviation, Northrop Corporation, Douglas Aircraft, and other firms about possible arms sales to South Africa under the "strategic exemption" clause in Stevenson's announcement. Analysts at the State and Defense departments estimated that approval of such purchases could generate as much as "$300–400 million in military sales to South Africa over the next five years."[23]

The obvious economic gains from the contract with Pretoria were balanced by the likelihood of a hostile domestic and foreign reaction. Bundy told Johnson, "Liberal and Negro groups . . . would criticize it as reneging on policy and support of South African racism." Approval would generate "highly emotional Afro-Asian adverse reaction and propaganda attacks on the U.S. that . . . might

20. Bundy to Rusk, 11 September 1964; Dillon to Rusk, 15 September 1964; Hodges to Rusk, 16 September 1964, ibid.
21. Robert L. McNeill, Deputy Assistant Secretary of Commerce, to Kitchen, 16 September 1964, ibid.
22. Bromley Smith, Executive Secretary, National Security Council, to Bundy, 18 September 1964; Brubeck to Bundy, 18 September 1964, ibid.
23. Memorandum for Mr. Bundy, "Proposed Lockheed Sale to South Africa," 22 September 1964, ibid.

shift enough votes for the U.S. to lose the Chinese representation issue in the November General Assembly." Bundy recommended postponing a decision until after the presidential election and the UN vote on the admission of mainland China.[24]

The National Security Council also advocated delay. It agreed that the sale was within the "strategic exemption clause" but cautioned that it would result in "considerable emotional reaction against the U.S. in Africa and Asia" and prompt attacks on the administration by "American liberal and Negro groups and many newspapers." It also warned that South Africa might well attach political strings to the deal such as demanding American support of Tshombe in the Congo. The NSC concluded that Pretoria was trying to buy the planes "largely for internal political reasons, respectability and membership in the Western Alliance" rather than for real security needs. Rusk, McNamara, and the others in the group suggested informing Lockheed that the deal probably would not be approved, but a final decision would be made in late November.[25]

Executives at Lockheed stepped up their lobbying efforts when they were informed of the delay. They asked former Secretary of State Christian Herter, now Johnson's special representative for trade negotiations, to work to "minimize the risk of losing the South African program to the French." Lockheed told Herter that if Johnson delayed his decision until after the election, South Africa would have already turned to the French. When Herter mentioned this point, some in the administration feared Lockheed would "go public" and accuse Johnson of playing politics with the sale. They claimed Lockheed was "using the election as a basis for a squeeze play" to force the president's approval.[26] On 1 October, Vernon Johnson, vice-president of Lockheed, met with White House officials. He said there were indications that South Africa might "be more flexible" on the deadline for the sale, but Lockheed needed some indication that the deal was still alive and that there was a possibility of "an ultimate favorable decision." Presidential aides merely reported that the case was still being reviewed.[27]

Immediately after Johnson's election in November, Commerce and Treasury officials renewed their demands for approval. On 20 November, the president asked McNamara for his opinion. The defense secretary concluded that the issue was "a political decision" and not "essential to our national defense." Johnson responded by rejecting the sale as not within the "strategic exemption" clause and not involving completion of a previous commitment. Bundy told disappointed Lockheed executives of the decision but assured them that they

24. Bundy to Johnson, undated, ibid.
25. Brubeck to Bundy, 22 September 1964; 23 September 1964, ibid.
26. Walter C. Smith, Director of Marketing, Lockheed Corporation, to Herter, 24 September 1964; Brubeck to Bundy, 28 September 1964, ibid.
27. Memorandum of Conversation, "Lockheed Sale to South Africa," 1 October 1964, ibid.

could reapply for future sales that were in the strategic interests of the United States.[28]

The veto of the Lockheed contract, despite the clear benefits to the American economy of the deal, showed the sincerity of Washington's efforts to disassociate from the Nationalist government and Johnson's commitment to live up to the spirit of the arms embargo. The certainty of severe international and internal criticism played an important role in the decision. Perhaps even more crucial was the conclusion that the weapons were not necessary for South African security. Johnson did not close the "escape clause" in America's arms policy but determined that it did not apply to the specific material in the Lockheed contract.

In contrast, the administration decided that atomic material for peaceful use was not covered by the weapons ban. South Africa had a long-standing agreement with the Allis-Chalmers Corporation for the construction and maintenance of a nuclear reactor. In August 1964, the company asked Washington for permission to ship fuel elements to South Africa. The Atomic Energy Commission told the State Department that the plant was designed completely for peaceful use and the United States should continue to cooperate in its maintenance. Officials at the State Department complained that shipment of atomic material would "unquestionably kick-up a nice propaganda storm . . . about U.S. nuclear cooperation with South Africa." They recommended avoiding sending the supplies until after the election and the UN session in the fall. In February 1965, America finally delivered the fuel elements. Ball informed the U.S. embassy in Pretoria, "We intend to give no publicity to this transaction and understand that the SAG [South African Government] will give no publicity to the receipt of the fuel."[29]

In addition to continuing Kennedy's arms policy, Johnson tried to duplicate his successful personal diplomacy. He invited a number of Africans to the signing of the civil-rights bill and sent autographed copies to all African leaders. In a message to a conference of non-aligned nations in Cairo in October 1964, the president followed the suggestions of Rowan that he "invoke the Kennedy name" because of "the astonishing emotional reaction to President Kennedy's death in the non-aligned countries." Johnson managed to make three references to Kennedy in his brief statement.[30]

Passage of the civil-rights bill, the rejection of the Lockheed deal, and the

28. Thomas Wyman, Assistant Secretary of Commerce for Domestic and International Business, to Bundy, 18 November 1964; Merlyn N. Trued, Acting Assistant Secretary of Treasury, to Francis M. Bator, Deputy Special Assistant to the President, 18 November 1964; McNamara to Johnson, 20 November 1964; Bundy, "Memorandum for the Record: Lockheed Aircraft," 30 November 1964, ibid.

29. Brubeck to Bundy, 17 August 1964; Ball to U.S. embassy, Pretoria, 10 February 1965, ibid.

30. Rowan to Robert Komer, Senior Staff Member, National Security Council, 1 October 1964; "Revised Message from the President to the Second Non-Aligned Conference in Cairo," NSF: International Meetings and Travel File, box 1, Johnson Library.

courting of African leaders by Johnson generated some good will for the administration among Africans. These minor gains, however, were suddenly dashed by American actions in the Congo in 1964. The factionalism and violence that plagued the Congo after its independence in 1960 had continued sporadically throughout its first four years of freedom. The Congo remained the one area of Africa most likely to produce direct conflict among the major powers. As such, it had a major impact on the overall U.S. approach to the continent. Just as Eisenhower's and Kennedy's support of a united but prowestern Congo had alienated some African leaders in the early 1960s, Johnson's actions in 1964 provoked renewed criticism and convinced many in Washington of the ingrained anti-Americanism of African leaders.

Like his predecessors, Johnson supported Congolese unity and the elimination of assumed radicals from its government. The United States had heavily financed both continued UN operations in the nation and the central government of Cyrille Adoula. America had also helped Adoula purge followers of murdered Congolese leader Patrice Lumumba from the government. By mid-1964, American officials assumed that their policy had been successful. The Congo seemed to be more stable, and the influence of "leftists" appeared to be diminished. In July 1964, the UN withdrew its forces from the Congo in hopes that the nation had achieved order. However, the fragile unity of the nation rapidly collapsed after the removal of UN troops, and revolts against the central government spread throughout the country. Nine days after the UN force left, Adoula resigned and Moise Tshombe, the former leader of the secessionist province of Katanga, was named prime minister. Although the United States had opposed Tshombe's earlier attempt to sever Katanga from the Congo, Washington reluctantly supported him in an attempt to maintain a central government. To most black Africans, however, Tshombe was an anathema. They dismissed him as a tool of Belgium.[31]

Washington's grudging support of Tshombe soon shifted to more active assistance as the revolt of "leftists" spread in the summer and fall. Repeating a policy he had used in Katanga, Tshombe finally hired four hundred white mercenaries from Rhodesia and South Africa to help restore the authority of the central government. The United States was in a bind; it did not want to seem to endorse the use of white mercenaries but also did not want the rebellion to destroy Congolese unity. Continued support of Tshombe would likely provoke the wrath of African leaders, while abandoning the Congolese prime minister might prolong the revolt and risk increased radicalism. However, concern about order soon outweighed all other considerations.[32] When rebels seized Stanleyville, proclaimed a "people's republic," and began executing govern-

31. Kalb, *The Congo Cables*, 377–79.
32. Weissman, *American Foreign Policy in the Congo, 1960–1964*, 234–36. See also G. Mennen Williams, *Africa for the Africans*, 98–101.

ment officials, teachers, and merchants, the United States decided it must act to support Tshombe. Washington supplied Tshombe with both combat and transport planes to be used against the revolt, and the CIA arranged for Cuban exile pilots to fly the planes. In November, the Stanleyville insurgents seized three hundred white hostages, including five U.S. consular officials, and threatened to kill them if Tshombe did not end air attacks and recall the white mercenaries. U.S. officials considered a unilateral raid to free the American hostages but rejected the idea when the CIA determined it would not work. Instead, Washington sent Wayne Fredericks to Narobi to meet with rebel leader Thomas Kanza to try to arrange for the hostages' release. When the talks failed to produce a firm agreement, Johnson ordered U.S. planes to transport Belgian troops to Stanleyville. On 24 November, U.S. pilots flying C–130 transports dropped five hundred Belgian paratroopers and their equipment over Stanleyville airport. As they fought their way into town, they were joined by Tshombe's white mercenaries. The rebels eventually fled the city, but they executed dozens of the hostages. American pilots later transported Belgian troops to other rebel strongholds. The disorganized rebel army eventually killed over three hundred whites, including eight Americans, as they retreated.[33]

To Lyndon Johnson and his advisers, American participation in the Stanleyville raid was a humanitarian act to free innocent hostages. They assumed that African leaders would recognize it as an isolated incident and not the beginning of direct U.S. intervention in the Congo. To the Africans, however, the airlift was an outrageous example of Washington's cooperation with Belgium and Belgium's "puppet," Tshombe, to violate African sovereignty. The administration had anticipated that some "radical" African leaders would denounce the airlift as support of the white mercenaries, but it was unprepared for the violent response of even "moderate" Africans. African leaders even called a special UN session to denounce the United States for "neocolonialism," intervening in the internal affairs of a sovereign state, and ignoring African diplomatic efforts to win release of the hostages. American officials sat in stoic silence as African representatives methodically marched to the podium to attack the airlift and the United States.[34]

Johnson and his aides were stunned by the African reaction. U.S. intelligence had predicted that the airlift might provoke demonstrations in some radical African countries and "the bill for glass breakage would probably be high," but it had estimated that "our losses are not likely to be irreparable." This proved to be a massive misreading of African sentiment. The sustained and emotional African attack on the U.S. actions in the Congo produced first disbelief and eventually bitterness in Washington. Stevenson announced that he was "stunned" by the African outburst. The president initially blamed "the

33. *SDB* 52 (8 February 1965): 220; *New York Times*, 25 November 1964, p. 1.
34. "U.S. Policy and the Congo Crisis," *Africa Today* 11 (December 1964): 3–4.

communists" for orchestrating the African protests but later attacked the African leaders themselves. To many American officials, the overreaction of the Africans was a prime example of their ingrained hostility to America, their obsession with the colonial past, and their "reverse racism," directed against any action by a white government.[35]

The bitterness in Washington resulting from the reaction to the Stanleyville incursion worked to drain what remained of American enthusiasm for any new efforts against the white regimes in Southern Africa. Little or no support remained for actions to win favor in black Africa, as black Africa had shown itself to be insensitive and irresponsible. There was even a feeling that the United States should clearly indicate its anger with the African states. Ball, for example, proposed that America publicly invite South African military officers to train at U.S. bases. Williams and the African Bureau managed to defeat the plan by arguing that the South Africans might end up as mercenaries fighting in the Congo or Rhodesia, but Ball's suggestion showed the depth of American disillusionment with black Africa by late 1964.[36]

As had happened earlier under Kennedy, the turmoil in the Congo led to a new emphasis on caution and inaction in dealing with the white governments and revived concerns about the ability of black Africans to maintain an orderly, anticommunist government. Administration reluctance to confront directly the issue of apartheid, in turn, produced renewed criticism from liberals and blacks in the United States. Martin Luther King was one of the first to charge that the Johnson administration had moved away from direct pressure on Pretoria. While in London on his way to accept the Nobel Peace Prize, King attacked the United States for "bolstering tyranny" in South Africa by refusing to use economic pressure. "Must they wait until there is a blood bath before they recognize a crisis?" King asked.[37]

King's remarks provoked some concern in the White House that blacks would turn against the administration. Lee White, Johnson's aide generally responsible for civil rights, told the president that King "has demonstrated a recent interest in South Africa" and was angered by Washington's lack of action against apartheid. When Johnson prepared to meet with Roy Wilkins of the NAACP, White mentioned that "the Negro leadership has taken a great interest in our African policy" and urged the president to be sure to mention America's continued opposition to apartheid.[38]

White Americans were even more vocal in their demands for action against

35. Department of State Intelligence and Research Memorandum, "Dragon Rouge: African Reactions and Other Estimates," November 1964, NSF: Congo, box 3, Johnson Library. *New Republic* 151 (26 December 1964): 9–10.
36. Williams to Harriman, 11 December 1964, Williams papers, box 4, National Archives.
37. *New York Times*, 8 December 1964, p. 53.
38. White to Johnson, 18 December 1964, CF: South Africa, box 71; White to Johnson, 28 December 1964, CF: Africa, box 6, Johnson Library.

apartheid. George Houser, executive director of the American Committee on Africa, charged that Washington had "backed-off" on the South African issue because of Pretoria's anticommunism. The refusal to challenge white rule had led Africans to see the United States as "the champion of reactionary status quos" on the continent.[39] The National Student's Association demanded sanctions and a boycott to end "the oppressive conditions that prevail today in Southern Africa." The African Studies Association, while narrowly defeating a resolution that called for complete U.S. "disassociation" from South Africa, did endorse a stepped-up diplomatic program to force changes in apartheid. Protestant church groups also urged some action. In 1963 the United Church of Christ called for sanctions. A year later a convention of the Methodist Church asked Johnson "to give serious consideration" to the idea. In 1965 the United Presbyterian Church also endorsed sanctions and compared apartheid to the Nazis' racial laws. The National Council of Churches called on its members to inform congregations of "the tragic situation in South Africa and the influence of the American economy on South African affairs" and to "review" church investments in corporations active in South Africa.[40]

More radical groups took more direct actions. In January 1965, protesters from the Students for a Democratic Society occupied the Chase Manhattan Bank in New York demanding cancellation of loans to South Africa. Chase's president, David Rockefeller, issued a statement that deplored apartheid but justified the bank's policies. He explained, "If we consider the receiver of a loan to be financially responsible, we do business with him, regardless of his nationality, religion, or political views." In March, the SDS organized demonstrations in New York, Boston, Detroit, San Francisco, and Washington against other banks and corporations involved in South Africa.[41]

For a number of reasons, protests by blacks lagged behind those by whites. Many black leaders appreciated Johnson's efforts on behalf of civil rights and other domestic programs. They did not want to alienate the administration by attacking its foreign policies. Others argued that the major interest of black groups should remain racism at home rather than discrimination abroad. Blacks were also divided on the issue of sanctions. Many agreed with the government that economic withdrawal from South Africa would harm blacks far more than it would harm the prosperous whites.

By 1965, however, younger, more militant blacks had begun to assert the importance of Africa and the need to work for foreign as well as domestic efforts to eliminate white supremacy. James Farmer of CORE delivered one of the

39. George Houser, "To Pretoria: Forward March," *Africa Today* 11 (October 1964): 4–6.

40. National Student Association to President Lyndon Johnson, 24 November 1965, CF: Africa, box 7, Johnson Library. Kenneth Carstens, "The Response of the Church in the USA to Apartheid," *Africa Today* 13 (December 1966): 19–22.

41. *Africa Today* 12 (February 1965): 16 and (March 1965): 11.

strongest condemnations of U.S. policy following a trip to Africa in early 1965. He concluded that Africans saw American diplomacy as "divisive and neo-colonialist." The Congo airlift was "an unmitigated disaster as far as our image in Africa is concerned." Equally important, Africans believed the United States was "at least tacitly supporting and helping to maintain apartheid." Farmer called on Washington to impose sanctions against Portugal and South Africa and to urge private banks to withdraw investments and cancel loans to both. He contended that continued normal relations with the Nationalists and Portugal forced Africans "into the arms of Peking and Moscow" for support in their struggle for freedom.[42] Even the more conservative NAACP adopted resolutions in 1965 endorsing "full economic sanctions" against South Africa, direct aid "to the South African freedom fighters," a boycott of South African products, an end to tourism and cultural exchanges, and all other means "not excluding collective military action" to end apartheid.[43]

The White House responded to the growth of criticism of its policies by stepping up its symbolic diplomacy. Johnson tried to demonstrate his concern with Africa by sending autographed copies of his speech in favor of the voting-rights bill to all African leaders. This posed a slight problem as the president had written, "Recognizing your personal interest in the great problems of achieving human dignity" on each copy, which hardly seemed appropriate for Verwoerd. The greeting to the South African leader was changed to "recognizing your Government's awareness of the importance of racial problems in the modern era."[44]

Bill Moyers, Johnson's aide and later his press secretary, urged the president to travel to Africa to "successfully project to the Africans his personal leadership for civil rights." Although he did not make the trip, Johnson suddenly invited African diplomats to join him for a cruise on the presidential yacht on 15 July 1965. Williams, Rusk, and a number of black governmental officials joined the voyage. Johnson told stories of his Texas boyhood friendships with blacks and defended the administration's opposition to racial discrimination abroad. Williams praised the president for the gesture and reported that the Africans "went away bubbling with enthusiasm."[45]

Johnson also continued the earlier U.S. policy of holding interracial receptions at facilities in South Africa. When Satterthwaite invited a number of blacks to an

42. Farmer, "An American Negro Leader's View of African Unity."

43. *Crisis* 72 (June–July 1965): 358–61.

44. Rowan to Johnson, 9 April 1965; Benjamin Read, Executive Secretary, Department of State, to Bundy, 22 April 1965, NSF: South Africa, box 2, Johnson Library. Later Johnson sent a collection of all of his speeches on civil rights to African leaders. See Jack Valenti, Special Assistant to the President, to Williams, 10 November 1965, CF: Africa, box 6, Johnson Library.

45. Moyers to Johnson, 14 June 1965, CF: Africa, box 6, Johnson Library; *New York Times*, 16 July 1965, p. 6; Williams to Johnson, 16 July 1965, CF: Africa, box 6.

official function at the American embassy, the South African minister of the interior berated him for the action. The minister noted that Pretoria's representatives abroad honored "the customs of those countries," and South Africa expected "the same courtesy."[46]

The multiracial receptions indirectly provoked another incident between the two nations when Verwoerd retaliated by announcing that U.S. servicemen aboard ships in South African ports would be subject to apartheid. The statement was aimed at the U.S. aircraft carrier *Independence*, due to stop in Capetown in a few days. Satterthwaite immediately asked for a clarification of Verwoerd's remarks. Officials told him that, while South Africa allowed "all ships of friendly nations" to use its ports, the crew of the *Independence* would be allowed ashore only if it observed local racial laws. The policy was necessary, they explained, because the United States "no longer observed social separation" as "a courtesy to the host country." Faced with the prospect of either accepting apartheid or creating a diplomatic incident, Washington cancelled the visit.[47]

Verwoerd, however, continued to attack the integration of American social affairs. He declared that the South African government would boycott all diplomatic receptions unless they were segregated. He also announced that he would not allow black Americans to work at the U.S. satellite tracking stations in South Africa. As there were no blacks employed at the facilities, the State Department ignored the prime minister's statement. White House officials explained to black groups that they had received no official policy statement and the agreement with South Africa contained no restrictions concerning race. Washington did protest South African attempts to censor the USIA movie on the life of John Kennedy, *Years of Lightning, Days of Drums*. The Nationalist government insisted scenes of peace corps volunteers in Africa, interracial education in America, and a long section on the civil-rights movement be removed. The State Department refused, and Pretoria banned the film.[48] Such diplomatic fencing was designed to show continued U.S. opposition to apartheid and particularly to attempts to apply apartheid to American citizens, but there was no attempt to transform this hostility into stronger official action. Public pressure for a tougher position on South Africa remained unorganized.

In contrast, conservative critics of U.S. diplomacy were well organized and extremely sensitive to any discussion of new initiatives against the Nationalists. Opponents of new efforts to confront Pretoria became enraged in July 1965 when the Carnegie Endowment for International Peace published a study on *Apartheid*

46. *New York Times*, 10 March 1965, p. 14.

47. Satterthwaite to Rusk, 14 May 1965; 5 June 1965, NSF: South Africa, box 2, Johnson Library.

48. *New York Times*, 28 June 1965, p. 1; James Williams, Director, American Negro Leadership Conference on Africa, to Johnson, 28 June 1965; White to Williams, 16 July 1965, CF: South Africa, box 71, Johnson Library; *New York Times*, 30 August 1965, p. 2.

and United Nations' Collective Measures. Although most of the book was a review of past efforts to deal with the issue of apartheid, the final chapter by Amelia Leiss of the Carnegie Endowment contained estimates of the cost of a blockade or actual invasion of South Africa. She calculated the price of an effective blockade at $165 million and predicted 19,000–38,000 casualties should there be a collective military effort to topple the Nationalists.[49] Pretoria labeled the document a plot to involve America in an invasion of South Africa. The South Africans sent copies of the book to conservative organizations, newspaper columnists, and politicians. There was an outcry against the Carnegie organization, the UN, and the U.S. government. Over fifty newspapers commented on the report. The *Chicago Tribune* charged that the UN and "a flock of blood-thirsty professors" were trying to engineer a war in Africa. Barry Goldwater reminded readers of his syndicated column that the Carnegie Endowment "has been headed by Alger Hiss." He suggested that the group now prepare an estimate of the cost of invading the Soviet Union and China. Other commentators saw a conspiracy by the Council on Foreign Relations, the Student Non-Violent Coordinating Committee, or the American Communist party to force the United States into a war with South Africa.[50]

Despite conservative fears of a major American confrontation with South Africa, the increasing involvement of the United States in Vietnam created a new emphasis on maintaining normal relations with all nations supportive of the effort. Like Portugal, South Africa used American intervention in Vietnam to emphasize its own militant anticommunism. Pretoria redirected its propaganda to stress South Africa's support of the war and opposition to communism. It greatly increased its cultural-exchange programs and was extremely successful in arranging favorable articles in American newspapers and magazines.[51]

The Nationalists also succeeded in convincing American military and business leaders to speak out on the importance of friendly relations between the two nations. Lauris Norstad, former supreme commander of NATO, visited South Africa in 1965 and called the country "critical" to U.S. economic and strategic interests. Charles Engelhard, chairman of the Rand Mines, an important contributor to the Democratic party, and a personal friend of Johnson, led the efforts of American business executives to assert the necessity of continued involvement in South Africa. Engelhard was a liberal among business leaders and received several awards for his support of civil rights in America. He was, however, a strong opponent of sanctions or any diplomatic break with South

49. Amelia C. Leiss, ed., *Apartheid and United Nations' Collective Measures: An Analysis*. The section that provoked the controversy was "Collective Military Measures: Some Calculations," 165–70.
50. Vernon McKay, "Africa and the American Right," *New Republic* 154 (26 March 1966): 13–15.
51. Francis Pollock, "Junkets to Apartheid: America's Press on Safari," *Nation* 203 (7 November 1966): 479–81.

Africa. Instead, he defended the idea of maintaining contacts with the country and working with the Nationalists for a gradual moderation of apartheid.[52]

Strong business opposition helped defeat the last major call within the administration for economic pressure on South Africa. In November 1965, Gordon Chase, deputy assistant to the president for national security affairs, urged the government to publicly announce that it no longer guaranteed "investments in South Africa" and would "discourage private American investment" in the country. The Commerce Department surveyed U.S. firms active in the area and found near unanimous opposition to the idea, but Chase argued that the State Department could "run it through" if Rusk and Ball supported it. He predicted, "If there is a major problem, it will be with Rusk and Ball themselves." Chase was correct. Both objected to the plan, and it never reached the president for his consideration.[53]

The dominance of strategic and economic concerns did not silence all debate over policy toward South Africa, but it did severely weaken demands for a tougher stance. In March 1966, the House Foreign Affairs Committee held extensive hearings on America and South Africa. Williams, who resigned two weeks later to run for the Senate, was the major administration witness. He denied that "economic and military interests . . . override this country's political interests in seeking an end to apartheid." He acknowledged that sanctions would greatly improve American relations with the third world but repeated the administration's position that sanctions would be ineffective, might push the Nationalists toward even more racial restrictions, and would threaten important "economic, scientific, and strategic interests."[54] Other officials gave similar justifications of existing policy. Alexander Trowbridge, assistant secretary of commerce, explained that the government "neither encourages nor discourages new investments" and considered sanctions unworkable. Satterthwaite warned that international pressure was already driving South African liberals into the Nationalist party as the only hope of white survival. William Lang of the Defense Department and two representatives from the National Aeronautics and Space Agency testified that the missile-tracking stations in South Africa and its ports remained important to American security.

On the other hand, academics, labor leaders, church officials, and others outside the government were generally critical of U.S. policy. Most demanded sanctions, discouragement of investments, and a general withdrawal of America from direct involvement in South Africa. Waldemar Nielsen, president of the African-American Institute, argued that apartheid was "not just another threat to

52. "Norstad Endorses Apartheid," *Africa Today* 12 (May 1965): 3; "The Engelhard Touch," *Forbes* (1 August 1965): 21–23; Paul Jacobs, "Our Man in South Africa: Charles Engelhard," *Ramparts* 5 (November 1966): 23–28.

53. Chase to Bundy, 3 November 1965, NSF: South Africa, box 2, Johnson Library.

54. U.S. Congress, House, Committee on Foreign Affairs, *Hearings on U.S.-Southern African Relations*, 1966, pts. 1–4.

human freedom. It is . . . the most flagrant and clearcut case in the world today of suppression of colored people by white people as a matter of official policy. It is the number 1 case in the world, therefore, of a threat to human freedom based on race." He defended American disengagement as an effective Cold War tactic to gain African support for U.S. foreign policy.[55]

The hearings produced no recommendations for legislation or new policies. Significantly, no blacks or businessmen appeared. Congress thus felt no great pressure on the issue. Rep. Donald Fraser of Minnesota, the most outspoken advocate in the House of a strong African policy, concluded that most members of Congress had "little interest in Africa" and would act only if prodded by their constituents. Fraser was especially upset by the lack of black lobbying. He attributed the silence of most civil-rights leaders to their concentration on domestic legislation. Similarly, white liberals were involved with the debate on Vietnam rather than with South Africa. As a result, what public pressure there was on Africa came largely from the right.[56]

The rivalries and infighting in the administration between Kennedy's appointees and those selected by Johnson also worked to limit any new approaches to South Africa. Although Johnson pleaded with many of Kennedy's advisers to remain in the government, he also brought in his own people. The inevitable conflicts were exacerbated by the distrust that many of the Kennedy officials had of Johnson and by the president's suspicions of many of his predecessor's staff. Despite his massive victory over Goldwater in 1964 and his success in enacting civil-rights legislation and the social programs of the Great Society, Johnson was still haunted by Kennedys both past and present. With the growth of liberal criticism of the war in Vietnam, his hatred of "the Harvards" became even more intense. Much of the president's wrath was aimed at Robert Kennedy. Even as attorney general, Robert Kennedy had a strong interest in the struggles for liberation in Africa. He had been influential in securing U.S. support for Mondlane in Mozambique and had generally defended the Africanist position. After he left the cabinet for the Senate, he maintained his ties in the administration. Williams and the African Bureau continued to send him weekly summaries of African affairs with special emphasis on developments in Angola and South Africa.[57]

In the fall of 1965, Ian Robertson, leader of the anti-apartheid National Union of South African Students, invited Kennedy to speak to his group in Capetown. Fredericks in the African Bureau urged the senator to accept in order to encourage white liberals in South Africa. Kennedy agreed to visit in 1966. When

55. Nielsen had written a book on the United States and southern Africa a year earlier that did not endorse sanctions but did call for other moves against apartheid. See *African Battleline*, 63–97. Before publication, he sent the manuscript to the African Bureau for comments. Most in the bureau were highly critical of the book as too "gloomy" and too harsh on U.S. policy. See Fredericks to Nielsen, 5 January 1965, Williams papers, box 15, National Archives.

56. Donald Fraser, "The Inert Congressional Watchdog," *Africa Today* 13 (December 1966): 6–8.

57. Williams to Hadsel, 11 March 1965, Williams papers, box 6, National Archives.

he announced plans to visit South Africa, Johnson was convinced the visit was an effort to embarrass the administration and perhaps even to court black votes for a Kennedy presidential campaign in 1968. For its part, South Africa promptly placed Robertson under house arrest and denied visas to U.S. reporters and television correspondents who wanted to cover the trip.[58]

As Kennedy prepared for his visit in the summer of 1966, Johnson and the White House staff became more convinced that the tour was largely for the senator's own political purposes. When Kennedy gave a speech in Ethiopia calling for Afro-Asian control of the UN, Vice-President Humphrey sent a copy of the address to Johnson with the comment, "rather interesting—and quite dangerous if it should happen." A week before Kennedy arrived in South Africa, the president suddenly invited the African diplomatic corps to the White House and delivered his first major speech on Africa. He denounced white supremacy as "odious" and promised that America would "not have a double standard— professing abroad what we do not practice at home or venerating at home what we ignore abroad."[59]

The State Department was also apprehensive about Kennedy's personal diplomacy. Rusk ordered Satterthwaite to attend the senator's speeches but to make it clear that Kennedy was not an official spokesman for the U.S. government. He also instructed the USIA to monitor Kennedy's comments throughout the trip and to analyze the reactions of the African press.[60]

Kennedy's actual visit was as dramatic as many had predicted. On 4 June he arrived in Johannesburg. Denied permission to see governmental officials, he met with South African businessmen in Pretoria. He visited Chief Albert Luthuli and gave him records of his brother's speeches on civil rights and called on Ian Robertson to present a copy of *Profiles in Courage* autographed by Jacqueline Kennedy. The senator also spoke to a hostile crowd of Afrikaner students at Stellenbosch University and defended U.S. progress on civil rights. He attacked apartheid and asked,"What if you found out God was black?" Kennedy concluded his tour with an unauthorized visit to the Soweto ghetto, where he urged nonviolent resistance to apartheid. The South African government and the Afrikaans-language press attacked Kennedy for "demagoguery," "electioneering," "meddling" in their internal affairs, and promoting a "mongrel world." English-language papers were less harsh but pointed out that the senator had little influence on American foreign policy.[61]

Kennedy's visit did not have a significant impact on U.S. diplomacy, but it

58. For details of Kennedy's trip, see Schlesinger, *Robert Kennedy*, 743–49; William V. Heuvel and Milton Gwirtzman, *On His Own*, 146–62; and Kennedy's "Suppose God Is Black," *Look* 30 (23 August 1966): 44–45.

59. Humphrey to Johnson, undated, CF: Africa, box 6, Johnson Library; *New York Times*, 27 May 1966, p. 1.

60. Rusk to Satterthwaite, 26 May 1966, NSF: South Africa, box 2, Johnson Library.

61. USIA to Rusk, "Media Comments on Senator Kennedy's Visit to South Africa," 16 June 1966, CF: Africa, box 6, Johnson Library.

widened the split between Johnson and the senator and increased the already strong White House distrust of liberals. When Prime Minister Verwoerd was assassinated in September, a newsman sarcastically wrote to Moyers, "The President always wants to do something nice for Bobbie [*sic*] Kennedy. Has he thought of sending him to Verwoerd's funeral?" Moyers included the note in his package of documents "for the President's Night Reading."[62]

By 1966 the growth of the antiwar movement and the increasing militancy of black protest had produced a new radical critique of U.S. foreign policy. Many antiwar activists saw all of American diplomacy as reactionary, racist, and motivated largely by profit. Similarly, some blacks rejected the traditional goals of the civil-rights movement for the abstract notion of black power and viewed themselves as part of a global struggle against white racism. Both black and white supporters of the new radicalism interpreted the continued cooperation with South Africa as symptomatic of larger flaws in the American system and took direct action to show their opposition. On 29 March, members of SNCC occupied the South African embassy in Washington chanting, "Death to apartheid." One White House aide predicted correctly: "This is only the beginning." Later, demonstrators from CORE and SNCC, led by black-power advocate Stokeley Carmichael, staged a sit-in at America's UN headquarters to protest "racism and hypocrisy" in U.S. policy toward southern Africa. They demanded sanctions, a break in diplomatic relations, and withdrawal of black soldiers from Vietnam to fight "for black majority rule in South Africa and Rhodesia."[63]

Although American officials rejected calls for any new pressure on South Africa for reform of apartheid, they were prepared for a diplomatic altercation over the major issue between the two nations in 1966: South West Africa. The international dispute over control of South West Africa (Namibia) dated from 1946. Throughout the 1950s, the UN had demanded that Pretoria withdraw from the territory and turn it over to international control in preparation for independence. South Africa argued that it governed the sparsely populated region under a mandate from the defunct League of Nations and the UN had no right to interfere with its administration. The United States had supported the right of the UN to monitor South Africa's rule but had not backed demands for collective action to drive the Afrikaners out.

In 1960, Liberia and Ethiopia brought suit in the International Court of Justice demanding that South Africa withdraw and turn the nation over to UN supervision. Washington vigorously supported the suit and worked to insure that South Africa comply with the court's ruling. In 1963, Rusk joined Great Britain in a strong communiqué warning South Africa to accept the court's judgment and

62. Ray Scherer to Moyers, 6 September 1966; Moyers to Johnson, 7 September 1966, CF: South Africa, box 71, Johnson Library.

63. Haynes to Komer, 29 March 1966, NSF: South Africa, box 2, Johnson Library; *New York Times*, 23 July 1966, p. 4.

indicating that both nations would support UN action if Pretoria ignored the opinion.[64]

America had also resisted the Nationalists' attempt to formally extend apartheid to South West Africa. In 1964, the Odendaal Commission of South Africa recommended full application of apartheid to the territory by 1967. Satterthwaite immediately notified Verwoerd that the United States opposed any extension of apartheid until after the world court ruled. America and Great Britain issued an aide-mémoire to Pretoria asking delay in implementing the recommendations of the Odendaal commission until after the ruling. Bundy met with Naude in Washington to emphasize the U.S. position that any consolidation of South African rule was "premature" until after the court decided the issue.[65]

Great Britain and the United States succeeded in postponing the imposition of apartheid, but some administration officials still worried that South Africa would defy the court's decision. Williams argued that the only reason Pretoria had even agreed to go to the world court was because of strong pressure from Washington and London. He urged that both nations prepare to force Pretoria to withdraw when the court ordered it. On 10 June 1964, the United States began discussions with Great Britain to coordinate policy to force South Africa to evacuate South West Africa after the court ruled. The State Department also urged Johnson to raise the issue with Prime Minister Harold Wilson to help "evolve a coordinated policy aimed at persuading South Africa to comply with the ruling." Rusk even told the British ambassador that the United States might reverse its traditional opposition to UN mandatory sanctions if Pretoria refused to accept the court's opinion on South West Africa.[66]

American planning and policy were based on the assumption that Liberia and Ethiopia would win the case. Legal experts in the State Department were certain that the court would follow an earlier advisory opinion that had found South Africa "in default of its obligations" toward the territory. Several American jurists helped the Africans prepare their case and were also convinced that South Africa had no real chance to win. Even many South Africans were resigned to an adverse ruling and to a confrontation with the United States and Great Britain.[67]

On 18 July 1966, after six years of deliberations and over 2,900 pages of

64. Rusk to U.S. embassies London and Pretoria, 7 February 1963, NSF: Africa, box 3, Kennedy Library.
65. Satterthwaite to the Department of State, 19 March 1964; Rusk to South African Foreign Ministry, 12 February 1964 and 19 March 1964; Brubeck to Bundy, 18 March 1964, NSF: South Africa, box 2, Johnson Library.
66. Williams to Harriman, 13 May 1964; Department of State, "Diplomatic Pressure on South Africa about South West Africa," 10 June 1964, ibid.; Department of State, "Visit of Prime Minister Harold Wilson, December 7–8, 1964: Regional Background Paper—Africa," 3 December 1964, NSF: United Kingdom, box 4; Department of State, "Memorandum of Conversation: Apartheid and the UN," 10 September 1965, ibid., box 2.
67. Department of State Memorandum, "The South West Africa Issue," undated, ibid. See also Barber, *South Africa's Foreign Policy*, 155–59 and C. W. De Kiewiet, "South Africa's Gamble with History," 1–17.

testimony, the court finally decided the longest case in its history. To the shock of nearly all observers, the judges ruled 8–7 that Liberia and Ethiopia did not have "sufficient legal interest" in the issue to bring suit. It did not decide on the merits of South Africa's claim to rule South West Africa, but only that the two African nations had failed to prove that they had adequate reason to be involved in the dispute.[68]

State Department officials were "shocked" by the decision. The American justice, Phillip Jessup, filed a 129-page dissent. Rusk announced that he was "surprised" by the ruling but rejected a suggestion that the United States suspend trade with South Africa until it withdrew from the territory. Pretoria was understandably jubilant. It distributed thousands of copies of the ruling within the United States along with Verwoerd's triumphant speech hailing the decision. It later rushed into print a book, *Ethiopia and Liberia versus South Africa*, with an extended analysis of the case and an extensive defense of apartheid for distribution in America and Great Britain. The South African ambassador sent a note to Ball citing the frequent U.S. demands that Pretoria accept the court's ruling and demanding that Washington now abide by the decision and resist UN efforts to bring "unwarranted pressure to bear on South Africa."[69]

Africans were outraged by the court's actions. They attacked the decision's "legalism" and the reluctance of the justices to come to grips with the real issues involved. The Namibian observer at the UN praised Jessup's dissent and his vote "against South African fascism" but cabled Johnson requesting American support of "strong political measures" against South Africa if it remained in the territory.[70]

Africans at the UN immediately introduced resolutions on the issue. American ambassador Arthur Goldberg warned South Africa "not to take refuge in a technical finding of the court which did not deal with the substantive merits of the case." Goldberg worked instead for a resolution appointing a special UN representative to "survey the situation" and report on progress toward independence. He argued that setting a date for self-rule, as the Africans wanted to do, was "coercion" and would provoke "an immediate confrontation with South Africa." The U.S. plan for a special observer offered a chance for "peaceful progress." However, the idea of a special representative was overwhelmingly defeated. Goldberg abstained when the General Assembly

68. The best analysis of the decision is Ernest A. Gross, "The South West Africa Case: What Happened?" See also Faye Carroll, *South West Africa and the United Nations*, 101–6.

69. *New York Times*, 19 July 1966, p. 1; 22 July 1966, p. 62; Vernon McKay, "South African Propaganda on the International Court's Decision," *African Forum* 2 (Fall 1966): 51–64; South African Department of Information, *Ethiopia and Liberia versus South Africa;* H. S. T. Taswell to Ball, 17 August 1966, *SDB* 55 (10 October 1966): 567–68.

70. Namibian Mission to the United Nations to President Lyndon Johnson, 21 July 1966; Read to Rostow, 23 July 1966, CF: Africa, box 7, Johnson Library.

passed a resolution on 19 May 1967 setting June 1968 as the date of Namibian freedom.[71]

The court's surprising decision removed the most likely source of direct conflict between America and South Africa. Previous actions indicate that the United States was prepared to join Great Britain in some sort of effort to make Pretoria obey the court's ruling. It is also likely that Washington would have supported UN efforts, short of binding sanctions, to pressure South Africa to comply. American policy since 1961 had been based on delaying the application of apartheid and preparing to force Pretoria to accept the court's authority. When the justices denied the African position, Washington was forced to improvise policy because it had no real contingency plans for a South African victory.

Although the 1966 decision did not end the problem of South West Africa, it did eliminate any direct diplomatic dispute between the United States and South Africa. America maintained its previous policy of normal relations with occasional protests of racial discrimination. However, in early 1967, Washington was again drawn into conflict with Pretoria over yet another quarrel concerning the treatment of U.S. military personnel. The controversy over the scheduled stop of the *Independence* in 1965 had led to a boycott of South African ports by the American navy. However, with the massive intervention in Vietnam, it became more difficult for U.S. ships to avoid South Africa. In February 1967, the USS *FDR*, returning to America after eight months in Vietnam, was ordered to dock at Capetown to refuel. American and South African officials worked out plans for the entertainment of the interracial crew, but Pretoria suddenly announced that all recreational facilities in Capetown would remain segregated. Word of the decision leaked to the American press, and blacks immediately protested that the visit was a "reversal of previous policy" and an "accommodation with apartheid."[72]

Congressman Fraser circulated a petition, eventually signed by thirty-eight representatives, asking Johnson to cancel the visit. Senators Clifford Case, Jacob Javits, Walter Mondale, and Charles Percy also protested the stop. Deputy Secretary of Defense Cyrus Vance met with congressional leaders and assured them the United States would not accept any form of racial discrimination. A spokesman for the navy said there were no plans to cancel the stop, as the navy had "reason to believe that there will be absolutely no discrimination against American personnel regardless of race." He noted it would cost $250,000 to send a tanker to refuel the *FDR* if it did not dock in Capetown.[73]

71. *SDB* 55 (15 August 1966): 321; (10 October 1966): 523; 56 (12 June 1967): 893–94. For a discussion of Goldberg's independent role and the confusion of the State Department, see Beichman, *The "Other" State Department*, 168–70.

72. *New York Times*, 2 February 1967, p. 12.

73. Ibid., 4 February 1967, p. 10; Vance to Javits, 3 February 1967, CF: South Africa, box 71, Johnson Library.

The next day, Vance and Nicholas Katzenbach of the State Department announced they had negotiated a "modified shore leave in connection with integrated activity only." South African officials quickly explained that this meant only integrated bus tours. All other facilities still were governed by apartheid. Faced with likely discrimination against U.S. servicemen, Washington ordered Capt. Martin O'Neil to cancel liberty for all his crew. American ambassador William Roundtree invited South Africans of all races to tour the vessel instead. Sixty American sailors also donated blood for South African hospitals as a "gesture of good will," but blacks protested when nurses marked each donation either "European" or "African" for separate use.[74]

On 7 February, the *FDR* cut short its visit and left for the United States, but another American ship, the missile-tracker *Sword Knot*, was scheduled to dock the next day in Durban. For eight days the *Sword Knot* cruised off the South African coast waiting for officials in Washington to decide if it should land. Finally, it was ordered to bypass Durban and land in Mombasa, Kenya.[75]

Black leaders in America applauded the decision to cancel leave for sailors on the *FDR* and to divert the *Sword Knot* but were indignant that the ships had been scheduled for South Africa in the first place. The State Department finally sent letters to Wilkins, A. Phillip Randolph, Theodore Brown of the American Negro Leadership Conference, and members of Congress explaining that the visits represented "no change in U.S. policy." American vessels would visit South Africa "as long as no racial conditions were imposed." Given the position of the Nationalists, no ships would be sent "in the foreseeable future."[76]

Despite the controversy over the *FDR*, South Africa was far from the center of concern in Washington in 1967. The war in Vietnam showed no signs of ending and had produced intense opposition. The battles in the ghettos continued, culminating in the bloody riots in Newark and Detroit.

South Africans explained the violence in America as the inevitable result of a misguided acceptance of racial equality. They used the riots to chide America for its long criticism of apartheid. After the uprising in Newark, the progovernment paper *Die Vaderland* concluded that the United States was "on the brink of racial civil war." The riots confirmed the Afrikaner interpretation that "America's obsession with integration only causes chaos, strife, and destruction." Rather than continue pressing South Africa to adopt its racial policies, the United States should consider emulating apartheid. After the Detroit riot, Prime Minister Vorster noted: "I ask prominent Americans whether they have solved their colour question and they tell me no . . . Have I not the right to ask: If the solution you offer is by your own admission no solution, what moral right do you have to

74. *New York Times*, 4 February 1967, p. 11; 5 February 1967, p. 1.

75. Ibid., 14 February 1967, p. 5; 16 February 1967, p. 11.

76. Joseph Palmer, Assistant Secretary of State for African Affairs, to Wilkins, Randolph, Brown, and Javits, 16 February 1967, CF: South Africa, box 71, Johnson Library.

impose it on me or my people?" He contrasted the "peaceful" situation in South Africa with the violence in American cities and offered apartheid as the only way to avoid total race war.[77]

While few in the United States considered apartheid a solution to racial problems, the riots did cause many whites to question the direction of the civil-rights movement and to reconsider their support of black protest. The alienation of many Americans from the new, more violent phase of the black struggle led some to become skeptical of U.S. support of black liberation in Africa as well. Just as the rhetoric and tactics of black Americans grew more inflammatory and militant, so did the position of liberation groups in Africa. Blacks in Angola, Mozambique, Rhodesia, and South Africa became more convinced that violence offered the only opportunity for their freedom and that whites, of all political philosophies, were the enemy. Many American liberals, church leaders, and politicians previously sympathetic to African liberation did not like the new tone and strategies of Africans in 1967 and 1968.[78]

Despite the impact of Vietnam and the ghetto riots, some in the United States continued to lobby for more active opposition to apartheid. In August 1967, Johnson met with a delegation of liberal congressmen led by Sen. Edward Kennedy of Massachusetts and Sen. Frank Moss of Utah, who urged "a harder stance against South Africa, Rhodesia, and Portugal." The president was sympathetic but offered no new policies. He noted that the problems of southern Africa were "among the most grim and intractable in the world" but rejected the suggestion of using economic pressure against the white regimes.[79]

Instead of sanctions, the administration renewed its call for negotiations and gradual reform. Goldberg explained that Washington was dedicated to "a genuine dialog on the basis of self-determination" in southern Africa. Neither violence nor economic pressure would reform apartheid, Goldberg concluded, as "no differences can be solved without contact, discussion, or negotiations."[80] Goldberg's statement was an accurate summary of the U.S. position that it should retain economic, military, and cultural contacts with South Africa in hopes of promoting gradual change.

In accord with this position, America consistently resisted attempts to ban South Africa from the Olympic games. Although the U.S. Olympic Committee was separate from the American government, few Africans accepted the distinction. The support of South Africa by the U.S. group, and by Avery Brundage, the American chairman of the International Olympic Committee, further alienated many African nations from Washington. South Africa had been

---

77. *New York Times*, 20 July 1967, p. 14; O. Geyser, ed., *B. J. Vorster: Selected Speeches*, 77, 84.
78. "Trends in African Liberation Movements," *Africa Today* 14 (August 1967): 3–18; Kenneth Carstens, "Christianity and Violent Revolution," ibid. 15 (June-July 1967): 6–7.
79. Rostow to Johnson, 10 August 1967; Edward K. Hamilton, National Security Council Staff, to Johnson, 16 August 1967, CF: Africa, box 6, Johnson Library.
80. *SDB* 56 (20 February 1967): 289–94.

allowed to participate in the 1960 games when it promised there would be no discrimination in the selection of its team. When this proved to be false, the OAU had passed a resolution demanding expulsion of South Africa from the 1964 Olympics. Brundage and the American delegation led the fight against the move. They argued that a nation's racial policy was an internal matter and the Olympics should not be involved in politics. The Africans prevailed, and South Africa was not invited in 1964. In 1967 Pretoria announced that it would comply with the rules and send an interracial team in 1968. Brundage and the IOC voted to allow the South Africans to participate. When over forty nations immediately threatened to boycott the games, the IOC ignored Brundage's vehement protests and reversed its decision, voting to ban South Africa from the 1968 games.[81]

Washington also continued its long-standing UN policy by abstaining on a 1967 resolution in the Special Political Committee calling for "universally-applied mandatory sanctions" against South Africa. The U.S. delegate criticized the statement as "too violent in tone" and unlikely to change apartheid. Columnist C. L. Sulzberger of the *New York Times* hailed the vote as a sign of a new realism in American policy toward apartheid. With the war in Vietnam and its own racial problems, Sulzberger felt it was "time for the United States to pipe down on South Africa" and stop "sticking our nose into its affairs."[82]

In contrast, liberals bemoaned the apparent decline of official interest in apartheid. One writer argued that, since the war in Vietnam, American policy toward South Africa had degenerated into "a tandem of lamentation and laissez-faire." Rep. Richard Ottinger of New York wrote to Johnson that U.S. inaction made "it appear that we pay more heed to our big business interests in South Africa than to our concern for Africa's future or our concern to resist racial injustice."[83]

Business and military leaders used the seeming relaxation in U.S. policy to push for elimination of the remaining restrictions on relations with South Africa. By 1968, many businessmen were openly critical of Washington's hostility to Pretoria. They predicted an economic boom in South Africa centering around Johannesburg, "the Detroit of South Africa," and argued that continued official opposition to apartheid restricted chances for American firms to capitalize on the new opportunities. A poll of U.S. executives in South Africa found 60 percent felt the nation "was attempting to solve the racial situation." Over 40 percent said they would vote for the Nationalist party if eligible, and only 9 percent saw apartheid as "altogether incorrect."[84] American military officials also criticized

81. Richard Espy, *The Politics of the Olympic Games*, 84–106.

82. *New York Times*, 23 November 1967, p. 10; 15 December 1967, p. 46.

83. John Marcum, "Southern Africa and United States' Policy: A Consideration of Alternatives," *Africa Today* 14 (October 1967): 5–13; Ottinger to Johnson, 22 July 1966, CF: Africa, box 7, Johnson Library.

84. "U.S. and South Africa: The Ties, the Differences," *U.S. News and World Report* 64 (22 April 1968): 96–99.

Washington's "isolation" of South Africa. Many advocated repeal of the arms embargo, and an unidentified U.S. military attaché in Pretoria claimed that, because of the ban on American ships in South Africa since the *FDR* incident, "lives are being lost in Vietnam because the navy can't use the ports down here."[85]

The policy battles that had characterized U.S. diplomacy toward southern Africa were largely over by 1967. Williams's resignation in 1966 removed the last strong advocate of new American efforts against apartheid. Vietnam and the internal racial violence destroyed what little pressure remained for a reevaluation of the U.S. position. Increasingly, the battle against apartheid took place not within the government but outside it. In 1968 the first major demonstrations against college and university investments in corporations and banks active in South Africa took place. Students at Cornell and Princeton demanded divestiture, and black students at Spelman College interrupted a speech by New York governor Nelson Rockefeller with chants of "get your money out of South Africa!"[86] Such protests foretold the more general debate over institutional divestiture in the 1970s that followed the government's rejection of any official disassociation.

The Kennedy and Johnson administrations had publicly and privately protested apartheid, integrated U.S. facilities in South Africa, defended the rights of black Americans, and embargoed weapons. Neither, however, had used all possible American power against the Nationalists. There were both practical and philosophical reasons for their rejection of sanctions, limits on investments, reduced diplomatic and cultural contacts, and other policy alternatives. There were no assurances that they would succeed in the major goal of forcing changes in the racial situation. There was a risk that South African retaliation would harm U.S. economic and strategic interests. To many officials, South African violations of human rights were no worse than those of any number of other regimes around the globe. To be consistent, they argued, Washington would have to "disassociate" from dozens of nations. Foreign policy would become nothing more than a well-intended but quixotic crusade to export American ideals.

Although some students of international relations strongly question the influence of idealism on foreign policy, there was a strong humanitarianism in America's hope for a moderation of apartheid. Most policymakers accepted diplomacy as a vehicle for international reform. In the case of South Africa, the dispute occurred when humanitarian desires threatened more immediate interests. The United States concluded that the risks involved in the pursuit of worthy goals outweighed the likely gains. Most high officials under both Kennedy and Johnson doubted that a "tough" policy would really influence the Afrikaners to change their racial laws. Liberals, blacks, and Africanists in the

85. Ibid.
86. *New York Times*, 21 April 1968, p. 74; 24 May 1968, p. 23.

government tried to convince the policymakers that American actions could produce significant changes in apartheid or at least generate other diplomatic benefits such as the strong support of the third world for U.S. objectives elsewhere. They were unable to convert either Kennedy or Johnson to their position.

8. THE U.S.A. AND UDI | America and Rhodesian Independence

In theory, foreign policy combines long-range planning with the management of immediate crises. Much of the vast bureaucracy of the State Department, White House, and CIA is involved in research, contingency planning, and educated predictions of possible international developments. Various "scenarios" circulate daily among those concerned with diplomacy, often with detailed forecasts of likely changes and potential American responses. By anticipating international developments, Washington supposedly is prepared to react instantly to any new major global problem. Despite the time and expense devoted to such efforts, however, it is the present rather than the future that generally occupies the attention of high-level officials. Although every new administration pays lip service to the need for more coordination and planning resulting in fewer unexpected crises, U.S. foreign policy concentrates on the most pressing and dangerous international issues. Unfortunately, most of the past studies and options become obsolete when an existing problem suddenly becomes an immediate crisis.

Rhodesia was Lyndon Johnson's "crisis," even though it had been a "problem" for American diplomats for nearly five years. In the cases of the Portuguese colonies and South Africa, Johnson inherited from the Kennedy administration a general diplomatic position and a series of ongoing policies. He occasionally altered prevailing diplomacy, but he was not forced to establish new objectives and tactics. With Rhodesia, Johnson and his advisers faced an issue nearly unencumbered by previous U.S. commitments. They worked within existing global priorities and domestic considerations similar to those affecting South Africa and the Portuguese colonies, but they also faced alternatives, pressures, and restraints unique to the new crisis.

Because Rhodesia had been a British colony, Rhodesia's Unilateral Declaration of Independence (UDI) on 11 November 1965 directly affected Anglo-American relations. The ties of language, culture, and history, as well as their generally shared international objectives, made consultation and cooperation between the United States and Great Britain an accepted procedure in any major diplomatic decision. Because of America's power, the "partnership" was far from equal, but the notion of working closely with London was almost a reflex action for U.S. diplomats. However, in the case of Rhodesia, London claimed leadership in the international response to the problem.

Washington agreed that Great Britain had a unique role in the crisis, yet the Johnson administration had its own international interests and domestic situation to consider. The problems of UDI forced America and Great Britain into even closer policy coordination than usual, but the crisis also showed the tension, jealousy, and rivalry within the "special relationship." America was unaccustomed to following any nation. It was often frustrated and impatient in its role as supporting actor to Great Britain's lead.

The situation in Rhodesia also raised again the question of the importance of the UN in American diplomacy. More than South Africa or the Portuguese territories, the Rhodesian dispute was dominated by the United Nations. All of the prevailing U.S. fears concerning the world organization again emerged, but Washington went much further in its acceptance of UN prerogatives on Rhodesia than it had on other African issues. Eventually, it even accepted the mandatory economic sanctions it had so vigorously rejected in other areas.

The Johnson administration agreed to stronger international involvement on Rhodesia largely because direct U.S. interests in the nation were not as significant as in other areas of white Africa. America had no bases, missile-tracking stations, or need for ports in Rhodesia. Unlike South Africa, the country was of only minor economic importance to the United States. There were no worries about weakening the NATO alliance. The direct economic and strategic risks of a "tough" policy were far less than in the other two areas of minority rule.

In spite of this lack of pressing interests, there were a number of pressures that complicated America's diplomatic decisions regarding Rhodesia. Dominant again was Vietnam. The war not only occupied the attention of the highest-level U.S. officials but also became a consideration in judging all other problems and nations. African hostility to the war in Asia made the administration less than zealous in its commitment to African concerns. More significant for the Rhodesian situation, Great Britain was hardly an enthusiastic backer of Washington's efforts in Vietnam. The "special relationship" supposedly worked both ways. The Johnson administration expected London's support in Vietnam just as much as the British demanded American help on Rhodesia. The refusal of the United Kingdom to give sustained diplomatic aid to the war, and its willingness to continue to trade with North Vietnam, severely strained relations between the two powers and affected their cooperation in Africa.

Other events in Africa and changes within the bureaucracy also shaped American actions on Rhodesia. The tribal conflict in Nigeria, culminating in the secession of the Ibos and the creation of the state of Biafra in 1967, demanded much of the attention of the African Bureau, often at the expense of the Rhodesian problem. In mid-1966, Williams left the government. His replacement, Joseph Palmer, was dedicated to the Africanist point of view but was not as willing as Williams had been to be an open advocate of black liberation or a crusader for the bureau's interpretation of the stakes involved in Rhodesia.

Rhodesia's break with Great Britain also created complex legal and moral problems for many Americans. As expected, Europeanists argued that, since the Rhodesian situation did not involve major American interests, active U.S. involvement would garner only minimum rewards. Others in Washington questioned the sudden reversal of the traditional U.S. opposition to European colonialism. The declaration of independence of a weak nation from Great Britain mirrored America's own actions in 1776. Many inside and outside the government objected to U.S. pressure to force any nation to return to colonial status. In addition, many were concerned that international efforts against whites in Rhodesia could set a precedent for attacks on the other two white regimes in Africa. To many conservatives, this would only encourage radicalism and communism on the continent. There was a risk of an African domino theory as opposition to the white government in Salisbury escalated into pressure on South Africa and the Portuguese colonies—areas of more immediate U.S. concern.

The crisis also forced Johnson to confront the persistent problem of public opinion. By 1965 blacks in the United States were more vocal on African issues than they had been even a few years before. They saw the situation in Rhodesia as a clear example of white exploitation and expected America to be equally clear in its support of black rule. As in the cases of South Africa and Portugal, however, there was a smaller but better organized group that fiercely resisted any U.S. efforts against the white minority. The administration again faced the challenge of balancing black, liberal, and African demands for action against conservative pressure by Congress and the general public for noninvolvement.

The "Rhodesian problem" began with the postwar rush to independence in Africa. As the British prepared to withdraw from Africa, they faced a dilemma in their handling of the white-ruled colony of southern Rhodesia. Throughout the late 1950s and early 1960s, decolonization was nearly synonymous with majority rule. It was assumed that the end of European control would transfer political and economic power to the black majority. In southern Rhodesia, this logic did not apply. Whites controlled the vote, the economy, and the armed forces. A British withdrawal without major reforms would only result in continued suppression of the black majority by the powerful white minority. The British had been pressured to get out of Africa to allow blacks their freedom. With Rhodesia, they faced demands to stay on the continent to prevent white control.

The obvious solution was for Great Britain to force whites to grant political and economic equality to the Africans. White Rhodesians, however, shared the conviction of the Afrikaners to the south that any compromise with the black majority would destroy the whites. They argued that London should be consistent and decolonize the entire African continent. The political and economic future of their nation was a Rhodesian, not a British issue. Years of negotiations were unable to resolve the dispute between Great Britain and its colony over the status of the African. As the rest of the continent gained independence, the future of Rhodesia remained unresolved. Great Britain faced the choice of abandoning the black majority by granting Rhodesia independence or trying to maintain its control in defiance of its decolonization efforts elsewhere.

In the United States, although the growing tension between Great Britain and Rhodesia from 1961 to 1964 did draw some attention to the area, prior to 1964 the "Rhodesian problem" was a distinctly secondary part of U.S. involvement in white Africa. Many of the reports and analyses of Africa in the early 1960s noted the deteriorating situation in Rhodesia, but they concentrated on the immediate crisis in Angola and on South Africa, the obvious major obstacle to majority rule. Rhodesia remained only a minor part of any official discussion of the problems of white Africa during the Kennedy years.

Nonetheless, Washington did have to choose how it would approach the "Rhodesian problem." It could stay out of the dispute by claiming it was an internal affair of the British Empire. This risked a possible violent effort by the Africans or the UN to force majority rule. It also was inconsistent with the U.S. position that the Portuguese colonies were an international and not an internal problem. Alternatively, America could support the British efforts to retain control of Rhodesia. This committed the United States to active opposition to any efforts by whites to unilaterally declare their independence. Throughout the ongoing dispute between Great Britain and Rhodesia in the early 1960s, America generally followed the second option and aided London.

In spite of the U.S. determination to aid the British, American diplomats were also critical of London's handling of its colony. In 1961, Great Britain and Rhodesia negotiated a new constitution that granted minor political power to the black majority in exchange for the abandonment of London's right to overturn the actions of the colony's assembly. Blacks protested the agreement and the fact that they were not consulted. The result was a crackdown on African organizations by Rhodesian Prime Minister Sir Edgar Whitehead, who emulated South Africa by dissolving black groups, banning black leaders, censoring the press, and using force to suppress any opposition. To Africanists in Washington, it was clear that Rhodesia's whites were totally unwililng to compromise on the issues of majority rule and racial equality. Many in the African Bureau were also suspicious of Great Britain's ultimate intentions in the area. They were certain that both British power and resolve were on the wane. Despite its claims that it was committed to racial equality in Rhodesia, some Americans feared London would eventually give in to white demands for independence without adequate guarantees of African rights. In early 1962, Williams warned Rusk that Great Britain might sacrifice the blacks to maintain close relations with the white minority. He recommended that Washington "be careful that the British don't pull out altogether" leaving the Africans unprotected in an independent Rhodesia.[1]

Other officials shared Williams's concerns. In a review of the "white redoubt" area of Africa in June 1962, State Department analysts warned of a possible alliance among whites in Rhodesia, South Africa, and Angola unless Great Britain was willing to exert control over the white regime in Salisbury. The National Security Council was also critical of London's management of the situation. In a report in October 1962, it concluded that the problem with Rhodesia was that Britain did "not have an overall African policy" but merely drifted" from crisis to crisis.[2] With the victory of Winston Field and the hard-line Rhodesian Front over the "liberal" Whitehead in late 1962, U.S. officials became even more alarmed. Bowles predicted imminent violence between blacks and whites in Rhodesia unless London acted decisively to curtail Field and "the diehards" in Salisbury. Williams claimed Rhodesia was "the new African time bomb." He explained to Rusk that the end of the Central African Federation would leave Rhodesia as the only remaining British colony in Africa. It would then demand its independence, and Williams feared that London would be unable to prevent it.[3]

In March 1963, Rhodesia formally requested independence. To the surprise of many in the State Department, Great Britain adamantly refused, and announced "five principles" that were conditions for independence: "progress toward" majority rule; no "retrogressive" amendment of the constitution; direct political participation by the Africans; major steps toward an end to racial discrimination; and evidence that the majority of Rhodesians, of all races, favored independence.

Africanists in Washington were impressed with Great Britain's resolve. Williams was delighted with the "five principles" and issued a public statement in their support. The Rhodesian assembly responded by attacking Williams for "encouraging chaos in Central Africa." Roy Welensky, former Rhodesian prime minister, charged that U.S. dedication to majority rule "actively assisted the fulfillment of Communist aims." Some whites even suggested that Great Britain's rejection of Rhodesian independence was the result of American pressure.[4] Although some U.S. diplomats were still unsure that Great Britain could handle the potential crisis in Central Africa, the announcement of the

1. Williams to Rusk, 16 April 1962, Williams Papers, box 2, National Archives.
2. State Department Planning Group, "The White Redoubt," 28 June 1962; National Security Council Memorandum, "Problems of Southern Africa," 4 October 1962, NSF: Africa, box 2, Kennedy Library.
3. Bowles, "Report on Mission to Africa, October 15–November 9, 1962," 13 November 1962, Bowles Papers, box 311, Yale University; Williams to Rusk, "Major Conclusions of Williams' African Trip," 24 February 1963, Williams Papers, box 3, National Archives.
4. *East Africa and Rhodesia* 39 (14 March 1963): 604; Roy Welensky, *4000 Days,* 111.

conditions for independence convinced most to support London on the Rhodesian issue.

In the fall of 1963, when African nations attacked Great Britain's plan for the dissolution of the Central African Federation, the United States did come to Britain's assistance. Africans were appalled that the final settlement gave the bulk of the federation's military supplies to the white regime in Salisbury, and they prepared a UN resolution demanding that Great Britain intervene to prevent the transfer of the equipment. Great Britain then requested America's help in defeating any "strong resolution on Rhodesia." Williams and Harlan Cleveland argued that it would take "vigorous American support" to block the resolution, since Great Britain's argument for the arms transfer was "both weak and impractical." They also noted that London's claim that the situation was an "internal matter" of no concern to the UN sounded quite similar to the position of Portugal and South Africa. Rusk, however, was convinced that the United States should back its European ally. He agreed to work against the African resolution with the tacit understanding that Great Britain would try to convince Commonwealth nations to vote against the admission of mainland China to the UN. The United States actively lobbied against the African statement and abstained when it passed. America was unable to defeat the measure, and Great Britain was forced to cast its first veto since the Suez crisis of 1956 to block the resolution.[5]

Two months later, when Parliament finally dissolved the federation, Rhodesia again pressed for independence, and Great Britain again refused. Extremist whites, angry at the "begging" of Field and the "cowardice" of London, reacted by electing the militant Ian Smith prime minister in April 1964. It was clear that Smith was determined to move toward independence regardless of London's reaction.

Smith's election caused U.S. officials to take a stronger interest in developments in Rhodesia. Ball sent a memo to all American embassies in Africa noting that Smith's victory "virtually wipes out . . . moderation or . . . the slim possibility of successful negotiations with the UK." He warned of the "dangers of a unilateral declaration of independence" and the fact that "the U.S. has virtually no leverage to exert that could directly influence SR [Southern Rhodesia] developments." Ball repeated the American view that "the UK is the responsible party to deal with the situation," but he also asked for recommendations of possible U.S. actions should Smith decide to defy London.[6]

In the spring of 1964, R. A. Butler, the British minister for central Africa,

5. Williams and Cleveland to Rusk, "United Kingdom Requests Further US Assistance on Southern Rhodesia Issue," 6 September 1963, Williams Papers, box 29, National Archives; David Nunnerley, *President Kennedy and Britain*, 206–7. See also CIA, "Special Report on the Breakup of the Federation of Rhodesia and Nyasaland," 27 December 1963, NSF: Rhodesia, box 1, Johnson Library.

6. Ball to all U.S. embassies in Africa, 15 April 1964, NSF: Rhodesia, box 1, Johnson Library.

traveled to Washington to confer with Rusk on the deteriorating situation in Rhodesia. Butler tried to allay American fears that Smith was preparing for an immediate declaration of independence. He explained that, although Smith was "a danger," he was "moving away from UDI." Butler affirmed his country's determination and ability to resist any plan for Rhodesian independence without firm guarantees of racial equality.[7]

American observers in Africa were not as optimistic. Satterthwaite sent a long, confidential note to Rusk warning of the "increasing possibility" of UDI and of the near certainty of strong economic support for an independent Rhodesia by South Africa. Although the U.S. envoy in Salisbury initially agreed with the British that Smith would not openly break with London, by the fall he was "not so sure." He predicted that Smith would declare an end to British control "within a year" unless London abandoned the existing conditions for independence.[8]

In October 1964, the Labour party under Harold Wilson gained power in Great Britain. Wilson immediately endorsed the "five principles." He also sent Foreign Secretary Patrick Walker to Washington with a plea for America "to do something to help the UK with its present problem with Southern Rhodesia." Rusk responded with a public statement that the United States was following the situation "with mounting concern" and fully supported London's requirements for decolonization. He declared that Washington had "no intention of recognizing an independent Rhodesian government which has declared its independence unilaterally and which is not acceptable to the majority of its people." When Wilson publicly warned Smith that UDI would be "an open act of defiance and rebellion," the United States immediately issued a statement that it was "encouraged by the forthright position taken by the British Government."[9]

Public statements in Great Britain and America had little impact on Ian Smith and his followers. By early 1965, they were convinced that their only alternative to eventual black rule was to defy Great Britain and declare independence. In the months prior to UDI, U.S. officials repeatedly warned Smith of the dangers of a break with London. America also made it clear that it would not act independently of England in any effort against Rhodesia. In the UN, Stevenson emphasized his government's view that Great Britain had "a particular role and special responsibility" to solve the crisis.[10]

American policy on Rhodesia consisted largely of vague warnings and verbal

7. Department of State, "Memorandum of Conversation: Southern Rhodesia," 27 April 1964, NSF: United Kingdom, box 3, Johnson Library.

8. Satterthwaite to Rusk, Confidential, 24 June 1964, NSF: South Africa, box 2; U.S. consul, Salisbury to the Secretary of State, 8 July 1964; 9 Septmeber 1964, NSF: Rhodesia, box 1, Johnson Library.

9. Belk to Bundy, 28 October 1964, NSF: United Kingdom, box 1; "Statement by the Secretary of State on Developments in Rhodesia," NSF: Rhodesia, box 1, Johnson Library.

10. *SDB* 53 (28 June 1965): 1061–66.

support of London. Williams effectively summarized the American stance on 15 June 1965 when he declared:

> Let me make our position crystal clear, so there will be no misunderstandings. The United States will support the British Government to the fullest extent . . . in its efforts to reach a solution. . . . We would also support the British Government to the fullest extent in case of a unilateral declaration of independence. . . . A unilateral break in the constitutional relation of Southern Rhodesia with the United Kingdom by the Southern Rhodesian Government would cause inevitable political, economic, and social chaos in the country. . . . We believe wholeheartedly in the correctness and validity of the present British position and are prepared to support it to the extent requested.[11]

Although America endorsed the "five principles" and promised support of London, it was still unclear what the United States would do and how closely it would work with Great Britain to prevent Smith from acting. According to Ulrich Haynes, a member of the NSC staff responsible for following the Rhodesian situation, the American "ace in the hole is a public announcement of a policy of total arms embargo on Southern Rhodesia. We'll save that ace for the most propitious time."[12] The hope that a U.S. arms embargo, for all practical purposes already in effect, would deter Smith was wishful thinking, however. By the summer of 1965, it was clear that much stronger measures would have to be considered either to force whites to compromise or to crush an independent Rhodesia.

When Smith's party won a landslide victory in general elections in May 1965, American officials began to seriously consider the implications of UDI. If Smith proclaimed independence as expected, it would not only create a diplomatic problem for Great Britain but also threaten the existence of the neighboring state of Zambia. As a landlocked nation, Zambia depended on Rhodesia for its economic links with the rest of the world. Over 95 percent of its imports and exports were routed through Rhodesia. Almost all of its electric power came from the Kariba Dam on the Zambezi, and its generators were on the Rhodesian side of the river. If Smith broke with London and Great Britain imposed economic sanctions, Zambia would be in a nearly impossible position. It would have to either continue its cooperation with Rhodesia or face economic ruin. The only other alternative was massive foreign aid. Throughout 1965, British and American diplomats considered possible assistance to Zambia should Smith carry out his threat of independence.

An obvious solution to the Zambian dilemma would be to construct a railroad to the coast bypassing Rhodesia. Prior to UDI, Zambian President Kenneth Kaunda pleaded with U.S. officials for aid in building a "Tan-Zam" railway to

11. Ibid. (12 July 1965): 75–76.
12. Haynes to Bundy, 29 April 1965, NSF: Rhodesia, box 1, Johnson Library.

carry his nation's products across Tanzania to Dar es Salaam rather than through Rhodesia. The African Bureau and some White House aides strongly supported Kaunda's request. They argued that any international action against Smith's regime would be disastrous for Zambia without the alternative railway. Robert Komer of the NSC staff compared the project with the Aswan Dam controversy in Egypt in the 1950s. When Washington rejected that project, Egypt turned to the communists for aid. According to Komer, an American refusal to support the Tan-Zam line would have similar repercussions, because the Chinese had already offered to finance the project.[13]

In May 1965, American and British representatives met in Washington to discuss Rhodesia and particularly the possible plight of Zambia. Europeanists in the State Department denounced the proposed Tan-Zam railroad as a "$500 million boon-doggle." They pointed to the increased costs of the war in Vietnam and to congressional opposition to such a massive foreign-aid project. Some also suspected that Kaunda was playing Washington off against the communists and doubted that China was serious in its offer. As a result of such arguments, Johnson rejected the proposal. Kaunda eventually accepted Chinese aid, but construction of the line was not completed for nearly eight years.[14]

By the fall of 1965, Wilson was engaged in frantic efforts to avoid the impending break with Rhodesia. He repeated Great Britain's five conditions for independence in negotiations with Smith at Salisbury. He also tried to mobilize international support to crush the rebellious colony if it took the final step. France and the Common Market nations rejected British appeals for economic assistance, but the United States agreed to supply Great Britain with tobacco and other products that would be cut off by an embargo on Rhodesia.[15] Washington hoped that such support of Great Britain would cause Smith to reconsider his rush toward independence. Ball ordered the U.S. representative in Salisbury to tell Rhodesian leaders that America did "not intend to deviate from its course of strong support for Her Majesty's Government now and—if it comes—after a unilateral declaration of independence."[16]

Despite the offer of economic assistance to Great Britain, many in the administration were unhappy with Wilson's handling of the crisis, fearing that Great Britain depended too strongly on the "U.S. threat" to crush a Rhodesian

13. Anthony Lake, *The "Tar Baby" Option*, 77–78. Lake's study is largely concerned with U.S. policy after 1969 but does have an excellent chapter on the period 1965–1968.
14. Robert Good, *UDI*, 93. Good was the U.S. ambassador in Zambia at the time of UDI, and his book is invaluable on the situation in that nation. See also Richard Hall, *The High Price of Principles*, 209–23.
15. Phillip Kaiser, U.S. chargé, London, to Rusk, 30 September 1965, NSF: United Kingdom, box 2; Komer to Bundy, 30 September 1965, NSF: Rhodesia, box 2, Johnson Library.
16. Ball to the American legation, Salisbury, 29 September 1965, NSF: Rhodesia, box 2, Johnson Library.

rebellion. On 29 September 1965, the same day he told Rhodesians of America's "strong support" of Great Britain, Ball bluntly warned London, "Our support for HMG [Her Majesty's Government] position on UDI is not, repeat not, without qualifications." He informed the British that America would not "make up the balance of payments losses" resulting from sanctions against Rhodesia. Ball also mentioned that he "was not sure" about increased tobacco sales and that any U.S. suspension of the Rhodesian sugar quota required "further study." He instructed American representatives in London to impress on Wilson that "our support is not to be construed as a blank check." Ball was highly critical of Wilson's vacillation between toughness and accommodation in his negotiations with Smith. He also was angry at London for pressing the United States for assurances of support when it had no clear program for responding to UDI. Ball was concerned that the repeated American promises of assistance would excuse the British "from taking action or permit them to place the blame for lack of action on our door."[17] Ball and others in Washington were willing to let Wilson use the threat of American action to confront Smith, but they were not willing to bear the burden of a tough reaction to UDI: America would "support" Great Britain but would not "carry " it. During the final, futile negotiations between Smith and Wilson, the United States repeatedly made vague threats to Smith of retaliation to UDI while simultaneously cautioning London that its help was not unlimited. Despite American opposition to UDI, Rhodesia was still "a British problem."

On 5 October, as Smith and Wilson were meeting in London, Johnson sent them both personal messages declaring America "would oppose vigorously" any Rhodesian attempt to declare independence. Three days later, the U.S. chargé in London personally told Smith that Washington "could not condone any political arrangement acceptable only to the minority and unresponsive to the interests or rights of the vast majority."[18]

Despite these efforts, the negotiations remained deadlocked, and there was growing impatience in Washington with Great Britain's inability to resolve the crisis. Haynes warned Bundy that Wilson's mismanagement of the situation was leading to "an international crisis along racial alignments which the communists, especially the Chinese, can exploit." He argued that Great Britain was simply unable to handle the problem. Continued support of London would only identify America with Wilson's failures. Haynes recommended that Washington undertake independent initiatives, since it was clear that British efforts were not working. He urged the United States to "pre-empt the field and stave off efforts to stir up more radical UN action."[19]

At this point, however, it was far too late for any decisive unilateral American action. Washington was locked into a position of "supporting Britain," even

17. Ball to Kaiser, 29 September 1965, NSF: United Kingdom, box 2, Johnson Library.
18. *SDB* 53 (6 December 1965): 913–14.
19. Haynes to Bundy, 8 October 1965, NSF: Rhodesia, box 2, Johnson Library.

though this position remained only a vague principle, since it was still unclear exactly what Wilson would do if Smith declared Rhodesia independent. The State Department continued to press London for details of its intended response to UDI so America could prepare its own policies. When Great Britain failed to provide specific information, U.S. officials were left in the difficult position of planning policy without knowing their ally's intentions.

The foreign-policy bureaucracy, reflecting the deep splits over the general importance of Africa, was divided over future American actions. Ball, disgusted with Great Britain's inability to resolve the crisis or to inform Washington of its plans, urged that America simply stay out of the entire affair. Predictably, Africanists advocated a strong response to UDI regardless of the British position. As a "minimum" American reaction to UDI, Williams proposed withdrawing the American consul, prohibiting new U.S. investments in Rhodesia, dumping American tobacco reserves on the world market to drive down the price of Rhodesia's major cash crop, and restricting all trade with the colony. In a note to Rusk, he urged the secretary immediately to inform both Great Britain and Rhodesia of the American program. If Smith knew that Washington would take such actions, he would be forced to abandon plans for independence and reach a settlement with Great Britain.[20]

On 19 October, Rusk sent Cleveland to meet with Williams to discuss Rhodesia. Cleveland conveyed Rusk's agreement that the United States should take action against Smith if he declared independence but told Williams that there would be no statement of administration intentions before UDI. Instead of pushing Rhodesia toward a settlement, announcement of the American response might drive "the Smith Government further into a corner," leaving it no option but independence.[21]

The next day the *St. Louis Post-Dispatch* ran a lengthy article on the ongoing debate in the administration over Rhodesia. The story was so detailed that it seemed clear it was based on sources within the government. It quoted Ball's opposition to any commitment to Great Britain and Williams's suggestions for a U.S. response to UDI. The article also mentioned that Bundy and others in the White House had reassured London of American support for nonrecognition and sanctions in the event of Rhodesian independence.[22] The leak provoked rage within the White House. Haynes was convinced that it was a ploy by the African Bureau to discredit Ball and gain support for the bureau's position. Komer agreed. He sent a copy of the piece to Bundy with the note, "This is lousy! I suspect some AF [African Bureau] hands!" The story created even more distrust of the Africanists in the government. It likely helped defeat Williams's idea of a

20. Haynes to Komer, 19 October 1965; Williams to Rusk, undated, NSF: Rhodesia, box 2, Johnson Library.

21. Rusk to Cleveland, 19 October 1965, NSF: United Kingdom, box 2, Johnson Library.

22. A copy of the article is in Haynes to Komer, 2 November 1965, NSF: Rhodesia, box 2, Johnson Library.

clear statement of U.S. intentions. Instead, the State Department issued a vague release that "hailed" Wilson's efforts to avert "a tragic confrontation" in Rhodesia, denounced any UDI, and declared that such an action "would cause the United States to sever the traditional close and friendly ties" with Rhodesia. The announcement made no mention of sanctions, embargoes, aid to Zambia, or any other specific actions suggested by the Africanists.[23]

The American position on the eve of UDI thus remained as it had been for nearly four years: dedicated to support of Great Britain yet unclear on any precise policies. On 29 October, Johnson cabled Smith urging compromise but without any threat of American action. In the UN, U.S. officials worked closely with the British to defeat resolutions calling on London to use force to block Rhodesian independence. On 5 November, final talks between Great Britain and Rhodesia broke down. Smith immediately declared a state of emergency. Rusk warned of the "dangers" of UDI at a press conference the same day, but he refused to spell out the American reaction. Four days later, the State Department prepared a draft statement for the president in the event of UDI. This statement also lacked any references to specific U.S. actions beyond nonrecognition.[24]

On 11 November 1965, Smith finally declared Rhodesia an independent nation with no formal ties to Great Britain. Despite over four years of predictions and several months of daily reports on the situation in Rhodesia, the final announcement of UDI caught the U.S. government unprepared. Johnson had scheduled a major review of Vietnam policy at his Texas ranch for 11 November. Rusk, McNamara, Bundy, Ball, and nearly all other high officials were in Austin when Smith issued his declaration. Those still in Washington were unwilling to make any statements or take any actions without clearance from top officials. Rusk finally came out on the porch of the ranch house to answer reporters' questions about Rhodesia. He announced that the United States was recalling its consul from Salisbury for consultations and suspending USIA activity in Rhodesia. He gave no other indications of American policy, telling the press that UN Ambassador Goldberg would give more details the next day "after we have seen what Britain does."[25]

After consultations with Rusk and Ball, Goldberg announced his government's response to UDI in New York on 12 November. America would halt all military supplies bound for Rhodesia, "discourage" travel there by its citizens, require British visas for all Rhodesians wishing to visit America, and suspend all loans and credits to the Smith regime. When questioned about the more crucial issue of sanctions, Goldberg replied that the administration "was considering additional steps."[26]

23. Ibid.; Komer to Bundy, 2 November 1965, ibid.; "Draft White House Statement on Southern Rhodesia, 21 October 1965," CF: Rhodesia, box 65, Johnson Library.

24. Johnson to Smith, 29 October 1965, ibid.; *SDB* 53 (6 December 1965): 908–09.

25. *New York Times*, 12 November 1965, p. 1.

26. Department of State, "Outline of the Rhodesian Problem," 1 December 1965, NSF: Rhodesia, box 2, Johnson Library.

Any action beyond the largely symbolic measures announced on 12 November faced a bureaucratic battle. Again, the Rhodesian situation brought to the surface the continuing conflicts over U.S. policy in white Africa. Further complicating the debate over Rhodesia was the fact that, by November 1965, much of the bureaucracy in the State Department was occupied with Vietnam.

Nonetheless, the Africanists, led by Williams and the African Bureau, were convinced that they had a strong case for decisive action. They argued that Smith had acted in defiance of international law and American ideals. His government was clearly illegal, racist, and in violation of such cherished U.S. goals as majority rule and self-determination. Perhaps more important, Rhodesia was extremely vulnerable to foreign pressure. Unlike South Africa, economic sanctions would be devastating to Rhodesia and would soon force Smith to come to terms with Great Britain. In addition, a tough policy had few risks for America. There were no worries about losing bases. U.S. trade with Rhodesia was relatively minor. World opinion was nearly unanimous in opposing the Smith regime. Washington could gain significant goodwill from black Africa at a minimum cost and also reassure black Americans disillusioned with U.S. compromises on Angola and South Africa. In addition, an uncompromising position against Smith would contribute to the international struggle with communism by taking the issue away from the Soviets and Chinese. If Washington did not stand up to Rhodesia, there would be immediate demands for the use of force and corresponding gains for radicalism in Africa.

The arguments of the African Bureau gained some allies. Like Stevenson, Goldberg at the UN was a strong supporter of the "Africa first" position and rapidly became a leader of the push for a tough policy on Rhodesia. More significant, Komer and Haynes of the NSC staff were very sympathetic to the Africanist view. Haynes, the former State Department official whose trip to South Africa produced Rusk's outburst against Pretoria in late 1963, had been closely monitoring the Rhodesian crisis throughout 1965. He was convinced that the United States must "get out in front" on the issue to retain the favor of the African nations and to avoid more radical solutions. Komer, a former CIA official, supported an aggressive policy largely from an anticommunist perspective. He was certain that an independent, white Rhodesia would provoke either guerrilla warfare or military intervention by the African states and the UN. Either move would contribute to communist influence throughout southern Africa. Haynes and Komer gave the Africanists strong representation in the White House—necessary because of continued opposition to their position from many in the State Department.

Within the State Department, Ball was responsible for the day-to-day coordination of policy on Rhodesia, although Rusk was involved in the major decisions. Ball's opinion of Williams and the Africanists had not changed. He still was skeptical of the importance of Africa and dubious of the advantages to the United States of any major involvement in the continent. Ball was also disdainful of Great Britain's handling of the problem. He feared Wilson might drag America ever deeper into an issue of minimal strategic and economic importance. Like many others in the department, Ball was concerned that sanctions against Rhodesia eventually would lead to the use of force to topple Smith's government, establishing a dangerous precedent for the other areas of white Africa with more direct U.S. interests. To Ball, and to others operating from a Europeanist perspective, the major American objective in Africa remained the containment of communism. Any policy that might encourage violence or radicalism on the continent weakened the free world. Rhodesia was simply not worth the risks involved in aggressive American actions.

Ball quickly recognized that the African Bureau and its supporters planned to try to use the Rhodesian crisis to implement all of the rejected options they had pushed for in the other areas of white rule. He knew that to restrain the Africanists he would have to control the decisionmaking process from the beginning. Immediately following UDI, the government followed its usual procedure by establishing a "working group" to handle the crisis. The committee included representatives from the State, Commerce, Defense, and Treasury departments as well as the National Security Council. Ball brought William D. Rogers, a Washington attorney, into the government to preside over the working group and serve as a "brake" on the Africanists.[27] Ball had wanted former Secretary of the Air Force Thomas Finletter to chair the group but settled on Rogers when Johnson vetoed Finletter. Rogers was clearly Ball's surrogate. The organization of the group made it nearly impossible for it to take any action without the approval of the coordinator—Rogers—which meant, in effect, the approval of George Ball. It is a maxim of administration that "he who controls the agenda controls the meeting." In the case of Rhodesia, Ball controlled the agenda.

Ian Smith's declaration of independence raised the immediate question of relations with Great Britain. Despite the generally dismal assessment of Wilson's performance by the administration, America was committed to "supporting Britain." The extent and nature of this support were uncertain, however. The United States was not happy with the effects of its subservient role in the period prior to UDI. It had to determine how closely it would work with London and how far it was willing to allow Wilson to control the situation now that Smith had acted.

Before deciding how it would assist the British, the Americans first had to know London's policy. This was not a simple task. Wilson had promised strong efforts to force Rhodesia back to its colonial status, but he had publicly ruled out military action. Great Britain expected the United States to help with economic sanctions, but it was uncertain what they would include or how they would be

27. Lake, *The "Tar Baby" Option*, 82–84.

enforced. Finally, it was unclear what the British saw the role of the UN to be in the situation. London had repeatedly claimed that Rhodesia was its problem, not that of the UN. Its veto of the 1963 resolution on the arms transfer was a clear illustration of its opinion that it held the major responsibility for dealing with the colony, but it was clear that the UN would demand swift and decisive action to topple Smith. America was left to ponder its relations with the UN should there be a conflict between the organization and Great Britain.

U.S. officials had complained that they were not kept informed of Great Britain's position in the period prior to UDI; they soon found that tracking London's hesitant and often inconsistent approach to Rhodesia after November 1965 was even more frustrating. Wilson faced pressure from a variety of sources and tried in vain to appease them all. The Commonwealth nations and many within his Labour party expected full use of British power to crush the rebel regime in Salisbury. Wilson, however, was dedicated to avoiding the use of force. He had a very small majority in parliament, and the conservatives adamantly opposed military action against their "kith and kin" in Rhodesia. A similar problem existed on sanctions. Liberals demanded total economic isolation of Rhodesia, while business leaders and many Tories opposed any embargo. Wilson engaged in a cautious balancing act to preserve both his leadership on the Rhodesian question and his shaky control of the British government. He tried to appear both decisive in order to blunt criticism from the African nations and the UN and also conciliatory in order to minimize attacks from conservative opponents at home.[28]

Wilson recognized that he needed to resolve the crisis as rapidly as possible if he was to avoid assault from both the left and the right. Thus, Great Britain adopted the strategy of the "quick kill": it would swiftly organize the economic isolation of Rhodesia and force Smith either out of office or back to the bargaining table. Having already rejected the use of force, Wilson was left with the hope that economic pressure would suffice. He faced problems, however, even in the use of sanctions. Effective economic pressure on Rhodesia would involve cutting off oil from South Africa. Given its large and favorable trade with South Africa, Great Britain was unwilling to confront Pretoria directly on the Rhodesian issue. London wanted a "quick kill," but not at the expense of its continued good relations with South Africa.

Although American officials also accepted the need for a rapid solution to the crisis to avoid third-world pressure for the use of force, they were not convinced that Great Britain was capable of implementing a "quick kill." After early discussions between Washington and London, Ball seriously doubted that the British plans would succeed. He recommended to Johnson that the United States

28. Good provides the best analysis of Wilson's handling of the Rhodesian problem. For details and many of the official statements of British policy, see Kenneth Young, *Rhodesia and Independence*.

adopt only "selective" economic sanctions rather than the complete ban on exports that Williams had suggested. Ball argued that "we must not cut off exports entirely" as it would place Washington "out in front" of Great Britain and restrain "flexibility." Ball reluctantly agreed that the United States needed to take steps against Smith to avoid a UN overreaction. "We could end up with a Communist-dominated United Nations' force attacking the white settlers in the heart of East Africa," he warned the president. "In order to avoid getting started down this road, we have been giving as much support as feasible to the British," he explained. Ball advocated suspending Rhodesia's sugar imports for both 1965 and 1966, even thought the 1965 crop was already en route to America. He also suggested denying diplomatic recognition and requiring special licenses for all exports to the colony. Johnson approved the recommendations on 18 November, and Goldberg announced them two days later.[29]

Even this compromise between inaction and major sanctions produced problems. Some State Department officials were upset that Johnson had suspended the sugar imports for both years. They asked Bundy if the president was "aware of the fact that such action would put us out in front of the British?" On the other side, Williams predictably contended the measures were too weak and would have only a slight impact on Rhodesia.[30]

On 19 November, the State Department circulated its first detailed analysis of the crisis and the range of U.S. options. Typical of the department's format, it first gave the rationale for "doing nothing," followed by a variety of possible actions culminating in the direct use of military force. The arguments for inaction were that Africa was a "European sphere of influence" with "no large U.S. interests." Sanctions would not work because black Africa was "too weak to resist South Africa and Portugal." Therefore, "inactivity is better policy than initiatives that fail." Those favoring no direct American involvement also mentioned the anticommunism argument that was very strong within the department: Action against Rhodesia would inevitably escalate into attacks on the entire area of white control. This must be avoided, since "free world interests demand a strong white bastion in South Africa, which will hold on when Black Africa has 'sold out' to the Communists."[31]

The arguments for an "active" policy emphasized that America was "inescapably involved" in Africa by reason of "its large and increasingly politically-conscious Negro minority." The study also noted that "sanctions have never been tried against a country as vulnerable as Rhodesia." Given the influence of the whites, and their dependence on foreign trade, economic

29. Ball to Johnson, 18 November 1965; "Outline of the Rhodesian Problem," 1 December 1965, NSF: Rhodesia, box 2, Johnson Library.

30. "BKS" (Bromley Smith, Executive Secretary of the National Security Council) to Bundy, 18 November 1965, ibid.

31. Department of State, "Memorandum for Mr. Bundy: the Rhodesian Crisis," 19 November 1965, NSF: Rhodesia, box 2, Johnson Library.

pressure would be very effective. Those supporting U.S. involvement also used anticommunism, arguing that strong Western response to Smith would undercut communist efforts to use the racial issue to gain influence in Africa. Likewise, a strong response would block UN efforts to send a peacekeeping force ("Red troops in blue berets") that would only foster radicalism.

In its final recommendations, the document followed a middle path between the two alternatives. It recommended limited economic sanctions accompanied by "guarantees against too speedy Africanization" of Rhodesia if Smith agreed to return to colonial status. It also urged major economic support of Zambia and the possible use of American troops if Smith cut off hydroelectric power.

Meanwhile, at the UN, America tried to work closely with Great Britain yet retain its influence with the Africans. On 20 November, the Security Council debated an African resolution calling on Great Britain immediately to end the rebellion in Rhodesia and asking all states to break diplomatic relations with Smith's regime. Goldberg labored effectively to make the motion acceptable to London. He arranged a change in the wording that avoided the chapter 7 language of "threats to international peace and security" by substituting a phrase that called the situation in Rhodesia "serious" and noted that "its continuation in time constitutes a threat to international peace and security." This placed the motion under a clause in the charter stating that "potential threats to international security" should be resolved through negotiations rather than by force or binding sanctions. Goldberg's efforts avoided a certain British veto yet allowed Africans to interpret the resolution as preparation for mandatory sanctions in the near future.[32]

Economic sanctions, the obvious key to any "quick kill," were understandably opposed by both Portugal and South Africa. In Portugal, Nogueira issued a statement welcoming Rhodesian independence and announcing that Lisbon would ignore any UN action against the new nation. In Pretoria, although Verwoerd had repeatedly cautioned the Rhodesians against UDI and the South African press had called Smith "hot-headed" and labeled UDI "ill-considered," officials had little choice but to support Smith. Sanctions against the white government in Salisbury were an obvious precedent for action against South Africa. Verwoerd thus proclaimed his "friendship and support of Rhodesia" and announced that his government would supply economic aid and diplomatic support. Pretoria also chided Wilson for trying to use the UN to solve what he himself had called a "British problem."[33]

While the Johnson administration considered what forms of economic pressure the United States would put on Rhodesia, it also waited for British

32. *SDB* 53 (6 December 1965): 915–16. See also Lake, *The "Tar Baby" Option*, 85–87.

33. Nogueira, "Portugal and the Question of Rhodesia," 25 November 1965, in *Portuguese Foreign Policy*, 33–35; Barber, *South Africa's Foreign Policy*, 177–80. The text of Verwoerd's statement on UDI is in NSF: South Africa, box 2, Johnson Library.

clarification of the exact details of the "quick kill." American observers in Salisbury warned that each day without decisive action "unites and solidifies the white community behind the Smith regime." Williams was particularly impatient. On 24 November, he finally asked Ball to inform Wilson, "The U.S. is anxious to support them [the British] but we do not understand the general outlines of their program or what their over-all thinking is."[34]

At meetings between U.S. and U.K. officials in Washington in late November, the British finally spelled out their program. It included an embargo on Rhodesian tobacco and sugar, an end to investments, and nonrecognition. Wilson's representatives also explained that they would expand the embargo gradually to include nearly all products from the rebellious colony. Williams's summary of the sessions emphasized America's doubts about the impact of the British proposals. He was disturbed that Wilson had no real alternatives given that "there is no positive indication anywhere that economic sanctions will bring down the Smith Government." He also was upset by the failure to develop a plan to end oil shipments to Rhodesia. Williams concluded that "the British expect to lean heavily on the U.S.," but, with America "heavily engaged in Vietnam," London would have to consider bolder measures against Rhodesia than it seemed prepared to accept.[35]

Rusk was also concerned by the apparent caution and indecisiveness of America's ally. He informed U.S. officials in London that the administration was willing to do its part in putting economic pressure on Salisbury, but America's leverage was far less than London's. U.S. imports from Rhodesia in 1964 were only $10 million, and exports to Rhodesia were about $20 million. Rusk noted that the State Department planned to rely on voluntary measures to curb American economic activity and was considering aiding U.S. companies that supported a boycott. He emphasized that Washington was not ready to accept mandatory sanctions or make any long-range commitment to supplying Zambia. These steps would be considered only when the Wilson government provided details of its long-range commitment to supplying Zambia. These steps would be considered only when the Wilson government provided details of its long-range strategy. "We are frankly dubious that the present UK program will provide a quick kill, if this implies the early expiration of the Smith rebellion," he concluded.[36]

Americans were not the only ones skeptical of the British plan. On 3 December 1965, the OAU met to consider the Rhodesian situation. Although

34. U.S. consul, Salisbury, to the Department of State, 29 November 1965, ibid.; Williams to Ball, 24 November 1965, Williams Papers, box 5, National Archives.
35. Williams, "Memo for the Files," 1 December 1965, Williams Papers, box 29, National Archives.
36. Rusk to U.S. embassy, London, 4 December 1965, NSF: United Kingdom, box 2, Johnson Library.

some African leaders, for purposes of domestic propaganda, demanded an invasion to topple Smith, the conference finally agreed only to end all economic and diplomatic contact with Rhodesia. The Africans also announced that they would break relations with London if Great Britain had not crushed the rebellion by 15 December. Both American and British analysts correctly predicted that only a few "hard-line" nations would carry out this threat. Wilson, however, recognized that the Africans did not consider his present program adequate. He knew that he would face strong pressure from Commonwealth countries to use force if economic sanctions did not resolve the situation.[37]

A month after UDI, it was clear the the "quick kill" was not working. American policy remained a mixture of public support of Wilson and private grumblings about his tentativeness and imprecision. State Department and White House officials were critical of London for not adopting stronger measures, but they also offered little U.S. support for any tougher actions. Washington continued to argue that Wilson must control the situation and not depend on America. Despite British urgings, the United States refused to commit itself to the two obvious steps necessary for any rapid end to the rebellion: mandatory sanctions and massive aid to Zambia.

Washington did continue its modest efforts to isolate the Smith government. On 8 December, the State Department announced that it would give control of Rhodesian assets in the United States to Great Britain. Rusk made it clear, however, that this was not preparatory to comprehensive economic sanctions. In a press conference the next day, he called sanctions "a rather complicated question" and refused to answer specific questions about the administration's next step in its economic program against Rhodesia.[38]

The United States also was cautious in its response to the critical situation in Zambia. American officials were sympathetic to Kaunda's plight but declared it was Great Britain's responsibility to lead efforts to aid its former colony. A group of British and American diplomats met in Washington in mid-December to consider the entire Rhodesian problem and particularly aid to Zambia. The meetings were cordial, but there was an underlying tension between the two delegations. The British were annoyed by Washington's reluctance to offer firm support of sanctions or significant aid to Zambia. The Americans were critical of Great Britain's management of the entire crisis and especially of their demands for a U.S. commitment to sanctions without any assurances that they would work. The group tentatively agreed to push for voluntary sanctions, including

37. Haynes to Bundy, "Situation Report: Rhodesian Crisis," 3 December 1965, 8 December 1965; CIA Intelligence Memorandum, "The Rhodesian Situation: African Pressure and British Dilemma," 11 December 1965, NSF: Rhodesia, box 2, Johnson Library.

38. Department of State Press Release, 8 December 1965, ibid.; *SDB* 53 (27 December 1965): 1008.

oil, and for a joint effort to supply Zambia. American representatives, however, made it clear that they were willing to accept only a "limited" commitment to Kuanda's nation of two months at a cost of "less than $300,000 a month." They reaffirmed that they were not "entering into a general, open-ended undertaking" because assistance to Zambia remained "a British concern."[39]

The agreement between the two nations was provisional since Wilson was scheduled to arrive in the United States on 16 December to address the UN and discuss Rhodesia with Johnson. On 15 December, the National Security Council reviewed the entire crisis and made recommendations to the president. The NSC predicted that Wilson would request massive U.S. aid for Zambia, sanctions, and direct economic assistance to London to help offset the costs of an embargo of Rhodesia. The group urged Johnson to pressure Wilson to take stronger steps and to mention that "we are not at all certain that the economic 'quick kill' strategy will work soon enough to hold off the African hotheads." They also suggested that the president make it clear that effective sanctions must include oil. In other words, Great Britain must confront South Africa.[40]

Relations between Wilson and Johnson had been rather cool prior to their discussions on 16 December. Johnson, however, was greatly impressed with Wilson at their meeting. The prime minister reaffirmed past British policy and told the president that he was optimistic that a coordinated U.S.-British program would end the rebellion by March 1966. The two leaders quickly resolved the broad outlines of policy: America would support an oil embargo and take a major role in an airlift of supplies to Zambia. Johnson was anxious to avoid "getting in front" of Great Britain but welcomed some strong new steps for both international and domestic reasons. First of all, his advisers had warned that the current efforts were not working. African countries identified the United States with British caution. Secondly, black leaders, most notably King, had criticized both nations for their "weak" position on Rhodesia. The president was thus willing to commit the United States to the British initiatives despite predictions from a number of his aides that they would not be successful.[41]

The next day Great Britain announced an embargo on all petroleum products for Rhodesia. The U.S. publicly "welcomed" the move, but again some officials privately questioned its effectiveness without direct pressure on South Africa. Washington next moved to implement Johnson's agreement to aid Zambia.[42]

39. Rusk to U.S. embassy, London, 13 December 1965, NSF: United Kingdom, box 2; Haynes to Bundy, "Situation Report: Rhodesian Crisis," 13 December 1965, NSF: Rhodesia, box 2, Johnson Library.

40. National Security Council Memorandum, "Talking Points for the Wilson Visit," 15 December 1965, NSF: United Kingdom, box 5, Johnson Library.

41. Harold Wilson, *The Labour Government 1964–1970: A Personal Record*, 186–88. See also Read to Bundy, 17 December 1965, NSF: Rhodesia, box 2, Johnson Library.

42. Department of State Press Release, 17 December 1965, NSF: Rhodesia, box 2, Johnson Library.

The situation in Zambia involved troops, oil, copper, and the fear that Rhodesia might invade the nation or cut off hydroelectric power. Kaunda had made several requests for British troops to protect his copper mines and the Kariba Dam. Wilson had agreed only to send an air-force squadron to defend Zambia from a Rhodesian invasion. Kaunda had next appealed to the United States for troops. Mindful of the disastrous effects of the Stanleyville airlift a year earlier, and heavily involved in Vietnam, Washington refused. Zambia remained nearly defenseless against possible attack from its white neighbor or a shutoff of its power. Great Britain and America were more willing to respond to the critical economic situation in the nation. On 27 December 1965, the State Department announced plans to join Canada in a massive airlift of oil and gasoline to Zambia. The fuel would be delivered to airfields in the Congo for overland transport. In January 1966, the airlift began. It was an impressive operation. Far from the "limited" two-month commitment that Rusk had agreed to, the shuttle continued for over four months. It eventually delivered over 3.5 million gallons of gasoline at a cost of over a dollar a gallon. The planes used more fuel than they actually delivered to Zambia, but the effort did keep the nation's economy from total collapse. In addition, Washington contracted with Lockheed Corporation to fly Zambian copper out of the country. The United States later provided $225,000 for Kaunda to hire an engineering team from Stanford University to study possible highway routes from Zambia to Tanzanian ports.[43]

Washington also kept Johnson's promise to Wilson to "tighten the economic screws" on Rhodesia. Rather than make a single announcement of U.S. plans, the administration decided it would be more effective to make periodic statements of American pressure. It was assumed that this would weaken the morale of the Smith government by repeatedly reminding it of U.S. determination. It would also keep American opposition to the white regime in public view for the African nations. In January 1966, Washington began to "dribble out" its economic program. On 10 January, the State Department announced a voluntary ban on imports of asbestos and lithium. Two weeks later, it asked American companies to end their purchases of Rhodesian chrome. On 9 February, the administration "informed" U.S. tobacco companies that Great Britain had embargoed Rhodesian tobacco and "requested" them to follow suit. The Commerce Department announced on 26 February that it would require licenses for nearly all exports to Rhodesia, and, on 18 March, Washington banned most exports under the Export Control Act.[44]

These steps may have had their intended psychological impact, but they did not inflict serious economic damage on Rhodesia. Legally, the administration could only "request" companies to end imports because there was no UN resolution

43. *SDB* 54 (17 January 1966): 85–86; *Business Week* (11 December 1965): 58.
44. Department of State Press Releases, NSF: Rhodesia, box 3, Johnson Library.

imposing mandatory sanctions. Many American firms were upset by the government's actions, particularly the request to end chrome imports. They pointed out that the alternative source for chrome was the Soviet Union. Washington was thus indirectly aiding Russia. In addition, Great Britain had allowed its companies to import over nine thousand tons of chrome ore from Rhodesia in January 1966. American corporations argued that they were being asked to make sacrifices while their British counterparts were prospering.[45]

The greatest difficulty with the Anglo-American effort against Smith was oil. South Africa was the major problem. Thomas Mann, the U.S. under-secretary of state for economic affairs, closely monitored the impact of the embargo on Rhodesia. In a long report to Johnson late in December he was extremely pessimistic. He reported that South Africa seemed capable of supplying Rhodesia with oil indefinitely. Unless Wilson ended the flow of oil from South Africa, Great Britain would "probably not achieve its objectives either in terms of maintaining the UK's relationship with the African Commonwealth States or of bringing down quickly the Smith regime." He warned that, because of the publicity given to American cooperation with Britain, "African resentment against the UK" would "inevitably rub off on the U.S."[46] American oil companies also were unconvinced of the effectiveness of the embargo. Mobil Corporation protested to Rusk that if it halted shipments of oil to South Africa for export to Rhodesia, Pretoria threatened lawsuits for breach of contract and even nationalization of Mobil subsidiaries. Rusk was also appalled by reports that some British oil firms were continuing to supply South African companies known to be front organizations for Rhodesia. He demanded that London "eliminate this chink in the embargo."[47] It also became clear that, regardless of U.S. and British actions, other nations were willing to supply oil to South Africa for delivery to Rhodesia. American intelligence agents reported that several dummy firms organized by Pretoria to aid Rhodesia were receiving oil from French companies "well known for financially shady deals." The U.S. consul in Salisbury noted on 22 January that, although there was gas rationing and some shortages, the oil embargo showed no signs of forcing Smith to compromise with Britain.[48]

Despite the glaring problems of economic sanctions, America was committed to support of the now "not-so-quick kill." Accordingly, the United States tried to

45. Rusk to U.S. embassy, London, 21 January 1966, NSF: United Kingdom, box 2, Johnson Library.

46. Mann to Johnson, "Memorandum for the President: The Rhodesian Crisis," 22 December 1965, White House Central Files: Confidential Files, Rhodesia, box 1, Johnson Library.

47. Rusk to U.S. embassy, London, 28 December 1965, NSF: United Kingdom, box 2, Johnson Library.

48. National Security Council, "Rhodesian/Zambian Situation Report, No. 17," 26–27 January 1966; American legation, Salisbury, to the Department of State, 22 January 1966, NSF: Rhodesia, box 4, Johnson Library.

end any diplomatic activity by Rhodesian agents in the country. On 4 February, Rhodesia opened an "information office" in Washington under the control of Henry J. C. Hooper. The State Department tried to close the facility and expel Hooper to symbolize U.S. nonrecognition of an "illegal government." The Justice Department, however, ruled that the office was legal and Hooper could stay. The State Department scored a symbolic victory when it forced Hooper to register as an agent of a "foreign principal" rather than of a "foreign nation," since America did not recognize Rhodesia as a "nation." Hooper and the Rhodesian information office remained and later became extremely active in propaganda efforts on behalf of the Smith regime.[49]

In its immediate response to UDI, the Johnson administration had enjoyed the diplomatic luxury of great freedom of action. The public pressure on the government that did exist came largely from blacks and liberals. Civil-rights, church, and academic groups had inundated Washington with letters, cables, and petitions demanding that the United States help force Smith back to London. The NAACP, the National Council of Churches, SNCC, CORE, King's Southern Christian Leadership Conference, and dozens of other organizations pressed Johnson to take immediate action following UDI. These groups generally approved of the administration's efforts in late 1965 and early 1966. Although some called for tighter sanctions, most applauded the decisions to impose voluntary sanctions, aid Zambia, and place an embargo on oil. Many accepted the "official" U.S. and British assurances that such actions would quickly end the rebellion in Rhodesia.[50]

As it became increasingly apparent that the "quick kill" was not working, the administration became caught in a wicked crossfire of public opinion. Opponents of Rhodesian independence began to criticize Johnson for being too cautious on the issue, while those sympathetic to Smith were able to organize effective opposition to any efforts against the colony. Each day that Rhodesia survived created more apprehension and impatience within the U.S. government. Officials feared America was being drawn into a long dispute with little certainty of success. As with Vietnam, what seemed to be a small commitment for a short time threatened to become an ever-expanding engagement with no sign of victory and the potential for domestic dissent.

Throughout late 1965 and early 1966, Washington fought a holding effort against both African and American critics. Williams again emerged as the major spokesman for U.S. policy. As in the cases of Angola and South Africa, he tried to explain the direct and indirect American interests involved. In a speech to the American Legion in Washington, he defended opposition to Smith as both humanitarian and practical. He claimed that it was contrary to American ideals

49. *New York Times*, 5 February 1966, p. 3; 11 March 1966, p. 9.
50. The correspondence between these groups and the White House is in CF: Rhodesia, boxes 12–13, and Africa, box 7, Johnson Library.

to allow "220,000 whites to maintain a 'Governor Wallace type' of racial supremacy over millions of black Africans." He also warned that, unless the West confronted Smith, "the Communists would be happy to rush into the situation." Rhodesia, Williams argued, was a test of the U.S. commitment to racial equality and a challenge to its determination to resist communism in Africa. "Unchecked, the Southern Rhodesian situation could well lead to the downfall of responsible, friendly African Governments . . . and their replacement by radical elements," he contended. Williams assured his audience that economic pressure would quickly end the crisis but criticized "the predatory tendencies of modern-day private buccaneers looking for a quick profit" by defying the oil embargo.[51]

Williams and other administration spokesmen implied a rapid solution to the situation. Blacks and liberals were thus willing to allow Johnson and Wilson time to end the rebellion. As Rhodesia endured, it became more difficult to restrain those impatient with voluntary sanctions. As early as one month after UDI, the CIA predicted that none of the intended British initiatives would have much of an impact on Rhodesia. The agency warned that time was running out for Wilson. He was attempting to "walk a tightrope" between African demands for decisive action and political pressures for moderation. Because of Great Britain's reluctance to provide the required aid for Zambia, the African nation would be forced to continue its trade with Rhodesia. London was unwilling to "stand up" to South Africa and stop the flow of oil. As a result, the African nations would "probably turn to radical methods." By its active support of Great Britain's cautious policy, America might well wind up involved in a major military confrontation in Africa.[52]

By mid-January, others in the government had begun to echo the CIA's earlier assessment. Bundy asked Rusk, McNamara, the CIA, and the Agency for International Development to prepare "a comprehensive analysis" of the Rhodesian situation including "alternative courses of action . . . which we might want to recommend to the UK or promote ourselves." He mentioned that the president was "concerned by the mounting gravity of the Rhodesian crisis and the apparent lack of any British plan which gives much confidence that the rebel regime will soon be brought to heel."[53]

Publicly, the administration still proclaimed its unity with Great Britain and the imminent success of the existing sanctions. On 28 January, Williams praised U.S. business leaders for their cooperation on Rhodesia. He offered a long litany of the dire problems of the Rhodesian economy. Two months of international pressure had "brought a drastic reduction in standards of living among whites,"

51. *SDB* 54 (3 January 1966): 13–15.
52. CIA Intelligence Memorandum, "The Rhodesian Situation: African Pressure and British Dilemma," 11 December 1965, NSF: Rhodesia, box 2, Johnson Library.
53. Bundy to Rusk, undated, ibid.

Williams claimed and "this is just the beginning!"[54] Privately, however, the government's analysis was the exact opposite. Daily "situation reports" on the crisis grew increasingly gloomy throughout January and February. The airlift to Zambia seemed to be working, but the efforts to "strangle" the Rhodesian economy were failing. By mid-February over thirty-five thousand gallons of oil were arriving each day from South Africa and Portugal. Lisbon was easily able to route petroleum to Salisbury through Mozambique, and South Africa had established a regular schedule of overland deliveries. American agents reported that Great Britain knew of the situation but was either unwilling or unable to do anything about it.[55]

As Smith continued in power, African leaders grew more incensed with the inability of Great Britain and America to end the crisis. Kaunda, in an article in *Punch* in March 1966, attacked both countries for their refusal to give him enough economic aid to cut trade with Rhodesia and for their reluctance to enforce the oil embargo. Tanzanian President Nyerere, one of only two African leaders to actually break diplomatic relations with London in protest of Wilson's refusal to send troops to Rhodesia, also lashed out at the "half-hearted" Anglo-American response. "Free Africa is now waiting, with some impatience, to see whether the West really intends to stand on the side of human equality and human freedom," he concluded.[56]

The continued survival of the Rhodesian regime also led to the first stirrings of criticism from the American right. Business leaders remained angered by the "voluntary" embargo. Several companies complained that they had been promised government aid if they went along with the boycott but, when they did cut trade, Washington refused any assistance. Congress also became more interested in the Rhodesian situation. In April, Rep. Joe Waggoner of Louisiana delivered a long attack on the administration's handling of the crisis. He defended Rhodesia as "the cornerstone of this nation's tenuous foothold in the entire Afro-Asian world." Waggoner predicted, "If we are successful in our treacherous subversion of Rhodesia," the Portuguese colonies and South Africa would soon collapse, and "we will have no friend on the continent."[57]

Congressional criticism became much stronger in 1967, but even in early 1966 there were signs of a major political battle over Rhodesia. Many politicians were angry at U.S. cooperation with Great Britain when London refused to support America in Vietnam. They were indignant that Great Britain continued to trade

54. *SDB* 54 (21 February 1966): 265–70.
55. *New York Times*, 25 February 1966, p. 12; 27 February 1966, p. 2.
56. Kenneth Kaunda, "A Racial Holocaust in Central Africa?" *Punch* 250 (9 March 1966): 334–35; Julius Nyerere, "Rhodesia in the Context of Southern Africa," *Foreign Affairs* 44 (1 April 1966): 373–86.
57. Department of State, "Memorandum of Conversation of Meeting of Under Secretary Mann with Tobacco Company Representatives on Rhodesia," 28 January 1966, NSF: Rhodesia, box 4, Johnson Library; McKay, "Southern Africa and Its Implications for American Policy," 24.

with North Vietnam at the same time that it pressured Washington to end economic relations with Rhodesia. In response to such attacks, Rusk sent a long message to the British Foreign Office noting, "Pressures from Congress are getting stronger" and it was becoming "difficult to explain what we are trying to do in Zambia and Rhodesia." He mentioned, "It is only too convenient, regardless of the merits, for critics of our measures in support of your Rhodesian policy to point to the continued appearance of ships of British registry in North Vietnamese ports." Rusk, who shared the congressional anger at Britain's trade with Vietnam, concluded that it was hard for Americans to understand "why the friendly flag of Britain flies over ships that . . . contribute to the material and financial strength of North Vietnam."[58]

Like many in Washington, Rusk was impatient with the lack of progress on Rhodesia and frustrated by the few apparent benefits of the close U.S. cooperation with Great Britain. Williams and the African Bureau shared many of the secretary's concerns but tried to gain more time to allow sanctions to work. They organized a special group within the African Bureau to explain American policy to Congress in hopes of heading off any resolution that might "embarrass Wilson." The bureau also tried, unsuccessfuly, to prevent "right-wingers" in Congress from visiting Rhodesia.[59]

Coinciding with the first significant domestic criticism of America's Rhodesian policy was a new international defiance of the oil embargo. In early April, there were numerous reports that Portugal would openly defy the oil embargo by allowing the Greek tanker *Manuela* to land in Mozambique with a shipment of oil for Rhodesia. Portugal had worked with South Africa before to channel petroleum to Rhodesia, but this time its actions were so openly contemptuous that the United States felt Great Britain had to react. On 5 April, State Department officials informed Lisbon that they had information that the *Manuela* was about to dock in Beria "in defiance of the UN embargo." Portugal first denied the report, but later Foreign Minister Nogueira admitted that the tanker was going to land. He explained that his nation did not recognize the UN's authority and "therefore . . . it cannot be asked to interfere in the activity of private enterprise."[60]

The State Department had expected Wilson to take a tougher approach to oil after the Labour party won a large majority in the 31 March 1966 general election. Thus, Washington waited impatiently for London to take some action concerning the *Manuela*. On 7 April, Great Britain finally responded. The Foreign Office

58. Rusk to Michael Stewart, British Foreign Secretary, enclosed in Rusk to U.S. embassy, London, 15 February 1966, NSF: United Kingdom, box 2, Johnson Library.

59. Williams to Fredericks, 26 January 1966, Williams Papers, box 5, National Archives.

60. Portuguese embassy, Washington, to the Department of State, 6 April 1966, CF: Portugal, box 64, Johnson Library; Nogueira, "Official Policy Statement," 6 April 1966, *Portuguese Foreign Policy*, 47–48.

told the United States that Britain was prepared to go to the UN to request permission to use force to stop delivery of the oil. The State Department was greatly relieved by its ally's sudden resolve. American representatives in London and intelligence analysts soon reported that Wilson was still being extremely cautious. The British would try only for a "carefully limited" UN resolution to cover the immediate situation. They would do nothing about the continued flow of oil from South Africa. London was willing to confront weak Portugal but remained determined not to challenge Pretoria.[61]

As it had done consistently since 11 November, America went along with Wilson's strategy. Goldberg and the British delegate, Lord Caradon, led a "sit-in" at the Security Council to force a special session on the problem. Goldberg was very influential in the defeat of various African resolutions demanding that Great Britain use force against Smith and end oil shipments from South Africa. Together, Caradon and Goldberg managed to limit the council to the current crisis of the tanker off Mozambique. On 9 April, the Security Council passed a unanimous resolution granting Great Britain permission to intercept the *Manuela*. The next day, HMS *Berwick* blocked the tanker from entering port, and the *Manuela* sailed on to South Africa.[62]

Initially, it seemed that Goldberg and Caradon had scored a major victory. They had managed to block any "radical" resolution yet demonstrated their determination to enforce the isolation of Rhodesia. However, it quickly became evident that the incident had unanticipated ramifications. The final UN resolution called the situation "a threat to the peace." This did not automatically invoke the dreaded chapter 7 of the charter, but it did authorize the Security Council to review the problem later. If the threat remained, the group was obligated to initiate whatever enforcement measures it deemed necessary under chapter 7. To Goldberg and Caradon, the "threat" was the tanker in Beria. To the Africans, however, the "threat" was Rhodesian independence. They contended that, as the "threat to the peace" still remained, the UN should proceed toward mandatory sanctions under chapter 7.[63]

It suddenly seemed that the "carefully limited" resolution supported by the United States would become the vehicle for direct UN intervention in Rhodesia. Great Britain repeatedly had argued that Rhodesia was not a UN problem, but its actions now seemed to invite the world organization to take control of the crisis. America repeatedly had opposed invoking chapter 7 and the resultant mandatory sanctions on any African issue. Its support of the 9 April resolution, however, seemed to imply that the United States would accept binding sanctions if the

61. George C. Denney, Department of State Intelligence Branch, to Rusk, "UK Asks for Security Council Meeting on Rhodesia," 7 April 1966, NSF: United Kingdom, box 2, Johnson Library.
62. *New York Times*, 8 April 1966, p. 1; 11 April 1966, p. 1; *SDB* 54 (2 May 1966): 713–18.
63. Good, *UDI*, 138–44; Lake, *The "Tar Baby" Option*, 94–95.

situation in Rhodesia was not resolved. In its efforts to encourage Great Britain to take a tougher policy, America had, almost unwittingly, opened the door to the obligatory economic pressure on white regimes that it had so long resisted.

When the implications of the UN action became clear, there was an immediate reaction within the administration. The press was suddenly full of stories of "serious misgivings" within the U.S. government over the UN resolution. The *New York Times* reported that "senior officials" in Washington feared that Great Britain was blundering toward the use of force in Rhodesia and was paving the way for mandatory sanctions against Portugal and South Africa as well. The article quoted "high-level spokesmen" as stating that the United States had no intention of accepting sanctions and would not provide any military support should Great Britain decide to intervene in Rhodesia.[64]

Ironically, American diplomats, many of whom had privately criticized Great Britain for its reluctance to take firm action, now were angered by the results of London's "tough" policy. They were concerned about the apparent inconsistency of British policy and feared that continued automatic support of Wilson might draw America too deeply into the crisis. Direct U.S. interests in Rhodesia were minimal, but its stakes in Portugal and South Africa were more significant. The administration had allowed Great Britain to lead the way on the Rhodesian issue, but U.S. officials were unwilling to "follow" London into a war in Africa, mandatory sanctions, or a sudden "sellout" to Smith.

By April 1966, it was clear that the "quick kill" was a failure. Washington was unsure of Wilson's next step. In fact, many U.S. officials were increasingly convinced that Great Britain had no overall strategy but was only "ad hocing" it—drifting from crisis to crisis. The obvious leaks to the press following the UN vote were designed to signal London that the policy of "supporting Britain" had its limits. America would not sacrifice its interests or influence to save British honor. The administration was angered by Great Britain's refusal to aid the U.S. effort in Vietnam and convinced that continuance of its deferential diplomacy on Rhodesia would generate increasing domestic and African criticism. It indirectly announced that it would not automatically continue to support London's Rhodesian policy if the policy led to force or sanctions against Portugal and South Africa. America did not end its cooperation with Great Britain, but it did give notice that future African diplomacy would be determined by its own pragmatic considerations.

A week after the orchestrated newspaper stories, Goldberg gave another indication of the new independence of U.S. policy. In a speech to the National Press Club on 19 April, he responded to the criticism of the 9 April resolution and its implications. He defended American actions but made it clear that the United States would not support the use of force or the application of mandatory

64. *New York Times*, 12 April 1966, p. 15.

sanctions against Portugal or South Africa. He also rejected the charge that American foreign policy was made in London. Goldberg contended that Washington had its own interests in the crisis and would shape its policies accordingly. He concluded his address by quoting the Spanish philosopher Salvador de Madariaga: "Our eyes must be idealistic and our feet realistic. We must walk in the right direction but we must walk step-by-step." In the summer of 1966, the United States tried to implement the "new realism" that Goldberg implied by pursuing its own diplomatic course independent of British actions.[65]

65. *SDB* 54 (9 May 1966): 753–54.

9. CONSENSUS AND COMPLACENCY | America and the "Long Haul" in Rhodesia

In the spring of 1966, it seemed that the prevailing policy of supporting Great Britain in Rhodesia would accomplish little more than an ever deeper American involvement in an unwinnable conflict. The situation was stalmated, but as time passed the crisis increased in complexity and importance and its global implications loomed ever larger. Rhodesia was simultaneously an issue between America and Great Britain, a problem for U.S. relations with black Africa, a possible source of confrontation between Washington and the UN, and a growing domestic dispute.

All of the possible ramifications of Rhodesia became apparent with the UN action in April authorizing Great Britain to use force. This was the first time since the Korean War that the Security Council had asked a nation to take military action to carry out its directives, and the first time ever that it had allowed a single country to take such a step. Given Wilson's reluctance to use force against Smith, it was highly unlikely that Great Britain would send troops to Rhodesia. There remained, however, the possibility that the UN would authorize military intervention by African nations. More probable, the group would go ahead with its announced intention to invoke mandatory sanctions against all three white regimes in southern Africa. Finally, there was a growing suspicion among U.S. diplomats that Wilson might negotiate a settlement with Smith that abandoned majority rule for a face-saving agreement that kept effective power in the hands of the whites. It was possible that continued U.S. support of Great Britain might lead to war, sanctions, or identification with a "sellout." The United States was not willing to let its commitment to aid London involve it in any of these options.

Throughout the crisis, Washington had been frustrated by Great Britain's serpentine diplomacy. By April it was even less clear what London's overall strategy was. Wilson had first denied that the UN had any right to be involved with Rhodesia, yet he seemed increasingly dependent on the organization. He had vowed not to negotiate with Smith, but in early 1966 there were persistent rumors that Great Britain was now prepared to talk. London had claimed it would not use force against Rhodesia, but it used military action to block delivery of oil. Wilson had assured America that sanctions would end the rebellion by March, yet in April he talked of the "long haul" rather than the "quick kill." The State Department had taken a tough position to force U.S. companies to embargo Rhodesia, only to watch British corporations evade the boycott with little governmental response. Finally, London had almost demanded U.S. support on

Rhodesia at the same time that it was increasingly critical of American actions in Vietnam.

A tempting solution to Washington's impatience and worries concerning the possible results of British policy was simply to "disengage" U.S. diplomacy from that of the United Kingdom. America could then respond to developments in Rhodesia in strict accordance with its own interests. This seemed to be the trend in Washington in the spring of 1966. Even before the 9 April Security Council resolution and the subsequent leaks to the press, there had been discussions within the government of a more independent position on Rhodesia. On 19 March, the *Christian Science Monitor* published an article entitled "U.S. Finds Dilemma on Rhodesia Road" by David Willis, its Washington correspondent. Willis noted a conflict between administration "hawks" and "doves" on the issue but found a consensus for a more unilateral U.S. stance free from dependence on London.[1]

The problem with an "independent" policy was that it involved more risks. It would either place America "in front" of Great Britain and, as a result, in the forefront of international criticism, or allow the United States to abandon the issue to the distress of blacks and liberals. To break from Great Britain required a consensus for a separate American policy where none existed. Both factions in the bureaucracy wanted a diplomatic divorce from London, but for opposite reasons. Africanists saw continued dependence on Great Britain as restraining strong U.S. initiatives and linking America with any negotiated settlement. They were convinced that Wilson would never defy Pretoria by enforcing the oil embargo. Thus, the existing economic sanctions would not topple Smith. Since he had ruled out force, Wilson's only alternative was to negotiate. As it was clear that Smith would not give in on majority rule, negotiations might well lead to a British betrayal of the Africans. Disengagement from Great Britain was necessary to avoid any identification of America with a weak and unpopular British settlement. To those, like Ball, who felt America had already devoted too much attention to Rhodesia, a break with London was required to block any "radical" UN action and to end the continued preoccupation with a largely peripheral issue. The Europeanists did not fear a "sell out" as much as a desperate British move to use force or UN sanctions against all white Africa. To them, disengagement from Great Britain would leave Washington free to pursue a course of inaction similar to its policies toward Portugal and South Africa after 1964. Divided on overall objectives, both sides temporarily agreed on immediate tactics: more independence in the U.S. position on Rhodesia.

On 15 April, Ball made his attempt to move America away from deference to London's leadership. In a long note to U.S. officials in Great Britain, he asked for recommendations for a possible unilateral American policy on Rhodesia. He emphasized that the officials were to make their suggestions "without consulting

1. *Christian Science Monitor*, 19 March 1966, p. 3.

HMG [Her Majesty's Government]."[2] Ball's action was consistent with his perceptions of both Africa and Europe. He was not only doubtful of the importance of Rhodesia to the United States but also disdainful of London's pretensions to the status of a world power. Wilson's inability to solve the crisis in Rhodesia only indicated the United Kingdom's global weakness. Ball previously had clashed with the British over the American-sponsored multilateral nuclear force. Wilson's rejection of the plan had infuriated Ball and convinced him of Great Britain's inflated opinion of its own power. Rhodesia was only a vehicle for the under-secretary to make clear his opinion that the United Kingdom would have to accept a drastically reduced role in international affairs. He had no intention of advocating any significant American efforts on Rhodesia; instead, he wanted to end London's outdated assumption of world leadership.[3]

While Ball waited for a response to his note, Wilson confirmed rumors that Great Britain would negotiate with Smith. On 27 April, he told parliament that representatives of the two governments would soon meet to discuss a solution to the rebellion. When Labour back-benchers cried "sellout," Wilson quickly reassured them that the negotiations were just "talks about talks"—informal conversations to determine if a basis existed for higher-level conferences.

Wilson's announcement again raised Africanist fears of an abandonment of the "five principles." The Africanists became more convinced that it was time for the United States to move toward an independent position. With the encouragement of the African Bureau, liberal American politicians conferred with British officials to try to determine Wilson's true intentions. Sen. Frank Church of Idaho met with Wilson on 10 May. The prime minister assured Church that Smith was "desperate for a settlement" and that there would be no agreement without firm guarantees of African rights. He evaded Church's questions about the specific conditions for any negotiated settlement.[4] A week later Donald Fraser, the most prominent Africanist in the House of Representatives, talked with Foreign Office officials in London. Fraser reported that the British expressed great concern that the United States was backing away from support of Great Britain on Rhodesia. He wrote Johnson of the need for continued American opposition to Smith to assure the goodwill of "liberal groups here in the U.S. and uncommitted nations abroad."[5]

Both Church and Fraser also commented on the growing problems that Vietnam posed for continued Anglo-American cooperation on Rhodesia. Wilson had initially given modest support to U.S. intervention in Vietnam. By late 1965,

2. Ball to U.S. embassay, London, 15 April 1966, NSF: United Kingdom, box 2, Johnson Library.
3. Ball elaborated on his ideas in his chapter "The Disadvantages of the Special Relationship," in *The Discipline of Power*, 90–117. See also Wilson, *The Labour Government*, 46–49.
4. Frank Church, "Memorandum of Conversation with Prime Minister Wilson, London, May 10, 1966" enclosed in U.S. embassay, London, to Mr. Walt Rostow, 1 June 1966, NSF: United Kingdom, box 2, Johnson Library.
5. Fraser to Johnson, 17 May 1966, ibid.

however, he had become opposed to American bombing in North Vietnam. Great Britain continued to trade with Hanoi despite repeated protests from Washington and refused Johnson's requests to "help us some in Vietnam" by sending a token force to the conflict. The president wanted "more flags" in the war and had urged Wilson to "send us some men . . . to deal with these guerrillas. And announce to the press that you are going to help us." The growing administration resentment over its ally's failure to give any assistance in the conflict in Vietnam made continued coordination of Rhodesian policy even more difficult.[6]

The beginning of low-level talks between Great Britain and Rhodesia and the continued tension between America and London over Vietnam provided a strong incentive for Washington to move away from its subordinate role on Rhodesia. There remained the question of where to move. The United States had no real alternatives to the existing policies of nonrecognition and voluntary sanctions. It did not want to become the sponsor of a tougher policy or the leader of a Western "retreat" on the issue.

The African nations were outraged by Wilson's decision to begin talks with Rhodesia and sponsored a UN resolution denouncing the negotiations, demanding mandatory sanctions, and authorizing the use of force to end the rebellion. Goldberg worked hard against the resolution. He cited the traditional U.S. position against sanctions and force. Goldberg found, however, that America was so closely identified with Great Britain that many countries assumed Washington had encouraged the negotiations with Rhodesia. African and communist delegates denounced "Anglo-American maneuverings" to block freedom in Rhodesia. Goldberg angrily denied charges that he was "in collusion with London" to go easy on Smith. He defended "the costly economic action, involving a wide variety of steps" that his nation had taken against Rhodesia. When the United States, Great Britain, and four other nations abstained, the resolution failed. The Soviet Union and several African states immediately attacked America and Great Britain for "vetoing the will of the African people."[7]

The angry UN debate convinced some in Washington that the United States should not only break away from Great Britain but also end its involvement in the Rhodesian problem. However, reactions to the UN demands also illustrated the difficulties in "disengagement" from London. Following the vote, Secretary of Defense McNamara gave an address in Montreal that strongly hinted at an American diplomatic withdrawal from the issue. "The United States has no mandate on high to police the world and no inclination to do so," he declared in a reference to Rhodesia. "There have been classic cases in which our deliberate nonaction has been the wisest action of all."[8] If McNamara's speech was a "trial

6. Wilson, *The Labour Government*, 80.
7. *New York Times*, 19 May 1966, p. 17; *SDB* 54 (20 June 1966): 987–89.
8. Quoted in Nielsen, *The Great Powers and Africa*, 313–14.

balloon" to test the reaction to inaction, it brought immediate response. Africans, blacks, and liberals claimed that Washington was preparing to "sell out" to Smith. The outcry was so strong that Johnson immediately arranged to speak to a meeting of African ambassadors on the anniversary of the Organization of African Unity. The president delivered an emotional speech defending his policy on Rhodesia. He attacked "the narrow-minded and outmoded policy which in some parts of Africa permits the few to rule at the expense of the many." Although he pointedly avoided any reference to Portugal or South Africa, he did single out Rhodesia. America was dedicated, he explained, "to open the full power and responsibility of nationhood to all the people of Rhodesia—not just 6 percent of them."[9]

Africanists were overjoyed at this rare display of direct presidential concern with Africa. Johnson's comments were his most specific public commitment to majority rule in Rhodesia. He clearly repudiated McNamara's suggestion of "nonaction." The president also signaled Wilson that the United States would not be a party to any agreement that did not include eventual majority rule. The new head of the African Bureau, Joseph Palmer, cited Johnson's remarks the next day in a letter to Roy Wilkins of the NAACP. Wilkins had written of his "deep concern" over the lack of progress in Rhodesia and asked that the United States "take an even stronger stance to identify itself with racial equality in Africa." He urged "a harder, bolder, more imaginative, more resourceful Rhodesian policy than is now in effect." Palmer responded by quoting Johnson's pledge to majority rule and assuring the black leader that America would rigorously enforce existing sanctions.[10]

Johnson's support of black rule left unclear what the United States would do to secure that goal. His speech, and later questions by the press to White House aides, failed to establish if Washington would continue its cooperation with Great Britain or undertake some independent actions. When Wilson launched a new attack on American policy in Vietnam, Ball and others immediately revived their arguments for "disengagement" from London.

In early June 1966, Johnson secretly informed Wilson that the United States would expand its bombing of North Vietnam to include targets within the city limits of Hanoi and Haiphong. On 28 June the attacks began. The next day, Wilson issued a public statement formally "disassociating" the British government from the bombings. Johnson, Rusk, and other top officials were incensed by Wilson's action. In the words of the U.S. ambassador in London, relations between the two powers became "extremely strained."[11]

9. *SDB* 54 (13 June 1966): 914.

10. Wilkins to Johnson, 4 May 1966; Palmer to Wilkins, 27 May 1966, CF: Rhodesia, box 65, Johnson Library.

11. David Bruce, U.S. ambassador to Great Britain, to Rusk, 12 July 1966, NSF: United Kingdom, box 2, Johnson Library.

Ball was now convinced that the president would be receptive to a major reassessment of the "special relationship." Although Ball also was a critic of the war, and would resign in September in opposition, he was well aware of Johnson's sense of betrayal at Wilson's statement. The under-secretary seized on the strains in the alliance to press Johnson for a complete break with Great Britain on Rhodesia as a first step toward a total reappraisal of Anglo-American relations.

The prime minister was scheduled to visit Washington at the end of July and knew of Johnson's rage. Wilson admitted that he expected "a frozen mitt from the President" in response to his criticism of the bombing. Ball intended to make certain that Wilson's reception was cool. He sent a long paper to Johnson on the eve of the prime minister's arrival stating the case for a new American unilateralism. Ball argued that Great Britain was a weak, declining power. Its financial problems, illustrated by the collapse of the pound, and its failures on Rhodesia made it time to "redefine the so-called special relationship." Ball urged Johnson to bluntly inform Wilson that the United States could no longer support him on Rhodesia. Moreover, this was only the beginning of a greatly reduced British role in world politics. "Sooner or later the British will be forced to abandon their pretensions to world power," Ball contended. London must curtail its diplomatic activities and concentrate on its pressing domestic problems. The president should explain that there was "a new world environment" with little room for continued British influence outside the European continent. Wilson's failures on Rhodesia illustrated the demise of British power in Africa. By ending Washington's acceptance of London's leadership on the issue, Johnson would signal Wilson that Great Britain's new position was as a European rather than an international power. Ball claimed that the president should consider his task "the opportunity for an act of statesmanship."[12]

Four days after Ball's memo to Johnson, Thomas L. Hughes, director of State Department intelligence and research, sent a long report to Rusk on "Implications of UK Disengagement from Southern Africa" that Ball had ordered to support his recommendations to the president for Great Britain's diminished role in world affairs. Hughes echoed the under-secretary's attack on British "weakness" and "lack of leadership." According to Hughes, the United Kingdom was greatly "over-committed" in the world. It was clear that the "quick kill was a failure," and strong evidence existed that Wilson was "softening on Rhodesia." As a result, London might well accept "a face-saving formula" that abandoned its earlier dedication to "strict constitutionality." This new weakness on Rhodesia had "a direct bearing on U.S. policy," since Washington was closely identified with its ally's action. Hughes suggested that Rusk recognize

12. Ball to Johnson, "Harold Wilson's Visit—The Opportunity for an Act of Statesmanship," 22 July 1966, ibid. See also Wilson, *The Labour Government*, 263.

"the growing divergence in UK and US policy towards Southern Africa" and consider how to end America's association with British actions.[13]

At the same time that Ball and Hughes were making their case for an end to British leadership on Rhodesia, Edward Korry, U.S. ambassador to Ethiopia, sent Johnson a long analysis of Africa in response to the president's orders to evaluate future American economic policy toward the continent. But Korry also discussed political developments and endorsed Ball's position: "We are persuaded that the role of Britain in Africa will be a diminishing one. . . . This has serious implications for U.S. policy in Africa." He argued that, since Washington had consistently supported Great Britain's handling of the Rhodesian situation, the United States could suffer if London's weakness led to an unpopular negotiated settlement.[14]

Despite the arguments of Ball and the others, Johnson did not suggest to Wilson that his nation accept a reduced role on Rhodesia or any other issue. The president's meeting with the prime minister produced no "act of statesmanship" as Ball had suggested. There was little discussion of either Rhodesia or Vietnam. The two leaders concentrated on the British financial situation and on joint efforts to support the foundering pound.[15]

There are a number of possible reasons for the failure of the United States to formally "disengage" from Great Britain's Rhodesian policies. First, there was no accepted alternative to the existing policy. Johnson's 26 May speech to the African ambassadors clearly indicated that the president would not accept any retreat on sanctions or nonrecognition, the obvious steps toward a policy of inaction. Second, with the ever-expanding U.S. involvement in Vietnam, there was little sympathy within the government for strong American initiatives on Rhodesia. Important also were the changes in personnel within the bureaucracy. The two major advocates of a reversal of Washington's position were Williams and Ball. By the summer of 1966, Williams had left the administration and Ball's influence had been eroded by his dissent on Vietnam. Finally, the administration found itself increasingly forced to defend what it had alredy done on the issue in the face of intense internal criticism.

Although Rhodesia declined somewhat as an international concern in the summer of 1966, it greatly expanded as a domestic dispute. The reaction from the American right that many in Washington had predicted if Smith survived arrived with a vengeance in mid-1966. Officials had little time to debate new strategy as they were strongly attacked for their support of sanctions and cooperation with London. The intense lobbying activities of Portugal and South Africa illustrated

13. Thomas L. Hughes to Rusk, "Implications of UK Disengagement from Southern Africa," 26 July 1966, ibid.
14. Edward Korry to Johnson, "Review of African Development Policies and Program as Directed by the President," July 1966, NSF: Africa, box 2, Johnson Library.
15. Wilson, *The Labour Government*, 263–66.

the power of those in the United States who opposed efforts against white regimes in Africa. To the surprise of many in Washington, the campaign in favor of Rhodesian independence was more wideread and sustained than the efforts of either Selvage & Lee on behalf of Portugal or the South African lobby.

The Rhodesian issue offered a variety of arguments for those opposed to the administration's position. First, there was the continuing view that Africa was outside the American sphere of influence or interests. Regardless of the legal or moral questions involved, the crisis was just not critical for the United States. Many Europeanists and former governmental officials attacked American involvement from a purely geopolitical perspective. The United States was engaged in a major war in Asia and should concentrate its efforts there. Africa was of only marginal concern. Opposition to Smith was of no real benefit to America's international strategy. Rhodesia was an internal matter for Great Britain that should not distract Washington from more significant issues.

Second, there was a dispute over the legality of the campaign against Smith's government. While the administration claimed Rhodesia was not a state and its declaration of independence was illegal, a number of Americans disagreed. Smith's separation from Great Britain was no more illegal than America's in 1776, they argued. Rhodesia had been virtually sovereign since 1923. It was thus as much of a "nation" as any other in Africa. Its political system was an issue for the people of Rhodesia, not for foreign powers. What was "illegal" was UN intervention into the domestic affairs of an independent nation.

Third, many Americans dissented from the argument that, because Smith's regime was racist and in violation of civil liberties, the United States should oppose it. By this standard, they contended, most nations were in defiance of American ideals. Washington recognized dozens of undemocratic countries yet refused to deal with Rhodesia. This was an unrealistic attempt to selectively impose U.S. values on a weak state while continuing to cooperate with dictatorships of both the left and right elsewhere in the world. Critics charged that the administration was being not only unrealistic but also inconsistent in its emphasis on "morality" and "democracy" as standards for recognition.

Fourth, some Americans attacked U.S. deference to Great Britain. They accused Johnson of allowing London to dictate American foreign policy. He was not only denying U.S. independence but also aligning Washington with a nation highly critical of the war in Vietnam. America had surrendered its diplomacy to a country that denounced the war and supplied material to the enemy.

Fifth, there was doubt among the public about UN involvement in the issue. Many conservatives had been highly dubious of the responsibility of the organization. They saw it as little more than a public forum for communists and third-world "fanatics." Many denied the right of the UN to determine standards of conduct for other nations. They pointed out that the UN was unwilling to condemn communist violations of freedom but was eager to attack Rhodesia. By cooperating with the group, America was encouraging a dual standard for international behavior, paving the way for a multilateral military operation in Africa, and, to a few Americans, leading toward a surrender of U.S. sovereignty to the world body.

Sixth, the fact that the Smith government was white, Christian, and anticommunist appealed to many in the United States. Rhodesia seemed an island of Western values in a continent of chaos and radicalism. To some Americans, the major standard for U.S. support was not domestic policy but anticommunism. By this criterion, Rhodesia should be an ally, not an enemy. Like Portugal and South Africa, it was a bastion against the spread of Soviet influence in the third world.

Last, part of the support for Smith was clearly racial. The belief in white supremacy was not limited to Africa. Many organizations and individuals opposed to the American civil-rights movement rallied to Rhodesia's cause. A sizable number of Americans knew nothing of the legal and diplomatic problems of the Rhodesian situation, but they did know that Smith was white. To some, this was reason enough for supporting him.

Because of the variety of possible justifications for dissent, the Rhodesian lobby was diverse. It included a number of foreign-policy experts who took seriously the legal and strategic issues involved. Businessmen joined the campaign because of their general opposition to governmental restrictions on free trade. Even those who were not directly active in trade with Rhodesia saw sanctions as a precedent for limits on business activity elsewhere. Congressional critics generally invoked the anticommunist argument, although some also expressed the racial attitudes of their districts. Religious organizations emphasized the Christian influence of whites in Rhodesia; antiblack groups used the racial argument; and a number of conservative organizations simply adopted the Rhodesian issue as a part of their general critique of American foreign policy. In addition, Rhodesia had an established constituency in existing groups supportive of Portugal, South Africa, and Katanga.

In its effort to duplicate the successful public-relations efforts of the other white regimes, the Rhodesian Information Office first concentrated on distributing pamphlets, films, and other material to established conservative organizations. Althought it had only a small budget (about $80,000 in 1966), the office managed to start a monthly journal, *Rhodesian Commentary*, and a weekly newsletter, *Rhodesian Viewpoint*, within a few weeks of UDI. By late 1966 the publications had a circulation of over thirteen thousand.[16] Rhodesian propaganda argued that America should accept UDI for reasons of both principle and self-interest. It repeatedly compared Rhodesia with the American colonies in 1776. The "patriots" in Salisbury were motivated by the same desire for freedom

16. The best summaries of the Rhodesian public-relations effort in the United States are Vernon McKay, "The Domino Theory of the Rhodesian Lobby," *Africa Report* 12 (June 1967): 55–58, and Lake, *The "Tar Baby" Option*, 103–12.

as were Jefferson, Adams, Franklin, and the others who rebelled against British tyranny. The material also offered an African form of the domino theory: If Britain and the UN managed to overthrow the Rhodesian government, it was inevitable that communism would follow, endangering the white regimes in Angola, Mozambique, and South Africa. Soon all of southern and central Africa would be communist, and it would only be a brief period until the whole continent was under the control of Moscow.[17]

A number of American groups came to support Rhodesia. The Rhodesians' first success was with the American-African Affairs Association, an outgrowth of the old "Katanga lobby." Many of its officers were tied to the conservative *National Review*. As a result, the journal became the most influential and vocal critic of U.S. policy. Rhodesians also found early support in the Young Americans for Freedom, the Liberty Lobby, and the John Birch Society. In early 1966, Smith's representatives helped establish new groups designed to concentrate solely on the issue of Rhodesian independence. Some, such as RIGHT (Rhodesian Independence Gung Ho Troops) and HISTORY (Hurray for Ian Smith, Titan of Rhodesian Yearning) soon collapsed. Two groups did become well organized and powerful: The Friends of Rhodesian Independence and the American-Southern African Council. Both sponsored American tours to Rhodesia, speakers, letter-writing campaigns, and a variety of fund-raising projects to finance lobbying efforts. A number of conservative radio commentators such as Carl McIntyre, Dan Smoot, and Fulton Lewis II also adopted the Rhodesian cause. Lewis visited Salisbury to tape interviews with Smith and several tribal chiefs to show Americans that both whites and blacks supported UDI. By mid-1966, dozens of congressmen, editors, religious leaders, and teachers had made the pilgrimage to Salisbury. Smith's government gave great publicity to such visits both in Rhodesia and in its American publications.[18]

By the spring of 1966, the propaganda campaign had begun to have an impact in Washington. Both Congress and the White House were flooded with letters from groups and individuals demanding an end to sanctions and the recognition of Rhodesia. The State Department was forced to hire extra secretaries to send a variety of form letters defending U.S. policy. One letter was designed for individuals, another for religious groups, and a third for "other" organizations. Communications from prominent individuals or large organizations were answered personally by officials in the African Bureau or by White House aides.[19]

Accompanying this mass public pressure were protests by influential foreign-

17. "A Message from Ian Smith to the American People," *Rhodesian Commentary* (January 1966): 1. See also Anthony Lejune, "Can Britain Stop Rhodesia?" *National Review* 18 (11 January 1966): 22–23.

18. "Report of American Missions to Rhodesia," *East Africa and Rhodesia* (24 March 1966): 540–42; (21 April 1966): 597–98.

19. Most of the correspondence for 1966 and 1967 is in CF: Rhodesia, box 65. Some can also be found in the Confidential Files: Rhodesia, box 11, Johnson Library.

policy experts. Former Secretary of State Dean Acheson led the Cold War establishment's critique of U.S. policy throughout 1966 and 1967. He quickly attached Rhodesia to his continued attack on American concern with Africa and the West's pandering to "the international juvenile delinquents" of the third world. By early 1967, Acheson had become almost fanatical on the issue.[20] John Roche, a professor at Brandeis and past president of the Americans for Democratic Action, made several attempts to influence Johnson to move away from opposition to Rhodesian independence. In 1966 he wrote to Moyers that pressure on the United States "to play world gendarme" and topple Smith would lead eventually to a war with South Africa. Roche admitted that the Rhodesians were "as nasty a crew of racist authoritarians as ever walked the earth," but he contended that they were no worse than the communists. "If we are not prepared to overthrow a communist dictatorship . . . why should we be available to liberate black Africans from white domination?" he asked. Like Ball, Roche advocated a policy of inaction: "There are times when the best policy is to sit things out on the sidelines. Africa is a shambles and will continue to be. . . . So let's be nice, generous, friendly—and aloof. If the Soviets and the Chicoms want to dabble around in those parts, they can have the privilege of making enemies for awhile."[21]

While Acheson, Roche, and others attacked U.S. policy for its strategic and theoretical shortcomings, business leaders responded to the issue out of direct self-interest. Most American companies had grudgingly gone along with sanctions only because they had been assured that they would be compensated for their losses and that the embargo would last only a few months. By the summer of 1966 they were angry because they had not received any governmental assistance and there seemed no early end to the restrictions. Although only a few U.S. firms were really harmed by sanctions, a number of businessmen objected to the government's blocking of trade with a noncommunist country. It seemed that Rhodesia was having little difficulty finding replacements for American products, and U.S. executives argued that they were sacrificing for an embargo that had no real impact on Rhodesia and only allowed other nations to profit at American expense.[22]

The pressures of public opinion were most evident in Congress. In March and April 1966, a number of conservatives in the House launched attacks on the "left-leaning press and Administration" for their denial of Rhodesia's right to independence. Congressional knowledge of the complexities of UDI and African politics was minimal. One member repeatedly referred to "Zambia,"

20. "Ambivalences of American Foreign Policy," speech at Indiana University, 5 March 1965, Acheson papers, box 141, Truman Library. For Acheson's efforts in 1966 and 1967, see below.
21. Roche to Moyers, 6 September 1966, CF: Rhodesia, box 65, Johnson Library. Moyers enclosed Roche's letter in the documents "For the President's Night Reading."
22. Anthony Solomon, Assistant Secretary of State for Economic Affairs, oral history interview, Johnson Library.

and others confused Southern Rhodesia with South Africa. Congressmen did, however, understand that Rhodesia was anticommunist and that Great Britain was not supporting the war in Vietnam. To Rep. H. R. Gross of Iowa, a leader of the pro-Rhodesian forces, Smith was being punished for opposing communism while Wilson was rewarded for aiding North Vietnam. John Ashbrook of Ohio, the first member of Congress to visit Rhodesia after UDI, argued that U.S. policy on Rhodesia was only part of a larger plot to turn over American sovereignty to the UN. Southern representatives railed away at the "savagery" of the black Africans and stressed the need for continued white control. In the words of Waggoner of Louisiana, the endless violence in black Africa showed that "the natives are not capable of producing any semblance of what we call civilization."[23] In the Senate, James Eastland of Mississippi, Strom Thurmond of South Carolina, Paul Fannin of Arizona, and Goldwater led the verbal campaign in defense of Smith. In the summer of 1966, Eastland introduced an unsuccessful resolution calling on the United States to end its "inhumane, illegal, arbitrary, unfair, harmful, and costly policy of economic sanctions against Rhodesia."[24]

Encouraged by such an immediate response to their efforts, Rhodesia's agents expanded their propaganda program. Like Portugal and South Africa, they attacked the news media's "slanted" coverage of Rhodesia and organized letter-writing campaigns to newspapers and TV networks. They also increased their financing of trips by Americans to Rhodesia. Throughout the spring and summer of 1966, dozens of fundamentalist church leaders visited with Smith. In July, Rhodesia paid for the journey to Salisbury of W. J. Simmons, editor of the White Citizens' Council *Citizen*. Simmons published a lengthy interview with Smith, and the Citizens' Council passed a unanimous resolution urging diplomatic recognition of Rhodesia.[25]

Although some within the administration dismissed the pro-Rhodesian lobby as reactionary and racist, public opposition to U.S. policy was not limited to extremists. A number of prominent conservatives and even some liberals had strong reservations about America's actions. Their organized and vocal criticism helped introduce a new caution in Washington's handling of the crisis in mid-1966.

Harold Wilson faced even more public-opinion problems than did Johnson. His announcement of talks with Smith infuriated some members of his Labour party as well as the African nations. When representatives of the Commonwealth countries met in London in September, there was a major split between the

23. The congressional debate on Rhodesia is well analyzed by Kenneth Grundy, "The Congressional Image of Africa," *Africa Today* 13 (December 1966): 8–13.
24. Lake, *The "Tar Baby" Option*, 118–19.
25. Calvin Trillin, "Letter from Salisbury," *New Yorker* (12 November 1966): 139; "A Conversation with Ian Smith," *Citizen* 10 (July–August 1966): 15–21.

African states and Great Britain. Canadian Prime Minister Lester Pearson worked frantically to try to find some common ground on Rhodesia. The stormy meeting finally produced a compromise. Wilson rejected demands for force, but he did endorse the African program for No Independence Before Majority Rule (NIBMAR). He also promised to seek binding sanctions at the UN if his negotiations with Smith failed.

Americans were again confused by Wilson's new tack. They had feared a British "sellout" in the summer, but now the prime minister seemed to be headed back toward a "tough" position that included mandatory sanctions. On 14 October, British Foreign Secretary George Brown arrived in Washington to try to explain the new strategy to Rusk and Johnson. Brown emphasized the growing pressure on Great Britain from the Commonwealth nations for stronger measures. He notified the Americans that Great Britain would have to ask for binding sanctions if there was not a rapid settlement. U.S. officials were noncommittal. They agreed that the present economic embargo was ineffective, but they also knew that domestic opposition to voluntary sanctions would be minor compared to the reaction to UN-sponsored mandatory actions.[26]

Despite American misgivings, it soon became apparent that Washington would support Wilson if he asked for the tougher economic measures. The push for an independent U.S. policy had failed by the fall, and the administration indicated that it would continue the traditional strategy of backing Great Britain. In November, Assistant Secretary of State for International Organization Joseph Sisco, an increasingly influential adviser on Rhodesian policy, admitted, "The voluntary sanctions have had some effect, but they have not succeeded in bringing about the desired political change." Sisco declared, "We may soon have to decide whether the authority of the Security Council to impose mandatory economic embargos should be invoked to put additional pressure on the present Rhodesian authorities."[27]

Sisco's remarks did not represent firm U.S. commitment to sanctions but only a recognition that the issue was likely to come up. African nations clearly intended to push for stronger UN pressure on Smith regardless of Wilson's actions. President Jomo Kenyatta of Kenya wrote Johnson in November expressing the African opinion that the situation in Rhodesia could not continue. Kenyatta told Johnson that the African states would demand more than verbal attacks and voluntary sanctions at the forthcoming UN session and that they expected U.S. support.[28]

There still remained an outside chance that Wilson could arrange a peaceful

26. National Security Council, "Memo for Mr. Bundy: Visit of UK Foreign Minister Brown," 15 October 1966, NSF: United Kingdom, box 5, Johnson Library.
27. *SDB* 55 (5 December 1966): 860–61.
28. Kenyatta to Johnson, 10 November 1965, Confidential File: Rhodesia, box 11, Johnson Library.

settlement before the UN convened. On 18 November, Michael Stewart, the British ambassador in Washington, gave Rusk a pessimistic report on the talks with Rhodesia. Stewart was doubtful that there could be any real breakthrough, since Smith refused to negotiate seriously until Wilson conceded Rhodesia's right to independence.[29] Based on Stewart's report, American officials assumed that the impasse remained and there would be no negotiated solution. Accordingly, they began deliberations on U.S. policy toward new economic sanctions. Suddenly the State Department received notice that Sir Saville Garner, under-secretary for commonwealth affairs, was flying to Washington to discuss Rhodesia.

Garner met with Sisco and Palmer on 30 November. He informed the Americans that London would announce plans the next day for a personal meeting between Smith and Wilson. The U.S. diplomats were surprised because only two weeks earlier Stewart had told them that there was no chance for successful negotiations. Sisco and Palmer were also worried that critics of the talks would accuse Washington of pressuring Wilson to meet with Smith. The Rhodesian press had recently reported that Johnson was cool to the idea of mandatory sanctions and was urging Great Britain to settle with Rhodesia. Although the State Department unequivocally denied the stories, American officials worried that the imminent British announcement of direct talks might support the charge of U.S. pressure. Palmer and Sisco immediately drafted a press release stating that their discussions with Garner were "a part of the regular consultations between the two governments on Africa which have been held periodically over the past two years." They wanted it clear that Washington had not forced negotiations and had only been informed of Wilson's decision a few hours before the general public.[30]

On 1 December, the day Wilson announced his intention to negotiate directly with Smith, American officials quizzed Garner about the talks and about sanctions. If Wilson could force Smith into an agreement, it would end the U.S. dilemma about mandatory sanctions. If the talks failed, Washington wanted to know what London would do at the UN. Garner assured the Americans that there would be no "sellout" to Rhodesia. He was vague on what exactly his government would ask for at the UN. Wilson wanted to avoid any mention of oil in the resolution. The Americans reminded Garner that sanctions without oil were meaningless. Britain also hoped to exclude South Africa from the resolution. Sisco pointed out that any formal exclusion of Pretoria would doom sanctions to failure. The U.S. representatives were most curious about Great Britain's plans if South Africa defied the new sanctions and the Africans pushed for military intervention. They received no firm answers.[31]

29. Stewart to Rusk, 18 November 1966, NSF: United Kingdom, box 3, Johnson Library.
30. *SDB* 55 (26 December 1966): 865. See also Good, *UDI*, 186–87.
31. Lake, *The "Tar Baby" Option*, 98–101.

On the evening of 1 December 1966, Wilson and Smith boarded the British vessel HMS *Tiger* off Gibraltar. Wilson commandeered the captain's rooms, while Smith and his delegation had to be content with the medical officer's quarters. The weather was stormy, and so, too, were the negotiations. There were immediate problems over Rhodesia's "return to constitutionality" as well as the major issue of black political rights. On 5 December, a document was tentatively agreed upon, but Smith refused to sign it until he had discussed it with officials in Salisbury. Still, Wilson was confident he had obtained a settlement. That evening, however, Smith repudiated the agreement and announced to a crowd of cheering Rhodesians, "The fight goes on!"[32]

Wilson now had no choice except to fulfill his promise to the Commonwealth nations to seek mandatory sanctions. From their talks with Garner, U.S. officials knew Great Britain would not try to extend sanctions to South Africa or Portugal and would oppose any call for the use of force. Still, Americans were understandably hesitant about the imminent UN resolution. They had managed to block sanctions aimed at South Africa and Portugal, but they now seemed committed to action against Rhodesia. Any new measures against Smith's regime would increase the already strong conservative criticism of the administration. Sisco warned that binding sanctions would "lead us into new and largely uncharted waters."[33] Yet Washington agreed to support Great Britain's efforts as long as it was clear that the action was not preparatory to pressure on the other two white governments and did not imply the use of force.

In determining its approach to any UN action on sanctions, the administration also recognized the domestic pressure from liberals and blacks for a tougher policy. While the government had been most concerned with conservative criticism, it had also been subjected to growing attacks from the left. Several major black groups had endorsed the African demands for the use of force against Smith. In 1966 the Urban League condemned the United States for adopting a "me too" position on Rhodesia rather than leading the campaign for majority rule. The NAACP had sent a letter to Goldberg calling for all action "short of the intervention by the armed forces of the United States" to oust Smith. It had even suggested that Washington provide arms to Rhodesian guerrillas. Some liberals had gone further still. Thomas Franck, director of international studies at New York University, had argued for direct American military intervention. According to Franck, the United States was more "psychologically committed" to military action than Great Britain and had no "kith and kin" in the colony. Therefore, it should lead an assault on the Smith government. Franck suggested "selective air strikes" against roads and bridges to South Africa as a first step.[34]

32. Wilson, *The Labour Government*, 307–31; Good, *UDI*, 188–97.
33. *SDB* 56 (9 January 1967): 68.
34. B. Vulindela Mtshali, *Rhodesia: Background to Conflict*, 175–76; Thomas Franck, "Must We Lose Zimbabwe?" *Africa Forum* 2 (Winter 1967): 17–33.

Although a vote for sanctions would infuriate the American right, it would at least pacify critics on the left.

Finally, a UN embargo of Rhodesia would have little impact on U.S. firms, as most had already accepted the voluntary sanctions imposed earlier. American exports to Rhodesia were already miniscule. Sanctions would affect only the few companies still dependent on imports from the colony. Many of the firms dealing with Rhodesia had already established alternative sources in anticipation of UN action.[35]

Despite its tradition of hostility to chapter 7 and its earlier intention to stop "following Britain," the United States supported the UN action on Rhodesia. Goldberg did manage to make known American dissatisfaction with Great Britain's handling of the crisis when he told the Security Council: "I do not say that if we had been the constituted authority we would have done everything exactly as it has been done every step of the way, by the British Government." He also noted that the American position was a major departure from past policy. Still, Goldberg promised, "The United States will apply the full force of our law to implementing this decision." On 16 December, the resolution passed by a vote of 11–0 with four abstentions.[36]

On 5 January 1967, Johnson issued Executive Order No. 11322 implementing the Security Council action under the United Nations' Participation Act. The order suspended all trade in arms, aircraft, motor vehicles, iron ore, chrome, sugar, tobacco, copper, and, most important, oil. Any violation of the embargo was a criminal offense. The Departments of State, Commerce, and Treasury were empowered to enforce the decree.[37] As anticipated, liberals and blacks hailed the U.S. decision while conservatives condemned the action. The pro-Rhodesian forces had been growing in number throughout 1966, but the UN resolution gave them a specific cause and brought thousands more into their ranks. The public displeasure with the administration's move was immediate and intense.

Acheson led the first wave of criticism. In only a few weeks, he managed to attack Goldberg, Johnson, the UN, the *Washington Post,* the *New York Times,* and the entire third world. In an interview in the *Washington Star* on 10 December, before sanctions were voted, Acheson called the UN "completely out of hand" and its anticipated action against Rhodesia "absolutely incomprehensible." To Acheson, the political and racial situation in Rhodesia was "totally an internal matter" of no business to Great Britain, the UN, or the United States.[38] The next day, the *Washington Post* published a letter from Acheson attacking an editorial

35. *Fortune* 74 (November 1966): 73–80.
36. *SDB* 57 (9 January 1967): 73–78.
37. Ibid. (23 January 1967): 145–47.
38. Copies of Acheson's correspondence, speeches, and articles on Rhodesia are in box 141 of his papers, Truman Library.

in support of sanctions. He ridiculed a reference to "the white minority's transgressions": "Transgressions against what? What international obligations have they violated?" Rhodesia had been "de facto independent" for "nearly half a century," he argued, and according to the UN Charter there should be no interference in the domestic matters of a sovereign state. To Acheson, the UN's reasoning was "worthy of the Red Queen in *Through the Looking Glass.*"

Goldberg replied to the former secretary of state first in a speech to the Association of American Law Schools and later in a letter to the *Post*. He denied that Rhodesia was "or had ever been" a state. Therefore, it was subject to UN action. He also insisted that the issue was a moral one: "America was dedicated to racial equality and could not adopt a double standard" in its foreign policy. Finally, Goldberg contended that the issue was "of highest importance" in maintaining good relations with the rest of the world and in blocking communist influence.[39]

Goldberg's reply only stirred Acheson to new efforts. The retired diplomat devoted almost all his time to his assault on the UN and U.S. policy. Throughout 1967 and 1968, he sent letters to newspapers, wrote articles, and solicited speaking engagements to talk on Rhodesia. His attacks became ever more shrill and personal. He compared Goldberg's reasoning to that of the communists in Russia and called Wilson "loony." Later he contended that there was a "conspiracy" in Great Britain and America to overthrow Smith. Eventually, Goldberg stopped responding. He stated that, while Acheson was "a very distinguished man," his ideas about Rhodesia were "sheer nonsense."[40]

Acheson was the most persistent and outspoken critic of sanctions, but many other Americans joined in the attack on the UN action and Washington's support. A group of conservative congressmen cabled Johnson asking why "a friendly government" such as Rhodesia was "boycotted and coerced and bludgeoned" while Great Britain gave "treacherous assistance to North Vietnam and North Korea" and received U.S. support. Sen. Sam Ervin of North Carolina wrote a long letter to Johnson, Rusk, and Goldberg declaring that sanctions were unconstitutional and in violation of the UN Charter. He contended that a UN action against "the sovereign state of Rhodesia" was identical with the group "intervening in Texas."[41] Other politicians, newspapers, and groups also expressed their strong dissent from U.S. policy. The Friends of Rhodesian Independence held rallies in Chicago, New York, and Washington to protest sanctions and raise money for Smith. Gov. George Wallace of Alabama claimed "Rhodesia is a fine country" and called it "ludicrous" for America to support

---

39. *SDB* 56 (23 January 1967): 140–44; *Washington Post*, 8 January 1967, p. 6.

40. Acheson papers, box 141, Truman Library. See also Lake, *The "Tar Baby" Option*, 115–16.

41. H. R. Gross and Durward Hall to President Lyndon Johnson, 7 January 1967; Douglas MacArthur, Jr., Department of State Congressional Relations Staff, to Gross, 21 January 1967; Ervin to Johnson, 12 December 1966, CF: Rhodesia, box 65, Johnson Library.

Great Britain while it aided "communism in Vietnam." Jesse Helms, a North Carolina radio executive and later a U.S. senator, contended American diplomats were "being played for suckers" by Wilson. Several state legislatures passed resolutions demanding repeal of sanctions and recognition of Smith's government.[42]

Occasionally, the rhetoric of the pro-Rhodesian forces got out of hand. Senator Thurmond, addressing a "Peace with Rhodesia" banquet in Washington, declared Ian Smith was ready "to make available immediately 5000 troops" to help in Vietnam. The entire Rhodesian army numbered less than 4,400. The *National Review* dubbed Smith "the George Washington of Africa" in an article urging recognition.[43]

Smith encouraged the image of Rhodesia as a stable, anticommunist state standing against violence and radicalism. He claimed that his nation was not racist, but only rewarded "merit." Smith also denied that majority rule was necessary for democracy: "The true principle of democracy is the maintenance of peace and economic viability." Those attacking Rhodesia were "communists" or Africans dedicated to "mau-mau violence" against the whites.[44]

The Rhodesian leader also tried to send a personal message to Johnson asking for recognition and an end to sanctions. He contacted L. L. "Tex" Colbert, the former head of Chrysler Corporation, and asked him to argue Rhodesia's case before the president. Johnson refused to see Colbert, but the executive did meet with the new national security adviser, Walt Rostow, whom the Rhodesians saw as one of the major "villains" in Washington because of his alleged "pro-British" views. Colbert tried to convince Rostow that Rhodesian independence was no different from the actions of the other former colonies of the British empire. He explained that whites in Rhodesia "had no place to go" if blacks gained power. Colbert also denied any similarities between the American civil-rights movement and the situation in Rhodesia. Unlike blacks in the United States, the Africans did not want integration and were grateful for white guidance and protection.[45]

The public response to the American vote for sanctions was far more organized and widespread than the administration had anticipated. Some officials worried that Congress might vote to repeal sanctions or to recognize Smith's government. White House aide Joseph Califano and Under-Secretary of State Nicholas Katzenbach (Ball's replacement) met in February to organize a "counteroffensive" against the pro-Rhodesian forces. Califano explained to Johnson that

42. *Citizen* 11 (February 1967): 19–21 and (June 1967): 17; Fredericks to the Arizona State Legislature, 3 February 1967, CF: Rhodesia, box 65, Johnson Library.
43. Hance, *Southern Africa*, 20–21; "How the U.S. Is Helping to Bring Down Rhodesia's George Washington," *National Review* 19 (16 May 1967): 513–26.
44. Ian Smith, "Rhodesia: A Personal View," *Punch* 250 (26 January 1966): 110–12.
45. Angus Graham, Rhodesian Minister of External Affairs, to Colbert, 5 May 1967; Colbert to Johnson, undated, CF: Rhodesia, box 65, Johnson Library.

many in Congress feared sanctions were the first step toward direct U.S. military involvement in Africa. He also noted that much of the vehement opposition to the administration's policy was in reaction to Great Britain's "less than satisfactory performance on Vietnam and Cuba."[46]

The State Department designated Katzenbach to help Congress "develop a better understanding of our position on Rhodesia." He arranged for Goldberg to meet with congressional leaders to explain the diplomatic benefits of opposition to Smith and to make it clear that sanctions did not imply any commitment to the use of force. The department also prepared a "Special Background Paper" on Rhodesia for distribution to Congress and the public. The document traced the history of the rebellion and Washington's response and justified the need for American encouragement of majority rule.[47] Douglas MacArthur, Jr., of the State Department's congressional relations staff handled the daily correspondence with U.S. political leaders on Rhodesia. He patiently responded to hundreds of letters and petitions throughout the spring of 1967. MacArthur defended the official U.S. position that Rhodesia was not a "state" but remained a colony of Great Britain. He also claimed that it was necessary to end the revolt through the UN or there might be "civil strife . . . involving other parties, including extremist elements."[48]

The government also entered into the public-opinion struggle. Goldberg, Palmer, and others in the State Department took to the lecture circuit to defend their actions. They concentrated on rebutting the three major criticisms offered by the pro-Rhodesian spokesmen: sanctions were a precedent for either military action or measures against South Africa and Portugal; U.S. policy was based on idealism rather than concrete interests; and Great Britain was determining American diplomacy.

In a speech on 29 December 1966, Goldberg responded to the first criticism. He admitted, "A number of individuals in our country have attacked, on both legal and policy grounds, the action of the Security Council and the support which the United States has given it." He explained that the Rhodesian situation had "a number of unique elements" that demanded the strong UN action. Golberg emphasized that this did not mean there would be similar steps against other nations. It was the "unique legal and factual elements" of UDI that caused America to accept sanctions. These elements did not exist in other areas. By stressing the "uniqueness" of Rhodesia, Goldberg tried to make it clear that

46. Califano to Johnson, 23 February 1967, Confidential Files: Rhodesia, box 11, Johnson Library.

47. Katzenbach to Johnson, 14 February 1967, ibid.; Department of State, "A Special Background Paper: Southern Rhodesia and the United Nations—the U.S. Position," *SDB* 56 (6 March 1967): 366–77.

48. MacArthur to Gross, 21 January 1967; MacArthur to Representative Donald Rumsfeld (Illinois), 30 January 1967, CF: Rhodesia, box 65, Johnson Library.

Washington had not abandoned its opposition to sanctions against the other white regimes in Africa.[49]

In response to the second criticism, the UN ambassador claimed that both the UN Charter and the U.S. Constitution were "embodied in moral principles." Goldberg denied that the Rhodesians' actions could be compared with those of America in 1776. He argued that a more apt historical parallel was the American Civil War: "We . . . learned over 100 years ago that any attempt to institutionalize and legalize a political principle of racial superiority in a new state was unacceptable." Smith was not a modern George Washington but a contemporary Jefferson Davis trying to use indepedence to continue racial exploitation.[50]

In a later address to black leaders in Washington, Goldberg turned to the third criticism, that the administration was dominated by Great Britain. "Contrary to propaganda assertions, we have not been engaged in pulling British chestnuts out of the fire," he declared. "We have acted, and shall continue to act, for good American reasons of our own." Goldberg cited "the practical interests" of economic and political influence in black Africa and "our domestic position on civil rights" as justifications for U.S. opposition to Smith.[51]

Palmer made a similar argument on 28 February when he noted:

> The question of Southern Rhodesia has lately attracted a great deal of attention here in the United States. Doubts have been cast on its [sanction's] wisdom. The line between informed opinion and misunderstanding has often been blurred. For example, we hear that U.S. support for the Security Council action derogates from our own sovereignty, that it constitutes misguided support of the British, and that its purpose is to curry favor with some members of the international community at the expense of others.

He denied that Great Britain had forced the United States to back sanctions. The administration had acted "only on the basis of a considered judgement that it was clearly in our national interests to do so." Palmer also stressed that the UN action was "limited" and created "no precedent or obligation with respect to similar measures anywhere either now or in the future."[52] Like Goldberg, Palmer tried to refute the analogy between UDI and the American Declaration of Independence: "The Rhodesian declaration is completely silent on human rights, that is the heart of the difference." He compared Jefferson's dedication to civil liberties with Smith's support of censorship. Ignoring Jefferson's commitment to slavery, Palmer emphasized that the Virginian's belief that "all men are

49. *SDB* 56 (23 January 1967): 140–44.
50. Ibid.
51. Ibid. (20 February 1967): 288–94.
52. Ibid. (20 March 1967): 449–58.

created equal" would have put him in direct opposition to the defense of white supremacy in the Rhodesian document.[53]

The State Department's "Special Background Paper" also defended U.S. policy as "grounded in practical considerations" as well as "our own democratic heritage." Sanctions were the only alternative to violence, it claimed. In a reference to Rhodesia in his State of the Union address, Johnson reaffirmed his dedication to "cooperation and harmony between the races" abroad as well as at home but also warned Africans to "reject the fools' gold of violence."[54]

Perhaps the public-relations efforts of the administration helped block any congressional resolution critical of U.S. policy, but they did little to end the public clamor on the issue. Throughout 1967, the strong opposition to American actions continued. Attempts by pro-Rhodesian demonstrators at UCLA to burn a UN flag led to a riot as black students clashed with members of the John Birch Society and the American Nazi party. Students at the University of Virginia provoked a minor crisis when they invited Ian Smith to speak on campus. State Department spokesman Robert McCloskey explained that Smith could not get a visa since the United States did not recognize Rhodesia as a state. The students accused the State Department of censorship. Late in 1967, Goldwater visited Rhodesia. He declared, "We need more men like Ian Smith," and called American policy "ridiculous."[55]

Along with the continued emotional public criticism, there was also a more carefully reasoned attack on U.S. policy. In March 1967, Charles Burton Marshall, a former associate of Acheson in the State Department and a professor at Johns Hopkins University, published *Crisis over Rhodesia: A Skeptical View*. The book summarized the legal critique of sanctions and their support by Washington. Marshall argued that Rhodesia was an independent nation because it had controlled its own affairs since 1923. The basis for diplomatic recognition was de facto rule. By that standard Rhodesia was a sovereign nation. He also denied that the situation in Rhodesia was "a threat to international peace," in which case the UN would have to invoke sanctions. The dispute in Rhodesia was a domestic concern, not an international problem. The UN Charter clearly denied the organization the right to intervene in internal matters. Marshall also warned that sanctions against Rhodesia were a dangerous precedent for the UN, allowing it to take action against any country whose domestic policies were objectionable to the majority of the UN members. Marshall concluded that the United States had supported this "illegal" action of the UN out of misguided moralism and for domestic political purposes.[56]

53. Ibid. See also (24 April 1967): 646–51.
54. Ibid. (30 January 1967): 158.
55. *New York Times*, 18 May 1967, p. 37; 27 September 1967, p. 5; 5 March 1968, p. 1; Stanley Uys, "Photography and Seeing 'Friends,'" *New Republic* 158 (6 January 1968): 15–16; Lake, *The "Tar Baby" Option*, 118–19.
56. Charles Burton Marshall, *Crisis over Rhodesia*. See also Acheson's review in the *Washington Post*, 4 June 1967, p. 6.

While the internal debate over American policy continued, the situation in Rhodesia deteriorated. The new sanctions soon proved to be as ineffective as the voluntary measures of 1965 and 1966 had been. After nearly two years of waiting for international pressure to topple Smith, black Rhodesians finally turned to violence.

Like the black liberation forces in Angola, those in Rhodesia were deeply divided. In 1961 Joshua Nkomo, a leader of the black trade-union movement, organized the Zimbabwe African People's Union (ZAPU) to replace the banned African National Congress and National Democratic party. In September 1962, ZAPU was also outlawed. Nkomo was restricted by the government and later sent to a detention camp. In August 1963, disgruntled members of ZAPU formed a rival organization, the Zimbabwe African National Union (ZANU) under the control of the Reverend Ndabaningi Sithole and Robert Mugabe.[57]

Prior to UDI, the two organizations spent most of their energies attacking each other in print and occasionally with their fists. Efforts by African leaders to unite the rival factions failed. By 1964, both groups had members in the Soviet Union, China, Cuba, North Korea, and Algeria training for guerrilla warfare. In April 1966, a small number of ZANU insurgents fought a brief battle with Rhodesian security forces. In August 1967, over one hundred guerrillas crossed the border from Zambia. Thirty-one were killed in clashes with Rhodesian forces. Three months later, about 160 nationalists tried to establish bases in a rugged region north of Salisbury. Rhodesian jets bombed the positions, and a helicopter assault destroyed the camps.

Despite the relatively easy defeat of these early guerrilla efforts, whites in Rhodesia recognized that they would face increasing black violence. With Smith's encouragement, South African police and helicopter units arrived in Rhodesia to help "maintain order." Verwoerd also threatened to retaliate against Zambia if it allowed commando forces to operate from its territory. In August 1967, in response to the first major guerrilla raids, Salisbury announced that it would execute three Africans convicted nearly four years earlier of the murder of a white farmer. The decision to hang the three was designed to serve as an example to African "extremists." On 6 March 1968, after lengthy appeals and worldwide protests, the three were hanged. Five days later, two more prisoners were executed.

Smith's actions revived the flagging international attention to Rhodesia. After the adoption of binding sanctions in December 1966, there had been little new pressure on Smith's regime. With the hangings, new demands surfaced for additional measures against Rhodesia. William Buffum of the United States joined the UN condemnations of the hangings on 20 March: "We dare not close our ears to the banging of the gallows trap in Salisbury."[58]

57. Gibson, *African Liberation Movements*, 145–96. See also *Zimbabwe To-Day* (March 1964): 2–3.
58. *SDB* 58 (24 June 1968): 846.

It remained uncertain, however, what America would do in the face of new African demands for force and even tougher sanctions. On 31 March 1968, as the UN considered new resolutions, Lyndon Johnson announced that he would not seek reelection. With the exception of Vietnam, American foreign policy quickly ground to a virtual halt. In contrast to the often-heated debates within the bureaucracy that preceded all other UN resolutions on Rhodesia, there was now little discussion of the American position. Washington was committed to sanctions and eventually went along with the new measures, but there is no evidence that anyone in the administration expected the action would alter the situation in Rhodesia. Goldberg abandoned his usually active role in drafting resolutions and remained nearly silent during the lengthy debates on a motion to cut all trade with Rhodesia except for medical and educational supplies. He did dissent from a clause "emphasizing the need" for all nations to end consular relations. Goldberg reminded the delegates that the need to end relations was "not of a mandatory character" and that the United States often maintained consular contacts with states it did not officially recognize. On 29 May 1968, the Security Council unanimously adopted the new sanctions. Even France ended its policy of abstaining on all resolutions dealing with Rhodesia and went along.[59]

The UN action rekindled protests from the Rhodesian lobby, but no one in the outgoing administration seemed to care. The State Department even stopped responding to correspondence on the issue. The dramatic events of 1968 quickly pushed Rhodesia out of the headlines. Johnson's announcement that he would not run, the assassination of Martin Luther King (and the riots that followed), the murder of Robert Kennedy, the violent confrontations at the Democratic convention in Chicago, and the campaign between Nixon and Humphrey all made the situation in Rhodesia seem insignificant to most Americans. George Wallace tried to make it an issue in his third-party campaign for the presidency when he vowed to end sanctions and recognize Smith. Reporters reacted by asking him about Vietnam.[60]

In October 1968, Wilson made a final attempt to negotiate a settlement when he met with Smith aboard HMS *Fearless* in the Mediterranean. The similarities with the *Tiger* talks were obvious, and as with the previous talks a stalemate resulted. Negotiations had failed. The strongest UN sanctions ever imposed had also failed. To many Africans, only violence remained. In August 1968, Kaunda told an American journalist that guerrilla war was the only solution to the Rhodesian problem. "To expect Africans . . . to continue to remain docile under minority rule is not being realistic," he argued. "History the world over shows that no matter how long it takes, the time does come when people refuse to be subjected to that type of rule." Kaunda predicted that the inevitable bloodshed would result in the very radicalism that the United States had so long feared:

59. Ibid., 847–48.
60. *New York Times*, 8 October 1968, p. 1.

"The people of the West have refused to help the freedom fighters. . . . This leaves these young men and women with no choice at all but to go to the only area where they will be supplied, namely the East."[61]

In October 1976, the two factions of Rhodesian liberation united to form the Patriotic Front. Four years and thousands of deaths later, Rhodesia became Zimbabwe, Robert Mugabe replaced Ian Smith, and blacks had finally obtained majority rule.

America's objectives in Rhodesia had been an end to Smith's rebellion, a negotiated return to colonial status, and a peaceful transition to majority rule. These goals remained constant from the announcement of UDI to the end of Johnson's presidency. With the exception of its willingness to endorse mandatory sanctions, the American position on Rhodesia was quite similar to its policy toward South Africa and the Portuguese colonies. Again the dominant consideration was to find some middle position between inaction and the encouragement of violence, to show a dedication to majority rule without contributing to the growth of radicalism. As Goldberg stated, the United States opposed both "those who would have the Rhodesian regime brought down in a single stroke and those who counsel a complete hands-off policy."[62]

Washington was again caught in the moderate role in a revolutionary situation. All of the traditional American commitments to negotiations, compromise, and peaceful change were ineffective given the obstinacy of the whites. Like the Portuguese and the Afrikaners, Smith's government viewed meaningful concessions to the black majority as an irrevocable first step toward white suicide. The Rhodesians were willing to accept economic hardship and international isolation as the price of their continued power. It was likely that nothing short of direct military intervention would have budged Smith and his followers.

Thus, in one sense, American policy failed: it did not achieve its major goal of ending the rebellion. Washington's opposition to Smith did succeed in achieving some secondary policy objectives, however. Its firm enforcement of sanctions, often more strictly monitored than in Great Britain, won the admiration of many African nations. Administration action against Rhodesia also regained the support of black Americans and liberals disillusioned by U.S. policy elsewhere in Africa. Finally, America demonstrated its solidarity with Great Britain. Even though the "special relationship" was often strained, it did endure. U.S. diplomacy did not "win" majority rule in Rhodesia, but it did not "lose" the good will of the third world. In this sense, it was more "successful" than policy toward either South Africa or the Portuguese territories.

61. Alan Rake, "Black Guerrillas in Rhodesia," *African Report* 13 (December 1968): 23–25.
62. *SDB* 54 (2 May 1966): 800–801.

10. EPILOGUE | From Nixon to Reagan

Although direct American diplomatic involvement in southern Africa waned in 1968, this proved to be an aberration. The rush of events in the area and the attempts of succeeding administrations to impose their own directions on foreign policy made the following sixteen years a time of sustained diplomatic activity in the region. While there is as yet no documentary record of U.S. policy in the post-Johnson years, published books, memoirs, and journalistic accounts allow for at least a tentative sketch of the shifts in policy.

The revival of American interest in southern Africa was in part a response to the dramatic military success of black rebels in Angola, Mozambique, and Rhodesia. A second source of policy was the attempt of each president to fit southern Africa into a more general approach to world affairs. Richard Nixon's celebrated "tilt" toward "communication" with the white regimes in 1970, Gerald Ford's attempt to involve Washington more directly in the war in Angola in 1975, Jimmy Carter's controversial emphasis on human rights, and Ronald Reagan's shift toward "more normal" relations with South Africa have all been extensions of more general approaches to international relations.

Despite the differences in style and substance among these four individuals, their policies have remained within the well-traveled "middle road" developed in the previous two decades. Even the seemingly sharp shift from Nixon to Carter was largely a modification of existing options developed long before either took office. Each of the four recent administrations has expressed a verbal commitment to racial equality and majority rule but has refused to adopt too aggressive a policy in pursuit of these goals. Each has also tried, with varying intensity, to work for gradual and peaceful change. They have all shared a general failure to achieve their objectives.

American hopes for a peaceful transition to a non-Marxist black regime in Angola were dashed in 1976 when MPLA forces, aided by Cuban troops, gained control of the nation. The goal of an orderly shift to majority rule in Rhodesia was achieved in 1980, but through the military success of the Patriotic Front and the diplomatic initiatives of Great Britain rather than through any action on the part of the United States. In South Africa, neither the accommodationist approach of Nixon and Reagan nor the confrontation policies of Carter succeeded in dissuading the Nationalists from apartheid or led to a settlement in Namibia. Although U.S. involvement in the region was sustained, successes remained as elusive as in the previous two decades.

The Nixon "Tilt"

When Richard Nixon took office in 1969, he and his national security adviser, Henry Kissinger, were convinced that America needed a new and more realistic approach to foreign policy. Fearful of the rise of a new isolationism following the phased American withdrawal from Vietnam, Nixon and Kissinger determined to shape U.S. diplomacy toward a clear defense of national interests. Both were relatively uninterested in and unknowledgeable about Africa. They saw southern Africa largely as an area of potential U.S.-Soviet conflict.

Determined to alter American policies, the Nixon administration ordered a review of U.S. diplomacy in all regions of the world. The National Security Council, under the demanding hand of Kissinger, assessed previous policies, current options, and future strategies. It was through this process that the now "infamous" *National Security Study Memorandum 39* (NSSM39) was drafted and adopted. When the document was leaked to the press in 1975, critics denounced it as a cynical example of indifference to the black majorities of southern Africa. Most commentators ignored the bulk of the study dealing with past policy and basic objectives and focused instead on the recommendations for future policy, in particular "option 2," the alternative eventually adopted. Dubbed "tar baby" by State Department critics, this position was based on the premise that "the whites are here to stay and the only way that constructive change can come about is through them. There is no hope for the blacks to gain the political rights they seek through violence, which will lead to chaos and increased opportunities for the communists."[1]

"Option 2" urged "selective relaxation of our stance against the white regimes" through the easing of arms embargoes on South Africa and Portugal, a weakening of sanctions against Rhodesia, and increased economic and political contacts with the government of South Africa. When the Nixon administration implemented these suggestions in 1970–1974, critics charged that there had been a major alteration of U.S. policy. Knowledge of the two decades prior to the Kissinger study suggests that the changes were far less momentous than many assumed. In fact, Washington had drifted away from any direct confrontation with the white regimes long before "tar baby" was adopted. The "tilt" toward the white governments was largely a tactical change consistent with assumptions and goals that had guided American policy for over twenty years.

The background of the Nixon-Kissinger "tilt" shows that the deep splits within the government over policy in southern Africa remained after the

1. *The Kissinger Study of Southern Africa: National Security Study Memorandum 39*, 66. The background of the study and an analysis of the debate within the government over the report are well covered by Roger Morris, *Uncertain Greatness*, 107–20. Morris was the National Security Council's African specialist.

Democrats departed. Kissinger and his staff were convinced that U.S. policy in the region was "aimless" and "in a shambles." They argued that Washington's efforts were designed to appease factions within the bureaucracy rather than national interests. In April 1969, Kissinger ordered his staff to prepare a total review of policy goals and alternatives in the area. After nine months, twenty meetings, and six drafts, the document was finally assembled. Throughout this process, the splits within the government that Kissinger had deplored were opened anew. Most within the State Department favored continuing Johnson's policies, while the CIA and the Defense Department wanted a much softer stance toward the white minorities.[2]

The strategy of a "more relaxed" approach was consistent with the view of the president. Nixon believed that American policy in the region was primarily the product of a "misguided idealism" that failed to recognize that the Soviets wanted southern Africa for its mineral wealth. He was certain that communists controlled the liberation groups in Rhodesia, Angola, and even South Africa.[3] The National Security Council shared Nixon's east-west view of the problem of race in southern Africa.

The NSC finally considered the report on southern Africa at a meeting on 17 December 1969. Although Vice-President Spiro Agnew perplexed the group by repeatedly confusing Rhodesia with South Africa, the council quickly approved the document. In January 1970, Nixon and Kissinger officially endorsed "option 2" and began their policy of "communication" with the white minorities.[4]

The major assumptions behind the decision to relax pressure on the whites were that external influences would not affect internal racial policy, that blacks in South Africa could not mount an effective opposition to white rule, that the Smith regime in Rhodesia could "hold out indefinitely" despite economic sanctions, and that there was "no solution in sight" on Namibia.[5] Given these perceptions, it was not surprising that Nixon and his advisers decided to move closer to the white regimes. The major belief that "the whites are here to stay" proved to be erroneous, as events in Angola, Mozambique, and Rhodesia illustrated, but the assumption that America could best secure its interests through closer cooperation with the white regimes was a logical response to the failures of diplomacy in the 1960s.

After adopting "tar baby," the Nixon administration moved quickly to implement it, making immediate symbolic and tangible changes in the American approach. Nixon appointed John Hurd, a conservative businessman and manager of the Nixon campaign in Texas, as the new U.S. ambassador to Pretoria. Hurd ingratiated himself to the South Africans by being the only foreign representative

2. Morris, *Uncertain Greatness*, 107–9.
3. Richard Nixon, *The Real War*, 30–31.
4. Tad Szulc, *The Illusion of Peace*, 220–23.
5. *The Kissinger Study of Southern Africa*, 62.

at the opening of a segregated theater and by joining a hunting trip on Robben Island with black prisoners serving as beaters.[6]

The shift in policy was also apparent in Washington. The White House welcomed the chief of South Africa's defense force at a reception, and Vice-President Gerald Ford received Pretoria's minister of the interior and information. The Commerce Department abandoned the existing policy of "neither encouraging nor discouraging" U.S. investments in South Africa and actively began to promote American economic involvement. At the UN, the United States abstained on resolutions critical of South Africa's occupation of Namibia.[7]

The "relaxed" policy also applied to Portugal. Washington approved the sale of a Boeing 707 plane to Lisbon to shuttle troops to Angola and accepted Portuguese soldiers for training at the U.S. Jungle Warfare School in the Panama Canal Zone. America also negotiated a new agreement for use of the Azores. The lease had expired in 1968, but the United States had continued to use the base with no agreement. In December 1971, Washington signed a new five-year lease that included $400 million in credits for Lisbon from the Export-Import Bank.[8]

While these and other examples of "tar baby" illustrated the U.S. move toward "communication" with the white governments, it was in American policy toward Rhodesia that the new approach was most evident. Even before the adoption of NSSM 39, there were indications that Nixon would soften economic pressure on Rhodesia. In May 1969, Union Carbide contacted Special Assistant to the President Patrick Buchanan and asked to be allowed to retrieve 150,000 tons of chromium ore it had purchased prior to the imposition of sanctions. Despite strong opposition from Kissinger and from Roger Morris, the NSC specialist on Africa, Nixon approved the plan. The administration also cast America's first veto in the UN against a measure calling for extension of sanctions to any nation aiding Rhodesia. In addition, the White House allowed the Rhodesian Information Office in Washington to arrange for travel by Americans to Rhodesia and to publish propaganda favorable to Smith.[9]

These actions paved the way for an amendment by Sen. Harry F. Byrd of Virginia that made a shambles of the U.S. sanctions policy by authorizing the importation of seventy-two "strategic and critical materials" from Rhodesia despite sanctions. Since the imposition of sanctions in 1965, conservatives in Congress had repeatedly introduced resolutions demanding repeal. With the election of a Republican president, corporations renewed their lobbying efforts to weaken or eliminate sanctions. Sen. Byrd and his supporters argued that

6. Study Commission on U.S. Policy Toward Southern Africa, *South Africa: Time Running Out* (Berkeley: University of California Press, 1981), 353–54.

7. Ibid.

8. Szulc, *The Illusion of Peace*, 461–62.

9. For a complete analysis of Nixon's policy toward Rhodesia and the background of the Byrd amendment, see Lake, *The "Tar Baby" Option*.

sanctions against Rhodesia made the United States dependent on the Soviet Union for chrome and other metals. American security demanded a relaxation of the embargo on Smith's regime. Although the Nixon administration did not sponsor the Byrd amendment, it was not opposed to its passage. Nixon, Kissinger, and others in the White House refused to support the State Department's efforts to defeat the bill. When the amendment passed, Nixon signed it immediately, on 17 November 1971. America thus joined South Africa and Portugal as the only nations to openly defy the UN sanctions.

Nixon's new approach was designed to make U.S. policy more "realistic" and to serve the national interests. The strategy revolved around the assumption that "the whites are here to stay." This proved to be its undoing. On 25 April 1974, young army officers in Portugal overthrew the dictatorship of Marcello Caetano and immediately promised to grant independence to Portugal's African colonies by the end of 1975. It was suddenly clear that, at least in the Portuguese territories, the whites were not "here to stay." The problem for Washington now shifted from establishing "communication" with the whites to trying to influence the make-up of the new black governments.

Gerald Ford and the End of "Tar Baby"

Following Nixon's resignation in 1974, Gerald Ford inherited the problem of Angola. The Portuguese coup had led to a chaotic and violent scramble in Angola among the three resistance groups and among outside powers concerned with the area. Zaire, South Africa, and the United States all tried to shape the composition of the new government. Strongly influenced by Kissinger, Ford accepted the need for Washington to try to shape events in Angola. Throughout the 1960s, the United States had offered aid to Holden Roberto and his FNLA and to Jonas Savimbi and UNITA. These funds were usually routed through Zaire. This assistance was small, since officials in Washington in the early 1970s were convinced that Portugal would continue the war and that rivalries among the three liberation groups would prevent any unified black movement. With the promise of independence, there was a new urgency in Washington to insure that the "proper" liberation group took power. More accurately, Ford and Kissinger were determined that the "improper" group, the Soviet-supported MPLA, not gain control.

In January 1975, the CIA requested $300,000 in emergency covert support for Roberto. The agency argued that the FNLA offered the "most stable and reliable government" and that Zaire would be threatened if the MPLA triumphed. The report also contended that the MPLA was a tool of the Soviets and its victory would be the first step toward communist control of southern Africa. Henry Kissinger, the chairman of the "40 Committee" that approved covert aid, found the CIA presentation "compelling," and the plan was approved. The committee did refuse a second CIA request for $100,000 for UNITA.[10]

Rather than insuring a "stable and reliable government," the U.S. decision helped escalate the conflict in Angola. The Soviet Union responded by greatly increasing its assistance to MPLA. From March to July, the Soviets supplied MPLA with over one hundred tons of weapons with an estimated value of nearly $30 million. Ford and Kissinger now sought to match the Soviet effort by increasing U.S. support for both FNLA and UNITA. Despite vehement opposition from the State Department and, in particular, from Assistant Secretary of State for African Affairs Nathaniel Davis, Washington approved $14 million more in military support for the rivals of MPLA in July. This was increased to $25 million in August and to $32 million in November. Davis resigned in protest.[11]

The deepening U.S. commitment in Angola prompted even more Soviet aid. This, in turn, led to direct military intervention by South Africa and Zaire. Threatened by two thousand Zairian troops in the north and five thousand South Africans in the south, by increased U.S. aid to its rivals and a South African strike into Angola in August 1975, MPLA appealed to Cuba for assistance. While there were only three hundred Cuban advisers in Angola in the summer, there were over one thousand by September. Following a second South African invasion in October, the number of Cubans had increased to over ten thousand by January 1976.[12] Whether the influx of Cubans was an offensive move by MPLA to destroy its rivals or a defensive move to preserve the territorial integrity of Angola, the effect on Ford and Kissinger was dramatic. The aftermath of the communist triumph in South Vietnam in April 1975 seemed to be a new communist assault in Africa. Ford was convinced that MPLA and the Cubans were mere "proxies" for the Soviets.[13]

To the administration, the solution in Angola was even more U.S. aid. Congress, however, had had enough. Despite pleas from Ford and Kissinger that abandonment of Angola would be appeasement of communism, the Senate rejected the administration's requests for more money. On 19 December 1975, the Senate went even further when it passed Sen. Dick Clark of Iowa's amendment prohibiting any future covert aid to Angola. Despite Ford's condemnation of the action as "an abdication of responsibility" by "liberal Democrats" and testimony by Kissinger that the United States would "emasculate itself in the face

10. For a summary of the U.S. effort in Angola in 1975-1976, see Gerald Bender, "Kissinger in Angola: Anatomy of Failure," and John Marcum, "Lessons of Angola," 407-25. For a firsthand account of CIA activities in the area, see John Stockwell, *In Search of Enemies*. Stockwell was the chief of the CIA Angola Task Force.

11. Nathaniel Davis, "The Angola Decision of 1975," 109-24.

12. Bender, "Kissinger in Angola," 90-94.

13. Gerald Ford, *A Time to Heal*, 358-59.

of massive, unprecedented Soviet and Cuban intervention," the House passed a similar resolution on 27 January 1976.[14]

The inability of America to control the course of the Angolan liberation struggle culminated sixteen years of frustration. Unable to budge Salazar toward granting independence in the 1960s, Washington finally accepted the idea of continued white control in the early 1970s. The Portuguese coup in 1974 forced a sudden reappraisal that led to increased covert aid. Rather than a peaceful transition to a pro-Western, independent Angola, the United States was faced with a Marxist regime, supported by the Soviet Union and Cuba and alienated from America. The lessons of the Angolan experience were unclear to American officials. Some contended that the results showed the folly of intervention in liberation struggles, while others argued that U.S. action had been too little too late. To Ford and Kissinger, it became clear that they would have to adopt a new approach to the second area of continued armed conflict, Rhodesia.

A decade after UDI, the Smith regime still survived, despite economic sanctions. Inspired by the success of violence in Angola, guerrilla leaders increased their military struggle in 1975 and 1976. Fearful of another Angolan situation, the Ford administration suddenly abandoned its policy of "communication" with the white minority and began a frantic search for a diplomatic solution in Rhodesia.

Following the cutoff of aid to Angola, Kissinger underwent a minor transformation in his perception of Africa. The U.S. failure in Angola and the collapse of South Vietnam both convinced the secretary of state that Washington needed to reassert its global influence. An American-sponsored settlement of the Rhodesian stalemate would demonstrate U.S. power and commitment abroad and, perhaps, improve Ford's chances for reelection at home.

In April 1976, Kissinger began a two-week, seven-nation tour of Africa. The trip culminated with a major address at Lusaka, Zambia, on 27 April. In his speech Kissinger repudiated the "tar baby" approach. He announced that there was going to be "a new era of American policy" toward southern Africa. Not only did he give the standard American defense of "self-determination, majority rule, equal rights, and human dignity for all peoples of southern Africa," but he also made it clear that Washington would no longer offer any support to the Smith government. Kissinger called for repeal of the Byrd amendment, promised economic aid to Mozambique to ease the hardships of maintaining sanctions against Rhodesia, and announced U.S. support for a new British effort to secure a black government in Salisbury.[15]

Action soon followed the secretary's rhetoric as he tried to apply his personal

14. Ibid., 345–46. See also U.S. Congress, Senate, Committee on Foreign Relations, *Hearings on U.S. Involvement in the Civil War in Angola*, 94th Congress, 2d Session, 29 January 1976 (Washington, D.C.: U.S. G.P.O., 1976), 14–21.
15. *SDB* 74 (31 May 1976): 672–79.

brand of shuttle diplomacy to Africa. In September, he raced between Pretoria, Zambia, and Tanzania trying to put together a plan to end the ten-year struggle in Rhodesia. Kissinger believed that South Africa was the key to any solution. He was sure that Pretoria would pressure Smith to negotiate if continued white influence could be guaranteed. To Kissinger, the problems in Rhodesia were largely technical: how to arrange a compromise between African nationalists and the white minority that would be supported by South Africa and by neighboring black nations. Kissinger displayed his usual stamina and negotiating brilliance, but he ultimately failed.

On 19 September, Kissinger, Vorster, and Smith met in Pretoria and worked out a plan for a two-year transition to majority rule. Whites would control defense and legal affairs during the transition, and there would be a dual legislature giving both blacks and whites a veto power. To Kissinger, it was a fair and workable solution, but the rebel leaders rejected the package. Africans were convinced that whites would dominate the transitional period and that a more complete victory could be won on the battlefield. Inspired by the victories in Angola and Mozambique, they demanded immediate black control. Although Kissinger did arrange a conference in Geneva of representatives of the two major guerrilla movements (aligned in the Patriotic Front), the Smith government, and Great Britain, it also failed.[16]

Although Kissinger was unable to overcome a decade of hate and violence with a month of shuttle diplomacy, his effort was notable as a new stage of American involvement. It was a clear departure from "tar baby" and a return to the traditional goal of peaceful change. It began a new activism in the region that would be intensified under the Carter administration.

Carter and the Diplomacy of Human Rights

Just as the Nixon and Ford administrations responded to the problems of southern Africa within a broader framework of east-west conflict, so did Jimmy Carter approach the area as an element of a larger policy. To Carter, southern Africa offered a perfect area in which to apply his stated concerns about racial equality and human rights in foreign affairs. Carter was convinced that he had a special sympathy for and understanding of the struggle for civil rights in America and that this affinity qualified him to deal with racial equality in Africa. His appointments of Andrew Young to the UN and Donald McHenry as Young's aide were designed to show his sympathy with blacks and to symbolize his intent to realign American policy toward Africa. Carter's controversial emphasis on human rights as a basis for U.S. diplomacy designated South Africa as a major target of this new approach.[17]

16. Larry Bowman, "U.S. Policy Toward Rhodesia," in *American Policy*, ed. Lemarchand, 171–201.

17. Sandy Vogelgesang, *American Dream, Global Nightmare*, 52–60.

Early in his term, Carter and his aides stressed that they wanted to make clear Washington's support of racial equality, majority rule, and basic freedoms in South Africa. Cyrus Vance, Carter's secretary of state, noted, "In no other area of foreign policy did our administration differ so fundamentally from that of our predecessors" as in relations with South Africa. At his confirmation hearings, Young suggested that the United States consider "limited sanctions" against South Africa. Later he publicly called the government of South Africa "illegitimate." When he visited South Africa in the spring of 1977, Young went to Soweto, the scene of black riots a year earlier, and urged Africans to engage in mass civil disobedience similar to that of American blacks in the 1960s. Vance, McHenry, and Assistant Secretary of State for African Affairs Richard Moose verbally attacked South Africa regularly during the first year of the administration.[18]

The new tone in Washington in 1977 provoked a strong reaction within South Africa and among conservatives in the United States. Rather than moderating their racial policies, the Nationalists intensified them. On 12 September 1977, black activist Steve Biko died while under police supervision in a South African jail. Biko's death provoked an outpouring of condemnation of the South African government nearly equal to that following Sharpeville seventeen years earlier. A month later, the government began mass arrests of black leaders and the banning of black organizations. The Carter administration condemned South Africa for its crackdown, Congress passed a "resolution of concern," and the United States voted in favor of a UN resolution protesting South Africa's actions.[19]

Despite the international outburst following the death of Biko and the arrests, the Nationalists showed no signs of moderation. The attacks by American officials provided a natural issue in South African elections. Vorster and his party campaigned against Carter and other "outside influences" in South Africa's affairs. A Nationalist party newspaper concluded, "Relations between South Africa and the United States of America have reached an all-time low." The "laager mentality" again prevailed as Vorster and his party were returned to office in November by the largest margin in South African history.[20]

Carter's human-rights campaign against South Africa also caused a reaction at home. Business leaders openly defied the president's call to curtail investments in South Africa. The U.S. Chamber of Commerce even made a point of opening an office in South Africa despite administration protests. Conservatives in Congress denounced Carter's attack on South Africa as selective enforcement and misguided idealism. Sen. Barry Goldwater told a South African audience that he was "ashamed" of U.S. policy. Even within the administration, strong doubts existed about the wisdom of the verbal assault on Pretoria. National

18. *South Africa: Time Running Out*, 357–58.
19. Ibid.
20. Ibid.

Security Adviser Zbigniew Brzezinski was skeptical of the anti–South African rhetoric. In the "Europeanist" tradition, Brzezinski worked against any strong pressure on South Africa and repeatedly called for more "flexibility" in dealing with the Nationalists.[21]

Although pleased with the verbal campaign for human rights, Vance, Moose, Young, and others wanted to do more than just make speeches. They urged some clear action to demonstrate their departure from the Nixon-Ford position. To Vance, recognition of Angola would be just such a move. Even though the government of Agostinho Neto was strongly supported by the Soviet Union and still had a large number of Cuban troops in its territory, Vance contended that Angola would expel the Cubans if the threats of intervention by Zaire and South Africa were removed. Young shared Vance's view. His statement that the Cubans represented "a force of stability" in Angola was widely ridiculed, but, to Young, the Cubans were in Angola only because of outside threats to the government.[22]

Despite the lobbying of Vance and Young, Carter did not recognize the Neto government. Brzezinski strongly opposed the move, and Carter feared that he would be accused of acknowledging a Soviet puppet government. The president decided that instead America should become directly involved in settling the persistent problems in Namibia and Rhodesia. Progress on these two issues, rather than recognition of Angola, would demonstrate the new approach to southern Africa. An American-sponsored settlement in Namibia would indicate the importance of black liberation to America, recapture the support of black African nations lost with U.S. involvement in Angola, and show the ability of Washington to replace violence with peaceful change.

When the UN Security Council passed a resolution calling for free elections in Namibia under UN supervision, Carter and his aides saw a chance to illustrate their concern. Young managed to avoid an African call for mandatory sanctions against South Africa if it violated the resolution. Instead, Young helped establish a "contact group" of the five western nations on the Security Council (Great Britain, France, West Germany, Canada, and the United States) to mediate between SWAPO and Pretoria. Young's deputy, Donald McHenry, emerged as a leader of the group.

Just as Henry Kissinger found in his negotiations over Rhodesia, the Carter officials discovered that the road to a peaceful solution in southern Africa is difficult. Despite lengthy and detailed negotiations throughout the fall of 1978, the "contact group" had little success. In October, Vance traveled to Pretoria with a private letter from Carter to new Prime Minister Pieter Botha calling for an international conference on Namibia. Carter threatened to "support

21. Cyrus Vance, *Hard Choices*, 70–72. Vance's book is the most complete and detailed account of Carter's African diplomacy. It contains lengthy sections on Namibia, Rhodesia, and Angola. For Brzezinski's views, see Zbigniew Brzezinski, *Power and Principle*, 139–45, 178–80.
22. Vance, *Hard Choices*, 91–92.

sanctions" if Botha refused. South Africa agreed to postpone its announced plans for an "internal settlement" in Namibia, and Carter withdrew his threat of sanctions. Pretoria, however, eventually balked at the idea of elections supervised by the UN. The South Africans claimed that, because the UN had already declared SWAPO the "sole representative of the people of Namibia," the organization could not be impartial in an election. Two years of active U.S. effort finally collapsed in 1980 when South Africa began punitive raids into Angola and Zambia against SWAPO forces. Confident that a new administration would be more sympathetic to their needs, the Nationalists simply ignored the protests of Carter officials.[23]

The frustrations over Namibia were repeated in even more sustained but equally futile U.S. efforts in Rhodesia. Convinced that their rhetoric on human rights and their repeal of the Byrd amendment in March 1977 would allow them to succeed where Ford and Kissinger had failed, Carter officials tried for a dramatic breakthrough in the Rhodesian impasse, although they faced the same problems in Rhodesia that had plagued the United States since 1965. Black leaders still believed they could win a military victory, while Smith and the whites were determined that they must have a "special position" in any new government. Carter's problems were compounded by the fact that all in Washington knew that South Africa was the key to any settlement in Rhodesia. The attacks on Pretoria by Carter officials made South Africa unlikely to favor any U.S. plan.

Despite these handicaps, Rhodesia occupied American diplomats more than any other African issue during the Carter years. Vance was certain that a joint U.S.-British plan could gain the support of South Africa and resolve the issue. Vance and British Foreign Secretary David Owen carefully worked out a plan calling for a caretaker government controlled by Great Britain to oversee the nation's peaceful transition to majority rule. Vice-President Walter Mondale went to Vienna to meet with South African officials while Vance and Owen met with Ian Smith. Richard Moose worked to mobilize support from other African states. After over a year of extensive negotiations, the plan collapsed in a maze of objections from both whites and blacks ranging from the make-up of parliament, to the length of the caretaker government, to how many rounds of ammunition the defense force would have. Smith still demanded guarantees of white seats in parliament, while black nationalists still insisted on immediate majority rule.

In a final attempt to salvage an agreement, Vance met with Patriotic Front leaders Robert Mugabe and Joshua Nkomo on Malta in early 1978. They rejected his terms. Smith followed by announcing an "internal settlement" calling for Rhodesia to be ruled by an executive council of Smith and three black "moderates"—Bishop Abel Muzorewa, Ndabaningi Sithole, and Chief Jeremiah

23. Ibid., 302–13.

Chivau. The plan also reserved 28 percent of the seats in parliament for whites, enough to block any constitutional changes.

Predictably, the Patriotic Front and other African leaders denounced Smith's proposal as a "sham." Jimmy Carter, however, frustrated by the inability to gain a peaceful settlement, favored it. The president was under strong conservative pressure to lift sanctions against Rhodesia and saw some hope that the Smith solution would lead to eventual majority rule. He ordered the U.S. delegation to abstain on a UN resolution condemning Smith's plan and even permitted the Rhodesian leader to come to Washington to explain his proposal.

Carter's endorsement of Smith's "internal settlement" and his decision to allow Smith to visit the United States outraged African leaders. A policy that was designed to regain the support of African nations had, by early 1979, alienated most black leaders on the continent. Although Carter refused to lift sanctions against Rhodesia, his actions seemed to align Washington with South Africa and the white minority in Rhodesia. The high hopes and good intentions of early 1977 had degenerated to confusion and frustration by 1979.

The final solution in Rhodesia was achieved without direct U.S. involvement. With the election of Margaret Thatcher and the Conservatives in Great Britain on 3 May 1979, the joint efforts of Washington and London ended. Thatcher and her new foreign secretary, Lord Peter Carrington, were convinced that Rhodesia was a British issue. As Vance recalled: "We had been full partners with the British, not only in shaping strategy, but in face-to-face negotiations with the parties. Thatcher and Carrington had a quite different conception of the Anglo-American relationship regarding Rhodesia."[24] The final negotiations over Rhodesia at Lancaster House in London in 1979 occurred without American participation or consultation. In February 1980, Rhodesians selected Robert Mugabe, a leader of the Patriotic Front, as prime minister, and on 18 April 1980 Zimbabwe became independent.

The Carter record in southern Africa was one of naiveté and failure. Determined to make a clear break with the preceding Republican administrations, Carter launched a verbal assault on South Africa's human-rights violations that enjoyed widespread support among black African leaders. The effort, however, alienated the Nationalists at the very time that Carter needed their cooperation for solutions in Namibia and Rhodesia. The intense U.S. involvement in negotiations for a solution in these two areas showed a willingness to commit energy and effort but a reluctance to use power. The half-hearted threat of sanctions against South Africa was never taken seriously by either Pretoria or the black African states. Carter managed to anger the South Africans with his rhetoric and anger black Africans with his refusal to use sanctions.

The abortive diplomatic attempt in Rhodesia was even less successful. After

24. Ibid., 297.

hundreds of trips by American officials, thousands of hours of negotiations, and seemingly endless position papers and draft constitutions, the United States remained caught between the intransigence of Smith and the whites and the confidence of the Africans in a military victory. Carter's support of Smith's "internal solution" alienated nearly all African leaders, especially Mugabe and others in the Patriotic Front. Carter did manage to show his concern with human rights and with peaceful change. His tangible accomplishments, however, were as minimal as those of his predecessors.

Ronald Reagan and "Constructive Engagement"

The inability of Carter to sustain his human-rights diplomacy and his lack of progress on Namibia and Rhodesia paved the way for another shift in American policy following the election of Ronald Reagan. Reagan had been a critic of both Ford and Carter in their dealings with southern Africa. He had accused Ford of being too harsh on Smith's government in Rhodesia and, at a press conference in 1976, had even suggested sending U.S. troops to Rhodesia to protect the whites. Reagan had attacked Carter's campaign against South Africa as unrealistic. The real violations of human rights were, Reagan argued, in the communist nations.

Reagan viewed southern Africa as an area of conflict between communism and stability. He indicated that he would return to the Nixon-Kissinger policies of more "communication" with the white regime in Pretoria. The president and his new assistant secretary of state for African affairs, Chester Crocker, announced that they would replace the "confrontation policy" of Carter with one of "constructive engagement" with the whites. Both Reagan and Crocker were careful to repeat the traditional U.S. condemnations of apartheid, but their early policies showed major changes from those of Carter.[25]

To signal the new emphasis on "communication" and "engagement," the administration immediately restored military attachés to the U.S. delegation in South Africa and allowed South African military officers to train at U.S. facilities. The Commerce Department also approved the sale to Pretoria of computers and other forms of technology that had been banned under Carter. Under administration prodding, the International Monetary Fund approved a $1.1 billion loan to South Africa despite protests from Democrats, the UN, and civil-rights groups.[26] The Reagan administration also restored cultural contacts with South Africa that had been eliminated by Carter. In one of its most controversial moves, the government permitted the famous South African rugby team, the Springboks, to enter the United States for a series of exhibition games. The Springboks had been met by violent protests when they toured New Zealand in

---

25. Chester Crocker, "Regional Strategy for Southern Africa," *SDB* 81 (October 1981): 24–27. See also Donald McHenry, "Southern African Policy," *New York Times*, 10 July 1981, p. 23.

26. *New York Times*, 15 October 1982, p. 1.

the fall of 1981, and there was pressure on the State Department to refuse the team admission to the United States for a five-city tour in September. The government, however, allowed the team to enter, despite fears that African nations would retaliate with a boycott of the 1984 olympics at Los Angeles. Although each of the five U.S. cities refused to allow the Springboks to play, the team did manage to engage in one match in Racine, Wisconsin, on 19 September.[27]

Despite these and other indications of "communication," the Reagan administration did continue to pursue a settlement on Namibia. Sensitive to charges that it had "tilted toward apartheid," the new administration launched a much publicized effort to arrive at a solution in Namibia. Reagan sent Crocker and a U.S. delegation to southern Africa in the spring of 1981. The group's announced intent was to work out a "Zimbabwe formula" for Namibia: a negotiated constitutional agreement between blacks and whites prior to any national elections.[28]

The South Africans, pleased with the shift from Carter to Reagan, were initially cooperative. By May, however, both Pretoria and Washington had introduced a new element into the Namibian dilemma: the continued presence of Cuban troops in Angola. South Africa had long tried to make a connection between a settlement in Namibia and the Cuban force in Angola. In the summer of 1981, the Reagan administration also joined the two issues. Crocker, and later the president, announced that the two questions were "empirically linked." The Cubans represented, in Crocker's words, "a major impediment to progress on Namibia." Although the administration denied that removal of the Cubans was an absolute precondition to continued talks on Namibia, State Department officials privately stated that any negotiations concerning Namibia were "dead in the water" until the Cubans left.[29]

The ties between the Cubans and Namibia were partly an outgrowth of the administration's deep concern about Angola. Reagan not only continued the U.S. nonrecognition of Angola but also tried to return to the Ford-Kissinger policy of aiding opponents of the Angolan government. Secretary of State Alexander Haig met with Jonas Savimbi of UNITA in December 1981 and hailed the guerrilla leader and his group as "a legitimate political force in Angola." Although Savimbi did not have the power to topple the government of Angola, he was able to control portions of the countryside and to harass trade and communication. The Reagan administration tried unsuccessfully to repeal the Clark amendment cutting off covert aid to Angola in the hopes of again supplying Savimbi.[30]

Reagan's positions on South Africa, Namibia, and Angola were consistent

27. Clive Gammon, "A Game They May Remember," *Sports Illustrated* 55 (28 September 1981): 34.
28. *New York Times*, 1 April 1981, p. 10.
29. Chester Crocker, "U.S. Interests in Africa," *SDB* 82 (January 1982): 23–26; *New York Times*, 1 May 1981, p. 2.
30. *SDB* 82 (March 1982): 34.

with his view of protracted global struggle between the free West and the communist East as the basis of world politics. Having denounced Carter's "softness" in foreign policy and repudiated the idea of detente with the Soviet Union, it was logical that he would see southern Africa in terms of a communist/anticommunist issue. Despite the talk about "constructive engagement," it was evident that Reagan and his advisers saw South Africa as a necessary evil. Despite its racism, it was stable and anticommunist. Angola was a Marxist regime supported by the USSR and Cuba. Thus it must be isolated or even overturned. Reagan's policies marked a return not to the Nixon "tilt" but to an even earlier Cold War perspective that viewed communism as the ultimate evil and judged all other regimes by their opposition to communism.

CONCLUSIONS | East and West, Black and White

The Reagan administration's return to a simplistic worldview of communism versus freedom illustrates the major premise that has controlled U.S. foreign policy since 1948: the containment of communism. This concern was at the heart of American actions throughout the world. In white Africa, however, American policy was also shaped by the desire to encourage a peaceful shift to black rule. Although this desire was related to the anticommunism impulse, it produced continuing dilemmas and problems. The attempt to strike the correct balance between change and stability while pursuing the overriding goal of containing communism was the major force in U.S. policy since 1948.

The Cold War view of international relations made it difficult for the United States to adapt to the changes brought about by the demise of European colonialism and the rise of race as an element in diplomacy. America had to adjust its policies of containment to accommodate dozens of new nations in Africa and Asia committed more to economic development and the end of white rule than to joining either the United States or the Soviet Union in the ideological battle.

Although Washington was slow to respond to the aspirations of the new nations, by the early 1960s hostility to decolonization had largely given way to support of independence and an acceptance of nonalignment. This shift did not indicate any abandonment of the prevailing Cold War view, however, but only a different tactic in the struggle. America accepted third-world independence because it was inevitable, generally peaceful, and resulted in governments that, while not necessarily "pro-West," at least were not "pro-Soviet." The United States could champion its traditional principles of self-determination and majority rule without fear of significant strategic loss.

Washington did not believe it had this option in the white redoubt region of southern Africa. Given the intractability of the whites in the region, it was far less likely that majority rule could be obtained peacefully. As a result, there was more danger of "radical regimes." To American diplomats, it was in the direct interests of the United States to work for a gradual and peaceful transition to black rule. To avoid opportunities for communism, America had to eliminate violence as the vehicle of political change. Thus, Washington had to force both blacks and whites to compromise. The United States wanted to achieve shared political and economic power rather than continued white exploitation of the African or the elimination of the whites by the black majority.

There remained the tactical problem of how America could foster the desired changes. Washington's rhetoric from Truman to Reagan was consistent in its encouragement of self-determination and majority rule. The United States was also willing to use limited economic pressure on the white regimes for change. It was not, however, ready to commit its power and prestige to black liberation. To do so would have threatened other "interests" and perhaps precipitated the very violence that Washington sought to avoid. America thus pursued the extremely difficult goal of achieving peaceful transition to majority rule accompanied by a continued white "presence," and it did so without a complete commitment of U.S. power. Washington did not want to impose a settlement but did accept the need to "encourage" the opposing parties to find a solution. America wanted discussions, compromise, gradualism, and nonviolence. It desperately tried to avoid rigidity and military solutions.

This "middle road" between noninvolvement and direct challenges to white rule began with Truman and continued under all his successors. It was the logical outcome of Cold War anticommunism and American attitudes toward political change. Alternative strategies, such as open support of the whites, encouragement of violent black struggle, or diplomatic inactivity in the region, were all rejected. Both American goals and policies in the region were thus moderate: The United States wanted neither continued white control nor immediate majority rule. Washington was convinced that it should be diplomatically active but not to the extent of jeopardizing more crucial international concerns.

America's "middle road" could succeed only if whites and blacks were willing or could be forced to make concessions and to substitute negotiations for force. To Americans, it was obvious that the alternative to gradual change was racial war. They assumed that the protagonists could be made to recognize this and adjust their demands to avoid it. Whites must abandon their fierce defense of the status quo, while Africans must modify their demands for immediate and total black rule. Such expectations proved to be false.

Whites saw meaningful concessions as suicidal. To the Portuguese, Afrikaners, and Rhodesians, the end of white Africa meant the end of whites in Africa. To Salazar, the African possessions were a part of Portugal. Compromise would lead to the dismemberment of the nation and the eventual end of Portugal as a world power. The Nationalists in South Africa saw concessions to the black majority as a denial of the Afrikaners' historic mission to preserve civilization on the continent and as a threat to white existence. The outnumbered whites in Rhodesia argued that their continued survival depended on maintaining political and economic control. Any significant acknowledgment of black rights would result in the rapid end of all white influence.

Because they lacked power, black Africans were initially more willing to accept the U.S. goal of peaceful change. They maintained, however, that there could be no compromise on the ultimate goal of majority rule. Africa belonged to the Africans—the black Africans. Continued white control was indefensible, independence inevitable, and freedom nonnegotiable.

Unable to agree on the fundamental question of who should rule, both sides eventually accepted violence. In Angola, Mozambique, and Rhodesia, Africans ultimately triumphed. In South Africa, whites remain in power even though signs of conflict are more obvious and ominous each year.

The whites' intransigence and the violent black response effectively doomed the major American objectives in southern Africa. Despite the growing futility of its efforts, Washington continued to be active in the area. The persistence of official interest in white Africa cannot be explained only by Cold War anticommunism. Policy was also influenced by domestic politics, liberal ideology, and the desire to gain support for America among the independent African states.

The rise of black activism in the United States and the decolonization of Africa both worked to broaden the idea of "national interests." Despite the dominance of "hard" strategic considerations, American diplomacy also reflected the nation's acceptance of legal equality at home and support of racial justice abroad. To some in Washington, this was justified simply because it was right: racial discrimination was a moral evil that demanded opposition whether in the American South or in southern Africa. To other U.S. officials, encouragement of equality overseas had the more "practical" benefit of gaining support for America from the third world and countering communist propaganda attacks on the United States as a racist nation. Support of equality was both "good principle" and "good strategy."

Failures and Successes of the Middle Road

Hindsight allows historians to praise or condemn past diplomats based on later events. In the case of white Africa, the United States failed in its major objectives of obtaining black rule through peaceful compromise. To dismiss American diplomacy in southern Africa as a complete failure, however, is erroneous. Washington succeeded in securing significant secondary benefits from the middle-of-the-road policy.

Although its limited opposition to the white regimes did not win the United States the unqualified praise of black Americans or Africans, it did produce a grudging admiration from both groups. America was far more consistent in its dedication to majority rule than were its European allies. Washington was not as "tough" as black and African groups wanted, but its efforts did gain general support from both. The United States managed to make its commitment to majority rule well known while retaining its other Cold War interests. This compromise policy alienated both whites and blacks in Africa but avoided identifying the United States with either white supremacy or violent revolution.

The Marxist triumphs in Africa in the 1970s were perceived by the Nixon and Ford administrations as defeats for America. These "losses" resulted more from actions after 1968 than from any policies in the two decades before. The shift in 1969 toward more "normal" relations with the white governments identified Washington more closely with Portugal and Rhodesia. As a result, the victories of black nationalists in Angola, Mozambique, and Zimbabwe became more direct "defeats" for America. The evasion of sanctions against Rhodesia, the restoration of military aid to Portugal, and, most important, the effort to join with South Africa to support "moderate" factions in Angola in 1975 did far more to alienate black Africa than had American efforts during 1948–1968. American diplomats can be criticized for their failure to recognize the inevitability of black control in the 1950s and 1960s. It is, however, perhaps even more legitimate to question the active American attempts to halt black liberation in the 1970s.

White Africa and America's Cold War Diplomacy

Africa rarely was at the center of U.S. foreign policy. Although American interest in the continent increased dramatically in the 1960s, Africa remained subservient to the more immediate crises in Cuba, Berlin, Vietnam, and elsewhere. Despite this secondary role, U.S. policy toward Africa illustrates several general trends applicable to other geographic areas.

There was a basic continuity in goals and assumptions throughout 1948–1968. Despite the differences in the personalities and styles of the presidents and their advisers, and the heightened importance of Africa after decolonization, stability, anticommunism, and the avoidance of violent conflict remained the overriding concerns. There were disputes over the correct tactics to obtain these objectives, but the prevailing view of Africa as an arena of U.S.-Soviet rivalry remained consistent. Even those in Washington most dedicated to racial equality and majority rule quickly learned to justify their arguments in Cold War, geopolitical rhetoric. The essential American objective in Africa, as in the other areas of the third world, was the containment of radicalism at a minimal risk to other global interests.

Given this perspective, it was not surprising that strategic considerations dominated policy. In the clash between "humanitarianism" and "realism," realism prevailed. The necessity of the Azores base and NATO unity exerted a dominant influence on U.S. relations with Portugal. South Africa's support of the Korean War, the importance of America's missile-tracking stations, and the need for minerals crucial to defense and other industries all worked to limit Washington's opposition to apartheid. In Rhodesia, where direct strategic interests were the least, the United States took a much stronger position. Even in

Rhodesia, however, the military struggle in Vietnam distracted official attention and eventually relegated the problem to secondary importance.

American policy toward black liberation also demonstrates the importance of bureaucratic politics in Cold War decisionmaking. The splits between Africanists and Europeanists, so noticeable in this study, suggest that internal rivalries and the flow of information within the government were quite significant in policy formation. The basic differences within the government over U.S. priorities in Africa forced a continuing compromise between decisive action and diplomatic inactivity. The bureaucratic battle occasionally produced a clear victory for the side with the most influence with the executive, but most often it reflected a compromise between the two factions. This lack of consensus within the government and the dominance of anticommunism combined to make major alterations of policy difficult. Once Washington began down the "middle road," it found it hard to abandon it. American policy toward Africa, as in other regions, most often consisted of minor adjustments of prevailing positions.

Analysis of U.S. diplomacy in southern Africa also reveals the conflicting impact of public opinion on foreign policy in the postwar decades. Historians disagree sharply on the importance of the public in the making of foreign policy. The example of white Africa offers some support to both sides of the debate. There is little doubt that the civil-rights movement was crucial in making Africa an area of importance in U.S. diplomacy. As noted, however, blacks and liberals were largely ineffective in shaping specific policies. The less numerous but far better organized supporters of the white regimes had the most impact on particular actions. General public opinion helped create the U.S. commitment to racial equality abroad, and much of the official rhetoric of U.S. officials was designed for internal consumption to illustrate that commitment. Nonetheless, the organized white lobby was effective in limiting direct actions to implement the promises contained in the rhetoric.

The Past and Future Policy

Those looking toward future U.S. policy will find that many of the problems that confronted Americans from 1948 to 1968 remain. White Africa has been reduced in size but not in its difficulty for America. As most U.S. officials predicted, South Africa has proved to be the last bastion of minority rule on the continent. The riots in the black ghetto of Soweto in 1976 and the triumph of the Patriotic Front in Zimbabwe have forced even the Afrikaners to make some adjustments. Recent attempts to eliminate "petty apartheid" (segregation of hotels, restaurants, recreational facilities, and so on), the recognition of black labor unions, and moves to establish separate legislatures for the coloreds and Asians all illustrate at least a minimal move away from the hard line that had prevailed since Malan's victory in 1948.

It is highly unlikely, however, that such gestures will have great impact on the fundamental problems of the nation. Blacks have denounced the moves as meaningless, while hard-line Afrikaners have condemned them as a dangerous drift toward black power. There is no indication that the Nationalists are prepared to make any significant alteration in apartheid. There is also strong evidence that blacks have learned well the lessons of Angola, Mozambique, and Zimbabwe.

The United States still faces the basic dilemma of how to encourage nonviolent evolution toward racial justice while maintaining effective relations with the white minority. It is unlikely that America can solve this policy problem. It seems doubtful that Washington can continue "normal" relations with the white government and not alienate the black opposition. It is even less realistic to assume that major change in South Africa will be achieved without violence. America's well-intended encouragement of peaceful change failed in Angola, Mozambique, and Zimbabwe. With a larger and more powerful white population, there seems even less chance for its success in South Africa.

BIBLIOGRAPHY

Unpublished documents

A. Materials in the Harry S. Truman Library, Independence, Missouri
    White House Central Files
        President's Personal Files
        Official File
    President's Secretary's Files
    Dean Acheson Papers
    Clark Clifford Papers
    George Elsey Papers
    John Sumner Papers
    Oral History Interviews
        George Elsey
        Loy Henderson
        John Maktos
        William Sanders
        Durward Sandifer

B. Materials in the Dwight D. Eisenhower Library, Abilene, Kansas
    White House Central Files (Records of the President)
        Central File
        Official File
    Ann Whitman Files (Papers of the President)
        Ann Whitman Diary Series
        Cabinet Series
        International Series
        National Security Council Series
    White House Office Files
        Office of the Special Assistant for National Security Affairs
        Office of the Staff Secretary
        Project "Clean-Up"
    U.S. Council on Foreign Economic Policy, Office of the Chairman
    Office of the Staff Secretary
    Frederick E. Fox Papers
    Gordon Gray Papers
    Christian Herter Papers
    Oral History Interviews
        Donald Dumont
        Gordon Gray
        Loy Henderson
        E. Frederick Morrow
        Francis Wilcox

C. Materials in the John F. Kennedy Library, Boston, Massachusetts
Pre-Presidential Papers: Transitional Files
  Task Force on Africa
President's Office Files
National Security Files
  Country Files
  Subject Files
  Carl Kasen File
  William Brubeck File
White House Central Files
  Foreign Affairs
  International Organizations
  Political Affairs
Roger Hilsman Papers
Arthur M. Schlesinger, Jr., Papers
James Thompson Papers
Oral History Interviews
  William Attwood
  Chester Bowles
  McGeorge Bundy
  Chester Cooper
  Charles Darlington
  Thomas Estes
  U. Alexis Johnson
  Phillip Kaiser
  Joseph Satterthwaite
  Leopold Senghor
  William Sullivan
  G. Mennen Williams
  Harris Wofford

D. Materials in the Lyndon B. Johnson Library, Austin, Texas
White House Central Files
  Confidential Files
  Country Files
  Launching Sites/Tracking Stations
  National Defense
  Religious Matters
National Security Files
  Country Files
  Heads of State Correspondence Files
International Meetings and Travel File
Vice-Presidential Security Files
Oral History Interviews
  Eugene Rostow
  Anthony Solomon

E. Materials in the National Archives, Washington, D.C.
General Records of the Department of State (Decimal File)
G. Mennen Williams Papers

F. Materials in the Sterling Library, Yale University, New Haven, Connecticut
Chester Bowles Papers

Published Documents

Ethiopia and Liberia versus South Africa. Pretoria: South African Department of Information, 1966.

Karis, Thomas, and Gwendolen Carter, eds. *From Protest to Challenge: A Documentary History of African Politics in South Africa, 1882–1964*. 3 Vols. Stanford: Hoover Institution Press, 1973.

The Kissinger Study of Southern Africa: National Security Study Memorandum 39. Westport, Conn.: Lawrence Hill, 1976.

Portuguese Foreign Policy. Lisbon: Ministry of Foreign Affairs, 1965.

U.S. Congress. House. Committee on Foreign Affairs. Subcommittee on Africa. *Activities of Private U.S. Organizations in Africa*. 87th Congress. 1st Session. 1961.

U.S. Congress. House. Committee on Foreign Affairs. *Hearings on U.S.-South African Relations*. 89th Congress. 2d Session. 1966.

U.S. Congress. Senate. Committee on Foreign Relations. *Activities of Non-Diplomatic Representatives of Foreign Powers in the U.S.* 88th Congress. 1st Session. 1963.

———. *Hearings on U.S. Involvement in the Civil War in Angola*. 94th Congress. 2d Session. 1976.

———. *United States in the United Nations 1960: A Turning Point*. 87th Congress. 1st Session. 1961.

U.S. Congress. Senate. Subcommittee on African Affairs. *Angola*. 94th Congress. 1st Session. 1976.

U.S. Congress. Senate. 85th Congress. 1st Session. *Congressional Record* 103, Pt. 8.

U.S. Department of State. *Foreign Relations of the United States, 1943, 1948, 1949, 1950, United Nations' Affairs: 1952–1954*. Washington, D.C.: G.P.O., 1970–1979.

———. *Sub-Saharan Africa and the United States*. Washington, D.C.: G.P.O., 1980.

Dissertations and Other Unpublished Materials

Baum, Edward. "The United States, Self-Government, and Africa: An Examination of the Nature of the American Policy on Self-Determination with Reference to Africa in the Postwar Era." Ph.D. diss., University of California, Los Angeles, 1964.

Chukwumerije, Ibezim. "The New Frontier and Africa, 1961–1963." Ph.D. diss., State University of New York at Stony Brook, 1976.

Farzanegan, Bahram. "United States' Response and Reaction to the Emergence of Arab and African States in International Politics." Ph.D. diss., American University, 1966.

Greenberg, Stanford D. "U.S. Policy toward the Republic of South Africa, 1945–1964." Ph.D. diss., Harvard University, 1965.

Katz, Milton. "E. Frederick Morrow and the Politics of Civil Rights in the Eisenhower Administration." Paper presented at the Missouri Valley History Conference, Omaha, Nebraska, 7 March 1980.

Miller, Jean-Donald. "The United States and Sub-Saharan Africa, 1939–1950: The Roots of American Policy toward Decolonization in Africa." Ph.D. diss., University of Connecticut, 1979.

Sakwa, Paul. Letters to the author, 24 September 1979, 11 January 1980.

Secrest, Donald. "American Policy toward Neutralism during the Truman and Eisenhower Administrations." Ph.D. diss., University of Michigan, 1967.

Spencer, Leon P. "The American Role in the South West Africa Question." Ph.D. diss., Indiana University, 1967.

Walters, Ronald W. "The Formulation of United States' Foreign Policy toward Africa, 1958–1963." Ph.D. diss., American University, 1971.
Williams, G. Mennen. Letter to the author, 15 January 1980.
Wouk, Jonathan. "U.S. Policy toward South Africa, 1960–1967: Foreign Policy in a Relatively Permissive Environment." Ph.D. diss., University of Pittsburgh, 1972.

Articles

I have relied on a number of periodicals and newspapers throughout the period of the study. Most useful were *Africa Forum, Africa Today, Atlantic, Christian Science Monitor, Commentary, Crisis, Harper's, Nation, National Review, New Republic, New York Times, State Department Bulletin, U.S. News and World Report,* and *Washington Post.* References to these and other periodicals are in the footnotes.

Acheson, Dean. "Fifty Years Later." *Yale Review* 5 (Fall 1961): 1–10.
Bender, Gerald. "Kissinger in Angola: Anatomy of Failure." In *American Policy in Southern Africa: The Stakes and the Stance*, ed. Rene Lemarchand. Washington, D.C.: University Press of America, 1978.
Bowman, Larry. "U.S. Policy Toward Rhodesia." In *American Policy in Southern Africa: The Stakes and the Stance*, ed. Rene Lemarchand. Washington, D.C.: University Press of America, 1978.
Brookes, Edgar. "South African Swing-Over." *Foreign Affairs* 27 (October 1958): 143–52.
Cotman, John Walton. "South African Strategic Minerals and U.S. Foreign Policy, 1961–1968." *Review of Black Political Economy* 8 (Spring 1978): 277–300.
Davidson, Nicol. "Africa and the U.S.A. in the United Nations." *Journal of Modern African Studies* 16 (1978): 365–95.
Davis, John. "Black Americans and United States Policy Toward Africa." *Journal of International Affairs* 23 (1969): 236–49.
Davis, Nathaniel. "The Angola Decision of 1975: A Personal Memoir." *Foreign Affairs* 57 (Fall 1978): 109–24.
De Kiewiet, C. W. "Loneliness in the Beloved Country." *Foreign Affairs* 42 (April 1964): 413–28.
———. "South Africa's Gamble with History." *The Virginia Quarterly Review* 41 (Winter 1965): 1–17.
Duncan, Patrick. "Towards a World Policy for South Africa." *Foreign Affairs* 42 (October 1963): 38–48.
Emerson, Rupert. "American Policy in Africa." *Foreign Affairs* 40 (January 1962): 303–15.
Emerson, Rupert, and Martin Kilson. "The American Dilemma in a Changing World: The Rise of Africa and the Negro American." *Daedalus* 94 (Fall 1965): 1055–84.
Farmer, James. "An American Negro Leader's View of African Unity." *African Forum* 1 (Fall 1965): 70–77.
Gelb, Leslie. "Vietnam: The System Worked." *Foreign Policy* 3 (Summer 1971): 140–67.
Gross, Ernest A. "The South West Africa Case: What Happened?" *Foreign Affairs* 45 (October 1966): 36–48.
Hero, Alfred. "The Negro Influence on U.S. Foreign Policy, 1937–1967." *Journal of Conflict Resolution* 13 (June 1969): 220–23.
Isaacman, Allen, and Jennifer Davis. "United States' Policy Toward Mozambique Since 1945: The Defense of Colonialism and Regional Stability." *Africa Today* 25 (January–March 1978): 29–55.

Kennan, George. "Hazardous Course in Southern Africa." *Foreign Affairs* 49 (January 1971): 218–36.

Lefever, Ernest W. "U.S. Policy, the UN and the Congo." *Orbis* 11 (Summer 1967): 394–413.

Lincoln, E. Eric. "The Race Problem and International Relations." In *Racial Influences on American Foreign Policy*, ed. George Shepherd. New York: Basic Books, 1970.

McKay, Vernon. "South Africa and Its Implications for American Policy." In *Southern Africa and the United States*, ed. William Hance. New York: Columbia University Press, 1968.

Marcum, John. "Lessons of Angola." *Foreign Affairs* 54 (April 1976): 407–25.

———. "The Politics of Indifference: Portugal and Africa, a Case Study in American Foreign Policy." *Syracuse University East African Studies* 5 (March 1972): 1–41.

Mason, Phillip. "Some Maxims and Axioms." *Foreign Affairs* 64 (October 1964): 150–64.

Moss, James. "The Civil Rights Movement and American Foreign Policy." In *Racial Influences on American Foreign Policy*, ed. George Shepherd. New York: Basic Books, 1970.

Padleford, Norman J. "The Organization of African Unity." *International Organization* 18 (Summer 1964): 521–42.

Rivkin, Arnold. "Lost Goals in Africa." *Foreign Affairs* 44 (October 1965): 111–26.

Roark, James. "American Black Leaders: The Response to Colonialism and the Cold War, 1943–1953." *African Historical Studies* 4 (1971): 253–70.

Scalapino, Robert. "Sino-Soviet Competition in Africa." *Foreign Affairs* 42 (July 1964): 640–54.

Weissman, Stephen. "The CIA and U.S. Policy in Zaire and Angola." In *American Policy in Southern Africa: The Stakes and the Stance*, ed. Rene Lemarchand. Washington, D.C.: University Press of America, 1978.

Books

Acheson, Dean. *Present at the Creation: My Years in the State Department*. New York: W. W. Norton, 1969.

Africa Research Group. *Race to Power: The Struggle for Southern Africa*. Garden City, N.Y.: Doubleday, 1974.

Akpan, Moses E. *African Goals and Diplomatic Strategies at the United Nations*. North Quincy, Mass.: Christopher Publishing House, 1976.

American Committee on Africa. *The South African Crisis and U.S. Policy*. New York: American Committee on Africa, 1962.

Annual Review of UN Affairs, 1955–1956. New York: New York University Press, 1957.

Arkhurst, Frederick S., ed. *U.S. Policy Toward Africa*. New York: Praeger, 1975.

Attwood, William. *The Reds and the Blacks: A Personal Adventure*. New York: Harper & Row, 1967.

Ball, George. *The Discipline of Power: Essentials of a Modern World Structure*. Boston: Little, Brown and Co., 1968.

Ballinger, Margaret. *From Union to Apartheid: A Trek to Isolation*. New York: Praeger, 1969.

Barber, James. *South Africa's Foreign Policy, 1945–1970*. London: Oxford University Press, 1973.

Barnet, Richard. *Intervention and Revolution: The United States in the Third World*. New York: World Publishing Co., 1968.

Bartlett, Vernon. *Struggle for Africa*. New York: Praeger, 1953.

Beichman, Arnold. *The "Other" State Department: The United States' Mission to the United Nations: Its Role in the Making of Foreign Policy*. New York: Basic Books, 1968.

Bender, Gerald J. *Angola under the Portuguese: The Myth and the Reality*. Berkeley: University of California Press, 1978.

Berman, William. *The Politics of Civil Rights in the Truman Administration*. Columbus: Ohio State University Press, 1970.

Bowles, Chester. *Africa's Challenge to America*. Berkeley: University of California Press, 1956.

———. *Promises to Keep: My Years in Public Office, 1941–1969*. New York: Harper & Row, 1971.

———. *The New Dimensions of Peace*. New York: Harper & Row, 1955.

Brauer, Carl. *John F. Kennedy and the Second Reconstruction*. New York: Columbia University Press, 1977.

Brookings Institute. *Major Problems of United States' Foreign Policy, 1949, 1951–1952, 1952–1953, 1954*. Washington, D.C.: Brookings Institute, 1950–1955.

Brzezinski, Zbigniew. *Power and Principle: Memoirs of the National Security Adviser 1977–1981*. New York: Farrar, Straus and Giroux, 1983.

Brzezinski, Zbigniew, ed. *Africa and the Communist World*. Stanford: Hoover Institute, 1963.

Bunting, Brian. *The Rise of the South African Reich*. London: Penguin, 1964.

Burgess, Julian. *The Great White Hoax: South Africa's International Propaganda Machine*. London: Africa Bureau, 1977.

Carroll, Faye. *South West Africa and the United Nations*. Lexington: University of Kentucky Press, 1967.

Carter, Gwendolen. *The Politics of Inequality: South Africa Since 1948*. New York: Praeger, 1958.

Chester, Edward. *Clash of Titans: Africa and U.S. Foreign Policy*. Maryknoll, N.Y.: Orbis Books, 1974.

Chilcote, Ronald H. *Portuguese Africa*. Englewood Cliffs, N.J.: Prentice-Hall, 1967.

Cleveland, Harlan. *The Obligations of Power*. New York: Harper & Row, 1966.

Council on Foreign Relations. *The United States in World Affairs, 1948–1949*. New York: Harper & Brothers, 1949.

Crollen, Luc. *Portugal, the U.S. and NATO*. Leuven: Leuven University Press, 1973.

Cry, Leo. *United States' Policy Toward Africa*. Athens, Ohio: Center for International Studies, 1966.

Davidson, Basil. *In the Eye of the Storm: Angola's People*. London: Longman, 1972.

Denoon, Donald. *Southern Africa Since 1800*. New York: Praeger, 1973.

De Villiers, H. H. W. *Rivonia: Operation Mayibuye*. Johannesburg: Afrikaanse Pers-Boekhandel, 1964.

Duffy, James. *Portugal in Africa*. Cambridge: Harvard University Press, 1962.

Eisenhower, Dwight D. *Peace with Justice*. New York: Columbia University Press, 1961.

———. *Waging Peace, 1956–1961*. Garden City, N.Y.: Doubleday, 1965.

El-Khawas, Mohamed A., and Francis A. Kornegay, eds. *American–Southern African Relations: Bibliographic Essays*. Westport, Conn.: Greenwood Press, 1975.

Emerson, Rupert. *Africa and United States' Policy*. Englewood Cliffs, N.J.: Prentice-Hall, 1967.

Emerson, Rupert, and Martin Kilson, eds. *The Political Awakening of Africa*. Englewood Cliffs, N.J.: Prentice-Hall, 1965.

Espy, Richard. *The Politics of the Olympic Games*. Berkeley: University of California Press, 1979.

Farlie, Henry. *The Kennedy Promise: The Politics of Expectation*. Garden City, N.Y.: Doubleday, 1973.

Ford, Gerald R. *A Time to Heal: The Autobiography of Gerald R. Ford*. New York: Harper & Row, 1979.

Ford Foundation Study Commission on U.S. Policy Toward Southern Africa. *South Africa: Time Running Out*. Berkeley: University of California Press, 1981.

Franck, T. M. *Race and Nationalism: The Struggle for Power in Rhodesia-Nyasaland*. New York: Fordham University Press, 1960.

Friendly Relations between Portugal and the United States: A Victory for Freedom. Washington, D.C.: G.P.O., 1962.

Frye, William R. *In Whitest Africa: The Dynamics of Apartheid*. Englewood Cliffs, N.J.: Prentice-Hall, 1968.

Gelb, Leslie, and Richard Botts. *The Irony of Vietnam: The System Worked*. Washington, D.C.: The Brookings Institute, 1979.

Geyelin, Phillip. *Lyndon B. Johnson and the World*. New York: Praeger, 1966.

Geyser, O., ed. *B. J. Vorster: Selected Speeches*. Bloemfontein: Institute for Contemporary History, 1977.

Gibson, Richard. *African Liberation Movements: Contemporary Struggles Against White Minority Rule*. London: Oxford University Press, 1972.

Goldman, Eric. *The Tragedy of Lyndon Johnson*. New York: Alfred A. Knopf, 1969.

Goldschmidt, Walter T., ed. *The United States and Africa*. New York: Praeger, 1963.

Good, Robert. *UDI: The International Politics of the Rhodesian Rebellion*. London: Faber & Faber, 1973.

Goold-Adams, Richard. *John Foster Dulles: A Reappraisal*. New York: Appleton-Century-Crofts, 1962.

Gurtov, Melvin. *The United States Against the Third World: Antinationalism and Intervention*. New York: Praeger, 1974.

Halberstam, David. *The Best and the Brightest*. New York: Random House, 1972.

Hall, Richard. *The High Price of Principles: Kaunda and the White South*. London: Hodder and Stoughton, 1969.

Hance, William, ed. *Southern Africa and the United States*. New York: Columbia University Press, 1968.

Hancock, William K. *Smuts*. 2 Vols. Cambridge: Cambridge University Press, 1968.

Helmreich, William B. *Afro-Americans and Africa: Black Nationalism at the Crossroads*. Westport, Conn.: Greenwood Press, 1977.

Heren, Louis. *No Hail, No Farewell*. New York: Harper & Row, 1970.

Heuvel, William V., and Milton Gwirtzman. *On His Own: Robert F. Kennedy, 1964–1968*. Garden City, N.Y.: Doubleday, 1970.

Hilsman, Roger. *To Move a Nation: The Politics of Foreign Policy in the Administration of John F. Kennedy*. Garden City, N.Y.: Doubleday, 1967.

Hilsman, Roger, and Robert Good, eds. *Foreign Policy in the Sixties: The Issues and the Instruments*. Baltimore: Johns Hopkins University Press, 1965.

Hoopes, Townsend. *The Devil and John Foster Dulles: The Diplomacy of the Eisenhower Era*. Boston: Little, Brown and Co., 1973.

Howe, Russell Warren. *Along the Afric Shore: An Historic Review of Two Centuries of U.S.–African Relations*. New York: Barnes & Noble, 1975.

Howe, Russell Warren, and Sarah Hays Trott. *The Power Peddlers: How Lobbyists Mold American Foreign Policy*. Garden City, N.Y.: Doubleday, 1977.

Hughes, John Emmet. *The Ordeal of Power: A Political Memoir of the Eisenhower Years.* New York: Atheneum, 1963.

Hull, Cordell. *The Memoirs of Cordell Hull.* 2 Vols. New York: Macmillan, 1948.

Johnson, Lyndon B. *The Vantage Point: Perspectives on the Presidency, 1963–1969.* New York: Holt, Rinehart and Winston, 1971.

Kalb, Madeleine. *The Congo Cables: The Cold War in Africa: From Eisenhower to Kennedy.* New York: Macmillan, 1982.

Kennan, George. *Memoirs: 1925–1950.* Boston: Little, Brown and Co., 1967.

Kuper, Leo. *Passive Resistance in South Africa.* New Haven: Yale University Press, 1957.

Lake, Anthony. *The "Tar Baby" Option: American Policy Toward Southern Rhodesia.* New York: Columbia University Press, 1976.

Lefever, Ernest. *Uncertain Mandate: Politics of the UN Congo Operation.* Baltimore: Johns Hopkins University Press, 1967.

Legum, Colin, and Margaret Legum. *South Africa: Crisis for the West.* New York: Praeger, 1964.

Leiss, Amelia, ed. *Apartheid and United Nations Collective Measures: An Analysis.* New York: Carnegie Endowment for International Peace, 1965.

Lemarchand, Rene, ed. *American Policy in Southern Africa: The Stakes and the Stance.* Washington, D.C.: University Press of America, 1978.

Loney, Martin. *Rhodesia: White Racism and Imperial Response.* London: Penguin Books, 1975.

Lord, Donald. *John F. Kennedy: The Politics of Confrontation and Conciliation.* Woodbury, N.Y.: Barrons, 1977.

Louis, William Roger. *Imperialism at Bay: The United States and the Decolonization of the British Empire, 1941–1945.* New York: Oxford University Press, 1978.

McKay, Vernon. *Africa in World Politics.* New York: Harper & Row, 1963.

Marchetti, Victor, and John D. Marks. *The CIA and the Cult of Intelligence.* New York: Alfred A. Knopf, 1974.

Marcum, John. Vol. 1. *The Angolan Revolution: The Anatomy of an Explosion, 1950-1962.* Cambridge: The M.I.T. Press, 1969.

———. Vol. 2. *The Angolan Revolution: Exile Politics and Guerrilla Warfare, 1962-1976.* Cambridge: The M.I.T. Press, 1978.

Marshall, Charles Burton. *Crisis over Rhodesia: A Skeptical View.* Baltimore: Johns Hopkins University Press, 1967.

———. *South Africa: The Strategic View.* New York: American-African Affairs Association, 1967.

Martin, John Bartlow. *Adlai Stevenson and the World: The Life of Adlai E. Stevenson.* Garden City, N.Y.: Doubleday & Co., 1977.

May, Ernest A. *"Lessons" of the Past: The Use and Misuse of History in American Foreign Policy.* New York: Oxford University Press, 1973.

Minter, William. *Portuguese Africa and the West.* New York: Monthly Review Press, 1972.

Mondlane, Eduardo. *The Struggle for Mozambique.* London: Penguin Books, 1969.

Morris, Roger. *Uncertain Greatness: Henry Kissinger and American Foreign Policy.* New York: Harper & Row, 1977.

Morrow, John. *First American Ambassador to Guinea.* New Brunswick, N.J.: Rutgers University Press, 1968.

Mtshali, B. Vulindela. *Rhodesia: Background to Conflict.* New York: Hawthorn Books, 1967.

Nielsen, Waldemar. *African Battleline: American Policy Choices in Southern Africa*. New York: Harper & Row, 1965.

————. *The Great Powers and Africa*. New York: Praeger, 1969.

Nixon, Richard. *The Real War*. New York: Warner Books, 1980.

Nolutshungu, Sam. *South Africa in Africa: A Study in Ideology and Foreign Policy*. New York: Africana Publishing Co., 1975.

Nunnerly, David. *President Kennedy and Britain*. London: Bodley Head, 1972.

Ogunsanwo, Alaba. *China's Policy in Africa, 1958–1971*. Cambridge: Cambridge University Press, 1974.

Padmore, George. *Pan Africanism or Communism?* New York: Roy Publishers, 1956.

Paper, Lewis. *The Promise and the Performance: The Leadership of John F. Kennedy*. New York: Crown Publishers, 1975.

Parmet, Herbert S. *Eisenhower and the American Crusades*. New York: Macmillan, 1972.

Richardson, Elmo. *The Presidency of Dwight D. Eisenhower*. Lawrence: University of Kansas Press, 1979.

Ritner, Peter. *The Death of Africa*. New York: Macmillan, 1960.

Rotberg, Robert. *Suffer the Future: Policy Choices in Southern Africa*. Cambridge: Harvard University Press, 1980.

Roux, Edward. *Time Longer than Rope: A History of the Black Man's Struggle for Freedom in South Africa*. Madison: University of Wisconsin Press, 1966.

Rubinstein, Alvin, and George Ginsburg, eds. *Soviet and American Policies in the United Nations: A Twenty-Five Year Perspective*. New York: New York University Press, 1971.

Schlesinger, Arthur M., Jr. *A Thousand Days: John F. Kennedy in the White House*. Boston: Houghton Mifflin Co., 1965.

————. *Robert Kennedy and His Times*. Boston: Houghton Mifflin Co., 1978.

Shah Harin. *The Great Abdication: American Foreign Policy in Asia and Africa*. New Delhi: Atma Ram, 1957.

Shepherd, George W. *Anti-Apartheid: Transnational Conflict and Western Policy in the Liberation of South Africa*. Westport, Conn.: Greenwood Press, 1977.

Shepherd, George W., ed. *Racial Influences on American Foreign Policy*. New York: Basic Books, 1970.

Siedman, Ann. *South Africa and U.S. Multinational Corporations*. Westport, Conn.: Lawrence Hill & Co., 1978.

Solberg, Carl. *Riding High: America in the Cold War*. New York: Mason & Lipscomb, 1973.

Sorenson, Theodore. *Kennedy*. New York: Harper & Row, 1965.

Stebbins, Richard. *The United States in World Affairs 1965*. New York: Harper & Row, 1966.

Stevens, Christopher. *The Soviet Union and Black Africa*. New York: Macmillan, 1976.

Steward, Alexander. *The World, the West, and Pretoria*. New York: David McKay, 1977.

Stockwell, John. *In Search of Enemies: A CIA Story*. New York: W. W. Norton, 1978.

Strydom, Lauritz. *Rivonia Unmasked*. Johannesburg: Voortrekkerpers, 1965.

Szulc, Tad. *The Illusion of Peace: Foreign Policy in the Nixon Years*. New York: Viking Press, 1978.

Thompson, W. Scott, *Ghana's Foreign Policy, 1957–1966: Diplomacy, Ideology, and the New State*. Princeton: Princeton University Press, 1969.

Vance, Cyrus. *Hard Choices: Critical Years in America's Foreign Policy*. New York: Simon and Schuster, 1983.

Vandenbosch, Amry. *South Africa and the World: The Foreign Policy of Apartheid.* Lexington: University of Kentucky Press, 1970.

Vatcher, William H. *White Laager: The Rise of Afrikaner Nationalism.* New York: Praeger, 1965.

Vogelgesang, Sandy. *American Dream, Global Nightmare: The Dilemma of U.S. Human Rights Policy.* New York: W. W. Norton, 1980.

Wallerstein, Immanuel. *Africa: The Politics of Unity.* New York: Random House, 1967.

Walton, Richard. *Cold War and Counterrevolution: The Foreign Policy of John F. Kennedy.* New York: Viking Press, 1972.

Washington Task Force on African Affairs. *Congress and Africa.* Washington, D.C.: African Bibliographic Center, 1975.

Weisbord, Robert G. *Ebony Kinship: Africa, Africans, and the Afro-American.* Westport, Conn.: Greenwood Press, 1973.

Weissman, Stephen. *American Foreign Policy in the Congo, 1960–1964.* Ithaca: Cornell University Press, 1974.

Welensky, Roy. *4000 Days: The Life and Death of the Federation of Rhodesia and Nyasaland.* London: Collins, 1964.

Williams, G. Mennen. *Africa for the Africans.* Grand Rapids, Mich.: William B. Eerdmans Publishing Co., 1969.

Wilson, Harold. *The Labour Government 1964–1970: A Personal Record.* London: Weidenfeld and Nicolson, 1971.

Windrich, Elaine. *Britain and the Politics of Rhodesian Independence.* New York: Africana Publishing Co., 1978.

Yarborough, William P. *Trial in Africa: The Failure of U.S. Policy.* Washington, D.C.: Heritage Foundation, 1976.

Young, Kenneth. *Rhodesia and Independence: A Study in British Colonial Policy.* London: Eyre & Spottiswoode, 1967.

Zacklin, Ralph. *The United Nations and Rhodesia: A Study in International Law.* New York: Praeger, 1974.

INDEX

Acheson, Dean, 26, 27, 65; and South Africa, 28-30; and UN, 31; and John Kennedy, 51, 63; criticism of U.S. policy toward Angola, 71; view of Salazar, 71n; Azores base, 89; criticism of U.S. policy toward Rhodesia, 224, 229-30

Adoula, Cyril, 85, 113, 166

Africanist-Europeanist split in U.S. government, 1, 64-66; and Angola, 88-89, 93-94; and Rhodesia, 187; effects of, 257

African National Congress (ANC), 50

Afrikaner Broederbond, 12

Agnew, Spiro, 240

Allen, George, 45

Allis-Chalmers Corporation, 165

American Committee on Africa, 42, 51, 91; and Mozambique, 121; and South Africa, 159, 169. *See also* Houser, George

American Federation of Labor, 42, 53

American Friends of Katanga, 75

American-Southern African Council, 223

Anderson, George: sympathy with Portugal, 114, 120; and LORAN-C, 118-19; criticism of U.S. policy toward Angola, 119

Anderson, Robert, 65

Andrews, H. T., 26

Angola: U.S. policy toward, 61-125 *passim;* U.S. weapons in, 81, 107

Angolan liberation groups: formation of, 67-68, 100-101; rivalries, 120-21, 242. *See also* FNLA, MPLA, UNITA, UPA

Apartheid: and 1948 election in South Africa, 19; U.S. reaction to, 19-20; implementation of, 23-24. *See also* South Africa

Atlantic Charter, 16-17

Attwood, William, 88-89, 150

Azores military base: history of, 69-70; and U.S. policy toward Portugal, 69-120 *passim;* Defense Department and, 79, 81; Acheson and, 79; John Kennedy and, 81-82, 90, 101-2, 116-17; Robert Kennedy and, 101; LORAN-C and, 118-20; CIA analysis of, 119. *See also* Salazar, Antonio de Oliveira

Ball, George: and "Africanists," 63; "Europeanist" view of Africa, 65; appointment as under-secretary of state, 82; and Salazar, 105-6; and South Africa, 130, 146, 150; and Stanleyville raid, 168; and Rhodesia, 193-200 *passim;* and Great Britain, 194, 215-16, 219-20

Belk, Sam, 79

Bennett, Tapley, 125

Berlin crisis and African policy, 77, 79, 81

Biko, Steve, 246

Black Americans: and apartheid, 21, 47, 137; and Angola, 93; and Rhodesia, 204, 207, 228. *See also* Civil rights movement and U.S. foreign policy

Black Sash, 51

Boer War, 7, 12

Bolton, Francis, 38-39

Botha, Pieter, 247-48

Bowles, Chester: criticism of Eisenhower, 43, 60; assessment of Kennedy's African policies, 61; appointment as under-secretary of state, 63; and Portugal, 69; and Angola, 79-97 *passim;* efforts to remove, 82; and Azores base, 84, 89; and Sakwa plan, 93, 97; and South Africa, 131-32, 134

British South Africa Company, 7

Brown, George, 226

Brundage, Avery, 181-82

Brzezinski, Zbigniew, 137, 246-47

Buchanan, Patrick, 241

Bunche, Ralph, 42

Bundy, McGeorge, 79; criticism of Stevenson, 82-83; and arms sales to South Africa, 145, 163-65

Bureau of African Affairs, 49, 49n

Burnham, James, 71

Business, American: and South Africa, 44, 128, 139, 157-58, 162-65, 172, 182-83, 246; and Rhodesia, 205-6, 224

Butler, R. A., 190-91

Byrd amendment, 241-42, 244, 248

Byroade, Henry, 45, 53

Caetano, Marcello, 242

Califano, Joseph, 231-32

Cannon, Clarence, 139-40

Caradon, Lord, 211-12

Carmichael, Stokely, 176

Randall, Clarence, 139, 141
Reagan, Ronald, 250-51
Redecker, Sydney, 25
Rhodes, Cecil, 7, 12
Rhodesia: history of, 7-10; U.S. policy toward, 185-250 *passim;* UDI, 187-96; propaganda efforts in U.S., 222-25. *See also* Smith, Ian
Rhodesian Front, 9
Rhodesian Information Office, 222-23
Rivonia trial, 160-62
Roberto, Holden: background of, 67-68; CIA aid to, 72, 72n, 85; U.S. support of, 72, 80, 87, 242-43; opposition to U.S. "rapporteur" plan, 92; criticism of U.S., 94, 98; forms Government of the Republic of Angola in Exile, 100-101; "tilt to the left," 109-11. *See also* Angola; FNLA; GRAE; UPA
Robertson, Ian, 174-75
Robeson, Paul, 41
Roche, John, 224
Rockefeller, David, 169
Rockefeller, Nelson, 183
Rogers, William, 198
Roosevelt, Franklin D., 15-16, 70
Rostow, Walter, 80, 83, 99-100, 136
Rowan, Carl, 161, 165
Ruether, Walter, 42, 51
Rusk, Dean: and Bowles, 63, 65; and Angola, 65-125 *passim;* and Portugal, 80-81, 110-11, 114, 118-19; and Congo, 85; meeting with Salazar, 90; and Chinese in Africa, 109-11; and South Africa, 126-77 *passim;* and arms embargo on South Africa, 147-48, 152-53; and Rivonia trial, 160-61; and South West Africa, 176-79; and Rhodesia, 190-210 *passim*

Salazar, Antonio de Oliveira: and African colonies, 5-6; personality, 6; U.S. relations with, 67-120 *passim;* criticism of U.S., 73, 76-77, 78, 91, 104; interview with, 76-77; and Azores base, 90, 94, 102, 118-20; meeting with Rusk, 90; rejection of U.S. aid for Angolan independence, 104, 112; and Ball, 105-6. *See also* Angola; Mozambique; Portugal
Sakwa, Paul, 86-88, 93
Sandifer, Durward, 27
Satterthwaite, Joseph: 65; and South Africa, 132-37, 152-58 *passim;* and segregation in U.S. facilities in South Africa, 143-44, 170-71; criticism of U.S. policy, 152; proposes "guarantee" of white security in South Africa, 156-58; and Rhodesia, 191
Savimbi, Jonas, 100, 120, 120n, 242, 251. *See also* UNITA
Sayre, Francis B., 26
Schlesinger, Arthur M.: assessment of Kennedy's

African policy, 64, 87; and Azores base, 101; and UN, 136; and arms embargo on South Africa, 151
Sears, Mason, 52
Segregation in U.S. *See* Civil rights movement and U.S. foreign policy
Segregation in U.S. facilities in South Africa, 53, 143-44, 170-71
Selvage & Lee: propaganda efforts in U.S., 74-76; and Congress, 83, 89
Separate Representation of Voters Act, 40
Sharpeville incident, 34, 54-56
Shepardson, Whitney, 21
Shepherd, George, 42
Simmons, W. J., 225
Sisco, Joseph, 108, 226-27
Sithole, Ndabaningi, 235, 248
Smith, Ian: election of, 9, 190; U.S. and, 190-237 *passim;* meetings with Harold Wilson, 194, 216, 228, 236; declares UDI, 196; and U.S. public opinion, 231; and Carter, 247-48. *See also* Rhodesia
Smuts, Jan Christiaan, 18-20, 30-31
South Africa: history of, 10-14; 1948 election, 18-22; U.S. policy toward, 20-60, 126-84, 238-58 *passim;* and Korean War, 28-29; sale of uranium to U.S., 28-29; constitutional crisis in, 40-41; censorship of U.S. authors, 46; propaganda efforts in U.S., 47, 56-57, 141, 178; and NATO, 47-48; and Sharpeville, 55-56; U.S. missile-tracking stations in, 59, 133-34; violence in, 138; U.S. arms embargo, 144-50, 162-65; and atomic energy, 165; and *Independence* incident, 171; and *FDR* incident, 179-80; and Olympic games, 181-82; and Rhodesia, 201-4, 206, 235. *See also* Apartheid
South Africa Foundation, 141
Southern Rhodesia. *See* Rhodesia
South West Africa: 24; and International Court of Justice, 176-79; Odendall commission and, 177; Carter and, 247-48; Reagan and, 251. *See also* United Nations
South West African Peoples' Organization (SWAPO), 247-48
"Spear of the Nation," 138
Sprague, Charles, 31
Springboks rugby team, 250-51
Stevenson, Adlai: criticism of Eisenhower, 43; and South Africa, 50, 146-69 *passim;* appointment as U.S. ambassador to UN, 63; and Angola, 79-89, 101-3, 108; split with John Kennedy on UN policy, 103; summary of Kennedy's South African policy, 154; and Congo, 167-68. *See also* United Nations
Steward, Michael, 227
Strijdom, J. G., 13, 41, 47